Treasures

A Reading/Language Arts Program

Program Authors

Dr. Donald R. Bear
University of Nevada, Reno
Reno, Nevada

Dr. Janice A. Dole
University of Utah
Salt Lake City, Utah

Dr. Jana Echevarria
California State University, Long Beach
Long Beach, California

Dr. Jan E. Hasbrouck
Educational Consultant - J.H. Consulting
Seattle, Washington

Dr. Scott G. Paris
University of Michigan
Ann Arbor, Michigan

Dr. Timothy Shanahan
University of Illinois at Chicago
Chicago, Illinois

Dr. Josefina V. Tinajero
University of Texas at El Paso
El Paso, Texas

Macmillan
McGraw-Hill

Contributor

Time Magazine, Accelerated Reader

B

The *McGraw-Hill* Companies

Macmillan McGraw-Hill

Published by Macmillan/McGraw-Hill, of McGraw-Hill Education, a division of The McGraw-Hill Companies, Inc., Two Penn Plaza, New York, New York 10121.

4 5 6 7 8 9 073/043 09 08 07

Program Authors

Dr. Donald R. Bear

Professor, Department of Curriculum and Instruction Director, E. L. Cord Foundation Center for Learning and Literacy University of Nevada, Reno

- Author of *Words Their Way* and *Words Their Way with English Learners*

Dr. Scott G. Paris

Professor, Department of Psychology University of Michigan, Ann Arbor

- Chair, Graduate Program in Psychology, University of Michigan
- Principal Investigator, CIERA, 1997–2004

Dr. Janice A. Dole

Associate Professor, Department of Teaching and Learning University of Utah

- Member, New Standards Literacy Project: Grades 4–5
- National Reading First Presenter

Dr. Timothy Shanahan

Professor, Urban Education Director, UIC Center for Literacy University of Illinois at Chicago

- Member, National Reading Panel
- President, International Reading Association, 2006
- Chair, National Literacy Panel and National Early Literacy Panel

Dr. Jana Echevarria

Professor, Educational Psychology, California State University, Long Beach

- Author of *Making Content Comprehensible for English Learners: The SIOP Model*
- Principal Researcher, National Research and Development Center on English Language Learners

Dr. Josefina V. Tinajero

Dean, College of Education University of Texas at El Paso

- NABE Board Member and Secretary, Past President

Dr. Jan E. Hasbrouck

Educational Consultant - J. H. Consulting, Seattle, WA

- Developed oral reading fluency norms for Grades 1–8
- Advisor to the National Reading First Technical Support Centers

Contributing Authors

Dr. Adria F. Klein

Professor Emeritus, Reading
Education, California State
University, San Bernardino

- President, California Reading
  Association, 1995
- Co-author of *Interactive
  Writing* and *Interactive
  Editing*

Dr. Doris Walker-Dalhouse

Professor, Department of Elementary &
Early Childhood Education
Minnesota State University, Moorhead

- Author of articles on multicultural
  literature and reading instruction
  in urban schools
- Co-chair of the Ethnicity, Race,
  and Multilingualism Committee,
  NRC

Dolores B. Malcolm

St. Louis Public Schools
St. Louis, MO

- Past President, International
  Reading Association
- Member, IRA Urban Diversity
  Initiatives Commission
- Member, RIF Advisory Board

In memory of our esteemed
colleague and friend,
Dr. Steven A. Stahl

Program Consultants

Dr. Stephanie Al Otaiba

Assistant Professor,
College of Education
Florida State University

Dr. Susan M. Brookhart

Brookhart Enterprises LLC - Helena, MT
Coordinator of Assessment and Evaluation
Duquesne University, Pittsburgh, PA

Kathy R. Bumgardner

Language Arts Instructional
Specialist
Gaston County Schools, NC

Dr. Lynn S. Fuchs

Dr. Douglas Fuchs

Professors, Department of Special
Education
Vanderbilt University, Nashville, TN

Dr. Vicki L. Gibson

Longmire Learning Center, Inc.
College Station, TX

Dr. Connie R. Hebert

National Literacy Consultant
Lesley University
The ReadWrite Place
West Springfield, MA

Dr. Sharon F. O'Neal

Associate Professor,
College of Education
Texas State University – San Marcos

Dinah Zike

Dinah-Might Adventures, L.P.
San Antonio, TX

Program Reviewers

Mable Alfred
Reading/Language Arts
Administrator
Chicago Public Schools, IL

Suzie Bean
Teacher, Kindergarten
Mary W. French Academy
Decatur, IL

Beverly Brown
Teacher, Kindergarten
Washington Irving School
Indianapolis, IN

Linda Burch
Teacher, Kindergarten
Public School 184
Brooklyn, NY

Ann Burton
Teacher, Grade 4
Cameron Park
Elementary School
Hillsborough, NC

Debra K. Casey
Assistant Principal
Weisser Park Arts
Magnet School
Ft. Wayne, IN

Robert J. Dandorph
Principal
John F. Kennedy
Elementary School
North Bergen, NJ

Suzanne Delacruz
Principal
Washington Elementary
School
Evanston, IL

Roberta Dobrzeniecki
Teacher, Grade 2
Lafayette Elementary School
Hammond, IN

Carol Dockery
Teacher, Grade 3
Mulberry Elementary
Milford, OH

Karryl Ellis
Teacher, Grade 1
Durfee School
Decatur, IL

Christina Fong
Teacher, Grade 3
William Moore Elementary
School
Las Vegas, NV

Lenore Furman
Teacher, Kindergarten
Abington Avenue School
Newark, NJ

Beth Holland
Teacher, Kindergarten
Jeffreys Grove Elementary
School
Raleigh, NC

Renee Jones
Curriculum and Instruction
Title I Director
Indianapolis Public Schools
Indianapolis, IN

Sister Miriam Kaeser
Assistant Superintendent
Archdiocese of Cincinnati
Cincinnati, OH

Toni Kring
Principal
Forest Park Elementary School
Ft. Wayne, IN

LaVonne Lee
Principal
Rozet Elementary School
Gillette, WY

Akida Kissane Lewis
Principal
54th Street Elementary School
Los Angeles, CA

Christi Lindeman
Teacher, Grade K/1
Veterans Park Elementary
Lexington, KY

SuEllen Mackey
Teacher, Grade 5
Washington Elementary
School
Decatur, IL

Jan Mayes
Curriculum Coordinator
Kent School District
Kent, WA

Robyn Morris
Teacher, Grade 2
Druid Hills Elementary School
Charlotte, NC

Bonnie Nelson
Teacher, Grade 1
Solano School, Osborn
Elementary District
Phoenix, AZ

Cyndi Nichols
Teacher, Grade K/1
North Ridge Elementary
School
Commack, NY

Sharron Norman
Curriculum Director
Lansing School District
Lansing, MI

Renee Ottinger
Literacy Leader, Grades K–5
Coronado Hills Elementary
School
Denver, CO

Cassandra L. Perez
Bilingual/ESL Instructional
Specialist
Remynse Elementary
Grand Prairie, TX

Effie J. Phillips
Teacher, Grade 1
Vance Elementary School
Asheville, NC

Michael Pragman
Principal
Woodland Elementary School
Lee's Summit, MO

Carol Rose
Teacher, Grade 2
Churchill Elementary School
Muskegon, MI

Monica Sandoval
Principal
Wharton Elementary
Houston, TX

Laura R. Schmidt-Watson
Director of Academic
Services
Parma City School District,
OH

Dianne L. Skoy
Literacy Coordinator,
Grades K–5
Minneapolis Public Schools
Minneapolis, MN

Charles Staszewski
ESL Teacher, Grades 3–5
John H. William School,
No. 5
Rochester, NY

Sandra Sunderland-Willis
Special Education
Specialist
Fort Wayne Community
School District
Fort Wayne, IN

Patricia Synan
New York City Department
of Education

Lynne Vitkus
Teacher, Grade 3
Ernest R. Elliott Elementary
School
Munster, IN

Beth Ware
Lead Literacy Teacher
Wake County School
District Raleigh, NC

Jackie West
Principal
Sea Breeze Elementary
Bradenton, FL

Charlotte Williams
Teacher, Grade 3
Durant Elementary
Raleigh, NC

Stephanie Yearian
Teacher, Grade 2
W. J. Zahnow Elementary
Waterloo, IL

Student Reviewers: Special thanks to the students of our program reviewers who reviewed the literature selections.

RESEARCH Why It Matters

Fluency

Jan E. Hasbrouck

Fluent readers can read text *accurately*, at a reasonable and appropriate *rate*, and with good *expression* and *phrasing*. Fluency is a critical component of skillful reading in part because it serves as a bridge between decoding and comprehension. Students with fluency problems read less than their peers and often fall further and further behind.

The benefits of reading practice can be optimized to build fluency by giving students frequent opportunities to read text orally, with corrective feedback and at an appropriate level of difficulty. Fluency-based assessments can be used as powerful "spot checks" of overall progress in reading because fluency is so highly related to comprehension. If a student's fluency is lower than expected levels, this can be an indicator of a variety of reading concerns.

Best Practices

Effective fluency instruction

- includes assessing children before instruction begins to determine their needs

- provides a model of fluent reading

- gives students repeated opportunities to read and reread text orally

- provides practice in text at an independent level

- uses a variety of practice formats, including partner reading, choral reading, and cloze reading practice

- has students time themselves and monitor their progress, giving them immediate and positive evidence that practice is making a difference in their fluency

Professional Development

- **READING, YES! K-3**
  Video Series: Module 2, *Beginning Reading/ Intervention*; Module 4, *Decoding and Spelling*

  Online Course: Accredited college course available at **www.macmillanmh.com**

- **TREASURES FOR TEACHERS**
  Video Series: *Fluency*

  Online: See **www.macmillanmh.com** for best practices in fluency.

References

- *Assessing Reading Fluency* (Rasinski, T., www.prel.org).
- *A Focus on Fluency* (Osborn, J., & Lehr, F., www.prel.org).
- Fuchs, L. S., Fuchs, D., Hosp, M. K., & Jenkins, J., (2001). Oral reading fluency as an indicator of reading competence: A theoretical, empirical, and historical analysis. *Scientific Studies of Reading*, 5(3), 239–256.
- Hasbrouck, J., & Tindal G., 2005. Oral reading fluency norms: A valuable tool for reading teachers. *The Reading Teacher*.
- *Report of the National Reading Panel*, National Institute of Child Health and Human Development (NICHD), 2000.

Theme: Challenges
Planning the Unit

Using the Student Book

Wrapping Up the Unit

Additional Lessons and Resources

Main Selections

Unit Assessment

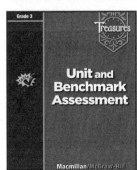

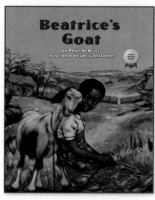

pages 150J–183V

pages 184A–217V

ORAL LANGUAGE

- **Listening, Speaking, Viewing**

WORD STUDY

- **Vocabulary**

- **Phonics/Decoding**

READING

- **Comprehension**

- **Fluency**

- **Leveled Readers/ELL Readers**

LANGUAGE ARTS

- **Writing**

- **Grammar**

- **Spelling**

WEEK 1

Theme
Making Money

Build Background

Vocabulary
sidewalks, grumbled, traders, blossomed, wailed, lonesome
Word Parts: Compound Words

Phonics
Compound Words

Comprehension
Strategy: Summarize
Skill: Sequence

Fluency
Repeated Reading

APPROACHING
Children at Work: Colonial America
ON LEVEL
Children at Work: On the Frontier
BEYOND
The Work They Did

ENGLISH LANGUAGE LEARNERS
Frontier Children

Writing
Compare/Contrast Paragraphs

Grammar
Pronouns

Spelling
Compound Words

WEEK 2

Theme
Making a Difference

Build Background

Vocabulary
gift, yearned, tend, produce, sturdy, schoolhouse, kindhearted
Word Parts: Word Families

Phonics
Inflected Endings

Comprehension
Strategy: Make Inferences and Analyze
Skill: Cause and Effect

Fluency
Repeated Reading

APPROACHING
Henry Bergh and the ASPCA
ON LEVEL
John Muir: Friend of Nature

BEYOND
Alexander Fleming and His Great Discovery
ENGLISH LANGUAGE LEARNERS
John Muir

Writing
Descriptive Paragraph

Grammar
Subject and Object Pronouns

Spelling
Inflected Endings

pages 218A–229V

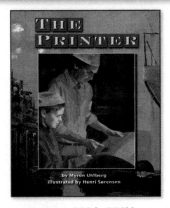

pages 230A–259V

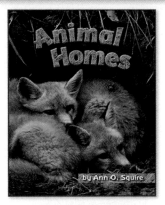

pages 260A–285V

Review and Assess

WEEK 3

Theme
In Motion

Build Background

Vocabulary
powered, declared, existed, artist's, pride
Word Parts: Possessives

Phonics
Endings *y* to *i*

Comprehension
Strategy: Make Inferences and Analyze
Skill: Fact and Opinion

Fluency
Repeated Reading

APPROACHING
Making Waves

ON LEVEL
Thrills and Chills

BEYOND
Up, Down, or Open-Moving Machines

ENGLISH LANGUAGE LEARNERS
What a Ride!

Writing
Personal Narrative

Grammar
Possessive Pronouns

Spelling
Endings *y* to *i*

WEEK 4

Theme
Heroes

Build Background

Vocabulary
screamed, numb, escape, fled, shuddered, image, newspaper
Context Clues:
Figurative Language

Phonics
The VC/CV Pattern

Comprehension
Strategy: Make Inferences and Analyze
Skill: Make and Confirm Predictions

Fluency
Repeated Reading

APPROACHING
Blizzard Heroes

ON LEVEL
Hurricane Heroes

BEYOND
Earthquake Heroes

ENGLISH LANGUAGE LEARNERS
Keeping Us Safe

Writing
Speech

Grammar
Pronoun-Verb Agreement

Spelling
The VC/CV Pattern

WEEK 5

Theme
Animal Architects

Build Background

Vocabulary
hives, architects, structures, contain, retreats, shallow, shelter
Analogies

Phonics
The V/CV and VC/V Pattern

Comprehension
Strategy: Summarize
Skill: Description

Fluency
Repeated Reading

APPROACHING
Amazing Mammal Builders

ON LEVEL
Amazing Bird Builders

BEYOND
Amazing Insect and Spider Builders

ENGLISH LANGUAGE LEARNERS
Bird Builders

Writing
Descriptive Poem

Grammar
Pronoun-Verb Contractions

Spelling
The V/CV and VC/V Pattern

WEEK 6

Test Strategy
Think and Search

Writing
Descriptive Writing

Unit 5 Assessment, 79–96

Comprehension
Sequence, Cause and Effect, Fact and Opinion, Make and Confirm Predictions, Description

Vocabulary Strategies
Word Parts: Compound Words, Word Families, Possessives; Context Clues: Figurative Language; Analogies

Text Features/Literary Elements/Study Skills
Calendar, Editorial, Skim and Scan, Map, Simile and Rhythmic Pattern

Grammar
Pronouns

Writing
Descriptive Writing

Fluency Assessment

Diagnose and Prescribe
Interpret Assessment Results

Literature

Read Big Book to introduce unit theme

Student Edition

Read-Aloud Anthology
- Folk Tales
- Poems
- Songs
- Plays

Intervention Anthology

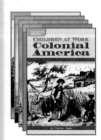

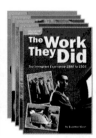

Leveled Readers

ELL Reader

Also Available

Classroom Library Tradebooks

Leveled Reader Program

Teaching Support

Teacher's Edition

Transparencies:
- Vocabulary
- Comprehension and Study Skills
- Daily Language Activities
- Graphic Organizers/ Fluency Passages
- Writing
- Grammar

ELL Teacher's Guide

Teacher's Resource Book
- Weekly Student Contracts
- Dinah Zike's Foldables™
- Blackline Masters for Vocabulary and Spelling Cards, writing rubrics, and picture prompts

traders   wailed

Vocabulary Cards

Student Practice

Approaching Level	On Level	Beyond Level	English Language Learners

Leveled Practice for Vocabulary, Skills, and Strategies

Spelling Practice Book　　**Grammar Practice Book**

Home-School Connection
Take–Home Stories
Homework Activities

 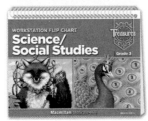

Cross–Curricular Workstation Activities

Technology

 AUDIO CD
- Listening Library
- Fluency Solutions

READING, YES!
- Videos
- Online Course

TREASURES FOR TEACHERS
- Videos
- Online Lessons

 CD-ROM
- Vocabulary PuzzleMaker
- Handwriting
- Instructional Navigator Interactive Lesson Planner
- StudentWorks

LOG ON www.macmillanmh.com
- Author/Illustrator Information
- Research and Inquiry Activities
- Vocabulary and Spelling Activities
- Oral Language Activities
- Computer Literacy
- Leveled Reader Database

READING
Triumphs
AN INTERVENTION PROGRAM

Treasure Chest
FOR ENGLISH LANGUAGE LEARNERS

Screening, Diagnostic, and Placement Assessments

Screening

Use your state or district screener to identify students at risk. See pages 5–12 in our **Screening, Diagnostic, Placement Assessment** book for information on using DIBELS and TPRI as screeners.

Diagnostic Tools for Instructional Placement

For individually-administered Diagnostics, use TPRI or your state or district diagnostic assessment. See pages 13–20 for diagnostic information, and the Informal Reading Inventory passages on pages 88–95 in our **Screening, Diagnostic, Placement Assessment** book.

For a group-administered Placement Test, see pages 199–208 in our **Screening, Diagnostic, Placement Assessment** book.

Use the results from these assessments to determine the instructional levels of your students for differentiated instruction grouping.

Monitoring Progress

Ongoing Informal Assessments

- Daily Quick Check Observations
- Weekly Comprehension Check
- Weekly Fluency Practice Passages

Formal Assessments

- **Weekly Assessment** includes

    On Level Assessments

    Approaching Level Assessments
- **Fluency Assessment**
- **Running Records**
- **Unit and Benchmark Assessment**
- **ELL Practice and Assessment**

    Weekly Tests

    Unit Progress Test

Managing and Reporting

- Assessment on CD-ROM or online

Instructional Navigator Interactive Lesson Planner

- All Teacher Edition pages
- Electronic Lesson Planner
- Student Blackline Masters

National Test Alignment

UNIT 5 ASSESSED SKILLS	NAEP	TerraNova/CAT6	ITBS	SAT10
COMPREHENSION STRATEGIES AND SKILLS				
• Strategies: Make Inferences and Analyze, Summarize	◆	◆	◆	◆
• Skills: Sequence, Cause and Effect, Fact and Opinion, Make and Confirm Predictions, Description	◆	◆	◆	◆
VOCABULARY STRATEGIES				
• Word Parts		◆	◆	◆
• Context Clues	◆	◆	◆	◆
• Analogies				
TEXT FEATURES AND STUDY SKILLS				
• Calendar	◆	◆	◆	◆
• Editorial	◆	◆	◆	◆
• Map	◆	◆	◆	◆
• Skim and scan a nonfiction article	◆	◆	◆	◆
GRAMMAR, MECHANICS, USAGE				
• Pronouns (subject and object, possessive)		◆	◆	◆
• Capitalizing I and proper nouns		◆	◆	◆
• Apostrophes		◆	◆	◆
• Pronoun-verb contractions		◆	◆	◆
• Pronoun-verb agreement		◆	◆	◆
• Contractions and possessive pronouns		◆	◆	◆
WRITING				
• Descriptive Writing	◆			

KEY

NAEP	National Assessment of Educational Progress	**ITBS**	Iowa Tests of Basic Skills
TerraNova/CAT6	TerraNova, the Second Edition	**SAT10**	Stanford Achievement Test

Theme Project

Build Background Write this theme statement on the board: We can use our hearts and minds to meet challenges. Ask:

- What kinds of challenges do you like?

- What hard challenges have you faced?

- Who are some people who have overcome great challenges?

Research and Inquiry
Self-Selected Theme Project

 State the Problem and Identify Needed Information Have students think of a kind of challenge that they would like to investigate. It could be a personal challenge, such as adjusting to a new school, or a community challenge, such as starting a recycling program or cleaning up a local park.

Step 2 Identify Resources for Finding Information Have students brainstorm to identify people and library resources that have information on the challenge they chose. People may include friends, family members, neighbors, teachers, and other community members.

Have students identify people who would provide the best information and would be available for an interview.

Step 3 Find the Information Have students do library research and contact the sources they identified to set up interviews. Students may find information about their challenge—or about people who have met it—in photographs, videos, diaries, journals, and letters.

Step 4 Organize the Information Students should take notes or record any interviews (with permission) so that they can use the information later.

See the Unit Closer on pages 289K–289L for **Step 5: Create the Presentation** and **Step 6: Review and Evaluate.**

RESEARCH STRATEGIES

Interview

- Telephone or write an e-mail describing your project and request an interview.
- Make a list of interview questions. Don't ask Yes or No questions.
- Listen carefully, and take good notes. Read back quotations to make sure you wrote them correctly.

Cross-Curricular Projects

Language Arts Activity

LANGUAGE DIFFERENCES

Have students work in cooperative groups. Have each group research one of the following:

How language varies between cultures, countries, regions, neighborhoods, and professions. Ask students to provide examples and reasons for these variations.

Have students share their findings with the rest of the group. Encourage questions and discussions about slang, dialect, jargon, and formal and informal language when appropriate.

Media Activity

EVALUATING MEDIA

With students, brainstorm two major events that have affected the lives of Americans in the last three years.

Ask students to identify the different ways that they or their parents heard about these events. Help students discuss the different ways that television, radio, movies, and the Internet affect the way that people think and express their point of view.

Help students with questions they can ask themselves when evaluating what they see and hear through different media. Two examples:

- Do I trust the person or persons giving me information? Why or why not?

- Is this person sharing his or her point of view or just giving information?

Have students use art and words to present their example. Tell them to cite their source.

CHARACTER BUILDING—TRUSTWORTHINESS

While students are investigating the impact of science and technology, discuss the importance of trustworthiness in people who do scientific research, in people who develop new technologies, and for us in daily life. Explain that trustworthiness includes being honest and building a good reputation.

DISCUSSION AND CONVERSATION GUIDELINES

Listening and Speaking

Remind students to:
- Show respect for others' ideas.
- Show respect when responding to others' ideas and opinions.
- Be a good listener and not interrupt while others are speaking.

 For Technology research and presentation strategies, see the Computer Literacy Lessons on pages 289I–289J.

Weekly Theme: Making Money

Week At A Glance

Whole Group

VOCABULARY
blossomed, grumbled, lonesome, sidewalks, traders, wailed

Word Parts/Compound Words

COMPREHENSION
Strategy: Summarize
Skill: Identify Sequence of Events

WRITING
Descriptive

Social Studies Link

Economics

Small Group Options

Differentiated Instruction for Tested Skills

Tested Skills for the Week

Main Selection
Genre Historical Fiction

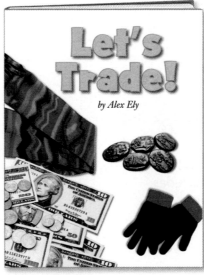

Vocabulary/ Comprehension

Social Studies Link
Genre Nonfiction Article

Leveled Readers

GR Levels M-R

Genre Informational Nonfiction

- Same Theme
- Same Vocabulary
- Same Comprehension Skills

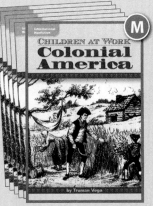

Approaching Level

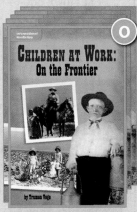

On Level

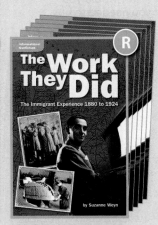

Beyond Level

On Level Reader sheltered for English Language Learner

ELL Teacher's Guide Available

English Language Leveled Reader

Also Available
LEVELED READER PROGRAM

CLASSROOM LIBRARY

Genre Historical Fiction

Approaching

On Level

Beyond

Trade books to apply Comprehension Skills

INTERVENTION ANTHOLOGY

- Phonics and Decoding
- Comprehension
- Vocabulary

Reading Triumphs, Intervention Program also available

LEVELED PRACTICE

Approaching

On Level

Beyond

ELL

Technology

www.macmillanmh.com

 LISTENING LIBRARY
- Main Selections
- Leveled Readers
- Intervention Anthology

FLUENCY SOLUTIONS

 VOCABULARY PuzzleMaker

NEW ADVENTURES WITH BUGGLES AND BEEZY

 ONLINE INSTRUCTION
- Meet the Author/Illustrator
- Computer Literacy Lessons
- Research and Inquiry Activities
- Oral Language Activities
- Vocabulary and Spelling Activities

Suggested Lesson Plan

**Boom Town,
154–175**

Leveled Readers

Whole Group

ORAL LANGUAGE

- **Listening**

- **Speaking**

- **Viewing**

WORD STUDY

- **Vocabulary**

- **Phonics/Decoding**

READING

- **Develop
  Comprehension**

- **Fluency**

LANGUAGE ARTS

- **Writing**

- **Grammar**

- **Spelling**

ASSESSMENT

- **Informal/Formal**

**Turn the Page for
Small Group Lesson Plan**

Day 1

Listening/Speaking/Viewing
❓Focus Question How would you
make money if you needed to buy
something?
Build Background, 150

  Read Aloud: "Music, Music for Everyone,"
151

Vocabulary
*sidewalks, grumbled, traders,
blossomed, wailed, lonesome,* 152

Practice Book A-O-B, 149

Strategy: Word Parts: Compound Words, 153

Read "Let's Trade!" 152–153

Comprehension, 153A–153B
  Strategy: Summarize
  Skill: Sequence
  Practice Book A-O-B, 150

Student Book

Fluency Partner Reading, 150R
Model Fluency, 151

Writing
Daily Writing Prompt Write about how you
can make money now. Then tell how it is
different than how adults earn money.

Prewrite a Comparison Piece, 183A

Grammar Daily Language Activities, 183I
Pronouns, 183I
Grammar Practice Book, 129

Spelling Pretest, 183G
Spelling Practice Book, 129–130

Quick Check Vocabulary, 152
  Comprehension, 153B

Differentiated Instruction 183M–183V

Day 2

Listening/Speaking
❓Focus Question How does Amanda help
her town boom?

Vocabulary
Review Vocabulary, 154
Phonics
Decode Compound Words, 183E

Practice Book A-O-B, 155

Read *Boom Town,* 154–175

Comprehension, 154–177
  Strategy: Summarize
  Skill: Sequence
  Practice Book A-O-B, 151

Student Book

Fluency Partner Reading, 150R
Echo-Reading, 162

Writing
Daily Writing Prompt Write a paragraph
telling how a parent or adult you know
earns money.

Draft a Comparison Piece, 183A

Grammar Daily Language Activities, 183I
Pronouns, 183I
Grammar Practice Book, 130

Spelling Compound Words, 183G
Spelling Practice Book, 131

Quick Check Comprehension, 163, 175
  Phonics, 183E

Differentiated Instruction 183M–183V

**Integrated
ELL
Support
Every Day**

Skills/Strategies

Vocabulary	Comprehension	Writing
Vocabulary Words	Strategy: Summarize	Descriptive Writing
Word Parts: Compound Words	Skill: Sequence	

Turn the Page for
Small Group Options

Day 3

Listening/Speaking

? **Focus Question** Compare "Let's Trade" with *Boom Town*. Compare how the characters got the things that they needed.

Summarize, 177

Vocabulary

Review Words in Context, 183C

Strategy: Word Parts/Compound Words, 183D

Practice Book A-O-B, 154

Phonics

Decode Multisyllable Words, 183E

Read *Boom Town*, 154–175

Student Book

Comprehension

Comprehension Check, 177
Maintain Skill: Draw Conclusions, 177B

Fluency Partner Reading, 150R
Practice Book A-O-B, 152
Repeated Reading, 177A

Writing

Daily Writing Prompt Write about two new businesses that Amanda describes. Who started them and what did they offer?

Writing Trait: Organization, 183
Revise a Comparison Piece, 183B

Grammar Daily Language Activities, 183I
Mechanics and Usage: Capitalization, 183J
Grammar Practice Book, 131

Spelling Compound Words, 183H
Spelling Practice Book, 132

Quick Check Fluency, 177A

Day 4

Listening/Speaking

? **Focus Question** What advice do you think Amanda could give kids who may want to start a business today?

Expand Vocabulary: How to Make Money, 183F

Vocabulary

Content Vocabulary: *business, services, batches, demand,* 178

Idioms, 183F

Apply Vocabulary to Writing, 183F

Phonics

Build Compound Words, 183E

Read "How to Earn Money," 178–181

Student Book

Comprehension

Social Studies: Nonfiction Article
Text Feature: Calendar, 178
Practice Book A-O-B, 153

Fluency Partner Reading, 150R

Writing

Daily Writing Prompt Write a letter to your favorite store near where you live. Explain why you like them and how they meet your needs.

Proofread a Comparison Piece, 183B

Grammar Daily Language Activities, 183I
Pronouns, 183J
Grammar Practice Book, 132

Spelling Compound Words, 183H
Spelling Practice Book, 133

Quick Check Vocabulary, 183D

Day 5

Review and Assess

Listening/Speaking

? **Focus Question** What steps would you take if you were starting a business? Use some of the tips in "Make Your Own Money!" in your answer.

Speaking and Listening Strategies, 183A

Presentation of Descriptive Writing, 183B

Vocabulary

Spiral Review: Vocabulary Game, 183F

Read Self-Selected Reading, 150R

Student Book

Comprehension

Connect and Compare, 181

Fluency Partner Reading, 150R

Writing

Daily Writing Prompt Amanda's father sings songs about being a miner and about Amanda's bakery business. Write a song about someone's business that you know.

Publish a Comparison Piece, 183B

Grammar Daily Language Activities, 183I
Pronouns, 183J
Grammar Practice Book, 133–134

Spelling Posttest, 183H
Spelling Practice Book, 134

Weekly Assessment, 261–268

Differentiated Instruction 183M-183V | **Differentiated Instruction 183M-183V** | **Differentiated Instruction 183M-183V**

Small Group Options

What do I do in small groups?

Additional Instruction, Practice, and Extend Activities are provided for this week's tested skills.

Phonics	Vocabulary	Comprehension	Fluency
Decode Compound Words	**Words:** sidewalks, grumbled, traders, blossomed, wailed, lonesome **Strategy:** Word Parts/Compound Words	**Strategy:** Summarize **Skill:** Sequence	

Lesson Plan
TEACHER-LED SMALL GROUP

 Instructional Navigator
Interactive Lesson Planner

	Day 1	**Day 2**
Approaching Level • **Additional Instruction/Practice** • **Tier 2 Instruction**	Leveled Reader Lesson 1, 183M • Vocabulary • Comprehension • Fluency	Leveled Reader Lesson 2, 183N • Vocabulary • Comprehension • Fluency **ELL** Compound Words, 183O
On Level • **Practice**	Leveled Reader Lesson, 183Q • Vocabulary • Comprehension • Fluency **ELL** Leveled Reader, 183U–183V	Leveled Reader Lesson, 183Q  • Vocabulary • Comprehension • Fluency
Beyond Level • **Extend**	Leveled Reader Lesson, 183S  • Vocabulary • Comprehension • Fluency	Leveled Reader Lesson, 183S • Vocabulary • Comprehension • Fluency

for Differentiated Instruction

Leveled Readers

GR Levels M–R
Matching students to text.

Also Available
LEVELED READER LIBRARY

Approaching Level
- Benchmark 28
- Use other guided reading titles, M–O

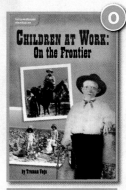

On Level
- Benchmark 34
- Use other guided reading titles, O–R

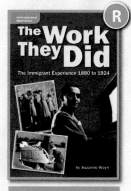

Beyond Level
- Benchmark 40
- Use other guided reading titles, R–T

English Language Leveled Reader

On Level Reader sheltered for English Language Learner

Leveled Reader Database
To search for additional Leveled Reader titles, go to www.macmillanmh.com

---

Day 3

Comprehension, 183O
Vocabulary, 183O

Vocabulary, 183R

Self-Selected Reading, 183T

Day 4

Phonics, 183P
Vocabulary, 183P

Text Feature, 183R

Vocabulary, 183T

Day 5

Fluency, 183N
Make Connections Across Texts, 183P

Make Connections Across Texts, 183R

Text Feature, 183T
ELL Categorize, 183T

Managing the Class

What do I do with the rest of my class?

Teacher-Led Small Groups

Cross-Curricular Workstations

Independent Activities

Leveled Reader Activities

M

CHILDREN AT WORK
Colonial America
by Truman Vega

Literacy Activities

Design a Picture Sign
Think of a trade for a shop. Write a paragraph describing the trade. Then design a sign that tells about the trade.

Word Web
Create a word web with the word apprentice in the center circle. For the circles around it, choose words that describe what life was like for an apprentice.

apprentice

Approaching

See inside back cover for activities

LEVELED PRACTICE

- Vocabulary, 149
- Comprehension: Sequence, 150
- Graphic Organizer, 151
- Fluency, 152
- Text Feature: Calendar, 153
- Vocabulary Strategy: Compound Words, 154
- Phonics, 155

⭐ **Approaching Practice Book A, 149–155**

A. Draw a line to match each word below with its definition.

1. lonesome — a. paths by side of a street or road
2. wailed — b. to grow or to develop
3. traders — c. unhappy from being alone
4. blossomed — d. cried out from grief or pain
5. sidewalks — e. people who exchange goods by selling, buying, or bartering
6. grumbled — f. complained in a low voice

B. Complete each sentence with one of the vocabulary words.

7. Adam's business __blossomed__ because people liked his fresh breads.
   a. (blossomed)   b. lonesome

8. At first Adam's brothers __grumbled__ because they didn't want to work in the bakery.
   a. blossomed   b. (grumbled)

9. We walked to the bakery on the __sidewalks__ because they were safer than walking in the street.
   a. (sidewalks)   b. traders

10. The baker was __lonesome__ because he was alone every night baking bread.
    a. wailed   b. (lonesome)

11. We went down to the market and watched the __traders__ showing off their goods.
    a. sidewalk   b. (traders)

12. The little boy __wailed__ when he dropped his cookie on the floor.
    a. (wailed)   b. blossomed

Weekly Contract

Name _____   Date _____

My To-Do List

✔ Put a check next to the activities you complete.

📖 **Reading**
☐ Practice fluency
☐ Choose a nonfiction book

🔤 **Word Study**
☐ Write compound words
☐ Build compound words

✏️ **Writing**
☐ Write two descriptions
☐ Write two diary entries

🔬 **Science**
☐ Research silver and gold
☐ Write from notes

🌎 **Social Studies**
☐ Write a business plan
☐ Put steps on a calendar

📖 **Leveled Readers**
☐ Write About It!
☐ Content Connection

💻 **Technology**
☐ Vocabulary Puzzlemaker
☐ Fluency Solutions
☐ Listening Library
☐ www.macmillanmh.com

📝 **Independent Practice**
☐ Practice Book, 149–155
☐ Grammar Practice Book, 129–134
☐ Spelling Practice Book, 129–134

Contracts   Unit 5 • Boom Town (23)

© Macmillan/McGraw-Hill

Teacher's Resource Book, page 23

• **Students use their Contracts to manage their time.**

HOME-SCHOOL CONNECTION

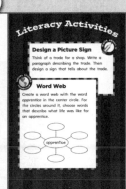

Grade 3

Treasures

Home-School Connection
• Parent Letters
• Homework Activities
• Take-Home Stories

Macmillan/McGraw-Hill

Pages 247–258

Independent Activities

On Level

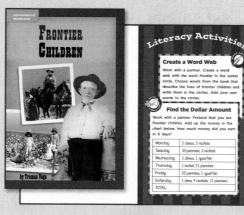

ELL

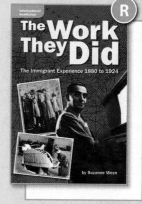

Beyond

On Level Practice Book O, 149–155

lonesome wailed traders blossomed sidewalks grumbled

A. Use a word from the box to answer each question. Use each word only once.

1. How might you feel if you moved to a new town where you did not know anyone? **lonesome**

2. What is another word for *complained in a low voice*?
   grumbled

3. What is the safest place for people to walk? **sidewalk**

4. What word might describe an idea that grew very quickly?
   blossomed

5. Who might be upset if they couldn't sell their goods?
   traders

6. What did the coyote do when it lifted its head toward the moon?
   wailed

Possible responses provided.
B. Write a sentence using each of the vocabulary words below.

7. lonesome **The guard was very lonesome when he worked by himself at night.**

8. grumbled **Many of the workers grumbled when the boss announced the new rules.**

Beyond Practice Book B, 149–155

Write the correct definition as a clue for each vocabulary word in the puzzle. Possible responses provided.

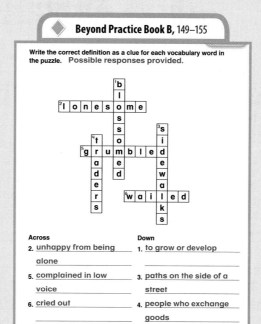

Across
2. unhappy from being alone
5. complained in low voice
6. cried out

Down
1. to grow or develop
3. paths on the side of a street
4. people who exchange goods

ELL Practice and Assessment, 134–135

Grade 3

TREASURES

ELL
Practice and Assessment

Macmillan/McGraw-Hill

Parent Letter

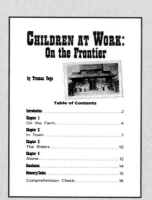

Take-Home Story

Turn the page for Cross-Curricular Activities.

Managing the Class

Cross-Curricular Activities

All activities reinforce this week's skills.

 ## Reading

Objectives

- Read aloud with a partner for fluency.
- Read a nonfiction chapter book about a historical event.
- Read independently daily.

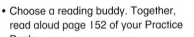 **Reading** | **Fluency** | 20 Minutes

- Choose a reading buddy. Together, read aloud page 152 of your Practice Book.
- Pause at commas and periods.

Extension

- How well did you and your partner read together? Discuss your reading. Did you both remember to pause for commas and periods?
- Listen to the Audio Disc.

Things you need:
- Practice Book
- Audio Disc

Fluency Solutions
Listening Library
41

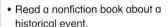 **Reading** | **Independent Reading** | 20 Minutes

- Read a nonfiction book about a historical event.
- Remember to check your understanding as you read. Use what you have learned about asking questions to help you understand the event.

Extension

- Tell a classmate about the event.
- Tell your classmate why you did or did not like the book.
- Write your opinion of the book in your response journal.

Things you need:
- nonfiction book
- journal and pencil

For more books about Making Money, go to the Author/Illustrator section at www.macmillanmh.com
42

Word Study

Objectives

- Use a dictionary to find the meanings of compound words.
- Make compound words.

Word Study | **Compound Words** | 20 Minutes

- Write these words on note cards: *side* and *walk*. Put them together to make a compound word.
- Then make cards for *step* and *line*. Put these words with the word *side* to make new words. Write all compound words on note cards.

Extension

- Use a dictionary. Look up the meanings of your new words.
- Write more compound words that begin with *side*. Use the dictionary.

side   step   walk   line

Things you need:
- note cards
- pencil
- dictionary

For additional vocabulary and spelling games, go to www.macmillanmh.com   Vocabulary PuzzleMaker
41

Word Study | **Compound Words** | 20 Minutes

- With a partner, write these words on note cards: *some, one, time, day, birth,* and *light.*
- Have a word building race. Build as many compound words as you can.
- List all your compound words. The one with the most compound words wins.

Extension

- Share your lists of words.
- What do the words mean? Check in a dictionary.

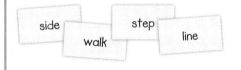

some   one   birth   day

Things you need:
- dictionary
- note cards
- pencil

For additional vocabulary and spelling games, go to www.macmillanmh.com   New Adventures with Buggles and Beezy
42

Independent Workstations

Objectives

- Write a descriptive paragraph.
- Write a diary entry.
- Write creatively for enjoyment.

Objectives

- Write sequence of events necessary for starting a business.
- Research the properties of silver and gold.

 Writing — **Descriptive Writing** — 20 Minutes

- How have you changed since you were a baby? Write a paragraph. Describe how you looked and what you did when you were little.
- Write another paragraph. Describe yourself now.

Extension

- Draw pictures for your paragraphs. Show how you looked as a baby and how you look today.

Things you need:
- paper
- pencil
- crayons or markers

41

Social Studies — **My Business Plan** — 20 Minutes

- With a partner, think of a business you could start. For example, you could mow lawns or do errands for neighbors.
- How would you start your business? Write the steps.

Extension

- Use a one-month calendar. Show when you would do each step. You might make flyers one week and give them out the next week.

Things you need:
- paper and pencil
- one-month calendar

 Internet Research and Inquiry Activity
Students can find more facts at www.macmillanmh.com

41

Writing — **Dear Journal** — 20 Minutes

- Pretend you were born in another country or in another time.
- In a journal, write about a day in your life in that time or place.
- Do research if you need more information.

Extension

- Write a second journal entry describing a day in your life now. How were descriptions different?

Things you need:
- paper
- pencil

42

Science — **Silver and Gold** — 20 Minutes

- American coins were once made of gold and silver.
- Use an encyclopedia, the Internet, or a science book. Learn about the metals silver and gold. They are both elements. What are their properties?

Extension

- Use your notes to write a paragraph about what you learned about either silver or gold.

Things you need:
- computer, science book, or encyclopedia
- paper
- pencil

42

ORAL LANGUAGE
- Build Background
- Read Aloud
- Expand Vocabulary

 VOCABULARY
- Teach Words in Context
- Compound Words

COMPREHENSION
- **Strategy:** Summarize
- **Skill:** Sequence

SMALL GROUP OPTIONS

- Differentiated Instruction, pp. 183M–183V

Oral Language

Build Background

ACCESS PRIOR KNOWLEDGE

Share the following information.

During the California Gold Rush from 1849 to 1864, half a million people traveled to California to find gold and make lots of money.

TALK ABOUT MAKING MONEY

Discuss the weekly theme.

- Do you think that looking for gold is a good way to earn money? Why or why not?

- Have you ever earned money? If so, how?

 FOCUS QUESTION Ask a volunteer to read "Talk About It" on **Student Book** page 151 and describe the photo. Ask:

- Why is it important to have a job?

ENGLISH LANGUAGE LEARNERS

Beginning Pantomime Have students say what they can about the photo. Act out throwing a paper and say: *He's a paper boy. He delivers papers.* Have students repeat. Ask: *Why is this boy delivering newspapers? Is that his job? Is he making money?* Help students say what they can.

Intermediate Ask Questions Establish that the boy in the photo is making money doing a job. Ask: *What other kinds of jobs can young people do? Do you make money doing any jobs?* Restate students' ideas using more complex language and description.

Advanced Categorize Do the Intermediate task. Then have students make two lists: Jobs they are paid to do and jobs they do voluntarily.

Talk About It

How would you make money if you needed to buy something?

LOG ON Find out more about money at **www.macmillanmh.com**

151

Picture Prompt

Tell students: Look at the picture. Write about what you see. You can write a poem, a story, a description, or use any other type of writing you like.

LOG ON Technology

For an extended lesson plan and Web site activities for **oral language development,** go to **www.macmillanmh.com**

Read Aloud
Read *Music, Music for Everyone*

GENRE: Realistic Fiction

Review features of realistic fiction:

- is an invented story that includes realistic characters and events

- could happen in real life

- has a clear sequence of events

LISTENING FOR A PURPOSE

Ask students to listen carefully for ways in which the author describes the main character, Rosa, in *Music, Music for Everyone* in the **Read-Aloud Anthology**. Choose from among the teaching suggestions.

Fluency Ask students to listen carefully as the story is read aloud. Tell students to listen to the phrasing, expression, and tone of voice.

RESPOND TO THE STORY

Ask students: If you wanted to earn money for something important, what would you do?

Expand Vocabulary

Ask students to choose three or more words from the story that relate to the theme of making money *(money jar, divide, equal shares)*. Have students work in groups and use their words to cooperatively write a story about friends who figure out a way to earn money to help someone. Students read their stories aloud to the class.

Vocabulary

TEACH WORDS IN CONTEXT

Use the following routine.

Routine

Define: **Sidewalks** are paths placed next to a road.

Example: Long ago, sidewalks were made of wood boards.

Ask: Why are sidewalks useful?

EXPLANATION

■ A person who **grumbled** about something, complained about it in a low voice. The neighbors grumbled about the noisy street repairs. What have you grumbled about? EXAMPLE

■ **Traders** are people who buy and sell things or exchange one thing for another. Ancient traders carried spices across Asia. How were ancient traders like modern business people?

PRIOR KNOWLEDGE

■ A person or a business that grows and develops has **blossomed**. We say that a tree has blossomed when its flowers appear in the spring. Why do you think blossomed can be used for both meanings? MULTIPLE/MEANING WORDS

■ **Wailed** means cried out with a long high sound. The baby wailed and could not be comforted. What is the difference between wailed and sobbed?

COMPARE AND CONTRAST

■ A **lonesome** place is a long way from where people live. Very few people visit that lonesome place. What comes to mind when you think of a lonesome place? DESCRIPTION

Vocabulary

sidewalks	blossomed
grumbled	wailed
traders	lonesome

Word Parts
Compound Words are words that are made up of two smaller words.

side + walks = *sidewalks*

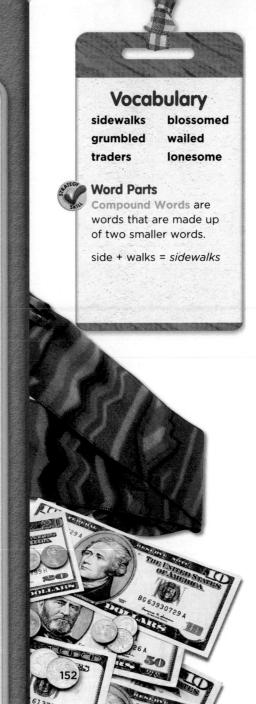

Let's Trade!

by Alex Ely

Elizabeth and Danny walked along newly paved **sidewalks** on a frosty winter morning. Elizabeth wore a hat and gloves but no scarf. Danny wore a hat and two scarves, but he didn't have any gloves. Both of them were freezing.

"I'm so cold," Elizabeth **grumbled** under her breath.

"Me too," Danny **wailed**.

Then Elizabeth had an idea! "What if I traded you one glove for one of your scarves?" Elizabeth said. "Then both of our necks would be warm, and we'd each have one warm hand. We could put the other hand in our pockets."

"Good idea!" said Danny.

After they shared the scarf and glove, they began to feel warmer.

A few minutes later Mrs. Baxter appeared. "Did I just see you barter?" she asked.

Elizabeth and Danny looked puzzled. "What's barter?" Elizabeth asked.

Quick Check

Do students understand word meanings?

During **Small Group Instruction**

If No → **Approaching Level** Vocabulary, p. 183P

If Yes → **On Level** Options, pp. 183Q–183R

Beyond Level Options, pp. 183S–183T

"Barter means trade," Mrs. Baxter explained. "You two traded a scarf and a glove so you could be warm. Did you know that **traders** bartered for thousands of years?"

"Really? How did it work?" Danny asked.

Mrs. Baxter said, "Well, traders who had too much of one thing, such as salt or cloth or pigs, would exchange them with other traders for other things that they needed. Trading grew and **blossomed**, but it had problems."

"Like what?" Elizabeth asked.

"Suppose you raised chickens. You could trade the chickens and eggs for what you needed. But if the chickens got away—"

"I wouldn't have anything to trade!"

"Exactly!" said Mrs. Baxter.

"And you'd be so **lonesome** without your poultry friends!" Danny said with a grin.

"Now you see why people began to use money to trade," Mrs. Baxter said.

"Is it true that silver and gold coins were used before paper money?" Danny asked.

"Yes, but they were too heavy to carry." Mrs. Baxter said. "People then began to write promises on paper instead of trading coins. That was how paper money got its start."

"Wow!" said Elizabeth, "but I guess people still trade sometimes, the way Danny and I did today!"

Reread for **Comprehension**

Summarize

Sequence

The sequence of events in a story is the order in which things take place. You can summarize the sequence of events in a story by paying close attention to when events happen.

A Sequence Chart helps you summarize story events in time order. Reread the story to find the order in which things happened.

Event
↓
↓
↓

153

Vocabulary

Using the Strategies To figure out unfamiliar words, students can

- decode words using phonics principles;
- look for word parts;
- look for context clues;
- use a dictionary.

STRATEGY
IDENTIFY WORD PARTS

Compound Words A compound word is made up of two shorter words, such as *space* and *ship* in *spaceship* or *base* and *ball* in *baseball*. A reader can often put together the meanings of the two words to figure out the meaning of the compound word.

Point to the word *sidewalks* on **Student Book** page 152. Point out the two smaller words that form it, *side* and *walks*. Ask students what they think the two words mean together. (walks along the side of something)

Point out that readers can't always figure out the meaning of a compound word from the two smaller words. When this happens, they need to look up the word in a dictionary.

Read "Let's Trade"

As students read "Let's Trade," ask them to identify clues to the meanings of the highlighted words. Tell students they will read these words again in *Boom Town*.

Vocabulary

Review last week's vocabulary words: **eparate, determination, storage, rate, exact, ruined,** and **luckiest.**

On Level Practice Book O, page 149

lonesome   wailed   traders   blossomed   sidewalks   grumbled

A. Use a word from the box to answer each question. Use each word only once.

1. How might you feel if you moved to a new town where you did not know anyone? _____ **lonesome**

2. What is another word for *complained in a low voice?*
   grumbled

3. What is the safest place for people to walk? _____ **sidewalk**

4. What word might describe an idea that grew very quickly?
   blossomed

5. Who might be upset if they couldn't sell their goods?
   traders

6. What did the coyote do when it lifted its head toward the moon?
   wailed

Possible responses provided.
B. Write a sentence using each of the vocabulary words below.

7. lonesome   The guard was very lonesome when he
   worked by himself at night.

8. grumbled   Many of the workers grumbled when the
   boss announced the new rules.

⭐ **Approaching Practice Book A,** page 149

◆ **Beyond Practice Book B,** page 149

Objectives

- Summarize important ideas
- Use academic language: *summarize, sequence of events*
- Identify the sequence of events in a story

Materials

- Comprehension Transparencies 21a and 21b
- Graphic Organizer Transparency 21
- Leveled Practice Books, p. 150

Skills Trace

Summarize: Sequence

Introduce	U3: 387A–B
Practice / Apply	U3: 388–409; Leveled Practice, 104–105
Reteach / Review	U3: 417M–T; U5: 153A–B, 154–175, 183M–T; Leveled Practice, 150–151
Assess	Weekly Tests; Unit 3, 5 Tests; Benchmark Tests A, B
Maintain	U4: 107B; U5: 253B

ELL
Access for All

Ask Questions Check students' comprehension of the text by asking questions as you do the Think Aloud: *What are Elizabeth and Danny doing? Where are they? What's the weather? What's the problem?* Write the signal words on the board as you identify them. For the last paragraph, help students restate the event orally using the signal words.

STRATEGY
SUMMARIZE

A **summary** is a short statement of the most important events in a story. When readers **summarize a story,** they tell the most important events in the story in sequence. Summarizing helps readers understand and remember what they read because they have to describe the important events in their own words.

SKILL
SEQUENCE

EXPLAIN

- In a fiction story, **sequence** is the order in which events happen.

- Signal words and phrases, such as *first, then, next, last, later,* and *after,* help a reader figure out when events take place. If there are no signal words, then use story clues and picture clues to figure out the sequence of events.

Transparency 21a

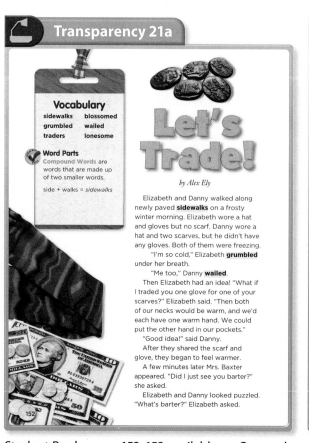

Vocabulary
sidewalks   blossomed
grumbled   wailed
traders   lonesome

Word Parts
Compound Words are words that are made up of two smaller words.
side + walks = *sidewalks*

Let's Trade!
by Alex Ely

Elizabeth and Danny walked along newly paved **sidewalks** on a frosty winter morning. Elizabeth wore a hat and gloves but no scarf. Danny wore a hat and two scarves, but he didn't have any gloves. Both of them were freezing.

"I'm so cold," Elizabeth **grumbled** under her breath.

"Me too," Danny **wailed**.

Then Elizabeth had an idea! "What if I traded you one glove for one of your scarves?" Elizabeth said. "Then both of our necks would be warm, and we'd each have one warm hand. We could put the other hand in our pockets."

"Good idea!" said Danny.

After they shared the scarf and glove, they began to feel warmer.

A few minutes later Mrs. Baxter appeared. "Did I just see you barter?" she asked.

Elizabeth and Danny looked puzzled. "What's barter?" Elizabeth asked.

152

Transparency 21b

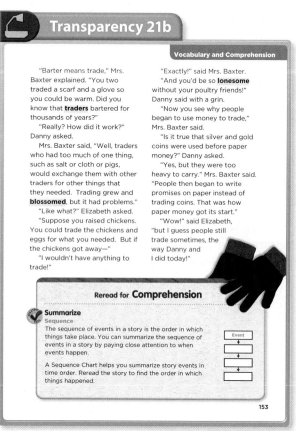

Vocabulary and Comprehension

"Barter means trade," Mrs. Baxter explained. "You two traded a scarf and a glove so you could be warm. Did you know that **traders** bartered for thousands of years?"

"Really? How did it work?" Danny asked.

Mrs. Baxter said, "Well, traders who had too much of one thing, such as salt or cloth or pigs, would exchange them with other traders for other things that they needed. Trading grew and **blossomed**, but it had problems."

"Like what?" Elizabeth asked.

"Suppose you raised chickens. You could trade the chickens and eggs for what you needed. But if the chickens got away—"

"I wouldn't have anything to trade!"

"Exactly!" said Mrs. Baxter.

"And you'd be so **lonesome** without your poultry friends!" Danny said with a grin.

"Now you see why people began to use money to trade," Mrs. Baxter said.

"Is it true that silver and gold coins were used before paper money?" Danny asked.

"Yes, but they were too heavy to carry." Mrs. Baxter said. "People then began to write promises on paper instead of trading coins. That was how paper money got its start."

"Wow!" said Elizabeth, "but I guess people still trade sometimes, the way Danny and I did today!"

Reread for Comprehension

Summarize
Sequence
The sequence of events in a story is the order in which things take place. You can summarize the sequence of events in a story by paying close attention to when events happen.

A Sequence Chart helps you summarize story events in time order. Reread the story to find the order in which things happened.

Event
↓
↓

153

Student Book pages 152–153 available on Comprehension Transparencies 21a and 21b

MODEL

Read aloud the first six paragraphs of "Let's Trade!" on **Student Book** page 152.

 Think Aloud I want to keep track of the order in which the events take place in this story. In the beginning, Elizabeth and Danny walk together. They are cold because they aren't wearing warm clothes. As I continue to read, I see the signal word *then*. It tells me what happens next: Elizabeth has an idea that they can share gloves and scarves to be warmer. Danny agrees that they should share.

GUIDED PRACTICE

Display the Sequence Chart on **Transparency 21.** Have students complete the chart using the first six paragraphs of "Let's Trade!" on page 152. Help students identify the first three events in the story and place each on the chart: (Elizabeth and Danny are walking and feeling cold. Then Elizabeth has an idea to share their scarves and gloves. After sharing the scarves and gloves, they feel warmer.) Have students place these events on their Sequence Charts.

APPLY

Have students read the last two paragraphs on page 152 and the first column on page 153. Ask them: *What happens next? What signal words help you figure this out?* (Mrs. Baxter asks Elizabeth and Danny if they were bartering. The signal words are *a few minutes later*.) Have students summarize the rest of this selection and place the last event in the bottom box on the Sequence Chart. Then have students use their charts to summarize what important events have happened in the story so far.

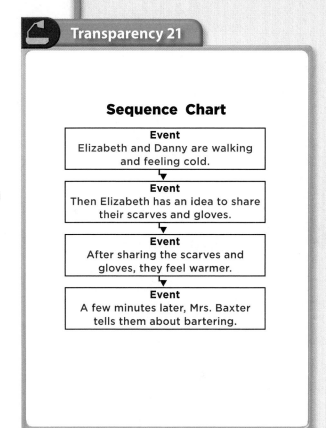

Transparency 21

Sequence Chart

| **Event** |
| Elizabeth and Danny are walking and feeling cold. |

↓

| **Event** |
| Then Elizabeth has an idea to share their scarves and gloves. |

↓

| **Event** |
| After sharing the scarves and gloves, they feel warmer. |

↓

| **Event** |
| A few minutes later, Mrs. Baxter tells them about bartering. |

Graphic Organizer Transparency 21

Quick Check Do students understand how to identify the sequence of events in a fiction story?

During **Small Group Instruction**

If No → **Approaching Level** Comprehension, p. 183O

If Yes → **On Level** Options, pp. 183Q–183R

Beyond Level Options, pp. 183S–183T

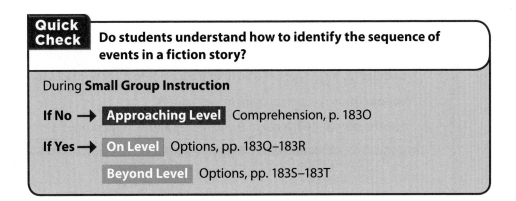

On Level Practice Book O, page 150

In a story, the events happen in a certain **sequence,** or order.

Read the events below, which are out of order. Then write the events in the order that they happened.

a. Many people liked the shirt that Jessica had sewn for her brother.
b. As the business grew, Jessica could not keep up with all the work.
c. Soon Jessica started a children's clothing business.
d. Jessica and her family moved to California to seek gold.
e. Jessica cut up an old sheet to make a shirt for her brother.
f. When Jessica convinced her brother and two friends to help, her business blossomed.

1. Jessica and her family moved to California to seek gold.
2. Jessica cut up an old sheet to make a shirt for her brother.
3. Many people liked the shirt that Jessica had sewn for her brother.
4. Soon Jessica started a children's clothing business.
5. As the business grew, Jessica could not keep up with all the work.
6. When Jessica convinced her brother and two friends to help, her business blossomed.

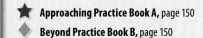

★ **Approaching Practice Book A,** page 150

◆ **Beyond Practice Book B,** page 150

Read

MAIN SELECTION
- *Boom Town*
- **Skill:** Sequence

PAIRED SELECTION
- "How to Earn Money!"
- **Study Skill:** Using a Calendar

WRITING
- Descriptive Writing
- **Writing Trait:** Organization

SMALL GROUP OPTIONS

- Differentiated Instruction, pp. 183M–183V

Comprehension

GENRE: HISTORICAL FICTION

Have a student read the definition of Historical Fiction on **Student Book** page 154. Students should look for details about the California Gold Rush as they read.

STRATEGY
SUMMARIZE

A summary tells about the most important events in a story. Good readers **summarize** as they read to help them understand the sequence of important events in a story.

SKILL
SEQUENCE

Sequence is the order in which events happen. Signal words and phrases, such as *first, then, next, last, after,* and *before,* help a reader figure out when each event takes place in a story.

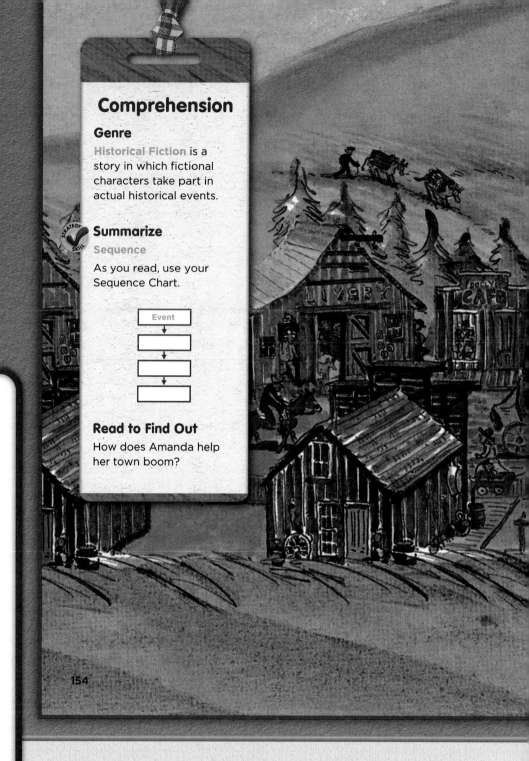

Comprehension

Genre

Historical Fiction is a story in which fictional characters take part in actual historical events.

Summarize

Sequence

As you read, use your Sequence Chart.

Event
↓
↓
↓

Read to Find Out

How does Amanda help her town boom?

154

Vocabulary

Vocabulary Words Review the tested vocabulary words: **sidewalks, grumbled, traders, blossomed, wailed,** and **lonesome.**

Story Words Students may find these words difficult. Pronounce the words and present the meanings as necessary.

stagecoach (p. 157): a carriage pulled by horses that carries people and mail

peddler (p. 166): a person who goes from place to place and sells things

cooper (p. 167): a person who makes barrels

apothecary (p. 168) a person who makes and sells medicine

BOOM TOWN

by Sonia Levitin

illustrated by Cat Bowman Smith

Award Winning Author

155

Read Together

If your students need support to read the Main Selection, use the prompts to guide comprehension and model how to complete the graphic organizer.

Read Independently

If your students can read the Main Selection independently, have them read and complete the graphic organizer. Have them set and modify their purposes when reading.

If your students need an alternate selection, choose the **Leveled Readers** that match their instructional level.

Technology

Story available on **Listening Library Audio CD**

Preview and Predict

Ask students to read the title, preview the illustrations and story topic, and note questions and predictions. Who is the main character? What will she do? Have students record their predictions and questions about the story.

Set Purposes

FOCUS QUESTION Talk about the "Read to Find Out" question and discuss with students how to look for the answer. Remind students to set their own purposes.

Point out the Sequence Chart in the **Student Book** and on **Leveled Practice Book** page 151. Explain that students will fill it in as they read.

Read *Boom Town*

Use the questions and Think Alouds for additional instruction to support the comprehension strategy and skill.

> **On Level Practice Book O,** page 151
>
> As you read *Boom Town*, fill in the Sequence Chart.
>
> **Sequence Chart**
>
> | Event |
> | --- |
>
> ↓
>
> | Event |
> | --- |
>
> **Sequence Chart**
>
> | Event |
> | --- |
>
> ↓
>
> | Event |
> | --- |
>
> ↓
>
> | Event |
> | --- |
>
> ↓
>
> | Event |
> | --- |
>
> ↓
>
> | Event |
> | --- |
>
> How does the information you wrote in this Sequence Chart help you summarize *Boom Town*?

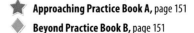

⭐ **Approaching Practice Book A,** page 151

◆ **Beyond Practice Book B,** page 151

Develop Comprehension

1 MAKE PREDICTIONS

Who do you think is the main character in this story? Why do you think this? Use the illustration to help make a prediction. (Answers may vary: Students will probably say that the main character will be the girl shown on pages 155 and 156. She is the person who stands out in the illustration.)

1

156

ELL   Access for All

Use Visuals Point out on page 157 the places and items the story mentions: the tents in the gold fields, the stagecoach, and the log cabins. Make sure students understand that Pa is going to work in the fields as a miner to look for gold. Have students guess which child in the picture is telling the story.

It took us twenty-one days on the stagecoach to get to California. When we got there, I thought we'd live with Pa in the gold fields. A whole tent city was built up. But Ma shook her head. "The gold fields are no place for children. We'll get a cabin and live in town."

2

What town? A stage stop, a pump house, a few log cabins— that was all. It was so wide and **lonesome** out west, even my shadow ran off.

3

157

Develop Comprehension

2 SEQUENCE

What are the first two events that happen in this story? Let's write these events on a Sequence Chart. (The first thing the narrator describes is the family's arrival in California by stagecoach. Next, Ma decides that the family will live in a cabin in town, not in a tent in the gold fields.)

> **Event**
> The family arrives in California.
>
> ↓
>
> **Event**
> Ma decides that the family will live in town.

3 GENRE: HISTORICAL FICTION

What clues tell you this story takes place in the past? (Characters travel by stagecoach, and some of them are looking for gold. The illustrations show people in old-fashioned clothes and land that has few people, roads, and buildings on it. This is how California looked long ago, not how it looks today.)

Comprehension

Narrator's Point of View

Explain Sometimes a character in a story is also the narrator. That character tells the story in his or her own words and uses the pronouns *I, me, my,* and *mine* to tell about what happens. Everything the reader finds out is from the narrator's point of view.

Discuss Help students see that a story character is the narrator. Point out the first paragraph of the story. Ask students: *How do you know that the narrator is a character in the story?* (The pronoun *I* tells me that the narrator is telling the story.)

Apply Have students find proof in the second paragraph on page 157 that the narrator is a story character. (The word *my* in "It was so wide and lonesome out west, even my shadow ran off" shows the narrator is telling the story.)

Vocabulary

Read the sentence that contains the word **lonesome**. Use *lonesome* in a sentence of your own. (I felt lonesome sitting at the table all by myself, but then my friends came along and sat with me.)

Develop Comprehension

4 NARRATOR'S POINT OF VIEW

Who is telling the story? How can you tell? (Amanda is telling the story. She tells her name and uses the pronoun *me* in the first paragraph.)

5 CONFIRM OR REVISE PREDICTIONS

Was your prediction correct about who the main character is? (Students may say that their prediction was correct. On page 158 they read that the narrator tells who the other members of the family are and says that her name is Amanda, so she is the main character. If students' predictions were not correct, they should revise them and understand that Amanda is the main character in the story.)

6 SEQUENCE

What does Pa do every Saturday night once he gets home? How can you tell the order in which he does these things? (First, Ma makes him take a bath. Then, he sings songs and tells stories. The words *first* and *then* show the sequence.)

4 5 Ma found a cabin big enough for all of us: Baby Betsy, brothers Billy, Joe, Ted, and me—Amanda. Pa came in from the gold fields every Saturday night, singing:

"So I got me a mule
And some mining tools,
A shovel and a pick and a pan;

But I work all day
Without no pay.
I guess I'm a foolish man."

6 First Ma made him take a bath in a tin tub set out under the stars. Then Pa sang songs and told stories he'd heard from the miners—stories about men finding big nuggets and striking it rich. But poor Pa, he had no luck at all. Still, every Monday morning he'd leave for the gold fields full of hope.

158

Comprehension

Sequence

Explain Sequence is the order in which events take place in a story. Signal words such as *first, second,* and *last,* help a reader understand the order in which events in a story take place. Knowing the sequence of events helps a reader understand the story.

Discuss Ask: *What did Amanda's family do before they came to California?* (They traveled for 21 days by stagecoach.) *What does Pa do after the weekend ends?* (Pa goes back to the gold fields every Monday morning.)

Apply As students continue reading, ask them to pay attention to the sequence in which events happen.

Days were long and lonely. The hills spread out as far as forever. Nights, me and Ma and my brothers and Baby Betsy would sit out and wait for a shooting star to sail across the sky. Once in a while a crow flew by. That's all the excitement there was.

My brothers worked up some furrows. They planted corn and potatoes and beans. Then they ran around climbing trees, skinning their knees. But after all the water was fetched and the wash was done, after the soap was made and the fire laid, after the beds were fixed and the floor was swept clean, I'd sit outside our cabin door with Baby Betsy, so bored I thought I'd die. Also, I hankered for some pie. I loved to bake pie. **7**

I asked Ma and she said, "Pie would be good, but we have no pie pans and no real oven, just the wood stove. How would you bake a pie?" **8**

159

Ways to Confirm Meaning

Semantic/Meaning Cues

Explain Tell students that good readers use their background knowledge and context clues to help them understand what they read.

Model Have students sound out *furrows* on page 159 and then predict the meaning. Then have them check the predicted meaning using context clues.

Think Aloud I've never seen the word *furrows* before, but clues tell me it has something to do with vegetables. The story says that Amanda's brothers planted corn, potatoes, and beans. I know that these vegetables are usually planted in rows. I think that *furrows* describes the rows of corn, potatoes, and beans.

Apply Encourage students to use phonics and context clues, background knowledge, and picture clues to help them with other difficult words or phrases, such as *lariat* on page 170.

Develop Comprehension

7 **STRATEGY**
MONITOR AND CLARIFY: READ AHEAD

Here Amanda mentions pie. How can reading ahead help you figure out if pie will be an important part of this story? (On pages 160-161 I see that the illustrations show Amanda making pie. If I read page 160, the text mentions gooseberries, a skillet, and crust. Looking ahead to page 163 I see more references to pie. I think pie will be an important part of this story.)

8 **REALISTIC FICTION**

Are the characters and their actions, the events in the story, and setting of the story realistic? How can you tell? (Yes they are realistic. I can tell because the characters talk like real people and their actions—looking for gold, planting gardens, cooking on wood stoves—are the kinds of things that people a long time ago did. The setting is California during the Gold Rush. I know that that was a real event that happened in a real part of the country that is now California.)

Develop Comprehension

9 **STRATEGY**
SUMMARIZE

Teacher Think Aloud Now that I've read a few pages of the story, I'll stop to summarize what has happened so far. This will help me understand and remember the events that have taken place. I'll include only the most important parts because a summary does not tell every detail. I know that Amanda and her family have traveled to California, where her father is mining for gold. Amanda is bored because there isn't much for her to do. She decides to make a pie in the family's skillet. In my summary, there is important information about the main character, the setting, and the plot, but I have left out details that are not important. I have also told the events in the order, or sequence, in which they happened. Now I understand what I've read, and I'm ready to read on.

9 **10**   I poked around in a big box of stuff and found an old iron skillet. I decided to make a pie crust and pick gooseberries to fill it.

Gooseberries grew on the bushes near town. I picked a big pailful and went back home. I made a crust with flour, butter, a little water, and a pinch of salt, and then I rolled it out.

Ma came in and said, "Looks good, Amanda. I knew you could make it. But tell me, how will you bake it?"

I showed Ma the skillet. She shook her head. "I don't think it will work, but you can try."

"It will work," I said.

Sequence
What steps does Amanda take to start baking her pie?

160

161

Develop Comprehension

 10 **SEQUENCE**

What steps does Amanda take to start baking her pies? (Amanda finds a skillet. She picks gooseberries. Then she makes and rolls out a crust made with flour, butter, water, and salt.)

STRATEGIES FOR EXTRA SUPPORT

Question 10 SEQUENCE
Explain that Amanda "takes steps," or, in other words, does a series of actions, to make a pie. Ask students to name each of Amanda's actions and write them on the board. Act out each action with students. Help students use the sequence words *first, then,* and *after that* to talk about the events in the correct sequence. Act out the actions with students as you restate each step.

Develop Comprehension

11 FIGURATIVE LANGUAGE: SIMILE

A simile compares two unlike things using *like* or *as*. What are two similes found on pages 162 and 163? How do they help you understand what is happening in the story? (The simile on page 162—"my pie, hard as a rock"—compares Amanda's pie to a rock and helps me understand how hard the pie is. The second simile on page 163—"she wailed like a coyote in the night"—helps me understand how loud and mournful Baby Betsy sounds when she cries.)

12 SEQUENCE

What events took place after Amanda decided to bake another pie? What words give you clues to the sequence? (Amanda made the pie, baked it, put it aside to cool, and did some mending. Then Baby Betsy ruined the pie, so Amanda made another one. *Next* and *that night* give clues.)

Brothers Billy and Joe and Ted stood there laughing. When the wood turned to coals, I pushed my pie inside the old stove. After a while I smelled a bad burning. I pulled out my pie, hard as a rock. Billy, Joe, and Ted whooped and slapped their sides. They snatched up my pie and tossed it high into the air. They ran outside and Billy whacked it hard with a stick. Pie pieces flew all over the place, and my brothers bent over, laughing.

162

Fluency

Echo-Reading

Explain Punctuation tells readers when they should pause and for how long. Commas often separate phrases from the rest of the sentence, making it easier to read aloud.

Model Model how to pause at commas and come to a stop at periods. Read the passage, available on **Fluency Transparency 21,** pausing appropriately to show punctuation.

Apply Ask students to raise their hands when they hear you pause, and lower them when you continue reading. Ask students to identify the punctuation marks after you finish reading a sentence.

I was so mad I went right back in to make another, and I swore none of them would get a bite. I rolled out my crust and filled it with berries, shoved the pie into the oven, and soon took it out. **12**

I set the pie down to cool. I went off to do some mending. Next thing I knew, Baby Betsy, just learning to walk, sat there with pie goo all over her face. Too soft, the filling ran down on Betsy, and she **wailed** like a coyote in the night. **13**

It took one more try, but I got it right. That night we ate my gooseberry pie, and it was delicious. **14**

163

Main Selection   Student page 163

Read

Develop Comprehension

13 MAKE INFERENCES

Why didn't Amanda know that Baby Betsy was trying to eat the pie? (Amanda left the pie to cool, then went off to do some mending. She was busy and didn't see Betsy go near the pie. Amanda didn't know what Betsy had done until she heard her crying.)

14 CHARACTER

What kind of person is Amanda? How do you know? (Amanda does not give up. She keeps trying even when her brothers do not think she will be able to make a good pie. She is not surprised when the third pie is delicious.)

Have students respond to the selection by confirming or revising their predictions and note additional questions.

Quick Check Can students identify the sequence of events as they read? If not, see the **Extra Support** on this page.

Extra Support

Sequence

If students have difficulty understanding the sequence in which events take place, have a student pantomime Amanda making a pie, placing it in the oven, taking it out, and leaving it on a counter to cool. Ask the student to walk to another part of the classroom and begin "mending," while another student pantomimes Baby Betsy walking in slow, careful steps to the "pie," pretending to eat it, and then crying. "Amanda" runs back in to see what has happened.

If students are still having trouble, have them reread the first two paragraphs on page 163. What did Amanda do to make the pie? (She rolled out the crust, filled it with berries, put it in the oven, and baked it.) Then what did Amanda do? (some mending) What did Betsy do after that? (She tried to eat the pie.)

Stop here if you wish to read this selection over two days.

Develop Comprehension

15 **STRATEGY**
SUMMARIZE

Teacher Think Aloud Summarizing a story's events in sequence helps me understand and remember what I read. To summarize, I tell the most important things that happen. How would you summarize the story up until now? How does this help you understand the story?

Encourage students to apply the strategy in a Think Aloud.

Student Think Aloud Amanda's family moved to California. Her father looks for gold. The rest of the family moves to a cabin in town. There is nothing to do but garden and do chores and watch the baby. Amanda is bored, so she decides to bake a pie. She gathers gooseberries, makes a crust, and bakes her first pie. It is as hard as a rock, and her brothers make fun of it. She makes another pie that the baby eats. Her third pie is delicious. Summarizing helped me understand and remember what is happening in the story.

16 **SEQUENCE**

What happens after Amanda bakes a pie for Pa to take to the gold fields? (Pa sells pieces of the pie to other miners. Then he takes pies to the gold fields every week. Soon miners come, looking for more pies.)

15

When Pa came home from the gold fields on Saturday night, there was a pie for him, too. "Amanda, you are the queen of the kitchen!" Pa scooped me up and whirled me around. I was proud.

The next week I made an extra pie for Pa to take with him to the gold fields.

Saturday night when he came home singing, coins jangled in his pocket.

We all ran out to ask, "Did you strike gold, Pa?"

"No," he said. "I sold Amanda's pie. The miners loved it. They paid me twenty-five cents a slice!"

After that, Pa took pies to the gold fields every week. **16** And every week he came home with coins in his pockets. Some miners walked right to our door looking for pie. They told Ma, "You should open a bakery."

Ma said, "It's my girl Amanda who is the baker. If she wants to make pies, that's fine. But I have no time."

164

Ma had a new baby on the way. It was up to me. I figured I could sell pies to the miners and fill up our money jar.

But I needed help. I rounded up my brothers and told them, "If you want to eat pie, you've got to work."

They **grumbled** and groaned, but they knew I meant it. So Billy built me a shelf, Joe made a sign, AMANDA'S FINE PIES, and Ted helped pick berries and sour apples.

17

165

Develop Comprehension

17 MAKE INFERENCES

What does Amanda mean when she says, "Ma had a new baby on the way. It was up to me"? (I know that babies need a lot of care, so Ma will be too busy to help with the baking business. Amanda knows she will have to do everything herself, if she wants the business to succeed.)

RESEARCH
Why It Matters

English Language Learners Having students encounter vocabulary words often and in various ways can have a significant effect. All the more so for ELLs who are learning a new language.

Jana Echevarria

 Log on to
www. macmillanmh.com

Vocabulary

Read the sentence that contains the word **grumbled**. What is another word that means the same as *grumbled*? (complained)

Develop Comprehension

18 SEQUENCE

What happens in the town after Amanda opens a bakery to sell her pies? Let's write the events on a Sequence Chart. (Peddler Pete opens a trading post. Travelers begin to stop in the town to go to the trading post and buy Amanda's pies. Some people decide to stay in the town. They open new businesses.)

Event Amanda opens a bakery.
↓
Event Peddler Pete opens a trading post.
↓
Event Travelers stop at the trading post and bakery.
↓
Event Some people decide to stay in the town.
↓
Event New businesses run by a cooper, a tanner, a miller, and a blacksmith open.

I needed more pans and another bucket. One day Peddler Pete came by, and with the money I'd made I bought them.

"You're a right smart little girl," said the peddler, "being in business like this."

I thought fast and told him, "Anybody can make money out here. Folks need things all the time, and there're no stores around. If you were to settle and start one, I'll bet you'd get rich."

Peddler Pete scratched his beard. "Not a bad idea," he said. "My feet are sore from roaming. I could use this cart and build my way up to having a store."

So pretty soon we had us a real store called PEDDLER PETE'S TRADING POST. Trappers and **traders** and travelers appeared. After shopping at Pete's, they were good and hungry.

166

ELL

STRATEGIES FOR EXTRA SUPPORT

Question 18 SEQUENCE

Ask: *What happened first after Amanda opened her bakery?* Help students say what they can about Peddler Pete. Use the illustration on page 166 to explain what a peddler is. Discuss the kinds of items that were sold in a trading post. Ask: *What happened after the trading post opened? Who came to buy things there? Did the people like the town? What did they decide to do? What businesses opened?* Use the illustrations on page 167 to explain the words *cooper, tanner, miller,* and *blacksmith.*

They came to our cabin, looking for pie. Some liked it here so well they decided to stay. Soon we had a cooper, a tanner, a miller, a blacksmith. A town was starting to grow. **18**

A prospector came in on the stage from St. Joe, his clothes covered with dirt. He looked around at the folks eating pie, and he asked, "Is there someone here who does washing?"

I stepped right up and I told him, "What we need is a laundry. Why don't you stay and start one? Why, the miners are sending their shirts clear to China. You'll make more money doing laundry than looking for gold." **19**

The man thought a while, then said with a smile, "You're right, little lady. It's a dandy idea. I'll send for my wife to help."

167

Develop Comprehension

19 **MAKE INFERENCES**

Why does Amanda tell the prospector that he should start a laundry instead of starting a laundry herself? (Amanda already has a business, but she thinks that someone should start a laundry. She knows that the people in town need to have their clothes washed, and that a laundry can help someone make a lot of money.)

Cross–Curricular Connection

STARTING A BUSINESS

Tell students that many successful businesses started with one popular product, just as Amanda's did. Then have students solve this math story and record it in a math journal.

A miner paid Amanda's father 25 cents for one slice of pie. Suppose the pie was cut into six pieces and sold. How much money did Amanda's father bring home? ($1.50) How much money would be made for one, then two, then three pies, cut into six slices each. ($1.50 for one; $3.00 for two; $4.50 for three) If the pies had been cut into eight slices instead of six, how much money would the family make? ($2.00 for one; $4.00 for two; $6.00 for three) Have students create their own math stories and record them in a math journal.

Develop Comprehension

20 MAINTAIN
DRAW CONCLUSIONS

Why does the town begin to change and grow? (Many of the miners stop by Amanda's house to buy pies and like the town so much that they decide to stay. Some of them, like Peddler Pete, start their own businesses. I know that when people move to town, they bring families with them. I know that families need to buy things, such as food and building supplies. They need places to wash their clothes. As a result, more people move to town and start more businesses. That is why Amanda's town begins to change and grow.)

Soon shirts and sheets fluttered on the line as people brought their washing in. A tailor came to make and mend clothes. A cobbler crafted shoes and boots. We heard the *tap tap* of his hammer and smelled the sweet leather. A barber moved in with shaving mugs, and an apothecary with herbs and healing drugs. So the town grew up all around us.

20

168

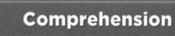

Comprehension

Reading Signs and Labels

Explain Most stores have signs that tell what they sell or do. Sometimes the signs include a picture of the item sold.

Discuss What signs do you see on pages 168–169? (Cobbler, Tailor Shop, The Boom Town Apothecary) What does each shop sell or do? (The cobbler makes and sells boots and shoes. The tailor makes and sells clothing. The apothecary makes and sells medicine.) Which store might have warning labels on its products? (the apothecary) What might these labels say? (Possible answer: Keep away from small children.)

Apply Invite students to choose another business for Boom Town and draw a picture of the store and its sign that would attract customers.

My pie business **blossomed**. Sometimes the line snaked clear around the house. Baby Betsy entertained the people while they waited. Billy added another shelf. Joe and Ted made a bench. We all picked berries and apples. Even Ma came to help. We had to get a bigger jar for all the money coming in.

21

Develop Comprehension

21 **GENRE: HISTORICAL FICTION**

What parts of the story tell about life in California long ago? What parts did the author make up? (The story tells about the kinds of jobs people had and how towns got started during the Gold Rush in California. The illustrations show what people's clothes and buildings in towns looked like. The author made up the characters, events, and the town Boom Town.)

Comprehension

Setting and Historical Fiction

Explain The setting in historical fiction often causes certain events to happen. Illustrations give readers clues about what it was like to live in the time and place in which the story is set.

Discuss What events in the story probably would not happen if this story were set in a different time? (There would not be gold miners if the story did not take place during the California Gold Rush. People would not use stagecoaches in a later time period. If the story setting were now, the town would already be settled and have many businesses. In a different time period, a young girl might not start her own business without help from adults.)

Apply Have students review the illustrations to find other examples of how the setting affects the events that take place.

Develop Comprehension

22 **FIGURATIVE LANGUAGE: IDIOMS**

What does Cowboy Charlie mean when he says, "I'd like to rest a spell"? (*Rest* means to relax and probably go to sleep. Cowboy Charlie asks where he can leave his horse for the night, so a *spell* must be a short period of time.)

23 **CHARACTER**

Who is the main character on page 170? Who is a minor character? How can you tell? (Amanda is the main character. The story is about her. Her actions determine the plot in the story. The minor character is Cowboy Charlie. He only helps Amanda move the plot along.)

22 One day our old friend Cowboy Charlie rode by. Like everyone else, he stopped for some pie. "I'd like to rest a spell," he said. "Where can I leave my horse for the night?"

"There's no livery stable," I said. "But why don't you start one? You'd rent out horses, and wagons too. That would be the perfect business for you."

"You're just full of great ideas, little lady," Cowboy Charlie said. He twirled his lariat. "I'd like to settle down. **23** I'll stay here and do just that."

170

Comprehension

Figurative Language: Idioms in Dialogue

Explain An idiom is a phrase whose meaning can't be understood from the ordinary meanings of the separate words in it. *You're pulling my leg* is an idiom. It means "you're not telling the truth." Idioms are a kind of informal language that people use more often in spoken than in written speech. Authors often use idioms to make dialogue more colorful and to give clues about characters' occupations or where and when they live.

Discuss Point out the idiom "rest a spell" on page 170. It means "rest for a short period of time." Explain that this idiom makes a cowboy like Charlie seem like a real person.

Apply Point out other idioms: *rounded up* (gathered together) on page 165 and *good and hungry* (very hungry) on page 166 and discuss how they add color to the story. Then have students figure out what they mean using context clues and a dictionary.

Soon a trail was worn right to Charlie's stable door. All day we heard the snorting of horses. Now Charlie needed hay. Farmers brought wagons and sacks full of feed. With all those people riding in, someone decided to build a hotel and a cafe. The town grew fast all around us.

The owner of the cafe bought pies from me, five or six at a time. I taught Billy how to roll the crust. Joe got wood for the stove. Ted washed the fruit, and Baby Betsy tried to stir in the sugar.

The money jar in our kitchen looked ready to bust. Where could we safely keep all that cash? Lucky us, one day Mr. Hooper, the banker, appeared.

"I'm building a bank," Mr. Hooper said to me. "This is getting to be a boom town."

"We'll use your bank," I told Mr. Hooper, "but the roads are so poor. In winter there's mud, and in summer there's dust. We need some **sidewalks** and better streets."

"You're a smart little lady," said Mr. Hooper, tipping his hat. "I'll see what I can do about that."

171

Develop Comprehension

24 **MAINTAIN**
DRAW CONCLUSIONS

Why does Amanda tell Mr. Hooper that the town needs some sidewalks and better streets? Why doesn't she tell someone else in town, such as Cowboy Charlie? (It costs money to make sidewalks and streets. A banker such as Mr. Hooper probably has enough money to build sidewalks, but Cowboy Charlie probably does not.)

Develop Comprehension

25 STRATEGY

Tested

IDENTIFY WORD PARTS

Can you figure out what the **compound word** *landmark* means by knowing what *land* and *mark* mean? Why or why not? (*Land* describes the ground. It is also an action verb that describes how a plane moves safely to the ground. A *mark* can be a spot made on something. *Mark* can also describe writing on something, such as "the teacher marks students' papers." When I put these two meanings together, I get "a spot made on a piece of land." That doesn't make sense. It's not possible to figure out which meanings of the two words are used in *landmark*. I will look up *landmark* in a dictionary.)

25 Before we knew it, the bank was built and wooden sidewalks were laid. One street was called Bank Street; the other was Main. Soon every lane and landmark had a name. Pa and my brothers built on a big room for our bakery.

Men sent for their families. New houses appeared everywhere. Babies and children filled up the town. We needed a school, and a good schoolmarm.

172

We knew Miss Camilla from our stagecoach days. She was living up the coast a ways. Cowboy Charlie rode off to fetch her, and she was glad to come.

Miss Camilla, the teacher, had married a preacher, and he came too. We all got together to build a church and a school. Bells rang out every day of the week. Now this was a real boom town!

One day Pa said to me, "Amanda, I'm through panning for gold. Will you let me be in business with you?" **26**

"Sure!" I said, happily. "I'd love to work with you, Pa, and I'd also like to go to school."

 Sequence
What sequence of events takes place to create this boom town? **27**

173

Develop Comprehension

26 **MAINTAIN**
DRAW CONCLUSIONS

Why do you think Pa decides to quit panning for gold to work with Amanda? (Earlier in the story, Pa sang about working all day without pay, meaning he doesn't find gold. He comes home each week with the money from selling pies, but no gold. He sees how quickly Amanda's business is growing. He wants to help her and work at something that is sure to pay off, unlike looking for gold.)

27 **SEQUENCE**

 What sequence of events takes place to create this boom town? (After people move to the town and start businesses, a bank opens. Then more families move to town. As the town grows, a school teacher and a preacher arrive. People then build a church and a school.)

 ## Research and Inquiry
Author Study

Sonia Levitin has written many books for children, including two more about Amanda—*Nine for California* and *Taking Charge.*

Have students do an author study on Sonia Levitin. They may wish to check the books out at the library. After they have finished reading, students can form literature circles, compare the books with *Boom Town*, discuss how the books are alike and different, and talk about how the character Amanda changes across the stories. Have them give specific examples to support their ideas about how she changes.

Students can extend their research and discussions to include other popular or favorite authors who have written series about the same character, such as Beverly Cleary's Ramona, Johanna Hurwitz's Ali Baba Bernstein, or Charlotte Herman's Max Malone. Students should keep a list of their reading accomplishments.

Develop Comprehension

28 MAINTAIN
DRAW CONCLUSIONS

Why does Amanda call the town a boom town? (Many people moved to the town and opened businesses that are "booming," or keeping all of the workers busy helping customers or making goods.)

29 STRATEGY
SUMMARIZE

How would you summarize what happens after Amanda gets her brothers to help her make pies to sell? What details would you include? Explain your thinking in a Think Aloud.

Student Think Aloud I know that I can't include every detail because not everything is important. I'll put only important parts of the story in my summary. People visit the town, and Amanda tells them to start businesses. More people move there, and soon the town has everything it needs. Amanda's baking business earns lots of money for the family. Pa gives up mining, so he can bake the pies while Amanda goes to the new school that the town has built. This summary tells me what happens as the story ends.

So Pa turned to baking, and we all worked together. Pa sang while he rolled out the dough:

"Amanda found a skillet
And berries to fill it,
Made pies without a pan;

Our pies are the best
In all the West.
I guess I'm a lucky man."

Now Pa is with us every day. There's excitement and bustle all around. Our house sits in the middle of a boom town! **28** **29**

174

Cultural Perspectives

COMMUNITY FESTIVAL

Tell students that Boom Town was like many real towns started during the California Gold Rush. Point out that the people worked hard but still had time to hold town festivals which celebrated special events or holidays, such as 4th of July or Cinco de Mayo.

Have students share their experiences with town festivals. Have them discuss these questions: *What is the town and where is it? What does the festival celebrate? What activities take place at the festival?* Have students research festivals in their area and make a book with a page for each festival, including the name of the festival, when and where it occurs, and what happens. Possible festivals might include: a Japanese cherry blossom festival, a Mexican Cinco de Mayo celebration, a Memorial Day celebration, a Korean cultural festival, and Chinese New Year.

And to think it all started with me, Amanda, baking pies!

175

Develop Comprehension

RETURN TO PREDICTIONS AND PURPOSES

Review students' predictions and purposes. Were they correct? Did students find out what the main character does to help her town?

REVIEW READING STRATEGIES

Ask students: Do you have any additional questions about the story? What strategies can you use to find answers? How did summarizing help you understand the sequence of events in the story? What strategies did you use when you came to unfamiliar or difficult words?

 PERSONAL RESPONSE

Ask students to write a paragraph describing the part of the story they liked best. You may also wish to have them reflect on themselves as readers. Then have them role play that scene with a partner for the class.

Quick Check **Can students keep track of the sequence of events in the story?**

During **Small Group Instruction**

If No → **Approaching Level**
Leveled Reader Lessons, pp. 183M–183N

If Yes → **On Level** Options, pp. 183Q–183R

Beyond Level Options, pp. 183S–183T

 Social Studies

Cross-Curricular Connection

THE CALIFORNIA GOLD RUSH

Boom Town takes place during the California Gold Rush, which lasted from 1849 to 1864. During this time about a half million people traveled to California to find gold. Many stayed, built towns, and started businesses. Wherever people gathered, culture—such as music, food, clothing—was an important part of their lives.

Have students research the history and culture of the Gold Rush. They can use books or the Internet, or watch a video about that time. Students may wish to find music and lyrics for the popular song of the time, "Oh My Darling Clementine," or research how blue jeans were invented, or the kinds of foods people ate. Students can also look at the personal journals of people involved in the Gold Rush. Have them share their information with the class, using visual aids if possible, and discuss what they found out.

Author and Illustrator

BANK ON SONIA AND CAT

Have students read the biographies of the author and illustrator.

DISCUSS

- Why did Sonia Levitin have to do research for this story?

- How do Cat Bowman Smith's illustrations help show the details of settling a western town?

Write About It

Call on a volunteer to read aloud the directions for the writing activity. Discuss with students their ideas and the results. Students may choose to write a letter, an essay, or some other mode—whatever best suits their purpose. Look for an understanding of sequence when you evaluate their work.

LOG ON **Technology**

Tell students they can find more information about Sonia Levitin and Cat Bowman Smith at **www.macmillanmh.com**

BANK ON SONIA AND CAT

AUTHOR
Sonia Levitin wrote this story after reading about a woman who made more than $10,000 by baking pies in a skillet during the California Gold Rush. Sonia loves research, so it is not surprising that she found such an interesting fact. History is just one of the things that Sonia likes to write about. She also writes mysteries, adventures, and funny stories.

ILLUSTRATOR
Cat Bowman Smith started out drawing magazine pictures. Her illustrations became very popular. Soon she was illustrating books. Today she has illustrated more than 40 of them.

LOG ON Find out more about Sonia Levitin and Cat Bowman Smith at **www.macmillanmh.com**

Other books by Sonia Levitin: *Nine for California* and *Taking Charge*

Write About It

In this story, Amanda's ideas help build a town. Describe an idea that you had. What happened as a result of your idea?

176

Author's Craft

Exaggeration or Hyperbole

Sonia Levitin uses exaggeration in *Boom Town* to show how characters felt about their new life in a western town.

- Exaggerations describe something as greater or more than it really is in order to be dramatic or humorous. For example: Amanda says she was "so bored I thought I'd die." (p. 159)

- Readers know that people do not die of boredom. They know Amanda means she was really bored.

Discuss how the exaggeration adds to the humorous tone of the story. Have students look for and discuss other examples of exaggeration, such as "even my shadow ran off" on page 157 and "the miners are sending their shirts clear to China" on page 167.

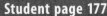

 ## Comprehension Check

 Summarize

Use your Sequence Chart to help you summarize *Boom Town*. Retell the story's events in the order in which they happen.

Event
↓
↓
↓

Think and Compare

1. Tell about two things that happened after Amanda's pie business **blossomed**. Use story details in your answer. **Summarize: Sequence**

2. Reread pages 162-163 of *Boom Town*. From those two pages, what conclusions can you draw about the kind of person Amanda is? Use story details to support your answer. **Analyze**

3. If you start your own business, what information from the story could help you to be successful? Explain. **Apply**

4. Based on this story, do you think new businesses are important to the growth of a town or a city? Use examples from the story. Explain. **Evaluate**

5. Read "Let's Trade" on pages 152-153. Compare how the characters in "Let's Trade!" and *Boom Town* got the things that they needed. **Reading/Writing Across Texts**

177

 ## Strategies for Answering Questions

Think and Search

Model the Think and Search strategy with question 1.

The answer to a Think and Search question can be found in more than one place in the selection. Remind students to keep reading until they have all the information they need and restate it to answer the question.

Think Aloud Question 1: I need to look for events that happened after Amanda's pie business blossomed. On page 167, I see the town grows because a cooper, a tanner, a miller, and a blacksmith bought pies and decided to stay. I'll keep reading. On page 173, Pa decides to work with Amanda, which means she'll have time to go to school. Looking in different places helped me find information to answer the question.

 ## Comprehension Check

SUMMARIZE

Have partners summarize *Boom Town* and paraphrase the main events. Remind students to use their Sequence Charts to help them organize their summaries.

THINK AND COMPARE

Sample answers are given.

1. **Sequence:** After Amanda's business blossomed, other people started businesses in the town. Because Amanda was so successful, she was able to go to school. USE THINK AND SEARCH

2. **Analyze:** Amanda made all three pies on the same day, so this shows that she works hard and does not give up easily. Amanda is also clever because she figured out how to make a pie without an oven.

3. **Text-to-Self:** Amanda takes small steps to make her business grow. She is also kind and helpful. This probably helped her business.

4. **Text-to-World:** New businesses are important to the growth of a town because people will move there if they can get what they need nearby. This is what happened in *Boom Town*. First there was the pie business, then Peddler Pete's Trading Post, and then more businesses and people moved to town.

 ### FOCUS QUESTION

5. **Text-to-Text:** In "Let's Trade," bartering helped keep Elizabeth and Danny warm. In *Boom Town*, businesses in the town helped people to get things they needed.

Objective
- Read fluently with proper phrasing
- 97–117 WCPM

Materials
- Fluency Transparency 21
- Fluency Solutions Audio CD
- Leveled Practice Books, p. 152

ELL
Access for All

Read with Expression
Review the meaning of the passage. Then choose several sentences, model reading them with expression, and have students practice reading those sentences. You may also want students to read along with the Fluency Solutions Audio CD.

On Level Practice Book O, page 152

As I read, I will pay attention to punctuation.

	They came by horse and wagon. They came by flatboat
10	down rivers. They came with everything they owned. Most
19	made the trip west with their parents. Some came alone.
29	From the 1780s to the 1880s, thousands of children
36	moved to the frontier. They started a new life at the
47	western edge of settled land in the United States.
56	Families moved west for many reasons. Some wanted
64	their own land to start a new life. Others wanted to find
76	gold. Still others came for adventure.
82	In 1862 the Homestead Act made moving to the frontier
91	possible for these families. They paid the government $18
99	for 160 acres of land. To keep the land, the family had to
111	build a house on it. Then they had to live in it for at least
126	five years. 128

Comprehension Check

1. Why did families move west? **Main Idea and Details** to get their own land and start a new life, some moved in search of gold, and others were in search of adventure
2. What was the Homestead Act? **Main Idea and Details** It gave 160 acres of land to families who paid $18 and who agreed to live on the land for 5 years.

	Words Read	−	Number of Errors	=	Words Correct Score
First Read		−		=	
Second Read		−		=	

★ **Approaching Practice Book A,** page 152

◆ **Beyond Practice Book B,** page 152

Fluency
Repeated Reading: Punctuation

EXPLAIN/MODEL Tell students that good readers learn to read groups of words together in phrases, paying special attention to punctuation. Explain that the text on **Transparency 21** has been marked with slashes that indicate pauses and stops. A single slash indicates a pause, usually between phrases. A double slash indicates a full stop, usually between sentences. Have the class listen carefully to your pauses and stops as you read.

Transparency 21

Brothers Billy and Joe and Ted stood there laughing.// When the wood turned to coals,/ I pushed my pie inside the old stove.// After a while I smelled a bad burning.// I pulled out my pie,/ hard as a rock.// Billy,/ Joe,/ and Ted whooped and slapped their sides.// They snatched up my pie and tossed it high into the air.// They ran outside and Billy whacked it hard with a stick.// Pie pieces flew all over the place,/ and my brothers bent over,/ laughing.//

from *Boom Town*, page 162
Fluency Transparency 21

PRACTICE Divide the class into two groups. Have the groups alternate reading the sentences. Remind them to pause at commas and come to a full stop at periods, as indicated by the slash marks. For additional practice, have students use **Leveled Practice Book** page 152 or Fluency Solutions.

Quick Check Can students echo-read fluently with proper phrasing?

During **Small Group Instruction**

If No → Approaching Level Fluency, pp. 183M–183N

If Yes → On Level Options, pp. 183Q–183R

Beyond Level Options, pp. 183S–183T

Comprehension

MAINTAIN SKILL
DRAW CONCLUSIONS

EXPLAIN/MODEL

■ To **draw conclusions**, readers look for two or more details about a character or an event, use their own experiences, and come to a new idea or understanding about it.

■ Drawing conclusions helps readers understand what happens in a story, and why characters act in a certain way.

Model how to draw conclusions about the characters in "Let's Trade!" on pages 152–153.

PRACTICE

Ask the following questions to help students draw conclusions about *Boom Town*.

■ What kind of person is Amanda? How do you know? (Amanda is a hard worker who believes in herself. She does not give up when she makes a mistake. She works very hard to bake lots of pies to sell, so she can make money for her family. My own experience tells me that people who try hard are a lot like Amanda.)

■ How did Amanda help the town become a real boom town? (Amanda's business gave people the chance to eat pies without having to do the baking. Amanda also showed that success was possible for people who worked hard to start their own businesses in new towns.)

■ What do you think California was like during the Gold Rush, based on details in *Boom Town*? (People traveled great distances to try to find gold. They may have felt lonesome sometimes. At first, there were no towns, so people had to build everything from homes to stores to schools. They had to make everything they needed, and worked together so that they could settle there.)

Have students form literature circles and compare *Boom Town* with other historical fiction they have read. During their discussion, challenge students to use new vocabulary words they have learned. Remind them to use **Discussion and Conversation Guidelines** on page 150I.

Objectives
- Draw conclusions about characters and events in a story
- Use academic language: *draw conclusions*

Skills Trace

Draw Conclusions

Introduce	U4: 49A–B
Practice / Apply	U4: 50–73; Leveled Practice, 120–121
Reteach / Review	U4: 77M–T; U6: 387A–B, 388–399, 403M–T; Leveled Practice, 215–216
Assess	Weekly Tests; Unit 4, 6 Tests; Benchmark Tests A, B
Maintain	U5: 177B; U6: 339B

Informational Text: Social Studies

GENRE: NONFICTION ARTICLE

Have students read the bookmark on **Student Book** page 178. Explain that a nonfiction article

- gives information and facts about a topic;

- usually contains boldface headings that tell the topic of the following section;

- may have graphic aids that help explain information, such as photographs, maps, charts, or calendars.

Text Feature: Calendar

EXPLAIN Point out the calendar on page 180. Tell students: A calendar shows the months, weeks, and days of the year. It helps organize and keep track of tasks that need to be done.

- **Calendars** are organized by the twelve months of the year.

- Dates are shown as numbers in the boxes.

- The month and the days of the week are written along the top of the page.

APPLY Have students identify what month the calendar on page 180 shows, how many days it has, and what day and date the dog-washing business will open. (May; 31 days; Saturday, May 31)

Social Studies

Genre

Nonfiction Articles give information about real people, places, or things.

Text Feature

Calendars show the months, weeks, and days of the year.

Content Vocabulary

business

services

batches

demand

How to Earn Money!

by R. J. Harkin

Would you like to do something new and exciting? Would you like to be looked up to and respected by kids and adults alike? Would you like to earn money in your free time? If you answered "Yes!" to any of these questions, then starting your own **business** might be right for you!

Content Vocabulary

Review the spelling and meaning of each content vocabulary word listed on Student Book page 178.

- **Business** means an activity that makes money and produces something that people want or need. If you could start a business, what would you sell?

- **Services** are the things you do for someone else for money. What services can you offer people in your neighborhood?

- **Batches** are groups of items that come together or are made together. How many batches of cookies can your classmates eat?

- A **demand** is a need that people have for goods and services. Is there a demand for baby-sitting in your neighborhood?

You Can Do It!

"My own business?" you might ask. "But I'm only a third-grader!" No problem! Even third-graders have plenty of talent and **services** to offer.

Do you enjoy cooking or baking? Then you may consider whipping up and selling a few **batches** of your fabulous blueberry muffins. Do you like arts and crafts? If so, why not make and sell artwork or jewelry? Do animals like you? Many busy families need responsible people to walk their dogs and feed their cats. The possibilities are endless! So, wash a car, plant a garden, or a lawn. If people want and need your special talents, you'll soon be in business!

2

179

Informational Text

Read "How to Earn Money!"

Access for All As students read, remind them to apply what they have learned about calendars. Also have them identify clues to the meanings of the highlighted words.

1 IMPORTANT DETAILS

What are some of the reasons people start a business? (People who start a business want to do something new and exciting, to be looked up to and respected, and to earn money.)

2 STRATEGY
MONITOR AND CLARIFY: READ AHEAD

The article says that even third-graders have talents and services to offer. If you are not sure what the author means, how can you figure it out? What are some of the services the author mentions? (Reading ahead can help me understand what the author means. By reading ahead, I learn more about the kinds of businesses young people can start. Some of the services are cooking, arts and crafts, and walking dogs.)

Informational Text

3 TEXT FEATURE: CALENDAR

What is being planned in May? How does the calendar help plan it? Why is the calendar helpful for the person starting this business? (It shows a schedule for starting a dog-washing business. The calendar can help keep track of the plan. When steps are recorded on a calendar, it is easier to see the sequence that should be followed.)

4 TEXT FEATURE: CALENDAR

According to the calendar, what date and day should the materials and supplies be gathered? Is this before or after the flyers are put up to advertise the business? Do you think this sequence of actions make sense? (The dog shampoo should be bought on Saturday, May 24. The tubs and towels should be collected from Tuesday, May 27 through May 30. These dates are after the flyers are put up, which happens from Monday, May 12 to Saturday, May 17. This sequence of actions makes sense because the person starting the business can figure out the right amount of supplies to get as people say they will bring their dogs on Saturday, May 31. This sequence also gives people enough time to find out about the business.)

Starting a Dog-Washing Business

 Using a Calendar

Before starting a business, you need to make a plan. A calendar can help you organize and keep track of what you need to do.

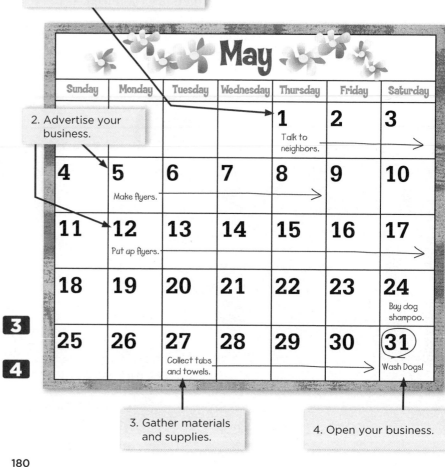

1. Find out if there is a **demand** for your business.

2. Advertise your business.

May

Sunday	Monday	Tuesday	Wednesday	Thursday	Friday	Saturday
				1 Talk to neighbors.	2	3
4	5 Make flyers.	6	7	8	9	10
11	12 Put up flyers.	13	14	15	16	17
18	19	20	21	22	23	24 Buy dog shampoo.
25	26	27 Collect tubs and towels.	28	29	30	31 Wash Dogs!

3
4

3. Gather materials and supplies.

4. Open your business.

180

On Level Practice Book O, page 153

A **calendar** helps you organize and keep track of important dates.

Use the information below to fill in the calendar. Enter the words in boldface type on the calendar.

July

Sunday	Monday	Tuesday	Wednesday	Thursday	Friday	Saturday
						1
2	3	4	5	6 ingredients	7 ingredients	8 make posters
9 put up posters	10 sell	11 sell	12 sell	13 sell	14 bank	15
16	17 vacation	18	19	20	21	22
23	24	25	26	27	28	29
30	31					

1. July 6 and 7: Buy **ingredients** for lemonade stand.

2. July 8: **Make posters** and signs to advertise lemonade stand.

3. July 9: **Put up posters** in town.

4. July 10, 11, 12, and 13: **Sell** lemonade at corner of Main and First Streets.

5. July 14: Count money earned and take it to **bank**.

6. July 17: Leave for family **vacation**.

 Approaching Practice Book A, page 153

Beyond Practice Book B, page 153

Informational Text

Connect and Compare

SUGGESTED ANSWERS

1. Four days are scheduled for making flyers and six for putting up flyers. So, ten days are scheduled in all for advertising. USING A CALENDAR

2. There might be a demand for businesses, such as mowing lawns, gardening, walking pets, and bathing pets. APPLY

 FOCUS QUESTION

3. Amanda figured out that there was a demand for pies in Boom Town. She might suggest that kids find out what there is a demand for in their neighborhood. Amanda also got her brothers to help her make a sign and pick fruit, so she might say it's important to find other people who can help with the business.

   READING/WRITING ACROSS TEXTS

Connect and Compare

1. Look at the calendar on page 180. How many days are scheduled for advertising? **Using a Calendar**

2. Suppose you live in a neighborhood where most people work all day. They aren't home to cook, work in the yard, or spend time with their pets. What businesses might there be a demand for? **Apply**

3. What advice do you think Amanda could give kids who may want to start a business today? **Reading/Writing Across Texts**

 Social Studies Activity

Research a business that interests you. Create a calendar that shows your preparations for opening that business.

 Find out more about businesses at **www.macmillanmh.com**

181

 Social Studies Activity

Ask students to present their business ideas to the class and explain how they organized their plans on a calendar.

 Technology

Internet Research and Inquiry Activity
Students can find more facts at **www.macmillanmh.com**

Research and Inquiry

Primary Sources

Primary sources are original documents, such as letters, diaries, old newspaper articles, songs, old photographs, recipes, and interviews, that give first-hand information about a variety of cultures and times. Primary sources can be found in reference books, on the Internet, and in library research centers. They help readers understand what it was like to live in another time or culture.

Have students find primary sources about the California Gold Rush with the help of a librarian. They may use resources, such as the Internet. Then have students analyze and evaluate the value of the sources and write short reports about them. They should name the topic, the type of source, the kind of information it gives, and why it is useful. Have students give oral reports about their findings to the class. Then have students orally compare the primary sources with *Boom Town* and tell how they are alike and different.

Writing

Descriptive Writing

OPTIONS FOR STUDENT WRITING

- Use these two pages for a short writing lesson focused on the features of Compare-and-Contrast Paragraphs and on the writing trait from **Student Book** pages 182–183.

- For a more detailed five-step writing process lesson, use the **Writing Workshop** on pages 183A–183B.

- Use the Daily Writing Prompts found in the Weekly Planner for brief writing assignments.

FEATURES

Present and discuss these features of Compare-and-Contrast Paragraphs with students.

- The purpose of Compare-and-Contrast Paragraphs is to tell how two things or people are alike and different.

- One paragraph compares the things or people. It shows how they are alike.

- Another paragraph contrasts them. It shows how they are different.

- Both paragraphs begin with a topic sentence and include supporting details.

Have students read "How Much Alike Are We?" on Student Book page 182. Explain that it is writing that compares and contrasts. Ask volunteers to point out examples of the features of Compare-and-Contrast Paragraphs in Sarah A.'s writing.

182

Writing

Organization
Some writing compares things that are alike and contrasts things that are different. Topic sentences can be used to highlight similarities and differences.

I compared Amanda in the story Boom Town to myself.

I wrote two topic sentences: one compares and the other contrasts.

Write Compare-and-Contrast Paragraphs

How Much Alike Are We?

by Sarah A.

Amanda and I are different because she lived a long time ago and I live in modern times. Amanda and her family traveled on a wagon. We have a minivan. She wears dresses. I wear jeans.

Amanda and I are also the same. We are girls who like to bake. Plus, Amanda started a pie business, and I walk dogs for the neighbors.

Amanda and I are probably more alike than we are different.

182

Your Turn

Write two paragraphs to compare and contrast life now to life when your parents were young. Use a Venn diagram to sort things that are alike and different. In one paragraph, compare things that are alike. In the other paragraph, contrast differences. Use the Writer's Checklist to check your writing.

Writer's Checklist

✓ **Ideas and Content:** Is it clear from my writing how the people are alike and different?

☑ **Organization:** Did I write a topic sentence to introduce each paragraph?

✓ **Voice:** Does my writing sound like something I would say?

✓ **Word Choice:** Did I use comparison words such as *same* and *different*?

✓ **Sentence Fluency:** Are my sentences too long?

✓ **Conventions:** Did I use pronouns correctly? Did I check my spelling?

183

Organization: Venn Diagram

Jim	Tanya
likes math	likes art
has a dog	has a cat
likes to hike	likes to hike

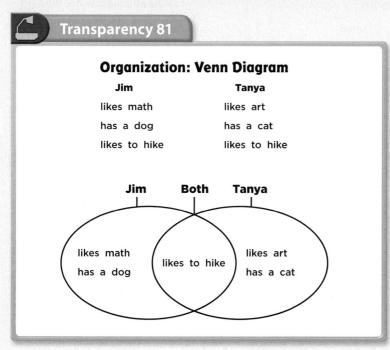

Jim   Both   Tanya

likes math, has a dog | likes to hike | likes art, has a cat

Writing Transparency 81

WRITING TRAIT: ORGANIZATION

Have a student read the bookmark on **Student Book** page 182. Discuss the Organization trait.

- To compare two different things, a writer needs to list details about them and then organize the details into two groups—things that are alike and things that are different— on a Venn diagram.

- After the details are sorted, the writer can figure out a topic sentence for each paragraph. One paragraph will be about how the things are alike. Another will be about how they are different.

Have students reread "How Much Alike Are We?" on Student Book page 182. Discuss the callouts on the left. Ask students whether Sarah A.'s paragraphs each begin with a topic sentence.

Use **Transparency 81** to show how to sort and organize ideas on a Venn diagram.

YOUR TURN

Read the "Your Turn" prompt on Student Book page 183 with students. Discuss what they might know about their parents' childhoods. Remind students to organize their ideas into two separate paragraphs.

WRITER'S CHECKLIST

Review the six Good Writing Traits on the Writer's Checklist. Have students give an example of Organization or Word Choice in Sarah A.'s writing. Then discuss how students can apply the traits to help them draft, revise, and proofread their Compare-and-Contrast Paragraphs.

Connect
Language Arts

WRITING WORKSHOP
- Descriptive: Comparison

WORD STUDY

- Words in Context
- **Word Parts:** Compound Words
- **Phonics:** Compound Words
- Vocabulary Building

SPELLING
- Compound Words

GRAMMAR
- Pronouns

SMALL GROUP OPTIONS
- Differentiated Instruction, pp. 183M–183V

Speaking and Listening

Have students read their paragraphs aloud. Share these strategies.

SPEAKING STRATEGIES
- Speak clearly and naturally.
- Emphasize words such as *alike* and *different* to stress major points.
- Make eye contact with your audience.

LISTENING STRATEGIES
- Listen for differences and similarities.
- Look at the speaker.
- Picture the people or things that are being compared and contrasted.

183A

Descriptive Writing: Comparison

Day 1 Prewrite

PURPOSE AND AUDIENCE

- The purpose of a Compare-and-Contrast Paragraph is to tell how two people or things are similar and different.

- The audience will be the teacher and classmates.

Display **Transparency 82** to show how Sarah A. used a Venn Diagram to plan her paragraphs. Tell students that they will use a Venn Diagram to plan their paragraphs.

Prompt *Write two paragraphs to compare and contrast life now with life when your parents were young.*

CHOOSE A TOPIC Students can compare and contrast their life now with their parents' childhood or self-select a topic.

Day 2 Draft

DRAFTING CHECKLIST

Display **Transparency 83.** Review Sarah A.'s draft of "How Much Alike Are We?" Discuss how the Venn Diagram was used. As students begin to draft:

- Review the features of Compare-and-Contrast Paragraphs.

- Encourage them to write a topic sentence and choose supporting sentences that fit the flow of ideas.

- Suggest that they use words such as *alike, different,* and *same* to show likenesses and differences.

- Remind students to refer to their Venn Diagrams and to the Good Writing Traits on the Writer's Checklist.

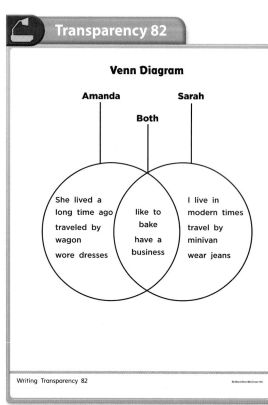

Transparency 82

Venn Diagram

Amanda — Sarah — Both

She lived a long time ago / traveled by wagon / wore dresses — like to bake / have a business — I live in modern times / travel by minivan / wear jeans

Writing Transparency 82

Transparency 83

How Much Alike Are We?

Amanda lived a long time ago and I live in modern times. We are different. And Amanda and her family traveled on a wagon. We have a minivan. She wears dresses. I wear jeans.

Amanda and I are also the same, girls who like to bake. Plus, Amanda started a pie business, and I walk dogs for the neighbors.

Amanda and I are alike and we are different.

Writing Transparency 83

Writing Transparency 82   Writing Transparency 83

Day 3 Revise

REVISING CHECKLIST

Display **Transparency 83.** Have students use what they have learned to discuss how they can revise Sarah A.'s draft.

Display **Transparency 84** and discuss Sarah A.'s changes:

- To improve the **Organization** she added information to the first topic sentence.

- She clarified and strengthened her concluding sentence.

Have students revise their paragraphs, making sure they have topic sentences, supporting details, and a concluding sentence. Partners may suggest where the **Organization** can be improved.

Transparency 84

How Much Alike Are We?

Amanda lived a long time ago and I live in modern times. We are different. And Amanda and her family traveled on a wagon. We have a minivan. She wears dresses. I wear jeans.

Amanda and I are also the same. girls who like to bake. Plus, Amanda started a pie business, and I walk dogs for the neighbors.

Amanda and I are alike and we are different.

Writing Transparency 84

Writing Transparency 84

Day 4 Proofread

REVIEW AND PROOFREAD

As they proofread, remind students to:

- Capitalize names of people.

- Use classroom resources, such as dictionaries, to check spelling.

- Indent each paragraph.

- Check that personal pronouns agree with the nouns they replace.

LOG ON Technology

Remind students that they can use the Copy and Paste features to move words instead of retyping them.

Day 5 Publish

PUBLISH AND PRESENT

To publish, students should make a neat copy using their best handwriting or a computer.

Review Speaking and Listening Strategies with students.

Handwriting For cursive models, see **Teacher's Resource Book** pages 168–173.

EVALUATE

To evaluate student writing, use the 6-point Scoring Rubric. Since students learned about **Organization** this week, check for that trait.

SCORING RUBRIC

4 Excellent	**3** Good	**2** Fair	**1** Unsatisfactory
Ideas and Content Clear distinction between similarities and differences; both are well-developed and supported with examples	**Ideas and Content** Clear and well-developed comparisons and contrasts	**Ideas and Content** Comparisons and contrasts not always clear	**Ideas and Content** Comparisons and contrasts mixed together and confusing
Organization One paragraph compares, and another contrasts; both have a strong topic sentence	**Organization** Topic sentences introduce purpose of each paragraph	**Organization** Missing a topic sentence in one paragraph	**Organization** No topic sentences; details not in logical order
Voice Original, natural, and strong	**Voice** Clear, engaging, and natural	**Voice** Not very engaging	**Voice** Flat and uninteresting
Word Choice Good use of comparison words	**Word Choice** Accurate use of comparison words	**Word Choice** Few comparison words used	**Word Choice** Inaccurate use of words that compare and contrast
Sentence Fluency Uses a variety of sentence lengths and types	**Sentence Fluency** Uses long and short sentences	**Sentence Fluency** Sentences are short and fragmented	**Sentence Fluency** Incomplete or confusing sentences
Conventions Mostly free of errors in spelling, mechanics, and usage	**Conventions** Few errors in spelling, mechanics, and usage	**Conventions** Many errors in spelling, mechanics, and usage	**Conventions** Repeated errors in spelling, mechanics, and usage

Word Study

Objectives

- Apply knowledge of word meanings and context clues
- Identify compound words
- Use academic language: *compound word*

Materials

- Vocabulary Transparency 41
- Vocabulary Strategy Transparency 42
- Leveled Practice Books, p. 154
- dictionary

Vocabulary

sidewalks (p. 171) paths by the side of the street or road

grumbled (p. 165) complained in a low voice

traders (p. 166) people who buy and sell things as a business

blossomed (p. 169) grew or developed

wailed (p. 163) made a long and sad cry

lonesome (p. 157) not often visited by people

ELL — Access for All

Use Vocabulary Prompt students to use the vocabulary: *Where can you see sidewalks? Name something you have grumbled about at school. What can traders exchange?* Help students answer in full sentences.

Review
Vocabulary

 Words in Context

EXPLAIN/MODEL

Review the meanings of the vocabulary words. Display **Transparency 41.** Model how to use word meanings and context clues to fill in the first missing word.

 Transparency 41

sidewalks   grumbled   lonesome
wailed   blossomed   traders

Once a man named Old Jim had a lot of problems. A weaker man might have (1) <u>wailed</u> about his troubles, but Old Jim didn't like to cry. He built a house where he could live alone in peace.

After awhile, Jim found his home (2) <u>lonesome</u>. One day, a pair of traveling salesmen came by. He liked the (3) <u>traders</u> so much that he invited them to stay. They moved in and set up a store. Word spread. People came from all around and the business (4) <u>blossomed</u>.

Soon other stores sprang up. People built (5) <u>sidewalks</u> next to the dusty roads. "It's too crowded," Old Jim (6) <u>grumbled</u>. Then he remembered how lonesome his old house had been. Maybe the new town was a good thing after all.

Vocabulary Transparency 41

Think Aloud The first paragraph tells me that things have not gone well for Old Jim. The phrase "Old Jim didn't like to cry" gives me another clue. The base word *wail* means the same as *cry* so the missing word must be *wailed*.

PRACTICE

 Help students complete item 2. Then have students use context clues to write the missing words for items 3–6 on a separate piece of paper. Students can exchange papers, check answers, and explain the clues they used to find the missing words.

Remind students that they can use the Glossary on pages 408–422 to confirm word meanings.

STRATEGY
WORD PARTS: COMPOUND WORDS

EXPLAIN/MODEL

■ A **compound word** is a word made of two smaller words.

■ Students can often figure out the meaning of a compound word by putting together the meanings of the smaller words. When this strategy doesn't work, as with the words *gooseberries* and *landmark*, students will need to check a dictionary.

 Display **Transparency 42.** Read the example sentence. Model identifying the two small words in *cookbook* and using them as clues to the compound word's meaning.

 Transparency 42

> **Compound Words**
>
> Amanda did not use a cookbook to make her pies.
>
> cook + book = cookbook: a book for a cook
>
> 1. A cobbler is a shoemaker. (shoemaker; shoe, maker; person who makes shoes)
>
> 2. The sign in front of the store was handmade. (handmade; hand, made; made by hand)
>
> 3. Do you think Amanda's town needs a newspaper? (newspaper; news, paper; a publication printed on paper with news stories)
>
> 4. The headline of the story read, "GOLD!" (headline; head, line; larger, top line of a news story)

Vocabulary Strategy Transparency 42

PRACTICE

On a separate sheet of paper, have students identify the compound word in items 1–4, write each smaller word, and use word parts or the dictionary to tell what the word means.

Quick Check Can students choose the correct meaning of a word and identify word parts and meanings of compound words?

During **Small Group Instruction**

If No → **Approaching Level** Vocabulary, p. 183O

If Yes → **On Level** Options, pp. 183Q–183R

Beyond Level Options, pp. 183S–183T

ELL **Access for All**

Give Examples Use known words to explain the concept. Write: *homework, bedroom, toothbrush.* Say each word and have students identify the two smaller words. Students may find it difficult to identify the smaller words in compound words. Have them work in groups to complete the Practice activity.

Vocabulary

Review last week's vocabulary words. Have students use each word in a sentence also containing a compound word.

☐ **On Level Practice Book O,** page 154

> Sometimes you can figure out the meaning of **compound words** from the meanings of the two smaller words. Other times you need to look up the words in a dictionary to find the meaning.
>
> Underline the compound word in each sentence. Then write its definition. Use a dictionary to help you.
> **Possible responses provided.**
> 1. Anna and her family traveled by <u>stagecoach</u> to California.
> **a coach or vehicle, usually pulled by horses, for carrying people and mail**
>
> 2. Anna spent her <u>daytime</u> hours sewing clothing.
> **the time when it is day; daylight, not nighttime**
>
> 3. Anna would use a <u>landmark</u> so she would not get lost while walking to the store. **a familiar object that serves as a guide**
>
> 4. The <u>blacksmith</u> in town traded some tools for a new shirt.
> **a person who makes and fixes iron objects, such as tools and horseshoes**
>
> 5. One day a <u>cowboy</u> rode into town and asked Anna to sew him a new shirt. **a person who herds and takes care of cattle on a ranch**

★ **Approaching Practice Book A,** page 154

◆ **Beyond Practice Book B,** page 154

Word Study

Phonics

Compound Words

Objectives

- Segment and blend compound words
- Decode compound words
- Decode a word with *qu*

Materials

- Leveled Practice Books, p. 155

ELL | **Access for All**

Game After the Practice activity, divide the students into two teams. Write a compound word from the lesson on the board. One player names the smaller words in the word for one point. The team scores an extra point if any member can give the word's meaning.

On Level Practice Book O, page 155

A **compound word** is made by joining two smaller words. You can use the meaning of the smaller words to help figure out the meaning of the compound word.

A. Read each definition. Then complete the chart.

Definition	Compound Word	Two Words	
1. case to store books	bookcase	book	case
2. material that covers a table	tablecloth	table	cloth
3. the part of a day after the morning	afternoon	after	noon
4. person who raises bees and collects honey	beekeeper	bee	keeper
5. no shoes or socks on your feet	barefoot	bare	foot
6. a book used for cooking	cookbook	cook	book

B. Write sentences for two of the compound words above.
Possible responses provided.

7. Walking around barefoot can be dangerous because you don't know what you are stepping on.

8. The afternoon is my favorite time of day.

 Approaching Practice Book A, page 155

◆ **Beyond Practice Book B,** page 155

EXPLAIN/MODEL

- A **compound word** is a word formed from two smaller words, as in *sailboat*. Knowing the meaning of the two smaller words can often help a reader figure out the meaning: *sail + boat = sailboat*, "a boat with a sail."

- Sometimes the small words' meanings don't help a reader figure out what a compound word means. You may have to look it up in a dictionary. Write the word *butterfly*.

Think Aloud I see that *butterfly* is a compound word. It is made up of the two smaller words, *butter* and *fly*. If I try to use the meanings of *butter* and *fly* to decode the meaning of the compound word, it does not make sense. So if I am unsure of the meaning, I must look up *butterfly* in a dictionary. A butterfly is an insect with a slender body and four bright-colored wings.

PRACTICE/APPLY

 Access for All

Write these words on the board: *football, airplane, snowshoes, birthday*. Have students identify the two words that make up each compound word and draw a line between them. Then have them read the compound words aloud and tell what each word means.

Decode Multisyllable Words Display these words: *earthquake, stomachache, grasshopper, eyeglasses, ladybug, supermarket*. Focus on identifying the two words that make up *earthquake* and figuring out the meaning. Remind students that *qu* in *quake* stands for the /kw/ sound. Have students decode the remaining words.

Build Compound Words Have students build compound words using *book* or *light* as one of the words. *(bookcase, cookbook, checkbook, textbook; lighthouse, flashlight)* They may wish to use a dictionary to help them.

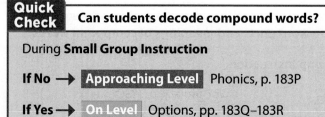

Quick Check | **Can students decode compound words?**

During **Small Group Instruction**

If No → **Approaching Level** Phonics, p. 183P

If Yes → **On Level** Options, pp. 183Q–183R

Beyond Level Options, pp. 183S–183T

Vocabulary Building

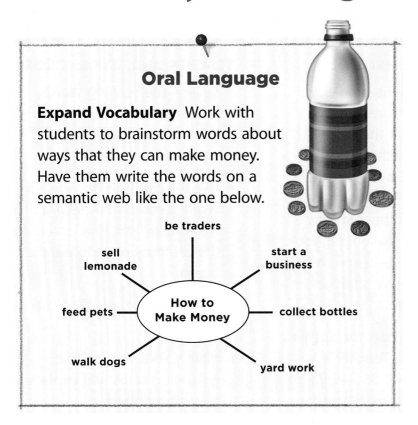

Oral Language

Expand Vocabulary Work with students to brainstorm words about ways that they can make money. Have them write the words on a semantic web like the one below.

How to Make Money
- be traders
- start a business
- collect bottles
- yard work
- walk dogs
- feed pets
- sell lemonade

Vocabulary Building

Idioms An idiom is an expression whose meaning is different from the usual meaning of the separate words in it. For example: the idiom *strike it rich* means "to get or find a lot of money suddenly." Help students figure out the meanings of these common idioms: *out of the blue* (suddenly), *piece of cake* and *easy as pie* (very easy), and *raining cats and dogs* (raining very hard). Review last week's words. Write on the board: *to a T*. Ask students to identify which word this idiom relates to. (exact) Have students illustrate these idioms.

Apply Vocabulary

Write a Paragraph Have small groups of students use the vocabulary words *sidewalks, grumbled, traders, blossomed, wailed,* and *lonesome* in a paragraph about a self-selected topic. Students can read their paragraphs aloud to the class.

Spiral Review

Vocabulary Game Have students play a word game using the following **Vocabulary Cards**: *crate, grownups, grumbled, luckiest, ruined, storage, traders.*

- Place **Vocabulary Cards** in a pile facedown.

- Ask two volunteers to select a word card. Have them work together to act out a brief scene with dialogue that shows the meaning of the word without saying the word. However, they can use synonyms. Ask the rest of the class to name the word and to explain how the scene shows the meaning of the word.

- Continue until all of the words have been used.

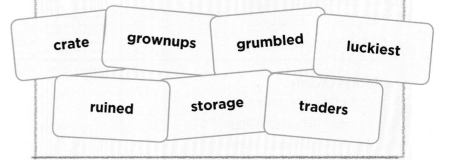

crate grownups grumbled luckiest

ruined storage traders

5 Day Spelling

Compound Words

airplane	notebook	someone
daytime	birdhouse	newspaper
birthday	barefoot	sidewalks
daylight	headlight	basketball
hairdo	sometime	stagecoach

Review states, inches, cities

Challenge somebody, handwriting

Dictation Sentences

1. Does that <u>airplane</u> fly?
2. We go to school in the <u>daytime</u>.
3. Today is Juan's <u>birthday</u>.
4. <u>Daylight</u> ended at six o'clock.
5. Erin's <u>hairdo</u> suits her.
6. I write stories in a <u>notebook</u>.
7. Dad built a <u>birdhouse</u>.
8. I went <u>barefoot</u> on the beach.
9. The car's <u>headlight</u> is broken.
10. I will arrive <u>sometime</u> tonight.
11. <u>Someone</u> opened the door.
12. Did you read the <u>newspaper</u>?
13. The **<u>sidewalks</u>** in town are wide.
14. Our coach handed us a <u>basketball</u>.
15. Two horses pulled the **<u>stagecoach</u>**.

Review Words
1. Iowa and Ohio are <u>states</u>.
2. The plant is ten <u>inches</u> tall.
3. Dad visited three <u>cities</u>.

Challenge Words
1. <u>Somebody</u> wrote me a note.
2. I can't read her <u>handwriting</u>.

Note: Words in **bold** type are from *Boom Town*.

Display the Spelling Words throughout the week.

Day 1 Pretest

ASSESS PRIOR KNOWLEDGE

Use the Dictation Sentences. Say the underlined word, read the sentence, and repeat the word. Have students write the words on **Spelling Practice Book** page 129. For a modified list, use the first 12 Spelling Words and the 3 Review Words. For a more challenging list, use Spelling Words 3–15 and the Challenge Words. Have students correct their own tests.

Have students cut apart the Spelling Word Cards BLM on **Teacher's Resource Book** page 86 and figure out a way to sort them. Have them save the cards for use throughout the week.

For independent practice, have students use Spelling Practice Book page 130.

Day 2 Word Sorts

TEACHER AND STUDENT SORTS

- Review the Spelling Words, pointing out the two words in each compound. Discuss meanings.

- Use the cards on the Spelling Word Cards BLM. Attach the key words *day, light, time, some,* and the category *other* to a bulletin board.

- Model sorting several compound words.

- Have volunteers sort the remaining cards and explain how they sorted them.

- Then have students use their own Spelling Word Cards. They place the key words on their desks and sort the Spelling Words three times. Have students write their last sort on Spelling Practice Book page 131.

Spelling Practice Book, pages 129–130

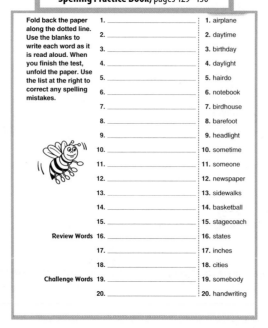

Fold back the paper along the dotted line. Use the blanks to write each word as it is read aloud. When you finish the test, unfold the paper. Use the list at the right to correct any spelling mistakes.

1. _____	1. airplane
2. _____	2. daytime
3. _____	3. birthday
4. _____	4. daylight
5. _____	5. hairdo
6. _____	6. notebook
7. _____	7. birdhouse
8. _____	8. barefoot
9. _____	9. headlight
10. _____	10. sometime
11. _____	11. someone
12. _____	12. newspaper
13. _____	13. sidewalks
14. _____	14. basketball
15. _____	15. stagecoach
Review Words 16. _____	16. states
17. _____	17. inches
18. _____	18. cities
Challenge Words 19. _____	19. somebody
20. _____	20. handwriting

Spelling Practice Book, page 131

airplane	daylight	birdhouse	sometime	sidewalks
daytime	hairdo	barefoot	someone	basketball
birthday	notebook	headlight	newspaper	stagecoach

What's in a Word?

Compound words are made up of smaller words. Write the spelling words that have the following words in them.

1. some   someone   sometime
2. light   headlight   daylight
3. time   daytime   sometime
4. day   daylight   birthday   daytime

Order Please!

Write each group of spelling words in alphabetical order.

birdhouse, airplane, basketball, barefoot, birthday

5. airplane
6. barefoot
7. basketball
8. birdhouse
9. birthday

notebook, hairdo, newspaper, headlight, daytime

10. daytime
11. hairdo
12. headlight
13. newspaper
14. notebook

someone, sometime, sidewalks, stagecoach

15. sidewalks
16. someone
17. sometime
18. stagecoach

Day 3 Word Meanings

DEFINITIONS

Display the definitions below. Have students write the clues and the Spelling Words that go with them in a word study notebook.

1. machine that flies (airplane)

2. day you were born (birthday)

3. without shoes or socks (barefoot)

4. places to walk next to streets (sidewalks)

5. a large ball (basketball)

Challenge students to come up with clues for other Spelling Words.

Have partners write a sentence for each Spelling Word, leaving a blank where the word should go. Then have them trade papers and write the missing word.

Day 4 Review and Proofread

SPIRAL REVIEW

Review plural nouns. Write *states, inches,* and *cities* on the board. Have students tell how the plurals are formed.

PROOFREAD AND WRITE

Write these sentences. Have students correct the errors.

1. The baby was barefot. (barefoot)

2. Pass me the basketbal. (basketball)

BLIND SORT

Partners use their Spelling Word Cards. They each write the key words *day, light, time, some,* and *other* on a sheet of paper. Then they take turns. One draws cards and says the words. The other writes them under the key words. After both have finished, they check each other's papers for errors.

Day 5 Assess and Reteach

POSTTEST

Use the Dictation Sentences on page 183G for the Posttest.

If students have difficulty with any words in the lesson, have them place them on a list called "Spelling Words I Want to Remember" in a word study notebook.

WORD STUDY NOTEBOOK

Challenge students to search for other compound words in their reading for the week and write them in a word study notebook under the heading "Other Compound Words."

Spelling Practice Book, page 132

airplane	daylight	birdhouse	sometime	sidewalks
daytime	hairdo	barefoot	someone	basketball
birthday	notebook	headlight	newspaper	stagecoach

What's the Word?

Complete each sentence with a spelling word.

1. My brother delivers the **newspaper** on our street to make money.

2. I wish **someone** would hire me.

3. Put on your shoes. You can't go to work **barefoot**.

4. I often wake up before **daylight**.

5. The woman went to the beauty salon for a new **hairdo**.

6. Write down your ideas in a **notebook** so you do not forget them.

7. The car's **headlight** was not working.

8. The **sidewalks** along the streets were full of people walking.

9. The store sells shoes for kids who play soccer, baseball, and **basketball**.

10. She works at night because she is too busy during the **daytime**.

11. My **birthday** is a day that I stay home from work and relax.

12. I would like to open my own business **sometime** in the future.

Where Would It Be?

Write the spelling word that would most likely be found in each of these places.

13. in the backyard **birdhouse**

14. at an airport **airplane**

15. in a movie about the old West **stagecoach**

Spelling Practice Book, page 133

There are six spelling mistakes in the letter. Circle the misspelled words. Write the words correctly on the lines below.

Dear Mr. Taylor,

I am writing to you for some advice on a business idea I had. I read about your sports store in the (nuespapper.) You seem like (sumone) who could help me.

I had the idea one day while I was walking home. My feet were hurting because I had been playing (basckettebal) (bearfoot.) My idea was to create a mailing list of customers. With each name, you could also list the person's (burthdea.) Your store could use the list to send letters reminding your customers to buy a new pair of shoes. You could even include a coupon! Maybe you could sell the list to different stores in town. The barber shop could send a coupon for a (haredoe.)

What do you think? If you are interested, please write to me.

Regards,
Josh Curtain

1.	**newspaper**		4.	**barefoot**
2.	**someone**		5.	**birthday**
3.	**basketball**		6.	**hairdo**

Writing Activity

Write a paragraph describing a business you would like to start. Use at least four spelling words in your description.

Spelling Practice Book, page 134

Look at the words in each set below. One word in each set is spelled correctly. Look at Sample A. The letter next to the correctly spelled word in Sample A has been shaded in. Do Sample B yourself. Shade the letter of the word that is spelled correctly. When you are sure you know what to do, go on with the rest of the page.

Sample A:	Sample B:
Ⓐ whithout	Ⓔ owtside
Ⓑ wittout	Ⓕ outsighted
Ⓒ without	Ⓖ ootside
Ⓓ wethout	Ⓗ outside

1. Ⓐ areplain	6. Ⓔ knotebook	11. Ⓐ someone
Ⓑ airplane	Ⓕ nootbook	Ⓑ sumwon
Ⓒ airplain	Ⓖ notebook	Ⓒ somewon
Ⓓ errplane	Ⓗ notbook	Ⓓ somewan
2. Ⓔ daytime	7. Ⓐ birdhause	12. Ⓐ newspaper
Ⓕ daytyme	Ⓑ birdhaus	Ⓑ newpaper
Ⓖ daitime	Ⓒ birdhous	Ⓒ newspapper
Ⓗ daytim	Ⓓ birdhouse	Ⓓ knewspaper
3. Ⓐ birthdai	8. Ⓔ barefut	13. Ⓐ sidewoks
Ⓑ birtday	Ⓕ barefoot	Ⓑ sidewalks
Ⓒ birthday	Ⓖ baerfoot	Ⓒ sydewalks
Ⓓ berthday	Ⓗ bairfoot	Ⓓ sidewaulks
4. Ⓔ daylite	9. Ⓔ headlite	14. Ⓐ basketbull
Ⓕ daelyte	Ⓕ hedlight	Ⓕ basketbal
Ⓖ daylight	Ⓖ headlyte	Ⓖ basketbol
Ⓗ deylight	Ⓗ headlight	Ⓗ basketball
5. Ⓐ hairdo	10. Ⓐ soumtime	15. Ⓐ stagcoche
Ⓑ hayredo	Ⓑ sometime	Ⓑ stajcoach
Ⓒ haredo	Ⓒ sumtime	Ⓒ stagecoah
Ⓓ herrdo	Ⓓ sometyme	Ⓓ stagecoach

Pronouns

Daily Language Activities

Daily Language Activities

Use these activities to introduce each day's lesson. Write the day's activities on the board or use **Transparency 21.**

DAY 1
1. Yesterday Mara run to the bake sail. 2. She seen phil there. 3. He were happy to see her (1: ran; sale; 2: saw Phil; 3: was; her.)

DAY 2
1. maria and I likes to bake. 2. Last week we maked two pie. 3. i eated a peace from both of them. (1: Maria; like; 2: made; pies; 3: I ate; piece)

DAY 3
1. Emma smith baught a good book. 2. it were about eleanor roosevelt. 3. she readed it in oklahoma. (1: Smith bought; 2: It was; Eleanor Roosevelt; 3: She read; Oklahoma)

DAY 4
1. kim and i work in the garden. 2. we like to plant Roses. 3. kims flowers are pretty. (1: Kim; I; 2: We; roses; 3: Kim's)

DAY 5
1. Jack and dan made a birdhows 2. they workd for hours. 3. Do you want to play in golden gate park! (1: Dan; birdhouse.; 2: They worked; 3: in Golden Gate Park?)

ELL · **Access for All**

Act It Out Pronouns are confusing for many students since many languages have different rules surrounding them. Practice them in a concrete way. Write sentences and have students act them out. *Maria gives the book to Carlos. She gives it to him.*

Day 1 — Introduce the Concept

INTRODUCE SINGULAR PRONOUNS

Present the following:

- A **pronoun** is a word that takes the place of one or more nouns.

- A **singular pronoun** replaces a singular noun.

- First person singular pronouns are *I* and *me*; the second person singular pronoun is *you*; the third person singular pronouns are *he, she, it, him,* and *her.*

Example:
Ana saw **Jack**. **She** saw **him**.

 See Grammar Transparency 101 for modeling and guided practice.

Grammar Practice Book, page 129

> - A **pronoun** is a word that takes the place of one or more nouns.
> - A **singular pronoun** replaces a singular noun.
> - First person singular pronouns are *I* and *me*; the second person singular pronoun is *you*; the third person singular pronouns are *he, she, it, him,* and *her.*
>   Example: *Boom Town* takes place in the 1800s. It takes place in the 1800s.

Read the sentences. Write the singular pronoun or pronouns you find in each sentence.

1. James gave me the book *Boom Town*. ___ me
2. He says it makes him want to live back in the Old West. ___ He, it, him
3. I read it from cover to cover in one afternoon. ___ I, it
4. I will tell you that it is about a girl named Amanda. ___ I, you, it
5. She starts a pie-selling business. ___ She
6. Many people buy pies from her. ___ her
7. I read how she gets other people to start businesses and help the town. ___ I, she
8. It makes me want to start a business, too! ___ It, me
9. Maybe I could open a bakery. ___ I
10. I could open it with my mom. ___ I, it

Day 2 — Teach the Concept

REVIEW SINGULAR PRONOUNS

Review with students what a pronoun is. Ask students to name singular pronouns that can replace the *girl.* (she, her)

INTRODUCE PLURAL PRONOUNS

Present the following:

- A **plural pronoun** replaces a plural noun or more than one noun. First person plural pronouns are *we* and *us*; the second person plural pronoun is *you*; the third person pronouns are *they* and *them.*

- A plural pronoun must match the noun or nouns that it replaces.

Examples:
Nate and **Kate** saw the **boys**.
They saw **them**.

 See Grammar Transparency 102 for modeling and guided practice.

Grammar Practice Book , page 130

> - Plural pronouns are *we, you, they, us,* and *them.*

Read each pair of sentences. Replace the underlined word or words with a plural pronoun. Use clues in the sentences to help you decide.

1. James, Sarah, and I decided to start a cookie business. ___ We
2. Have you and your friends ever tried to start a business? ___ you
3. James and Sarah made the cookies. ___ They
4. I painted signs while I waited for James and Sarah. ___ them
5. Then there was a phone call for James, Sarah, and me. ___ us
6. James, Sarah, and I had our first customers! ___ We
7. The cookies were still warm from the oven. ___ They
8. Sarah carefully wrapped the cookies. ___ them
9. James, Sarah, and I delivered the cookies to our customers. ___ We
10. The people were delighted and promised to order more. ___ They

Day 3 · Review and Practice

REVIEW PLURAL PRONOUNS

Review with students how to use plural pronouns. Remind them that the pronoun must match the nouns it replaces.

MECHANICS AND USAGE: CAPITALIZING I AND PROPER NOUNS

- **Proper nouns** name specific people, places, and things.

- Always begin a proper noun with a capital letter.

- Always capitalize the pronoun *I*.

Examples:
Cat Bowman is an artist.
Central Park is beautiful.
I will visit **Ohio** this summer.

 See Grammar Transparency 103 for modeling and guided practice.

Grammar Practice Book, page 131

> - A **proper noun** names a special person, place, or thing.
> - A proper noun begins with a capital letter.
> - The pronoun *I* is always capitalized.

Rewrite each sentence correctly. Write each proper noun and *I* with a capital letter.

1. In the book *Boom Town*, amanda starts a pie-selling business.
   In the book Boom Town, Amanda starts a pie-selling business.

2. Like amanda, i live in california.
   Like Amanda, I live in California.

3. My family has a bakery in the town of marlton.
   My family has a bakery in the town of Marlton.

4. It is called the little red bakery.
   It is called the Little Red Bakery.

5. It is in a red building on maple street.
   It is in a red building on Maple Street.

6. My brother chris works there with mom and dad.
   My brother Chris works there with Mom and Dad.

7. Our biggest seller is a pie called the incredible peach experience.
   Our biggest seller is a pie called the Incredible Peach Experience.

8. I like to bring my friends steve and rebecca to the bakery.
   I like to bring my friends Steve and Rebecca to the bakery.

Day 4 · Review and Proofread

REVIEW PRONOUNS

Ask students to name singular and plural pronouns. Ask what kinds of nouns begin with capital letters.

PROOFREAD

Write these sentences. Have students correct the errors.

1. Does jeff like to travel? (Jeff)

2. Sue and i read the same book. (I)

3. Ed and ann took the bus (Ann; bus.)

4. Are they going to peg's party (Peg's; party?)

5. Can i see the drawing? (I)

 See Grammar Transparency 104 for modeling and guided practice.

Grammar Practice Book, page 132

> - A **pronoun** is a word that takes the place of one or more nouns.
> - A **singular pronoun** replaces a singular noun. A **plural pronoun** replaces a plural noun or more than one noun.
> - Singular pronouns are *I, you, he, she, it, me, him,* and *her*.
> - Plural pronouns are *we, you, they, us,* and *them*.

Proofread the paragraph. Circle any incorrect pronouns.

We recently read *Boom Town*. (They) is the story of a girl named amanda. (Her) helped her town grow by starting a pie business. (Us) decided to try the gooseberry pie recipe in the book. Mom suggested using blueberries instead. Then Mom thought there wasn't enough sugar. (Him) kept adding more. I thought there weren't enough berries. (You) piled them so high that there wasn't enough dough to cover them. Then (me) forgot to turn on the oven. No wonder the pie took so long to bake!

Rewrite the paragraph with the correct pronouns. Make sure all proper nouns and *I* are capitalized.

We recently read *Boom Town*. It is the story of a girl named Amanda. She helped her town grow by starting a pie business. We decided to try the gooseberry pie recipe in the book. Mom suggested using blueberries instead. Then Mom thought there wasn't enough sugar. She kept adding more. I thought there weren't enough berries. I piled them so high that there wasn't enough dough to cover them. Then I forgot to turn on the oven. No wonder the pie took so long to bake!

Day 5 · Assess and Reteach

ASSESS

Use the Daily Language Activity and **Grammar Practice Book** page 133 for assessment.

RETEACH

Write sentences on the board using singular and plural pronouns. Ask students to identify the pronouns and tell if they are singular or plural. For example: *She sits near the window.* (She-singular) *They cleaned up the art center.* (They-plural)

Have students write the sentences with the pronouns underlined on sentence strips and display them.

Use page 134 of the Grammar Practice Book for additional reteaching.

 See Grammar Transparency 105 for modeling and guided practice.

Grammar Practice Book, pages 133–134

A. Write *yes* if the underlined word is a pronoun. Write *no* if the underlined word is not a pronoun.

1. Have you read about Amanda and her pie business? _____ yes

2. She started making gooseberry pies for the settlers in California. _____ yes

3. They bought many pies from Amanda. _____ no

4. The settlers in her town realized there was a need for other businesses. _____ no

5. Amanda helped them think of ideas. _____ yes

6. Soon they had built a busy town. _____ no

B. Underline the pronoun in each sentence. Then write *S* if it is singular or *P* if it is plural.

7. We visited a museum over the weekend. _____ P

8. The guide showed us how people lived during the California Gold Rush. _____ P

9. She said that towns sprang up where people searched for gold. _____ S

10. I had read about the Gold Rush in the book *Boom Town*. _____ S

11. It has become one of my favorite books. _____ S

12. We read it during class _____ P

Administer the Test

Weekly Reading Assessment,
Passage and questions, pages 261–268

ASSESSED SKILLS

- Sequence
- Vocabulary Words
- Word Parts/Compound Words
- Compound Words
- Pronouns

Macmillan/McGraw-Hill

Administer the **Weekly Assessment** from
the CD-ROM or online.

Weekly Assessment, 261–268

Fluency

Assess fluency for one group of students per week.
Use the Oral Fluency Record Sheet to track the number
of words read correctly. Fluency goal for all students:
97–117 words correct per minute (WCPM).

Approaching Level	Weeks 1, 3, 5
On Level	Weeks 2, 4
Beyond Level	Week 6

Fluency Assessment

Alternative Assessments

- **Leveled Weekly Assessment,**
  for Approaching Level,
  pages 269–276
- **ELL Assessment**, pages 136–137

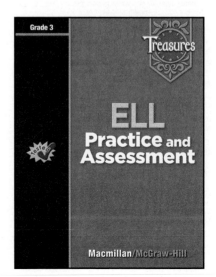

ELL Assessment, 136–137

Diagnose	IF . . .	Prescribe — THEN . . .
VOCABULARY WORDS **VOCABULARY STRATEGY** Word Parts: Compound Words Items 1, 2, 3	0–1 items correct . . .	Reteach skills using the **Additional Lessons,** page T6 Reteach skills: Go to **www.macmillanmh.com** Vocabulary PuzzleMaker Evaluate for Intervention.
COMPREHENSION Skill: Sequence Items 4, 5, 6,	0–1 items correct . . .	Reteach skills using the **Additional Lessons**, page T1 Evaluate for Intervention.
GRAMMAR Pronouns Items 7, 8, 9	0–1 items correct . . .	Reteach skills: **Grammar Practice Book**, page 134
SPELLING Compound Words Items 10, 11, 12	0–1 items correct . . .	Reteach skills: Go to **www.macmillanmh.com**
FLUENCY	89–96 WCPM	Fluency Solutions
	0–88 WCPM	Evaluate for Intervention.

READING
Triumphs
AN INTERVENTION PROGRAM

Also Available

To place students in the Intervention Program, use the **Diagnostic Assessment** in the Intervention Teacher's Edition.

Leveled Reader Lesson 1

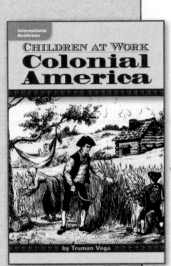

Informational Nonfiction

CHILDREN AT WORK
Colonial America

by Truman Vega

Leveled Reader

Objective	Read to apply strategies and skills
Materials	• **Leveled Reader** *Children at Work: Colonial America* • chart paper
	• **Approaching Practice Book A,** p. 152

PREVIEW AND PREDICT

Show the cover. Discuss the title, table of contents, and art and photos. Ask what students think this book will be about and what questions it might answer. Encourage them to revise their predictions as they read.

VOCABULARY WORDS

Review the vocabulary words. As you read together, have students raise their hands when each word comes up: *lonesome, grumbled, wailed,* p. 5; *traders, blossomed,* p. 7; *sidewalk,* p. 13. Discuss how the word is used in that sentence.

STRATEGY
SUMMARIZE

Discuss how summarizing can help readers understand what they read. As students read, they should look for important ideas they would include in a summary and keep track of the order in which events happen.

Read pages 2–3 aloud. Model summarizing.

Think Aloud On page 3, I read that colonists started making their own goods and that boys began to learn a trade at a young age. That information seems important enough to go in a summary of the book. I'll keep reading to make sure and to look for other important ideas.

SKILL
SEQUENCE

Remind students that sequence means time order. As you continue reading, discuss how boys learned to work in colonial America. Talk about the sequence of events related to their jobs. Help students identify sequence signal words and create a Sequence Chart on chart paper.

READ AND RESPOND

Have students read orally through the end of Chapter 2. Offer fluency help as needed. Suggest that students read to find out what children did after they became apprentices. Allow time for students to share ideas.

Fluency: REPEATED READING

Model reading the passage on **Practice Book** page 152. Have the group echo-read the passage. Then have partners practice reading it to each other, paying attention to punctuation. Coach students as needed.

⭐ **Approaching Practice Book A,** page 152

As I read, I will pay attention to punctuation.

	Most colonial families were large. Everyone had chores
8	to do. Boys learned to farm, hunt, build, and fix things.
19	Girls learned to garden, cook, sew, and take care of
29	animals.
30	At first the colonists got their goods from
38	England. Then they began making their own.
45	The colonists built houses and ships. They made shoes
54	and hats and wigs. They also made bricks and baskets. All
65	kinds of trades, or crafts, developed.
71	A boy began to learn a craft at a young age.
82	To do so, he would become an apprentice. He would work
93	with his father or another tradesman. 99

Comprehension Check

1. What kinds of chores did girls and boys do during colonial times? **Main Idea and Details** Boys learned to farm, hunt, and build and fix things. Girls learned to garden, cook, sew, and take care of animals.
2. How did a boy learn a trade in colonial times? **Main Idea and Details** by becoming an apprentice to his father or another tradesman.

	Words Read	–	Number of Errors	=	Words Correct Score
First Read		–		=	
Second Read		–		=	

Leveled Reader Lesson 2

Objective   Read to apply strategies and skills
Materials   • **Leveled Reader** *Children at Work: Colonial America*   • chart paper

VOCABULARY WORDS

Review the vocabulary words: *sidewalk, grumbled, traders, blossomed, wailed, lonesome,* and how they are used in the Leveled Reader. When you read page 13, discuss how *sidewalk* is used and any context clues students can find.

SUMMARIZE AND PREDICT

Have volunteers summarize the book so far and recount the process of becoming an apprentice. Ask students to predict what happens next. What do they think happened to the boys after they learned their trade?

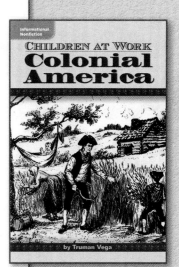

Leveled Reader

SKILL
SEQUENCE

Remind students to identify the most important events, in the correct order, to help them summarize what they read. Display the Sequence Chart from the previous day and direct students to add to it as you read. Discuss questions such as these during and after reading.

■ For how many years did a boy often have to work as an apprentice?

■ What did a boy do during his last year as an apprentice?

READ AND RESPOND

Have the group read aloud to the end of the selection. Discuss what happened after a boy was no longer thought of as an apprentice and help students identify signal words and phrases for sequence. Afterward, have students respond to these questions and share questions of their own.

■ If you lived in colonial America, what job would you choose? Why?

■ What seems like the hardest part of being an apprentice? Explain.

Fluency

Objective   Read with increasing fluency
Materials   • stopwatch   • **Approaching Practice Book A,** p. 152

TIMED READING

At the end of the week, have students do a final timed reading of the fluency passage. Students should read aloud for one minute, starting when you say "Go" and ending when you say "Stop." Help students graph the number of words they read correctly. Analyze and address miscues.

Let's Trade!
by Alex Ely

Student Book

Compound Words Review that compound words are words composed of smaller words. Write the examples *birthday*, *newspaper*, and *birdhouse* on the board. Have students brainstorm other compound words that are familiar to them. As they volunteer words, write them on the board. For each compound word, ask what smaller words make up the word. Then place slash marks dividing the words. Pronounce each word and have students repeat.

Comprehension

Objective   Identify the sequence of events in a story
Materials   • **Comprehension Transparencies 21a** and **21b**

SKILL
SEQUENCE

Remind students that sequence means the order in which events happen in a story or article. "Let's Trade!" tells a story about two friends who barter and gives information on the history of trading.

Display **Transparencies 21a** and **21b**. Read the opening paragraphs.

Think Aloud The fourth paragraph begins with the word *then*. I know *then* is a sequence clue word. I will look for the event that comes before *then* and the event that comes right after.

Have students underline sequence words and phrases such as *after, a few minutes later,* and *then* and write numbers beside the main events to show the sequence.

Vocabulary

Objective   Apply vocabulary word meanings and analyze compound words
Materials   • **Vocabulary Cards**   • **Student Book** *Boom Town*

VOCABULARY WORDS

Review the words using the **Vocabulary Cards.** Help students locate the words in *Boom Town*. Focus on words students do not know well. Read the words aloud in context and ask students to restate the meanings. Then have students use each word in a silly sentence that expresses the meaning.

COMPOUND WORDS

Write *sidewalks* on the board. Review that *side* means "next to" and *walks* here means "paths." *Sidewalks,* then, are paths next to a road.

Have students work in pairs to define these compound words: *birthday, newspaper, birdhouse,* and *everywhere.* Challenge them to write each definition in the form of an explanation based on the combined meaning of the two smaller words. Encourage students to scan previous selections in their textbook and list compound words. How often can they figure out the meaning of the compound word by analyzing its two parts? Discuss a compound word such as *gooseberry* where the meaning differs from the meaning of the two parts.

Phonics

Objective   Decode compound words
Materials   • chart paper

DECODE COMPOUND WORDS

Write *doorbell* and *basketball* on chart paper. Show how each word is formed by joining two smaller words. Say each smaller word and have students repeat it. Then say each compound word and have students repeat it. Have students write and say *airplane, sometime, notebook, haircut, birthday,* and *daylight.* They should draw a slash between the two words within each to show how each compound word is formed.

Additional Lessons

Use your **Quick Check** observations to help you identify students who might benefit from additional instruction. See page T1 for comprehension support and page T6 for vocabulary support.

Vocabulary

Objective   Use vocabulary words in sentences
Materials   • **Vocabulary Cards**   • sentence strips

VOCABULARY WORDS

Read each vocabulary word from this week and last and discuss its definition. Have students work in pairs to write a definition card for each word.

Partners can shuffle the **Vocabulary Cards** and definition cards and arrange them facedown on a surface. The first player turns over one word card and one definition card. If the cards match, the player keeps the cards. If they don't match, the player turns the cards facedown again. Then the partner takes a turn.

sidewalks   grumbled   traders   blossomed   wailed   lonesome

Make Connections Across Texts

Objective   Compare sequences of events and make connections across texts
Materials   • **Student Book** *Boom Town*
                 • **Leveled Reader** *Children at Work: Colonial America*

SKILL
SEQUENCE

Summarize and discuss *Boom Town* and *Children at Work: Colonial America.* Have students use sequence to put three main events in order that would occur in the life of an apprentice in colonial America. Then have groups compare the work of an apprentice with Amanda's work at the bakery. Which do they think would be harder? Why? What questions would they ask each author?

Student Book

Leveled Reader

Leveled Reader Lesson

Objective   Read to apply strategies and skills

Materials   • **Leveled Reader** *Children at Work: On the Frontier*   • chart paper
                   • **On Level Practice Book O,** p. 152

PREVIEW AND PREDICT

Show the cover and read the title. Ask students if they know what the word *frontier* means. Review vocabulary word meanings as they appear in the selection.

STRATEGY
SUMMARIZE

Explain that summarizing a nonfiction text as they read helps readers understand the passage's most important events. Read pages 2–3 aloud. Model how you summarize.

Think Aloud   The introduction says that children on the frontier had to work hard to help their families. That information seems important enough to go in a summary. I'll keep reading and pay attention to what the children did to help out.

SKILL
SEQUENCE

As students read, discuss and summarize the events that happened during the gold rush that led different children to move west and pursue work. Students can create a Sequence Chart on chart paper. Discuss the kind of work available to children, based on their age and gender.

READ AND RESPOND

Have students read to the end of Chapter 2 and look for information that tells what kind of work children did. Discuss the main ideas and events.

Then have students read to the end of the book. Remind them to pause often to summarize and identify the sequence of events. Discuss the kind of work children did in frontier towns and whether children would still be allowed to do that kind of work today. Ask students what was the most unexpected fact they learned.

Fluency: REPEATED READING

Use the fluency passage on **Practice Book** page 152 to model reading narrative nonfiction aloud. Have students echo-read each sentence.

As students take turns reading in pairs, remind them to pause at commas and periods. Listeners should praise their partner when he or she has done well. Offer fluency support as needed.

Informational Nonfiction

CHILDREN AT WORK: On the Frontier

by Truman Vega

Leveled Reader

ELL
Leveled Reader
Go to pages 183U–183V.

On Level Practice Book O, page 152

As I read, I will pay attention to punctuation.

	They came by horse and wagon. They came by flatboat
10	down rivers. They came with everything they owned. Most
19	made the trip west with their parents. Some came alone.
29	From the 1780s to the 1880s, thousands of children
36	moved to the frontier. They started a new life at the
47	western edge of settled land in the United States.
56	Families moved west for many reasons. Some wanted
64	their own land to start a new life. Others wanted to find
76	gold. Still others came for adventure.
82	In 1862 the Homestead Act made moving to the frontier
91	possible for these families. They paid the government $18
99	for 160 acres of land. To keep the land, the family had to
111	build a house on it. Then they had to live in it for at least
126	five years. 128

Comprehension Check

1. Why did families move west? **Main Idea and Details**   to get their own land and start a new life, some moved in search of gold, and others were in search of adventure.
2. What was the Homestead Act? **Main Idea and Details**   It gave 160 acres of land to families who paid $18 and who agreed to live on the land for 5 years.

	Words Read	–	Number of Errors	=	Words Correct Score
First Read		–		=	
Second Read		–		=	

Vocabulary

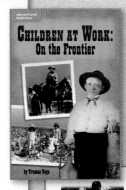
Leveled Reader

Objective Apply vocabulary words and identify and define compound words

Materials
- **Leveled Reader** *Children at Work: On the Frontier*
- **Vocabulary Cards** • chart paper

VOCABULARY WORDS

Show the **Vocabulary Cards** for *sidewalks, grumbled, traders, blossomed, wailed,* and *lonesome.* Have students use each word in a sentence that shows the meaning of the word.

Then have the group collaborate on creating a crossword puzzle using the vocabulary words for this week and previous weeks on chart paper. After they write the clues they should prepare at least three copies of the puzzle for classmates to solve.

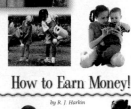
Student Book

COMPOUND WORDS

Ask students to locate these compound words in the leveled reader: *fireplaces* (p. 5), *cornhusk* (p. 6), *shopkeepers, horseshoes* (p. 9), and *steamboats* (p. 13). Challenge students to write definitions of each based on the combined meaning of their word parts. Example: *Fireplaces are* places *in a house where you can have a* fire.

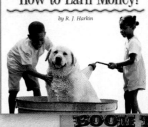
Student Book

Text Feature

Objective Read and understand a calendar

Materials
- **Student Book** "How to Earn Money!"

CALENDARS

Discuss how calendars are organized and the information that they typically include (months, weeks, days of the year, holidays). Have students look at the calendar on **Student Book** page 180 and discuss why calendars are useful to people who run businesses. Ask them to create a calendar for themselves that shows their plans for a month.

Make Connections Across Texts

Objective Make connections across texts and identify sequence of events

Materials
- **Student Book** *Boom Town*
- **Leveled Reader** *Children at Work: On the Frontier*

SKILL

SEQUENCE

Discuss the sequence of events in *Boom Town* and *Children at Work: On the Frontier* and point out the frontier time line. Discuss which book makes living and working in frontier times sound more enjoyable.

Leveled Reader Library

Leveled Reader Lesson

Objective	Read to apply strategies and skills
Materials	• **Leveled Reader** *The Work They Did* • chart paper
	• **Beyond Practice Book B**, p. 152

Informational Nonfiction

The Work They Did

The Immigrant Experience 1880 to 1924

by Suzanne Weyn

Leveled Reader

PREVIEW AND PREDICT

Show the cover. Read the title and the chapter headings. Ask students if they know what an immigrant is. Discuss what the book might be about. Challenge students to identify vocabulary words.

STRATEGY
SUMMARIZE

Remind students that summarizing nonfiction can help them understand and remember the most important events in a text. As students read, they should try to summarize the sequence of events that led to immigrant workers moving to the United States.

SKILL
SEQUENCE

As students read, discuss the kinds of jobs that were available to immigrants in the late 1800s. Ask why immigrants from certain countries sought out specific kinds of jobs. Discuss the sequence of events that led to the jobs female immigrants had in the early 1900s.

READ AND RESPOND

Have students first read orally to the end of Chapter 2 and listen for fluency. Encourage them to read to find out if immigrants got jobs outside of blue-collar industries like mining and farming. Monitor comprehension.

After students finish reading, have them share personal responses.

- Was anything surprising about the jobs immigrants found? Explain.

- What do you think is the most interesting contribution these immigrants made to United States culture? Explain and support your opinion.

Fluency: REPEATED READING

Read the fluency passage from the Leveled Reader, reproduced on **Practice Book** page 152, and model pausing at punctuation marks. Then have partners take turns reading the passage and offering corrective feedback. Observe and offer feedback, too.

Students should continue to practice reading the passage during independent time throughout the week. At the end of the week, have them do a timed reading to measure improvement.

◆ Beyond Practice Book B, page 152

As I read, I will pay attention to punctuation.

	In the 1890s, cities were booming. Many immigrants lived in
9	tenements. They got jobs in nearby factories and mills where iron
20	and steel was produced or factories that made thread, fabric, clothing,
31	and other goods.
34	The work was long and hard and wages were low. The workrooms
46	were dimly lit and crowded. People grew tired and often grumbled
57	about their jobs. They worked long hours, and there were often
68	accidents and fires.
71	By 1880 there was a great need for steel. Steel is made
82	from iron ore that is found in the earth. Many miners were
94	needed to dig out the iron. That was hard work. Miners
105	worked long hours for little pay. Young boys were paid
115	even less.
117	Coal was also important in the early 1900s. It provided
126	most of the country's energy. Miners worked hundreds of
135	feet below the surface of the earth to dig it out.
146	Both iron and coal miners helped our country to grow. Iron
157	was used for buildings, railroads, and other goods. Coal kept
167	people warm and fueled steam engines. 173

Comprehension Check

1. What does the word **wages** mean? **Context Clues** *pay or payment for work done*

2. Why were young boys paid less? **Make Inferences** *because they were younger and not as strong*

	Words Read	−	Number of Errors	=	Words Correct Score
First Read		−		=	
Second Read		−		=	

Vocabulary

Objective   Apply content vocabulary words
Materials   • **Student Book** "How to Earn Money!"

CONTENT VOCABULARY

Have students use at least three of the content vocabulary words on **Student Book** page 178 to write a plan for a business they envision. Tell them that their plan must explain what their business is, how people would benefit from it, and how they would advertise. Ask them to underline the content words and check their spelling.

Text Feature

Objective   Interpret calendars and create a calendar
Materials   • **Student Book** "How to Earn Money!"   • chart or graph paper

CALENDARS

Ask students to reread "How to Earn Money!" on **Student Book** pages 178–181 and summarize the main ideas. Review and discuss the calendar for starting a dog-washing business.

■ How can calendars help keep events organized?

■ What other things are calendars useful for?

Ask students to make a calendar of things they would need to do before opening the business they wrote about earlier. Have them decide how much time they need for each task and mark the task on the calendar and the number of days for each task. Students may work with a partner.

Self-Selected Reading

Objective   Read independently and identify the sequence of events
Materials   • Leveled Readers or trade books at students' reading level

READ TO SUMMARIZE THE SEQUENCE OF EVENTS

Invite students to choose a fiction book to read independently for enjoyment. Have them think about their personal needs and interests as well as recommendations from others. For a list of theme-related titles, see pages T19–T20. As students read, have them note the sequence of events in the story.

Afterward, partners should discuss how the outcome of the story might be different if the plot had skipped one or two steps in the sequence. Invite them to revise the story with an alternate sequence of events and to share their revisions with the group.

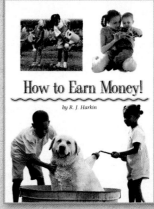

Student Book

ELL   Access for All

Categorize Review that calendars help keep events organized. Explain that other things help us to organize other parts of our lives. For example, drawers in a dresser help us keep clothes organized. Folders or notebooks help us keep school papers organized. Ask: *What other things in our lives help us to stay organized?* Write the items on the board. Next to each item write how it helps students stay organized.

Academic Language

Throughout the week the English language learners will need help in building their understanding of the academic language used in daily instruction and assessment instruments. The following strategies will help to increase their language proficiency and comprehension of content and instructional words.

LOG ON **Technology**

Oral Language For additional language support and oral vocabulary development, go to
www.macmillanmh.com

Strategies to Reinforce Academic Language

- **Use Context** Academic Language (see chart below) should be explained in the context of the task during Whole Group. Use gestures, expressions, and visuals to support meaning.

- **Use Visuals** Use charts, transparencies, and graphic organizers to explain key labels to help students understand classroom language.

- **Model** Demonstrate the task using academic language in order for students to understand instruction.

Academic Language Used in Whole Group Instruction

Content/Theme Words	Skill/Strategy Words	Writing/Grammar Words
making money (p. 151)	compound words (p. 152)	descriptive (p. 182)
business (p. 178)	summarize (p. 153)	compare-and-contrast paragraphs (p. 182)
services (p. 178)	sequence (p. 153)	similar and different (p. 182)
batches (p. 178)	draw conclusions (p. 177B)	topic sentences (p. 182)
demand (p. 178)	reading a calendar (p. 178)	Venn diagram (p. 183)
talent (p. 179)	months, weeks, and days of the year (p. 178)	singular and plural pronouns (p. 183I)
		capitalizing I and proper nouns (p. 183J)

ELL Leveled Reader Lesson

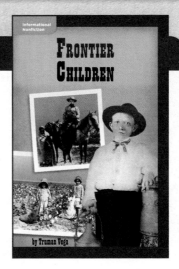

FRONTIER CHILDREN

by Truman Vega

Before Reading

DEVELOP ORAL LANGUAGE

Build Background Brainstorm activities that students do every day, such as go to school and play. Then, write the date 1800 on the board and ask: *How do you think life was different for children who lived in 1800?*

Review Vocabulary Write the vocabulary and support words on the board and discuss their meanings. Write a sentence for each of the words; however, leave a blank space in place of the word. *My mom works to ____.* (make a living)

PREVIEW AND PREDICT

Point to the cover photographs and read the title aloud. Explain that the children in the photographs lived in the 1800s in an area called the "frontier." Show this area on a map. *How do you think the children are feeling? Why?* Have students discuss.

Set a Purpose for Reading Show the Sequence Chart. Ask students to do a similar chart to record key information and summarize the story.

During Reading

Choose from among the differentiated strategies below to support students' reading at all stages of language acquisition.

Beginning	Intermediate	Advanced
Shared Reading As you read, model how to identify key information. Number the events to show their order. As you fill in the chart, use this information to summarize each chapter. Discuss the time line in the conclusion.	**Read Together** Read Chapter 1. Help students write key information in the chart. Number the events to show sequence. Have students take turns reading the rest and use the strategy to fill in the chart and then summarize.	**Independent Reading** Have students read the selection. After each chapter, ask them to record information in their charts. Guide them to look for words or dates that show the sequence of events. Have students summarize each chapter.

After Reading

Remind students to use the vocabulary and story words in their whole group activities.

Objective

- To apply vocabulary and comprehension skills

Materials

- ELL Leveled Reader

ELL 5 Day Planner

DAY 1	• Academic Language • Oral Language and Vocabulary Review
DAY 2	• Academic Language • ELL Leveled Reader
DAY 3	• Academic Language • ELL Leveled Reader
DAY 4	• Academic Language • ELL Leveled Reader
DAY 5	• Academic Language • ELL Leveled Reader Comprehension Check and Literacy Activities

ELL Teacher's Guide
for students who need additional instruction

Weekly Theme: Making a Difference

Week At A Glance

Whole Group

 VOCABULARY
gift, kindhearted, produce, schoolhouse, sturdy, tend, yearned

 Word Parts/Word Families

 COMPREHENSION
Strategy: Make Inferences and Analyze
Skill: Identify Cause and Effect

 WRITING
Descriptive

 Social Studies Link

Economics

Small Group Options

Differentiated Instruction for Tested Skills

Main Selection
Genre Nonfiction Article

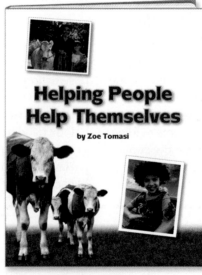

Vocabulary/ Comprehension

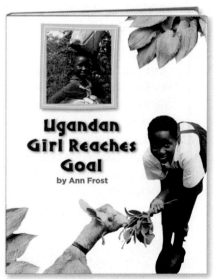

Social Studies Link
Genre Newspaper Article

 Tested Skills for the Week

Resources for Differentiated Instruction

Leveled Readers
GR Levels M–R

Genre Biography

- Same Theme
- Same Vocabulary
- Same Comprehension Skills

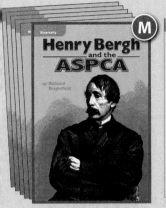
(M) Henry Bergh and the ASPCA
by Richard Brightfield

Approaching Level

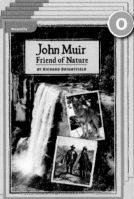
(O) John Muir: Friend of Nature
BY RICHARD BRIGHTFIELD

On Level

(R) Alexander Fleming and His Great Discovery
by Richard Brightfield

Beyond Level

John Muir: Friend of Nature
BY RICHARD BRIGHTFIELD

English Language Leveled Reader

On Level Reader sheltered for English Language Learner

ELL Teacher's Guide Available

Also Available
LEVELED READER PROGRAM

CLASSROOM LIBRARY

Genre Historical Fiction

Approaching

The Year of Miss Agnes
On Level

Amelia and Eleanor Go For A Ride
Beyond

Trade books to apply Comprehension Skills

INTERVENTION ANTHOLOGY

- Phonics and Decoding
- Comprehension
- Vocabulary

Reading Triumphs

Reading Triumphs, Intervention Program also available

LEVELED PRACTICE

Practice Book A
Approaching

Practice Book O
On Level

Practice Book B
Beyond

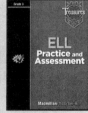
ELL Practice and Assessment
ELL

Technology

www.macmillanmh.com

 LISTENING LIBRARY
- Main Selections
- Leveled Readers
- Intervention Anthology

FLUENCY SOLUTIONS

 VOCABULARY PuzzleMaker

NEW ADVENTURES WITH BUGGLES AND BEEZY

 ONLINE INSTRUCTION
- Meet the Author/Illustrator
- Computer Literacy Lessons
- Research and Inquiry Activities
- Oral Language Activities
- Vocabulary and Spelling Activities

Beatrice's Goat **184B**

Suggested Lesson Plan

   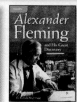

Beatrice's Goat, 188–209

Leveled Readers

Whole Group

Integrated ELL Support Every Day

ORAL LANGUAGE
- **Listening**
- **Speaking**
- **Viewing**

WORD STUDY
- **Vocabulary**
- **Phonics/Decoding**

READING
- **Develop Comprehension**

- **Fluency**

LANGUAGE ARTS
- **Writing**

- **Grammar**

- **Spelling**

ASSESSMENT
- **Informal/Formal**

Turn the Page for Small Group Lesson Plan

Day 1

Listening/Speaking/Viewing

❓ Focus Question What person has made a difference in your life or in your community?

Build Background, 184

Read Aloud: "Frog and Locust," 185

Vocabulary

gift, yearned, tend, produce, sturdy, schoolhouse, kindhearted, 186

Practice Book A-O-B, 156

Strategy: Word Parts: Word Families, 187

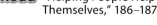 **Read** "Helping People Help Themselves," 186–187

Helping People Help Themselves by Zee Tamari

Comprehension, 187A–187B

Strategy: Make Inferences and Analyze

Skill: Cause and Effect
Practice Book A-O-B, 157

Student Book

Fluency Partner Reading, 184I
Model Fluency, 185

 Writing

Daily Writing Prompt Write a paragraph about how you can make a difference in your neighborhood.

Prewrite a Descriptive Paragraph, 217A

Grammar Daily Language Activities, 217I
Subject and Object Pronouns, 217I
Grammar Practice Book, 135

Spelling Pretest, 217G
Spelling Practice Book, 135–136

Quick Check Vocabulary, 186

Comprehension, 187B

Differentiated Instruction 217M-217V

Day 2

Listening/Speaking

❓ Focus Question Does Beatrice ever get to go to school?

Vocabulary
Review Vocabulary, 188

Phonics
Decode Words with Inflected Endings, 217E

Practice Book A-O-B, 162

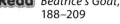 **Read** *Beatrice's Goat,* 188–209

Comprehension, 188–211
Strategy: Make Inferences and Analyze
Skill: Cause and Effect
Practice Book A-O-B, 158

Student Book

Fluency Partner Reading, 184I
Phrase-Cued Text, 205

Writing

Daily Writing Prompt Imagine you are on the beach in the photograph on pages 184–185. Write a paragraph about how you would make a difference there.

Draft a Descriptive Paragraph, 217A

Grammar Daily Language Activities, 217I
Subject and Object Pronouns, 217I
Grammar Practice Book, 136

Spelling Word Sorts, 217G
Spelling Practice Book, 135–136

Quick Check Comprehension, 201, 209

Phonics, 217E

Differentiated Instruction 217M-217V

Vocabulary
Vocabulary Words
Word Parts/
Word Families

Comprehension
Strategy: Make Inferences and Analyze
Skill: Cause and Effect

Writing
Descriptive Writing

Turn the Page for
Small Group Options

Day 3

Listening/Speaking
❷ Focus Question Read "Helping People Help Themselves." How is this selection like *Beatrice's Goat*? How are the two selections different?
Summarize, 211

Vocabulary
Review Words in Context, 217C
Strategy: Word Parts: Word Families, 217D
Practice Book A-O-B, 161

Phonics
Decode Multisyllable Words, 217E

Read *Beatrice's Goat,* 188–209

Student Book

Comprehension
Comprehension Check, 211
Maintain Skill: Making Inferences, 211B

Fluency Practice Book A-O-B, 159
Partner Reading, 184I
Repeated Reading, 211A

Writing
Daily Writing Prompt Write a thank-you letter to someone who treated you in a kindhearted and caring way.

Writing Trait: Ideas and Content, 217
Revise a Descriptive Paragraph, 217B

Grammar Daily Language Activities, 217I
Mechanics and Usage, 217J
Grammar Practice Book, 137

Spelling Word Meanings, 217H
Spelling Practice Book, 138

Quick Check Fluency, 211A

Differentiated Instruction 217M-217V

Day 4

Listening/Speaking
❷ Focus Question Think about *Beatrice's Goat* and this article. Which parts let you know how Beatrice feels about getting an education?
Expand Vocabulary: Making a Difference, 217F

Vocabulary
Content Vocabulary: *achieve, determined, encourages,* 212
Word History, 217F
Apply Vocabulary to Writing, 217F

Read "Ugandan Girl Reaches Goal," 212–215

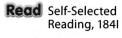
Student Book

Comprehension
Social Studies: Newspaper Article
Text Feature: Editorials, 212
Practice Book A-O-B, 160

Fluency Partner Reading, 184I

Writing
Daily Writing Prompt Write a letter to the editor asking readers to help a non-profit organization like the one that helped Beatrice.

Proofread a Descriptive Paragraph, 217B

Grammar Daily Language Activities, 217I
Subject and Object Pronouns, 217J
Grammar Practice Book, 138

Spelling Review and Proofread, 217H
Spelling Practice Book, 139

Quick Check Vocabulary, 217D

Differentiated Instruction 217M-217V

Day 5
Review and Assess

Listening/Speaking
❷ Focus Question Based on what you have read in *Beatrice's Goat*, "Ugandan Girl Reaches Goal," and "Helping People Help Themselves," how can the gift of a goat affect someone's life?
Speaking and Listening Strategies, 217A

Presentation of Descriptive Paragraph, 217B

Vocabulary
Spiral Review: Vocabulary Game, 217F

Read Self-Selected Reading, 184I

Student Book

Comprehension
Connect and Compare, 215

Fluency Partner Reading, 184I

Writing
Daily Writing Prompt Imagine that your family moved to Kisinga and that you lived like Beatrice's family. Compare your new life with the life you had before.

Publish a Descriptive Paragraph, 217B

Grammar Daily Language Activities, 217I
Subject and Object Pronouns, 217J
Grammar Practice Book, 139–140

Spelling Posttest, 217H
Spelling Practice Book, 140

Weekly Assessment, 277–284

Differentiated Instruction 217M-217V

Small Group Options

What do I do in small groups?

Quick Check

Use your Quick Checks to inform instruction.

Additional Instruction, Practice, and Extend Activities are provided for this week's tested skills.

Phonics	Vocabulary	Comprehension	Fluency
Decode Words with Inflected Endings	**Words:** gift, yearned, tend, produce, sturdy, schoolhouse, kindhearted **Strategy:** Word Parts/ Word Families	**Strategy:** Make Inferences and Analyze **Skill:** Cause and Effect	

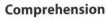

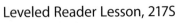

starry

Lesson Plan
TEACHER–LED SMALL GROUP

 Instructional Navigator
Interactive Lesson Planner

	Day 1	**Day 2**
Approaching Level • **Additional Instruction/Practice** • **Tier 2 Instruction**	Leveled Reader Lesson 1, 217M • Vocabulary • Comprehension • Fluency	Leveled Reader Lesson 2, 217N • Vocabulary • Comprehension • Fluency **ELL** Drawing, 217O
On Level • **Practice**	Leveled Reader Lesson, 217Q • Vocabulary • Comprehension • Fluency **ELL** Leveled Reader, 217U–V	Leveled Reader Lesson, 217Q • Vocabulary • Comprehension • Fluency
Beyond Level • **Extend**	Leveled Reader Lesson, 217S • Vocabulary • Comprehension • Fluency	Leveled Reader Lesson, 217S • Vocabulary • Comprehension • Fluency

for Differentiated Instruction

Leveled Readers

GR Levels M–R

Matching students to text.

Also Available
LEVELED READER LIBRARY

LOG ON **Leveled Reader Database**
To search for additional Leveled Reader titles, go to **www.macmillanmh.com**

M

Approaching Level

• Benchmark 28
• Use other guided reading titles, M–O

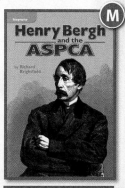

O

On Level

• Benchmark 34
• Use other guided reading titles, O–R

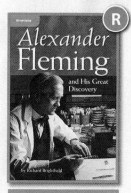

R

Beyond Level

• Benchmark 40
• Use other guided reading titles, R–T

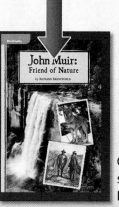

English Language Leveled Reader

On Level Reader sheltered for English Language Learner.

Day 3

Comprehension, 217O
Vocabulary, 217O

Vocabulary, 217R

Self-Selected Reading, 217T

Day 4

Phonics, 217P
Vocabulary, 217P

Text Feature, 217R

Vocabulary, 217T

Day 5

Fluency, 217N
Make Connections Across Texts, 217P

Make Connections Across Texts, 217R

Text Feature, 217T
ELL Partnered Reading, 217T

Managing the Class

What do I do with the rest of my class?

Teacher-Led Small Groups

Cross-Curricular Workstations

Independent Activities

See inside back cover for activities

Leveled Reader Activities

Approaching

LEVELED PRACTICE

- Vocabulary, 156
- Comprehension: Cause and Effect, 157
- Graphic Organizer, 158
- Fluency, 159
- Text Feature: Editorial, 160
- Vocabulary Strategy: Word Families, 161
- Phonics, 162

★ **Approaching Practice Book A, 156–162**

A. Write the letter of each definition in front of the correct vocabulary word.

- c 1. sturdy
- g 2. yearned
- f 3. produce
- e 4. gift
- d 5. tend
- b 6. kindhearted
- a 7. schoolhouse

  a. a building used as a school
  b. generous and kind towards people
  c. strong
  d. to look after or take care of
  e. a present
  f. to make or create something
  g. had a strong want for something

B. Circle the vocabulary word that correctly completes each sentence.

8. My brother ___yearned___ for a puppy all winter, and my parents gave him one for his birthday.
   a. yearned   b. kindhearted

9. The storm knocked over everything except for the ___sturdy___ hut.
   a. gift   b. sturdy

10. The artist received an award because she was able to ___produce___ so many excellent paintings.
    a. yearned   b. produce

Weekly Contract

Name _____ **Date** _____

My To-Do List

✔ Put a check next to the activities you complete.

📖 **Reading**
- ☐ Practice fluency
- ☐ Read a news report

🔤 **Word Study**
- ☐ Make words from word families
- ☐ Work with inflected endings

✏️ **Writing**
- ☐ Write a description
- ☐ Write a headline

🔬 **Science**
- ☐ Read a science article
- ☐ Write about a discovery

🌐 **Social Studies**
- ☐ Find an editorial opinion
- ☐ Write an opinion

⚓ **Leveled Readers**
- ☐ Write About It!
- ☐ Content Connection

💻 **Technology**
- ☐ Vocabulary Puzzlemaker
- ☐ Fluency Solutions
- ☐ Listening Library
- ☐ www.macmillanmh.com

✍️ **Independent Practice**
- ☐ Practice Book, 156–162
- ☐ Grammar Practice Book, 135–140
- ☐ Spelling Practice Book, 135–140

㉔ Unit 5 • Beatrice's Ghost   Contracts

Teacher's Resource Book, page 24

• Students use their Contracts to manage their time.

HOME-SCHOOL CONNECTION

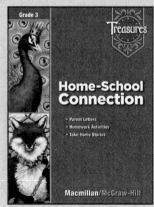

Pages 259–270

Independent Activities

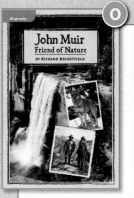

On Level

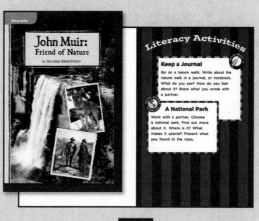

ELL

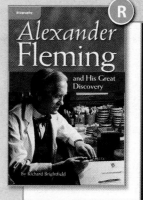

Beyond

On Level Practice Book O, 156–162

Use the words in the box to complete the puzzle.

sturdy	yearned	produce	gift
tend	kindhearted	schoolhouse	

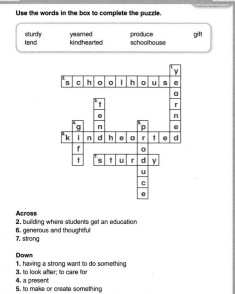

Across
2. building where students get an education
6. generous and thoughtful
7. strong

Down
1. having a strong want to do something
3. to look after; to care for
4. a present
5. to make or create something

Beyond Practice Book B, 156–162

Use vocabulary words to fill in the missing letters in the crossword puzzle below. Then write the correct definition as a clue for each vocabulary word. **Possible responses provided.**

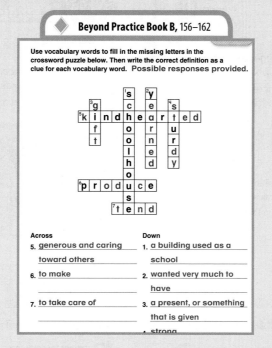

Across
5. generous and caring toward others
6. to make _____
7. to take care of _____

Down
1. a building used as a school
2. wanted very much to have
3. a present, or something that is given
4. strong

ELL Practice and Assessment, 138–139

Parent Letter

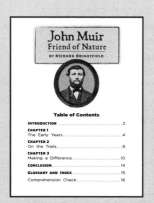

Take-Home Story

Turn the page for Cross-Curricular Activities.

Managing the Class

Cross-Curricular Activities

All activities reinforce this week's skills.

 Reading

Objectives

- Read aloud with a partner.
- Make a Sequence Chart for a news report.
- Read for a purpose.

 **Word Study**

Objectives

- Make compound words.
- Sort words with double consonants and similar word endings.

Reading — FLUENCY — *20 Minutes*

- Choose a reading buddy. Read aloud page 159 of your Practice Book.
- You read the narration. Your partner reads the dialogue.

Extension

- Read the page aloud again. This time, switch roles.
- Talk about the differences between narration and dialogue.
- Listen to the Audio Disc.

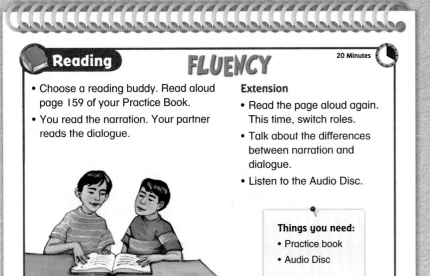

Things you need:
- Practice book
- Audio Disc

Fluency Solutions Listening Library

43

Word Study — **Word Families** — *20 Minutes*

- Write these words on note cards: *house, book.*
- Add the word *school* to each word. Write the new words you made.
- Use both words in one sentence.

Extension

- Write a short paragraph describing your school day. Use three compound words you know.

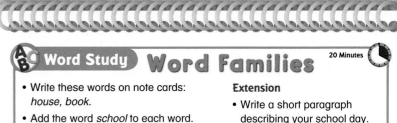

Hartwell School

Things you need:
- note cards
- dictionary
- paper
- pencil

 For additional vocabulary and spelling games, go to www.macmillanmh.com   Vocabulary PuzzleMaker

43

Reading **Independent Reading** — *20 Minutes*

- Find a news report about something that happened in your school or community.
- Fill out a Sequence Chart for the news report. Write events in order.

Extension

- Tell a partner about the news report. Talk about your opinion about the news reports.

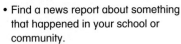

Things you need:
- newspaper
- paper
- pencil

For more books about Making a Difference, go to the Author/Illustrator section at www.macmillanmh.com

44

Word Study **Inflected Endings** — *20 Minutes*

- Write these words on note cards: *drop, drops, dropped,* and *dropping.*
- Now make note cards for *wrap, wraps, wrapped,* and *wrapping.*
- Use the same spelling rules to make note cards with *-s, -ed,* and *-ing* endings for these words: *flip* and *chop.*

Extension

- Sort your cards into two piles: words with double consonants and words without double consonants.
- Then sort your cards into four piles by word endings.

drop
drops
dropped
dropping

Things you need:
- note cards
- pencil

For additional vocabulary and spelling games, go to www.macmillanmh.com   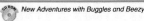 New Adventures with Buggles and Beezy

44

Independent Workstations

Objectives

- Write a paragraph describing how to reach a goal.
- Write a headline for a newspaper story.

Science/Social Studies

Objectives

- Identify persuasive parts of an editorial.
- Identify the *who, what, where, when,* and *why* in a science article.

Writing — Descriptive Writing · 20 Minutes

- Think of a goal you have reached. Maybe you read a long book. Maybe you learned to ride a bike.
- Write a paragraph. Describe your goal. What was it? How did you reach it? How did you feel afterwards?

Extension

- Read your paragraph to a partner. Did you include descriptive details? Could your partner picture what happened?

Things you need:
- paper
- pencil

43

Social Studies — Newspaper Knowledge · 20 Minutes

- Find an editorial in your local or school newspaper. The editorial should give an opinion about something.
- What is the writer's opinion? Underline persuasive parts of the editorial.

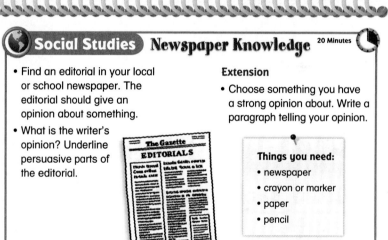

Extension

- Choose something you have a strong opinion about. Write a paragraph telling your opinion.

Things you need:
- newspaper
- crayon or marker
- paper
- pencil

LOG ON — Internet Research and Inquiry Activity
Students can find more facts at www.macmillanmh.com

43

Writing — A Hero Saves the Day! · 20 Minutes

- Think of something a hero might do. What would it be?
- Write a headline for a newspaper story about this heroic act. Make people want to find out more.

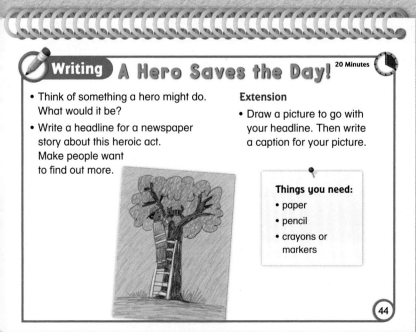

Extension

- Draw a picture to go with your headline. Then write a caption for your picture.

Things you need:
- paper
- pencil
- crayons or markers

44

Science — Discoveries in the News · 20 Minutes

- Find a science article in a newspaper or magazine. It might be about a recent discovery or an invention.
- Underline the parts that tell *who, what, where, when,* and *why.*

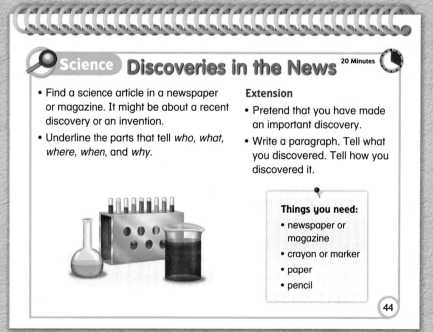

Extension

- Pretend that you have made an important discovery.
- Write a paragraph. Tell what you discovered. Tell how you discovered it.

Things you need:
- newspaper or magazine
- crayon or marker
- paper
- pencil

44

ORAL LANGUAGE
- Build Background
- Read Aloud
- Expand Vocabulary

 VOCABULARY
- Teach Words in Context
- **Word Parts:** Word Families

COMPREHENSION
- **Strategy:** Make Inferences and Analyze
- **Skill:** Cause and Effect

SMALL GROUP OPTIONS
- Differentiated Instruction, pp. 217M–217V

Oral Language

Build Background

ACCESS PRIOR KNOWLEDGE

Share the following information.

UNICEF, the United Nations Children's Fund, is an organization that provides medicine, schooling, and clean water for children in more than 150 countries.

TALK ABOUT MAKING A DIFFERENCE

Discuss the weekly theme.

- What do you think "making a difference" means? Who has made a difference in your life?

 FOCUS QUESTION Ask a volunteer to read "Talk About It" on **Student Book** page 185 and describe the photo.

- Would you like to help the people in the photograph? Why or why not?

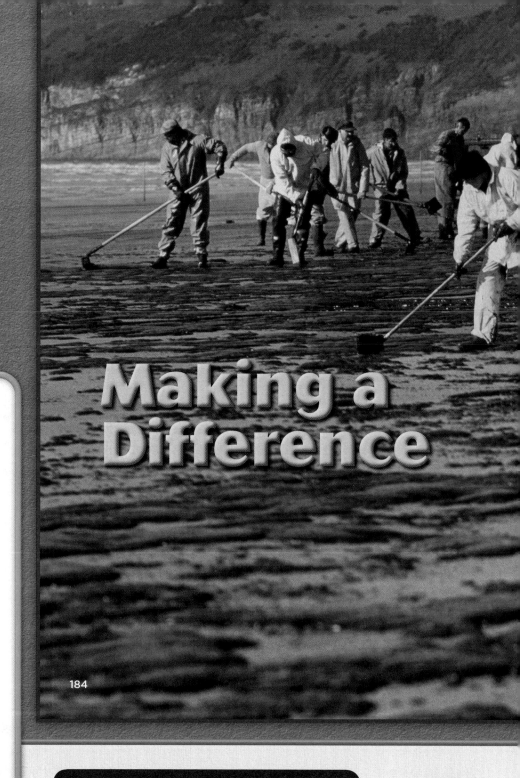

Making a Difference

184

 ENGLISH LANGUAGE LEARNERS

Beginning **Use Visual Information** Ask: *What do you see?* Identify what the people are doing. Explain that the duck needs help and that the person is helping the duck. Ask: *What will the person do with the duck?* Help students answer through words and gestures.

Intermediate **Discuss Ideas** Have students describe what is happening in the photograph. Explain *make a difference*. Have students discuss how people have made a difference in their lives. List the ways.

Advanced **Relate to Personal Experience** Complete the Intermediate task. As students talk about people who have made a difference in their lives, help them use descriptive and varied vocabulary.

Talk About It

What person has made a difference in your life or in your community?

LOG ON Find out more about making a difference at **www.macmillanmh.com**

185

Picture Prompt

Tell students: look at the picture. Write about what you see. You can write a poem, a story, a description, or use any other type of writing you like.

LOG ON Technology

For an extended lesson plan and Web site activities for **oral language development,** go to www.macmillanmh.com

Read Aloud
Read "Frog and Locust"

GENRE: Folk Tale
Review features of a folk tale:

- is made-up stories based on customs and traditions of a people or a region

- often has animal characters

- is handed down orally from one generation to the next

LISTENING FOR A PURPOSE

Ask students to identify the problem and the solution as they listen to "Frog and Locust" in the **Read-Aloud Anthology**. Choose from among the teaching suggestions.

Fluency Ask students to listen carefully for phrasing, expression, and tone of voice.

RESPOND TO THE FOLK TALE

Ask students to state their opinion about the quality of this story. Did they like the way the author described the characters and plot?

Expand Vocabulary

Ask students to choose words or phrases from the folk tale that relate to making a difference, such as *together, gather together, join,* and *one heart.* Have students collect other words during the week and then have a discussion with all the words about how working together can make a difference.

Vocabulary

 TEACH WORDS IN CONTEXT

Use the following routine.

Routine

Define: A **gift** is something that is given to someone on a special occasion or as a thank you.

Example: We gave Grandma flowers as a birthday gift.

Ask: What word means about the same as *gift*? (present) SYNONYM

- If you **yearned** to do something, you wanted to do it very much. I yearned to visit my best friend. What have you yearned to do? EXAMPLE

- If you **tend** to something, you take care of it. Farmers tend their crops. In what ways do parents tend to their children? EXPLANATION

 - To **produce** something is to make it. Dairy cows produce milk. What do chickens produce? PRIOR KNOWLEDGE

- If something is **sturdy**, it is strong. The firefighter climbed the sturdy ladder. What is the opposite of *sturdy*? (weak) ANTONYM

- A **schoolhouse** is a building used as a school. In a one-room schoolhouse, all students are in the same class. What is your schoolhouse like? DESCRIPTION

- A **kindhearted** person cares about others. The volunteers who work in the soup kitchen are kindhearted. Whom do you know that is kindhearted? EXAMPLE

Vocabulary

gift	sturdy
yearned	schoolhouse
tend	kindhearted
produce	

Word Parts

Word Families are groups of words that have the same base word.

Schoolhouse, preschool, and *schoolgirl* belong to the same word family.

An Armenian family with a cow

Helping People Help Themselves

by Zoe Tomasi

In the 1930s, Dan West was farming in Spain. It was wartime, and people were starving. As he handed out cups of milk to children, an idea hit him. "These children don't need a cup. They need a cow." This was the start of Heifer International.

Send Some Cows

Do you think a nice **gift** is a bike or CD? Heifer International gives different kinds of presents. Its presents might say "quack" or "moo." Dan West asked friends in the United States to give gifts of heifers, or young cows. Since then, Heifer International has given animals to four million families. It gives people the chance to feed themselves.

186

Quick Check

Do students understand word meanings?

During **Small Group Instruction**

If No → **Approaching Level** Vocabulary, p. 217P

If Yes → **On Level** Options, pp. 217Q–217R

Beyond Level Options, pp. 217S–217T

ELL   Access for All

Sentence Frames For the word *produce*, write: *Cows produce milk. Hens produce _____.* Help students answer. Ask: *What other animals produce milk? Eggs?* Say: *A kindhearted person does things for other people. My sister is kindhearted. She babysits for her friend.* Ask students to give other examples using the sentence frame: *_____ is a kindhearted person. He/She _____.*

Pass on the Gift

Heifer International wants the people they help to help others. For one project, the group sent chickens to some children in Asia. The children **yearned** for the day when they could help others.

Nine-year-old Julie said, "I want other girls like me to take care of chickens and their families. I want to share and give many away."

Julie knew she had to **tend** to her chickens well so they would **produce** new eggs and healthy chicks. She took good care of them, and they gave birth to strong, **sturdy** chicks. Julie then passed on the gift of chicks to other families.

This girl will care for her chicks so they grow up to be healthy.

Letting Children Learn

Because of Heifer International, children can spend their days in a **schoolhouse** instead of working in the fields. They can use the money they earn from their animals to pay for school.

Heifer International has made a huge difference in people's lives for many years, thanks to a **kindhearted** farmer named Dan West.

Reread for **Comprehension**

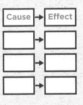

Make Inferences and Analyze
Cause and Effect
Why something happens is the cause. What happens is the effect. Recognizing these two things can help you make inferences about what you are reading.

A Cause and Effect Chart helps you analyze what happened in a story and make inferences about why it happened. Reread the selection to find several effects and their causes.

Cause	→	Effect
	→	
	→	
	→	

187

Vocabulary

eview last week's vocabulary words:
lossomed, grumbled, lonesome, idewalks, traders, and **wailed**.

On Level Practice Book O, page 156

Use the words in the box to complete the puzzle.

sturdy	yearned	produce	gift
tend	kindhearted	schoolhouse	

[crossword puzzle: schoolhouse, kindhearted, sturdy, with letters y-e-a-r-n-e-d down, t-e-n-d down, g, p-r-o-d-u-c-e]

Across
2. building where students get an education
6. generous and thoughtful
7. strong

Down
1. having a strong want to do something
3. to look after; to care for
4. a present
5. to make or create something

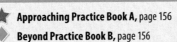

⭐ **Approaching Practice Book A,** page 156
◆ **Beyond Practice Book B,** page 156

Vocabulary

Using the Strategies To figure out unfamiliar words, students can use phonics to decode words, look for word parts, look for context clues, or use a dictionary.

STRATEGY
WORD PARTS

Word Families Some words are related to other words because they share a common word. They belong to word families. For example, *bookcase, copybook,* and *booking* are related. If readers can identify a common word, they can often figure out the meaning of the entire word.

Point to the word *schoolhouse* on **Student Book** page 187. The word *school* is in the first part of the word and the second part of the word is *house.* Ask students: What do you think these two words mean together? (possible answer: a school in a house) The actual meaning is "a building used as a school."

Write the words *schoolgirl, schoolbook, schooling, preschool,* and *schools.* Have students identify the common words in these related words and have them predict the meanings of the words.

Read "Helping People Help Themselves"

As students read "Helping People Help Themselves," have them identify clues to the meanings of the highlighted words. Tell students they will read these words again in *Beatrice's Goat.*

Objectives

- Make inferences and analyze
- Use academic language: *inference, analyze, cause, effect*
- Identify cause and effect

Materials

- Comprehension Transparencies 22a and 22b
- Graphic Organizer Transparency 22
- Leveled Practice Books, p. 157

Skills Trace

Cause and Effect

Introduce	U3: 343A–B
Practice / Apply	U3: 344–347; Leveled Practice, 90–91
Reteach / Review	U3: 351M–T; U5: 187A–B, 188–209, 217M–T; Leveled Practice, 157–158
Assess	Weekly Tests; Unit 3, 5 Tests; Benchmark Tests A, B
Maintain	U4: 85A; U6: 315B

ELL   Access for All

Give Context Write this story to illustrate *cause* and *effect*: *Some children were playing on the playground when it started to rain. They got soaking wet.* Ask: *Why did the children get wet? Rain is the cause.* Circle the word *rain* and label it *cause. What happened to the children? They got wet is the effect.* Circle the word *wet* and label it *effect*.

Reread for Comprehension

STRATEGY
MAKE INFERENCES AND ANALYZE

Authors don't always tell a reader every detail. Readers often have to **analyze,** or carefully look at, the information in the story and **make inferences** about it. To make inferences, good readers use what they know and clues in the story to figure out what is missing. When readers make inferences they better understand the characters and events and can identify causes and effects.

SKILL
CAUSE AND EFFECT

Access for All

- A **cause** is an event that makes something else happen. An **effect** is something that happens because of an earlier event.

- To find causes and effects, readers can ask these questions: What happened? (This is the effect.) Why did it happen? (This is the cause.)

- Sometimes readers can find signal words, such as *so, because, due to, since,* and *as a result,* to help them find causes and effects.

Transparency 22a

Vocabulary

gift	sturdy
yearned	schoolhouse
tend	kindhearted
produce	

Word Parts
Word Families are groups of words that have the same base word.

Schoolhouse, preschool, and *schoolgirl* belong to the same word family.

An Armenian family with a cow

Helping People Help Themselves
by Zoe Tomasi

In the 1930s, Dan West was farming in Spain. It was wartime, and people were starving. As he handed out cups of milk to children, an idea hit him. "These children don't need a cup. They need a cow." This was the start of Heifer International.

Send Some Cows
Do you think a nice **gift** is a bike or CD? Heifer International gives different kinds of presents. Its presents might say "quack" or "moo." Dan West asked friends in the United States to give gifts of heifers, or young cows. Since then, Heifer International has given animals to four million families. It gives people the chance to feed themselves.

186

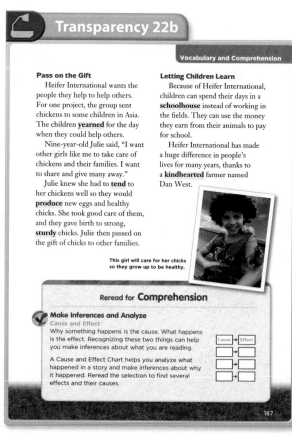

Transparency 22b

Vocabulary and Comprehension

Pass on the Gift
Heifer International wants the people they help to help others. For one project, the group sent chickens to some children in Asia. The children **yearned** for the day when they could help others.
Nine-year-old Julie said, "I want other girls like me to take care of chickens and their families. I want to share and give many away."
Julie knew she had to **tend** to her chickens well so they would **produce** new eggs and healthy chicks. She took good care of them, and they gave birth to strong, **sturdy** chicks. Julie then passed on the gift of chicks to other families.

Letting Children Learn
Because of Heifer International, children can spend their days in a **schoolhouse** instead of working in the fields. They can use the money they earn from their animals to pay for school.
Heifer International has made a huge difference in people's lives for many years, thanks to a **kindhearted** farmer named Dan West.

This girl will care for her chicks so they grow up to be healthy.

Reread for **Comprehension**

Make Inferences and Analyze
Cause and Effect
Why something happens is the cause. What happens is the effect. Recognizing these two things can help you make inferences about what you are reading.

A Cause and Effect Chart helps you analyze what happened in a story and make inferences about why it happened. Reread the selection to find several effects and their causes.

Cause	→	Effect

187

Student Book pages 186–187 available on Comprehension Transparencies 22a and 22b

MODEL

Write on the board: Dan West realized that the children in Spain could use cows more than cups of milk. As a result, he started Heifer International, which gives animals to families all around the world.

Think Aloud When I read these sentences, I notice the signal words *as a result* in the second sentence. This tells me that one event happened because of another event. I will look at the second sentence again and ask myself, "What happened?" The clue words *as a result* show me that Dan West started Heifer International. Now I will ask myself "Why did this happen?" Dan West realized that cows would help the children more than cups. As I read, I will look for clue words that signal other causes and effects.

GUIDED PRACTICE

- Display the Cause and Effect Chart on **Transparency 22.** For the first effect, write: *Dan West started Heifer International.* Then fill in the first cause: *Dan West realized that cows would help the children more than cups.*

- Have students reread the second paragraph on page 186. Have them ask themselves "What happened?" (Heifer International has given animals to four million families.) "Why?" (Dan West asked people in the United States to give gifts of heifers.) Have them add this cause and effect to the chart.

APPLY

- Have students reread the remainder of "Helping People Help Themselves," and identify the clue word and the cause and effect in the first paragraph of the last section on page 187. (Cause: Heifer International gave people heifers so they could earn money. Effect: Children could go to school instead of working in the fields. Clue word: *because*)

Quick Check Can students identify the causes and effects in a nonfiction article?

During **Small Group Instruction**

If No → **Approaching Level** Comprehension, p. 217O

If Yes → **On Level** Options, pp. 217Q–217R

Beyond Level Options, pp. 217S–217T

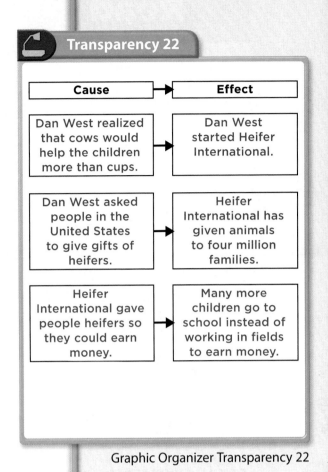

Transparency 22

Cause	→	Effect
Dan West realized that cows would help the children more than cups.	→	Dan West started Heifer International.
Dan West asked people in the United States to give gifts of heifers.	→	Heifer International has given animals to four million families.
Heifer International gave people heifers so they could earn money.	→	Many more children go to school instead of working in fields to earn money.

Graphic Organizer Transparency 22

On Level Practice Book O, page 157

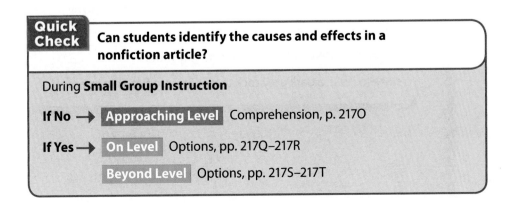

Approaching Practice Book A, page 157

Beyond Practice Book B, page 157

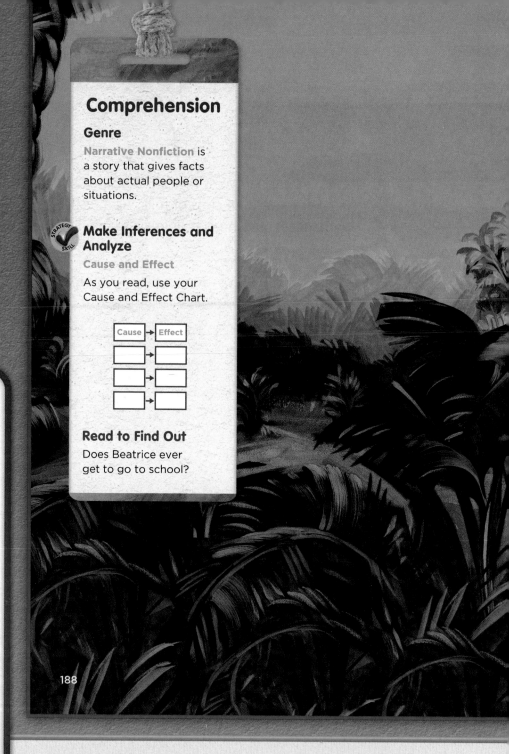

Read

MAIN SELECTION
- *Beatrice's Goat*
- **Skill:** Cause and Effect

PAIRED SELECTION
- "Ugandan Girl Reaches Goal"
- **Text Feature:** Editorial

WRITING
- Descriptive Paragraph
- **Writing Trait:** Ideas and Content

SMALL GROUP OPTIONS

- Differentiated Instruction, pp. 217M–217V

Comprehension

GENRE: NARRATIVE NONFICTION

Have a student read the definition of Narrative Nonfiction on **Student Book** page 188. Students should look for facts about how Beatrice got her goat and how it changed her life.

STRATEGY
MAKE INFERENCES AND ANALYZE

Good readers use their experiences and story clues to figure out information the author has left out. This is called **making inferences**.

SKILL
CAUSE AND EFFECT

A **cause** is an action that makes something happen. An **effect** is something that happens because of an action. Sometimes readers can use signal words, such as *because, due to,* and *as a result,* to find a cause and effect. Sometimes they will have to make inferences to figure it out.

188

Comprehension

Genre

Narrative Nonfiction is a story that gives facts about actual people or situations.

Make Inferences and Analyze

Cause and Effect

As you read, use your Cause and Effect Chart.

Cause	→	Effect
	→	
	→	
	→	

Read to Find Out

Does Beatrice ever get to go to school?

188

Vocabulary

Vocabulary Words Review the tested vocabulary words: **gift, yearned, tend, produce, sturdy, schoolhouse, kindhearted.**

Selection Words Students may find these words difficult. Pronounce the words and present the meanings as necessary.

groves (p. 190): large groups of trees

cassava (p. 193): a plant that has starchy roots

slate (p. 193): a dark grey rock that splits into flat, thin layers

Beatrice's Goat

by Page McBrier
illustrated by Lori Lohstoeter

Award Winning Author

189

Read Together

If your students need support to read the Main Selection, use the prompts to guide comprehension and model how to complete the graphic organizer.

Read Independently

If your students can read the Main Selection independently, have them read and complete the graphic organizer. Have students set and adjust their reading rate based on their purpose for reading.

If your students need an alternate selection, choose the **Leveled Readers** that match their instructional level.

Technology

Story available on **Listening Library Audio CD**

Preview and Predict

Ask students to read the title, preview the illustrations, and note questions and predictions about the story. Do they think this story is about real people and events? Have students write their predictions and anything else they want to know about the story.

Set Purposes

FOCUS QUESTION Discuss the "Read to Find Out" question on **Student Book** page 188. Remind students to look for the answer as they read.

Point out the Cause and Effect Chart in the Student Book and on **Leveled Practice Book** page 158. Explain that students will fill it in as they read.

Read *Beatrice's Goat*

Use the questions and Think Alouds for additional instruction to support the comprehension strategy and skill.

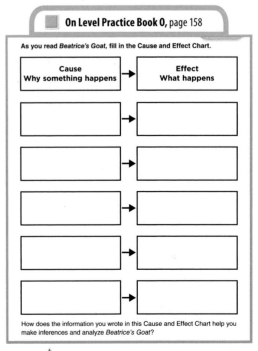

On Level Practice Book O, page 158

As you read *Beatrice's Goat*, fill in the Cause and Effect Chart.

| Cause
Why something happens | → | Effect
What happens |
|---|---|---|
| | → | |
| | → | |
| | → | |
| | → | |

How does the information you wrote in this Cause and Effect Chart help you make inferences and analyze *Beatrice's Goat*?

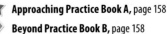

⭐ **Approaching Practice Book A,** page 158

◆ **Beyond Practice Book B,** page 158

Develop Comprehension

1 STRATEGY
MONITOR AND CLARIFY: SEEK HELP

Suppose you want to know more about where Uganda is. How can you find out? (First I would read ahead to see if there is more information. If there isn't, then I will seek help. I can use a map, an atlas, an encyclopedia, the Internet, or ask my teacher or librarian.)

2 CAUSE AND EFFECT

 Why does Beatrice's family live in a new house? (The story says that it's all because of a goat named Mugisa.)

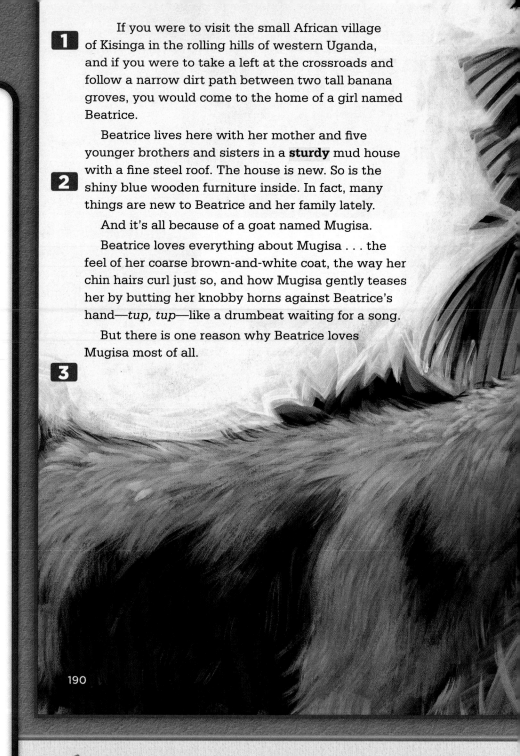

1 If you were to visit the small African village of Kisinga in the rolling hills of western Uganda, and if you were to take a left at the crossroads and follow a narrow dirt path between two tall banana groves, you would come to the home of a girl named Beatrice.

Beatrice lives here with her mother and five younger brothers and sisters in a **sturdy** mud house with a fine steel roof. The house is new. So is the **2** shiny blue wooden furniture inside. In fact, many things are new to Beatrice and her family lately.

And it's all because of a goat named Mugisa.

Beatrice loves everything about Mugisa . . . the feel of her coarse brown-and-white coat, the way her chin hairs curl just so, and how Mugisa gently teases her by butting her knobby horns against Beatrice's hand—*tup, tup*—like a drumbeat waiting for a song.

But there is one reason why Beatrice loves Mugisa most of all.

3

190

Comprehension

Sensory Details

Explain Tell students that **sensory details** describe things that people can taste, touch, smell, see, or hear.

Discuss Look at the sensory details about Mugisa on page 190. Ask: *What does Mugisa's coat look like? How does it feel?* (It is brown and white. It feels coarse.) *How do Mugisa's horns feel?* (They feel knobby.) Point out that these sensory details help the reader understand what Mugisa is like.

Apply Have students look at page 193. Have them identify the sensory details about the area around the schoolhouse. (sight: the long bench; touch: the cool shade under the jackfruit trees) Help them see that these details show how appealing the school is to Beatrice.

191

Develop Comprehension

3 STRATEGY
MAKE INFERENCES AND ANALYZE

Teacher Think Aloud Sometimes the author doesn't tell the reader everything. When this happens, I can use story clues and my own knowledge to figure out the missing information. I can also pay attention to how some events in the story might make other events happen. For example, on page 190 I see that the goat Mugisa is the reason Beatrice's family has a new house with new furniture. I also see that there is one reason why Beatrice loves Mugisa most of all. But the author doesn't tell me why. From my own experience, I know that I like people or animals who make me feel good, so I think that Mugisa must have caused something to happen that makes Beatrice feel good. I will keep reading to find out.

Cross–Curricular Connection

UGANDA

Have students locate Uganda on a map or globe. Tell them it is the country where this story is set. Point out that Uganda is a nation mostly made up of villages just like Beatrice's.

List with students the things they would like to learn about Uganda, such as geography, wildlife, and food. Then divide students into groups to research a topic of their choice. Allow students to present their data to the class.

Develop Comprehension

4 VOCABULARY STRATEGY
WORD PARTS

On page 193, the word *school* is combined with other words. They all belong to the same **word family.** What are those new words? How can you use the meaning of the word parts to figure out the meaning of the whole word? (The two new words are *schoolhouse* and *schoolgirl*. A schoolhouse is a house, or building, where children go to school. A schoolgirl is a girl who goes to school.)

RESEARCH
Why It Matters

Vocabulary
Research indicates that learning word meanings also means learning how words connect together. Categorization activities, semantic mapping, and other procedures that guide students to think about the connections among words stimulate valuable vocabulary learning.

Timothy Shanahan

Log on to
www.macmillanmh.com

192

In the time before Mugisa, Beatrice spent her days helping her mama hoe and plant in the fields, **tend** the chickens, watch the younger children, and grind the cassava flour that they would take to market to sell.

Once in a while, when she was tending baby Paskavia, Beatrice would stop by the **schoolhouse**. Often, the students had carried their long wooden benches outside to work under the cool shade of the jackfruit trees. Then Beatrice would stand quietly off to one side, pretending she was a student, too.

Oh, how she longed to be a schoolgirl! How she **yearned** to sit on one of the benches and figure sums on a small slate chalkboard. How she wished to turn the pages of a worn copybook and study each word over and over until it stuck in her mind like a burr.

"I'll never be able to go to school," she would sigh. "How could I ever save enough money to pay for books or a uniform?"

4

5

193

Develop Comprehension

5 CAUSE AND EFFECT

Why can't Beatrice go to school? Identify the cause and effect in this part of the story. Then fill in the first row of your Cause and Effect Chart. (The cause is that Beatrice doesn't have enough money to buy books or a uniform. The effect is that Beatrice cannot go to school.)

Cause	Effect
Beatrice does not have enough money to buy books or a uniform.	Beatrice cannot go to school.

Comprehension

Cause and Effect

Explain A **cause** is an action that makes something else happen. An **effect** is something that happens because of an earlier action. To find the effect, ask: "What happened?" To find the cause, ask: "Why did it happen?" Look for clue words *because, due to, as a result,* and *cause.*

Discuss Talk about why Beatrice can't go to school. Is it because she doesn't want to? (No.) Is it because her mother won't let her? (No.) Does it cost money? (Yes, she needs to pay for books and a uniform.) Does her family have enough money for these things? (No.) Discuss how this is the cause that makes something else happen.

Apply Have students think about what happens because Beatrice does not have enough money for books or a uniform. (Beatrice can't go to school.) Is this a cause or an effect? Why? (It's an effect. It's something that happened because of an earlier action—the cause.)

Vocabulary

Read the sentence with the word **yearned** in it. What is another word or words that mean nearly the same thing? (really wanted, wished)

Develop Comprehension

6 **MAINTAIN**
MAKE INFERENCES

Does Beatrice think the goat will be a good gift? How do you know? (She doesn't think the goat will be a very good gift. It won't be able to help her with any of her work, such as starting the charcoal fire or washing her clothes in the river. If I were Beatrice, I would want a gift that would be more helpful.)

Vocabulary

Read the sentence with the word **kindhearted**. What two words do you see? What kind of word is kindhearted? (*Kind* and *hearted*. Kindhearted is a compound word.)

One day while Beatrice was busy pulling weeds, Mama came to her with dancing eyes. "Beatrice, some **kindhearted** people from far away have given us a lucky **gift**. We are one of twelve village families to receive a goat."

6 Beatrice was puzzled. A goat? What kind of gift was a goat? It couldn't get up each morning and start their charcoal fire for cooking. It couldn't hike down to the stream each week and scrub their dirty clothes clean. It couldn't keep an eye on Grace, Moses, Harriet, Joash, and Paskavia.

Her long fingers tugged patiently at the weeds. "That's very nice, Mama," she said politely.

Then Mama added, "It will be your job to take care of our goat. If you do, it can bring wonderful things."

Beatrice looked up at her mother. "Will this goat come soon?" she asked. "Because I would like to meet such a goat."

Mama laughed. "Good things take time. First I must plant pastures and build our goat a shed."

Beatrice nodded slowly. Surely Mama knew what she was doing. "I will help you," she declared.

7

194

194

195

Develop Comprehension

7 **GENRE: NARRATIVE NONFICTION**

What facts and information have you learned about the girl named Beatrice? (Beatrice wants to go to school. She lives with her family in a house. She helps her mother by cooking, washing clothes, and looking after her brothers and sisters. She is not happy about her family getting a goat.)

Develop Comprehension

8 **USE ILLUSTRATIONS**

What details does the illustration on pages 196 and 197 give about Beatrice and her family? (It shows a straw hut where they probably live, the kind of clothes they wear, and what the land is like. There are a lot of plants. It looks a little like a jungle.)

196

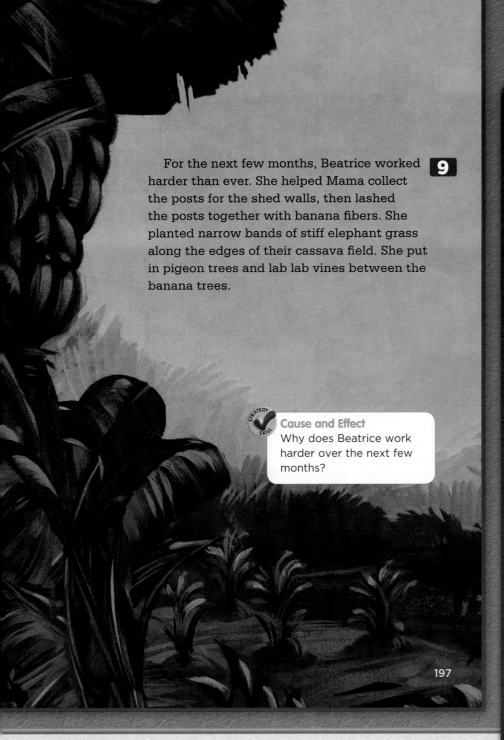

For the next few months, Beatrice worked **9** harder than ever. She helped Mama collect the posts for the shed walls, then lashed the posts together with banana fibers. She planted narrow bands of stiff elephant grass along the edges of their cassava field. She put in pigeon trees and lab lab vines between the banana trees.

Cause and Effect
Why does Beatrice work harder over the next few months?

197

Develop Comprehension

9 CAUSE AND EFFECT

 Why does Beatrice work harder over the next few months? Continue filling in your Cause and Effect Chart. (Cause: Beatrice's family is chosen to receive a goat. Effect: Beatrice works harder than ever to get ready for the goat.)

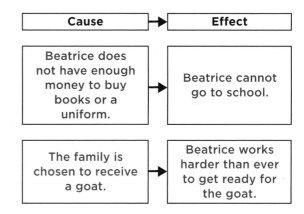

ELL Access for All

STRATEGIES FOR EXTRA SUPPORT

Question 9 CAUSE AND EFFECT
Explain that the expression, "Beatrice worked harder than ever" means that Beatrice worked more than she had worked before. Have students turn to page 194. Ask: *What does Mama say the goat can bring?* (wonderful things) *What does Beatrice say?* (I will help.) *What wonderful things do you think the goat will bring Beatrice and her family?*

Beatrice's Goat **197**

Develop Comprehension

10 **WRITING TRAIT: ADDING DETAILS**

What details does the author use to describe the goat? How do they help the reader understand this part of the selection? (The author says the goat is fat and sleek like a ripe mango. Her belly is round like a ripe mango because she will soon give birth. These details help the reader picture what is happening in the story and what the characters look like.)

10   Finally, one day Beatrice's goat arrived, fat and sleek as a ripe mango. Beatrice stood shyly with her brothers and sisters, then stepped forward and circled the goat once. She knelt close, inspecting its round belly, and ran her hand along its smooth back. "Mama says you are our lucky gift," she whispered. "So that is what I will name you. *Mugisa* ... luck."

    Two weeks later, Mugisa gave birth. It was Beatrice who discovered first one kid and then, to her surprise, another. "Twins!" she exclaimed, stooping down to examine them. "See that, my Mugisa? You have already brought us *two* wonderful things." Beatrice named the first kid *Mulindwa*, which means expected, and the second *Kihembo*, or surprise.

11   Each day Beatrice made sure Mugisa got extra elephant grass and water to help her **produce** lots of milk, even though it meant another long trip down to the stream and back.

    When the kids no longer needed it, Beatrice took her own first taste of Mugisa's milk. "Mmm. Sweet," she said, mixing the rest into her cup of breakfast porridge. Beatrice knew Mugisa's milk would keep them all much healthier.

198

Cultural Perspectives

LIFE IN UGANDA

Remind students that *Beatrice's Goat* tells the true story of Beatrice Biira, a girl from the rural village of Kisinga in Uganda. Explain that the events in the story took place in 1993.

Help students identify details about the geography and culture of Uganda. Then have them compare trees and houses there with ones in your region. Ask students: About 80% of the people in Uganda are farmers in small villages. What details in the story tell about farming and village life? Beatrice did not begin school until she was nine. At what age did you start school? How would you have felt if you were Beatrice before she got Mugisa? How is Beatrice's life with her family similar to and different from yours? What do you think of Beatrice? What message does her story teach? Explain.

199

Develop Comprehension

11 **MAINTAIN**

MAKE INFERENCES

What did Beatrice do each day for Mugisa? What does this tell you about the type of person she is? (Beatrice made sure Mugisa got extra elephant grass and water, even though it meant another long trip to the stream and back. This shows that she is hard-working and caring. She wanted to make sure Mugisa produced a lot of milk for her two kids. This also shows that Beatrice is smart. She is making sure that all the goats are healthy. If they are healthy, they will produce a lot of sweet milk.)

Develop Comprehension

12 MAINTAIN
MAKE INFERENCES

Do you think other people, besides
Bunane, are buying Mugisa's milk from
Beatrice? How do you know? (Day
after day and week after week the
purse was getting fuller. I know that
when a purse gets fuller, more money
is coming in. This means there were
probably a lot of people buying the milk.)

200

Now, each morning after breakfast, Beatrice would head off to the shed to sell whatever milk was left over. "Open for business," she would say, in case anyone was listening.

Often she would spy her friend Bunane coming through the banana groves.

"Good morning, Beatrice, Mugisa, Expected, and Surprise," Bunane would always say. Then he would hand Beatrice a tall pail that she would fill to the top with Mugisa's milk.

When Beatrice finished pouring, Bunane would hand her a shiny coin, and Beatrice would carefully tuck the money into the small woven purse at her side.

Day after day, week after week, Beatrice watched the purse get fuller. Soon there would be enough money for a new shirt for Moses and a warm blanket for the bed she shared with Grace.

 12 **13**

Cause and Effect
How is Mugisa helping Beatrice and her family?

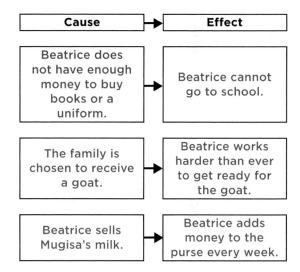

201

Stop here if you wish to read this selection over two days.

Extra Support

Monitor Comprehension

To help students answer question 13, ask: *What does Mugisa give the family every day?* (milk) *What does Beatrice do with the milk?* (She sells it.) *What do people give Beatrice for the milk?* (money) Help students see that Mugisa is helping Beatrice and her family earn money.

If students have difficulty, review the definitions of cause and effect. Review other cause and effect relationships that have been presented earlier in the selection. Have them read the third paragraph on page 198. Ask: *What does Beatrice do for Mugisa?* (She gets her extra elephant grass and water.) *Why does she do this?* (So that Mugisa will produce lots of milk.) *Do Beatrice's actions make something else happen?* (Yes. When she gets extra grass and water, this makes Mugisa produce more milk.) Discuss how one action is a cause and the other is an effect.

Develop Comprehension

13 **CAUSE AND EFFECT**

 How is Mugisa helping Beatrice and her family? Continue filling in your Cause and Effect Chart. (Mugisa produces milk. The family can drink the milk and get healthier. Beatrice also sells the milk and makes money. So the cause is that Beatrice sells Mugisa's milk and the effect is that Beatrice adds money to the purse every week.)

Cause	→	Effect
Beatrice does not have enough money to buy books or a uniform.	→	Beatrice cannot go to school.
The family is chosen to receive a goat.	→	Beatrice works harder than ever to get ready for the goat.
Beatrice sells Mugisa's milk.	→	Beatrice adds money to the purse every week.

 Have students respond to the selection by confirming or revising their predictions and purposes and noting any new questions they have.

 **Quick Check** Can students find cause and effect in the story? If not, see the **Extra Support** on this page.

Develop Comprehension

14 SUMMARIZE

What has happened in the story so far? Think about main events in the story as you summarize. (Beatrice wants to go to school, but she doesn't have enough money. Beatrice's family is going to get a goat. Beatrice does a lot of work to prepare for the goat. The goat, named Mugisa, has twins and produces a lot of milk. Beatrice starts selling Mugisa's milk and making money.)

15 STRATEGY
MAKE INFERENCES AND ANALYZE

Teacher Think Aloud Sometimes an author leaves out details or doesn't tell everything. When this happens, I can look for clues in the story and think about my own experiences to figure out what is missing. This helps me understand the story better. On page 202, Beatrice's mother is frowning and Beatrice acts upset. What is the cause for this? What clues can help you figure it out?

Encourage students to apply the strategy in a Think Aloud.

Student Think Aloud I think that something is wrong, because Mama is counting the money and frowning at the purse and Beatrice's words show she is concerned. People usually frown when something is wrong. Maybe some of the money is missing. I think this is why Mama is frowning. I will keep reading to find out.

14

One day, Beatrice returned from collecting water and noticed Mama frowning and counting the money in her woven purse. Beatrice put down the water can and rushed to her mother's side. "Mama! What is it?" **15** she asked. "What's wrong?"

202

16

203

Develop Comprehension

16 **USE ILLUSTRATIONS**

How does the illustration on pages 202 and 203 help you understand this part of the story? (I can see how carefully Mama is counting the money and how Beatrice's face looks when she sees Mama. I can see that Beatrice has suddenly stopped and dropped the water cans she was carrying. The illustration helps me picture exactly what is happening in the story.)

Develop Comprehension

17 CAUSE AND EFFECT

What happens the next day because Beatrice has saved money from selling Mugisa's milk? Continue filling in your Cause and Effect Chart. (Beatrice saved enough money from selling Mugisa's milk to pay for school. This is the cause. The effect is that she starts school.)

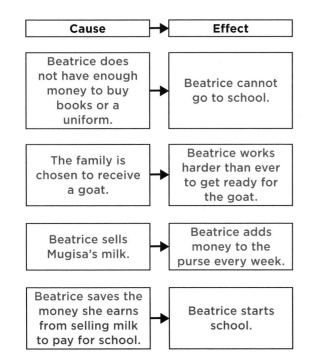

Cause	→	Effect
Beatrice does not have enough money to buy books or a uniform.	→	Beatrice cannot go to school.
The family is chosen to receive a goat.	→	Beatrice works harder than ever to get ready for the goat.
Beatrice sells Mugisa's milk.	→	Beatrice adds money to the purse every week.
Beatrice saves the money she earns from selling milk to pay for school.	→	Beatrice starts school.

204

As she looked up, Mama's frown turned to a small smile. "I think," she said, "you may just have saved enough to pay for school."   **17**

"School?" Beatrice gasped in disbelief. "But what about all the other things we need?"

"First things first," Mama said.

Beatrice threw her arms around her mother's neck. "Oh, Mama, thank you." Then she ran to where her goat stood chewing her cud and hugged her tight. "Oh, Mugisa!" she whispered. "Today *I* am the lucky one. You have given me the gift I wanted most."   **18**

The very next week Beatrice started school. On the first morning that she was to attend, she sat proudly waiting for milk customers in her new yellow blouse and blue jumper, Mugisa by her side.

205

Develop Comprehension

18 DRAW CONCLUSIONS

How does Beatrice feel about going to school? How do you know? (Beatrice is very happy about going to school. When she finds out she can go, she gives her mother a big hug. When I feel happy, I hug people, too. Then Beatrice tells Mugisa she is a lucky girl. The goat has given her the gift she wanted most. Also, the first morning she is going to school, Beatrice sits "proudly." This shows that she is happy, too.)

Fluency

Phrase-Cued Text

Explain   Tell students: Punctuation helps you know when to pause. You pause for a short time after a comma and for a slightly longer time after a period or other end punctuation mark.

Model   Read aloud the passage on **Student Book** page 205, available on **Transparency 22.** Model how to pause after different punctuation marks. Ask: *When did I pause for a short time as I read?* (after a comma) *When did I pause longer to let you know I finished a sentence?* (after a period, question mark, or exclamation point) In this passage, ask students where you should mark the pauses with slashes. Mark the pause after a comma with one slash, and the pause after a period with two slashes.

Apply   Have students reread the passage chorally and then with a partner. Students should take turns reading aloud, focusing on how long they pause after different punctuation marks. Partners can offer corrective feedback.

Develop Comprehension

19 **STRATEGY**
MAKE INFERENCES AND ANALYZE

How can you figure out what caused Beatrice to feel both nervous and excited? Explain your thinking.

Student Think Aloud To answer this question, I will think about everything I know about Beatrice. I will also think about how I would feel if I were Beatrice. I know that Beatrice has wanted to go to school for a long time. Now she is able to. This is probably why she feels excited. When I want something and finally get it, I feel very excited, too. This is also Beatrice's first day at school. I know doing something new causes most people to feel nervous. Beatrice has never been to school so she doesn't know exactly what will happen. This is probably why she is nervous.

20 **STRATEGY**
DICTIONARY

Beatrice's mother says they will "tear down this old house." What does the **homograph** *tear* mean in this sentence? What is another way to say this word? What does it mean? How can you confirm the meaning? (In this sentence the verb *tear* rhymes with bear, and means "to pull apart or destroy." The word *tear*, which rhymes with dear, means "a drop of salty water that comes from your eye when you cry." I can confirm the meaning by looking up the noun *tear* and the verb *tear* in a dictionary.)

206

206

Beatrice felt nervous and excited at the same time. Mugisa pressed close, letting her coarse coat brush softly against Beatrice's cheek. "Oh, Mugisa," Beatrice cried. "I'll miss you today!"

19

Then she thought again about all the good things Mugisa was bringing. Mama said that soon Surprise would be sold for a lot of money. "It will be enough to tear down this old house," she had explained. "We will be able to put up a new one with a steel roof that won't leak during the rains."

20

21

Beatrice heard a rustle and noticed Bunane heading toward her with his empty milk pail. He eyed her new uniform and sighed. "You're so lucky. I wish *I* could go to school."

Beatrice reached out and touched Bunane's arm. "I've heard that your family is next in line to receive a goat."

A smile crossed Bunane's face. "Really?"

"Really."

207

Develop Comprehension

21 CAUSE AND EFFECT

What is another good thing that will happen for Beatrice and her family because of Mugisa? Continue filling in your Cause and Effect Chart. (The family will sell Mugisa's kid, Surprise, for a lot of money. The effect is that Beatrice's family will have enough money to build a new house.)

Cause	→	Effect
Beatrice does not have enough money to buy books or a uniform.	→	Beatrice cannot go to school.
The family is chosen to receive a goat.	→	Beatrice works harder than ever to get ready for the goat.
Beatrice sells Mugisa's milk.	→	Beatrice adds money to the purse every week.
Beatrice saves the money she earns from selling milk.	→	Beatrice can go to school.
The family will sell Surprise to get money.	→	The family will use the money to build a new house.

Develop Comprehension

22 DRAW CONCLUSIONS

At the beginning of the story, the narrator says that "there is one reason why Beatrice loves Mugisa most of all." What do you think the reason is? (Mugisa made it possible for Beatrice to go to school. This is something she had really wanted to do for a long time, so that is probably why she loves Mugisa most of all.)

23 AUTHOR'S PURPOSE

Why do you think the author wrote this selection? (Answers may vary. Some students may think the author wrote this story to entertain the reader and to tell a good story. Others may say the purpose was to inform because the selection presents information about Beatrice and how the goat Mugisa helped her to go to school.)

Then Beatrice kissed Mugisa on the soft part of her nose, close to where her chin hairs curled just **22** so, and started off to school.

23

208

Research and Inquiry

Nonprofit Organizations

Tell students there are many nonprofit organizations throughout the world. Have them brainstorm some they may already know about, for example, the Red Cross and Goodwill.

Divide students into groups and assign each a problem, such as education or health. Have groups find information about a nonprofit that helps their cause, using the Internet or library resources.

When their research is complete, have each group create and share a presentation about the nonprofit organization. They should tell what the problem is and what the nonprofit provides. Then have students discuss any current events or news reports about nonprofits' efforts at home or in other countries.

Beatrice felt nervous and excited at the same time. Mugisa pressed close, letting her coarse coat brush softly against Beatrice's cheek. "Oh, Mugisa," Beatrice cried. "I'll miss you today!"

19

Then she thought again about all the good things Mugisa was bringing. Mama said that soon Surprise would be sold for a lot of money. "It will be enough to tear down this old house," she had explained. "We will be able to put up a new one with a steel roof that won't leak during the rains."

20

Beatrice heard a rustle and noticed Bunane heading toward her with his empty milk pail. He eyed her new uniform and sighed. "You're so lucky. I wish *I* could go to school."

21

Beatrice reached out and touched Bunane's arm. "I've heard that your family is next in line to receive a goat."

A smile crossed Bunane's face. "Really?"

"Really."

207

Develop Comprehension

21 **CAUSE AND EFFECT**

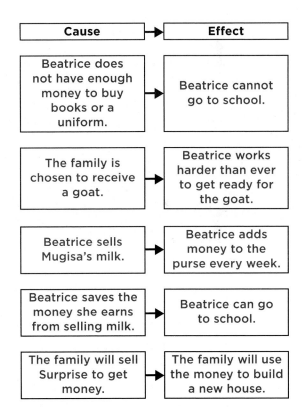

What is another good thing that will happen for Beatrice and her family because of Mugisa? Continue filling in your Cause and Effect Chart. (The family will sell Mugisa's kid, Surprise, for a lot of money. The effect is that Beatrice's family will have enough money to build a new house.)

Cause →	Effect
Beatrice does not have enough money to buy books or a uniform.	Beatrice cannot go to school.
The family is chosen to receive a goat.	Beatrice works harder than ever to get ready for the goat.
Beatrice sells Mugisa's milk.	Beatrice adds money to the purse every week.
Beatrice saves the money she earns from selling milk.	Beatrice can go to school.
The family will sell Surprise to get money.	The family will use the money to build a new house.

Develop Comprehension

22 DRAW CONCLUSIONS

At the beginning of the story, the narrator says that "there is one reason why Beatrice loves Mugisa most of all." What do you think the reason is? (Mugisa made it possible for Beatrice to go to school. This is something she had really wanted to do for a long time, so that is probably why she loves Mugisa most of all.)

23 AUTHOR'S PURPOSE

Why do you think the author wrote this selection? (Answers may vary. Some students may think the author wrote this story to entertain the reader and to tell a good story. Others may say the purpose was to inform because the selection presents information about Beatrice and how the goat Mugisa helped her to go to school.)

22 Then Beatrice kissed Mugisa on the soft part of her nose, close to where her chin hairs curled just so, and started off to school.

23

208

Research and Inquiry

Nonprofit Organizations

Tell students there are many nonprofit organizations throughout the world. Have them brainstorm some they may already know about, for example, the Red Cross and Goodwill.

Divide students into groups and assign each a problem, such as education or health. Have groups find information about a nonprofit that helps their cause, using the Internet or library resources.

When their research is complete, have each group create and share a presentation about the nonprofit organization. They should tell what the problem is and what the nonprofit provides. Then have students discuss any current events or news reports about nonprofits' efforts at home or in other countries.

Comprehension Check

Summarize

 Use the Cause and Effect Chart to help you summarize *Beatrice's Goat*. Tell how and why Beatrice was finally able to go to school.

Cause	→	Effect
	→	
	→	
	→	

Think and Compare

1. The **gift** of the goat caused many changes. Use your Cause and Effect Chart to show the effects of this gift on Beatrice and her family. **Make Inferences and Analyze: Cause and Effect**

2. Reread the first paragraph on page 194. Why do you think people from far away gave goats to families in Beatrice's village? **Analyze**

3. Before you read the story, what would you have thought about receiving a goat as a gift? Did your opinion change after reading the story? Explain your answer. **Evaluate**

4. What would have happened if the villagers had never been given goats? Explain. **Synthesize**

5. Read "Helping People Help Themselves" on pages 186–187. How is this selection like *Beatrice's Goat*? How are the two selections different? Use details from both selections in your answer. **Reading/Writing Across Texts**

211

Strategies for Answering Questions

On My Own

Model the On My Own strategy with question 3. Students will not find the answers to On My Own questions in the selection. Sometimes they will have to form an opinion. Other times they will use information they already know.

Think Aloud Question 3: I can't find the answer in the story because it's asking for my opinion. I will think about my own experiences. Before I read the story, I would have been confused about a family getting a goat as a gift. I probably would have thought they were getting it as a pet. I'll think about what happened in the story. This story changed my opinion because I see how the goat was more than a pet. Because of Mugisa, Beatrice's family was able to make money, get things they needed, fix their house, and send Beatrice to school. Now I see how a goat can be an important gift.

Comprehension Check

 SUMMARIZE Have students write a summary of *Beatrice's Goat* by paraphrasing the main events. Remind students that their Cause and Effect Charts can help them organize their ideas.

THINK AND COMPARE

Sample answers are given.

1. **Cause and Effect:** Getting Mugisa was a cause, and the effects were that Beatrice's family had milk to sell and they were able to make money. Another effect is that they were able to send Beatrice to school. Also, selling one of Mugisa's kids gave the family money to build a new house.

2. **Analyze:** Beatrice's family was very poor. People from far away donated the goats to try and help.

3. **Text-to-Self:** Students may say that they thought a goat might make a nice pet for Beatrice, but they didn't know how it would help her. After reading the story, students should see how the goat helped the family in many ways. For example, they were able to fix their house and send Beatrice to school. USE ON MY OWN

4. **Text-to-World:** Without the goats' milk, the villagers would not have gotten healthier and would not have been able to pay for what they need.

 FOCUS QUESTION

5. **Text-to-Text:** Both stories are about helping people. "Helping People Help Themselves" is about a group that gives animals to families. *Beatrice's Goat* is about what happens to one family when they receive a goat as a gift.

Objective

- Read fluently with echo-reading
- 97–117 WCPM

Materials

- Fluency Transparency 22
- Fluency Solutions Audio CD
- Leveled Practice Books, p. 159

ELL   **Access for All**

Track Print Review the meaning of the passage. Discuss the characters' feelings. Remind students that quotation marks mean someone is speaking. Have students give you examples of sentences that use quotation marks. Write them on the board.

On Level Practice Book O, page 159

As I read, I will pay attention to the genre of the passage.

	One man who came to the United States as a boy helped
12	to save Yosemite's natural wonders for you to enjoy. His
22	name was John Muir.
26	John Muir was born in a small town in Scotland in
37	1838. His family moved to the United States when he was
47	eleven. They moved to what is now Wisconsin and set up a
59	farm there. They were pioneers.
64	Muir went to school in a small schoolhouse. He liked
74	being a schoolboy. The rest of the time he worked on the
86	farm. He was busy from sunup until sundown. But Muir
96	yearned for more. He knew he didn't want to tend the farm
108	all his life. Muir liked to read and he read often. He also
121	liked to invent things. He made a special thermometer.
130	And he made something he called his "early-rising
138	machine." 139

Comprehension Check

1. What interests did John Muir have? **Main Idea and Details**
   John enjoyed school, reading, and inventing things.
2. What does the word pioneer mean? **Context Clues**
   A pioneer is someone who settles in land that is
   unknown or that has not been claimed.

	Words Read	–	Number of Errors	=	Words Correct Score
First Read		–		=	
Second Read		–		=	

★ **Approaching Practice Book A,** page 159

◆ **Beyond Practice Book B,** page 159

Fluency

Repeated Reading: Pauses and Intonation

EXPLAIN/MODEL Model the text on **Transparency 22.** Emphasize stopping at periods, pausing at commas, and raising your pitch at question marks. Show students the difference in your intonation when you read the text in quotes and the text without quotes. Model the passage again, one sentence at a time, while students echo-read.

Teacher Think Aloud I want my reading of Mama's words to be different from what Beatrice says. Maybe if I make Mama's voice a little lower sounding and Beatrice's voice higher in pitch, that might work.

 Transparency 22

> As she looked up, Mama's frown turned to a small smile. "I think," she said, "you may just have saved enough to pay for school."
>
> "School?" Beatrice gasped in disbelief. "But what about all the other things we need?"
>
> "First things first," Mama said.
>
> Beatrice threw her arms around her mother's neck. "Oh, Mama, thank you." Then she ran to where her goat stood chewing her cud and hugged her tight. "Oh, Mugisa!" she whispered. "Today I am the lucky one. You have given me the gift I wanted most."

Fluency Transparency 22
from *Beatrice's Goat,* page 205

 PRACTICE Divide the class into two groups. Have one group read a sentence at a time. Have the other echo-read. Then they switch roles. For additional practice, have students use **Leveled Practice Book** page 159 or Fluency Solutions.

Quick Check   **Can students read fluently with echo-reading?**

During **Small Group Instruction**

If No →   Approaching Level   Fluency, pp. 217M–217N

If Yes →   On Level   Options, pp. 217Q–217R

        Beyond Level   Options, pp. 217S–217T

Comprehension

MAINTAIN SKILL
MAKE INFERENCES

EXPLAIN/MODEL

- An author does not always tell readers everything that takes place in a story. Readers must **make inferences** to help them understand the information that the writer has left out.

- Inferences are good guesses readers make by using clues from the selection and their own experiences.

- Making inferences helps readers understand events and characters' actions that are not stated directly.

Model how to make inferences about what kind of person nine-year-old Julie is on page 187 of "Helping People Help Themselves."

PRACTICE

Ask students these questions about *Beatrice's Goat*.

- How can you tell that Beatrice is patient and hard-working? (Even though Beatrice isn't sure a goat will be a helpful gift, she still works hard to get ready for it. For example, she helps her mother collect and lash together posts for the shed walls, and she plants elephant grass.)

- At the end of the story, why does Bunane smile when he thinks about getting a goat? (He has seen how Mugisa helped Beatrice and her family. He probably knows that a goat will make his life better, too.)

- What kind of person is Beatrice's mother? How do you know? (She is very busy because she has six children. She is also caring. She knows that Beatrice wants to go to school, so once they have enough money saved she decides to spend it on a uniform and books for Beatrice.)

Have partners take turns reading the story aloud.

Objectives

- Make inferences about a story
- Use academic language: *make inferences*

Skills Trace

Make Inferences	
Introduce	U3: 285A–B
Practice / Apply	U3: 286–307, Leveled Practice, 76–77
Reteach / Review	U3: 313M–T, 355A–B, 356–379, Leveled Practice, 171–172
Assess	Weekly Tests; Unit 3 Test; Benchmark Tests A, B
Maintain	U3: 411B; U5: 211B

Informational Text: Social Studies

GENRE: NEWSPAPER ARTICLE

Have students read the bookmark on **Student Book** page 212. Explain that newspaper articles

- are printed daily or weekly in a newspaper;

- usually contain facts about an event or a person in the news;

- often have photographs and captions;

- have headlines that tell the topic of the news story.

Text Feature: Editorial

EXPLAIN Point out the editorial on page 214. Explain that this editorial is about Beatrice Biira.

- An **editorial** is a newspaper article that gives the editor's or publisher's opinion about something.

- The purpose of an editorial is to persuade readers to think or believe a certain way.

APPLY Have students identify the headline of the editorial on page 214, the date it was written, and the person who wrote it. (Headline: "How Important Is Education? Ask Beatrice!" Date: April 17, 2007. Writer: Earl Clements, Jr.) Ask: Is the first sentence a fact or an opinion? How do you know? (It is an opinion, because it tells the way the author feels about getting an education.)

Social Studies

Genre
Newspaper Articles tell about important people and events and are part of daily or weekly newspapers.

 Text Feature
Editorials are newspaper articles that present the opinions of the publisher or editors. They try to persuade the reader to do or believe something.

Content Vocabulary
achieve

determined

encourages

Ugandan Girl Reaches Goal

by Ann Frost

To Beatrice Biira, getting an education is the most important goal a person can have. Even when she was a little girl growing up in Uganda, she saw how important it is to get a good education. A goat named Mugisa helped her **achieve**, or reach, that goal.

Content Vocabulary

Review the spelling and meaning of each content vocabulary word for "Ugandan Girl Reaches Goal" on Student Book page 212: *achieve, determined,* and *encourages.*

- To **achieve** means to successfully complete something by working hard. What would you most like to achieve as a third grader?

- Being **determined** means wanting to do something very much. Have you ever been determined to learn something? What was it? What made you so determined?

- A person who **encourages** you to do something, gives you courage or confidence to do it. Who encourages you to do well in school?

After receiving Mugisa from the charity group Heifer International, Beatrice's family took care of the goat and the goat's young, which are called kids. With the money they made from selling milk and one of the kids, the Biiras were able to buy things they needed. Many people would have been satisfied with that, but Beatrice wanted more. She wanted to go to school.

Ten-year-old Beatrice had to start first grade with much younger students. This just made her more **determined** to work harder. Soon she caught up with her friends. Beatrice's good grades made it possible for her to go to school in the United States.

Even though it was hard for Beatrice to live so far away from her family, it has been worth it to her to get a good education.

Beatrice feeds Mugisa.

213

Informational Text

Read "Ugandan Girl Reaches Goal"

Access for All As students read, remind them to apply what they have learned about editorials. Also have them identify clues to the meanings of highlighted words.

1 STRATEGY

MONITOR AND CLARIFY: SEEK HELP

If you don't know what a charity group is, how can you figure it out? (If I can't figure something out by rereading or reading ahead, I can ask for help from my teacher or librarian. A charity group gives different things, such as food and clothing, to people in need. Heifer International gives farm animals.)

2 DRAW CONCLUSIONS

Beatrice was very determined to do well in school. How did this determination change her life? (She was able to go to school in the United States because her grades were very good.)

3 SUMMARIZE

What helped Beatrice Biira achieve her goals when she was growing up in Uganda? (Hard work, smart choices, and a goat named Mugisa helped her.)

ENGLISH LANGUAGE LEARNERS

Access for All

Beginning Point and Say Establish that the article is about Beatrice and remind students of the story, *Beatrice's Goat*. Ask: *What did Beatrice want to do? Who helped Beatrice go to school?* Help students answer. When you introduce the editorial on page 214, point out each part and have students point and repeat.

Intermediate Explain and Discuss Complete the Beginning task. As you read the article, encourage students to explain their thinking as you discuss and evaluate facts and opinions.

Advanced Share Opinions Complete the Intermediate task. Pause as you read and ask students to share their opinions about what they have read. What do they think of Mugisa?

Informational Text

4 **TEXT FEATURE: EDITORIAL**

What is the topic of this editorial? Why did the author write it? (This editorial is about Beatrice Biira's life and how hard she had to work to get an education. The author wrote it to persuade the reader that getting an education is an important goal for everyone.)

5 **TEXT FEATURE: EDITORIAL**

Which sentences give facts? How do you know they are facts? (The writer shares many facts. For example, he wrote that Heifer International gave Beatrice's family a goat and that Beatrice earned enough money to buy books and a uniform. These are facts because they tell about events that really happened and can be proved true.)

6 **AUTHOR'S PURPOSE**

Identify persuasive vocabulary used in the editorial to influence the reader. (Words and phrases such as *most important* and *a better life* are used to persuade the reader.)

About Beatrice

Reading an Editorial

Editorials contain facts, as well as the opinions of the publisher or editor.

4 **5**

6

The News

Vol. 3   **LATE CITY EDITION**   **April 17, 2007**

> The title of a newspaper article or editorial is called the headline.

How Important Is Education? Ask Beatrice!

by Earl Clements, Jr.

> This expresses an opinion.

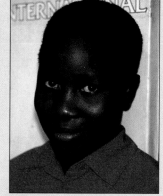

Getting an education should be one of the most important goals a person has. Beatrice Biira knew this when she was a little girl growing up in Uganda. Beatrice's family could not afford to buy the uniform and books she needed for school. When Heifer International gave her family a goat, Beatrice worked hard to take care of it and sell its milk. She earned enough money to buy books and a uniform. She worked hard at school and eventually went to college in the United States. Beatrice plans to help others reach their goals of getting an education and a better life.

214

On Level Practice Book O, page 160

Newspapers include factual articles, columns, and **editorials.** Persuasive editorials are articles that give opinions of the publisher or editor of the paper. Editorials use words such as *should, must, need,* and *ought* to persuade the reader to do or believe something.

A. Read the article below. Then underline the words or phrases that are meant to persuade you.

Vegetables to Help the Community

There are people from our community that are in need. We <u>should</u> not think only about ourselves, but about each member of our community. Planting a school vegetable garden is one way to help the people in need from our community. Together, we <u>should</u> plant a large garden in the empty lot near the elementary school. Everyone <u>ought</u> to help to take care of it. That way the community is working together to help others. When we give the ripe vegetables to the food bank in town, we will be making a difference in the life of a hungry person.

B. Use the article to answer the following questions.
Possible responses provided.
1. Why is the author of the article trying to persuade people to plant vegetables? to help the people in the community who don't have enough to eat

2. Why is working together a good way to help? that way everyone feels like he or she helped someone in the community

---

 Approaching Practice Book A, page 160

Beyond Practice Book B, page 160

Education has changed Beatrice Biira's life. She has appeared on television to tell her story and has visited schools to talk about how Mugisa the goat changed her life.

Beatrice worked hard. She didn't give up. Today, she **encourages**, or urges, students to read and help make the world a better place.

Beatrice visits classrooms to talk about her experiences.

Connect and Compare

1. Which sentences in the editorial express opinions? **Reading an Editorial**

2. Do you agree with the opinion in the editorial about the importance of education? Explain. **Evaluate**

3. Think about *Beatrice's Goat* and this article. Which parts let you know how Beatrice feels about getting an education? **Reading/Writing Across Texts**

Social Studies Activity

Find out about an organization, like Heifer International, that helps people. Write an editorial that tries to convince people to donate money or time to that organization.

LOG ON Find out more about charitable organizations at **www.macmillanmh.com**

215

LOG ON Technology

Internet Research and Inquiry Activity Students can find more facts at www.macmillanmh.com

Informational Text

Connect and Compare

SUGGESTED ANSWERS

1. The first sentence expresses an opinion. It tells how the author feels about getting an education. READING AN EDITORIAL

2. Answers will vary. Sample: I agree with the author's opinion because it is hard to get a good job without an education. EVALUATE

FOCUS QUESTION

3. The beginning of *Beatrice's Goat* shows how much Beatrice wanted to go to school. Later in the story, she is excited and thankful that she can go to school. The first sentence of "Ugandan Girl Reaches Goal" tells that Beatrice believes getting an education is the most important goal a person can have. The last sentence explains that Beatrice encourages other students to read. READING/WRITING ACROSS TEXTS

Social Studies Activity

Have students design newspaper pages for their editorials. Remind them to use a headline and date, along with the name of the newspaper.

Writing

Descriptive Writing

OPTIONS FOR STUDENT WRITING

- Use these two pages for a short writing lesson focused on the features of descriptive writing and on the writing trait from **Student Book** pages 216–217.

- For a more detailed five-step writing process lesson, use the **Writing Workshop** on pages 217A–217B.

- Use the Daily Writing Prompts in the Weekly Planner for brief writing assignments.

FEATURES

Present and discuss these features of descriptive writing with students.

- It paints a clear picture with words.

- It includes vivid details that support the main ideas.

- Colorful words and phrases help a reader see, feel, taste, touch, and smell what the writer is describing.

Have students read "How Bert Changed My Life" on Student Book page 216. Ask volunteers to point out examples of the features of descriptive writing in Danielle L.'s paragraph.

Writing

Ideas and Content
Good writing includes vivid details to support the main ideas. Good writers elaborate by adding interesting or unusual examples and descriptions.

Write About Someone or Something That Changed Your Life

How Bert Changed My Life

by Danielle L.

I wanted to describe how Bert changed my life. Here is what I wrote.

I added vivid details so the reader can picture what happened.

Bert, my new baby brother, changed my life. I used to have my own room. Now Bert sleeps in my room in his crib. He likes to throw his stuffed animals on the floor. If I don't give them back to him, he cries. Now Bert can crawl. He knocks down my block castles and chews on my books! I know he is just a baby, so I put my books on shelves and build new castles. Things change when you are a big sister!

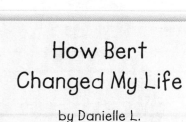

216

Your Turn

Write a paragraph about someone or something that has changed your life. You can write about something you did. You can also tell about a person you know or have read about. Be sure to include vivid details that tell about your topic. Use the Writer's Checklist to check your writing.

Writer's Checklist

☑ **Ideas and Content:** Did I include vivid details that tell about the topic?

 Organization: Did I write a good topic sentence?

 Voice: Did I show how I feel about the topic?

 Word Choice: Did I use colorful words and phrases that the reader will remember?

 Sentence Fluency: Did I vary the kinds of sentences I used?

 Conventions: Did I use subject and object pronouns correctly? Did I check my spelling?

217

WRITING TRAIT: IDEAS AND CONTENT

Have a student read the bookmark on **Student Book** page 216. Discuss the Ideas and Content trait.

■ Good descriptive writing includes vivid details that support the main ideas.

■ Writers elaborate by adding lively and colorful examples and descriptions.

■ Ideas and details together create a clear picture for the reader.

Have students reread "How Bert Changed My Life" on Student Book page 216. Discuss the callouts on the left. Is the main idea of Danielle L.'s paragraph supported by vivid details? Do the details help create a clear picture for the reader?

Display **Transparency 85.** Have students elaborate on the sentences by adding vivid details that make the writing livelier and more colorful.

YOUR TURN

Read the "Your Turn" prompt on Student Book page 217 with students. Talk about people or events that changed their lives. Encourage students to be sure to elaborate and add vivid details when they write their descriptive paragraph. Remind students to use classroom resources to check spelling and help with word choice.

WRITER'S CHECKLIST

Review the six Good Writing Traits on the Writer's Checklist. Have students give an example of Organization or Ideas and Content in Danielle L.'s paragraph. Then discuss how students can apply the traits to help them draft, revise, and proofread their descriptive paragraph.

Transparency 85

Ideas and Content

1. My neighbor is nice.

2. My baby brother cries at night.

3. The flowers are pretty.

4. My dog is loving.

Sample Answers: 1: She always smiles and says hello.; 2: He wakes up and screams really loudly when he's hungry.; 3: The yellow and red roses look like a summer sunset.; 4: He always jumps in my lap and licks me in the face.

Writing Transparency 85

Writing Workshop

WRITING WORKSHOP
- Descriptive Writing

WORD STUDY
- Words in Context
- **Word Parts:** Word Families
- **Phonics:** Inflected Endings
- Vocabulary Building

SPELLING
- Inflected Endings

GRAMMAR
- Subject and Object Pronouns

SMALL GROUP OPTIONS
- Differentiated Instruction, pp. 217M–217V

Speaking and Listening

Have students read their descriptive paragraphs aloud. Share these strategies.

SPEAKING STRATEGIES

- Speak clearly and at a smooth pace to convey details.
- Speak naturally, as though you were talking to a friend.
- Look often at your audience.

LISTENING STRATEGIES

- Prepare to listen without interruption.
- Listen for and picture descriptive words and details.
- Set a purpose for listening.

Descriptive Writing: Paragraph

Day 1 Prewrite

PURPOSE AND AUDIENCE

- Explain that the purpose of a descriptive paragraph is to create a vivid picture in readers' minds.

- The audience will be classmates or the teacher.

Display **Transparency 86** to show how Danielle L. used a Main Idea and Details Chart. Tell students that they will create a chart to plan their paragraphs.

Prompt *Write a descriptive paragraph about someone or something that changed your life.*

CHOOSE A TOPIC

Students can write about someone they admire or self-select a topic.

Day 2 Draft

DRAFTING CHECKLIST

Display **Transparency 87.** Review Danielle L.'s draft of "How Bert Changed My Life." Discuss how the Main Idea and Details Chart helped her organize her writing. As students begin to draft:

- Encourage them to write a topic sentence with a clear main idea that captures the reader's interest.

- Review the features of descriptive paragraphs.

- Emphasize the importance of vivid, colorful details.

- Remind students to refer to their Main Idea and Details Chart and the Good Writing Traits on the Writer's Checklist.

 Transparency 86

Main Idea and Details Chart

Main Idea	Details
My baby brother changed my life.	He sleeps in my room.
	He throws things on the floor.
	He knocks down my blocks. He eats my books.
	He is just a baby!

Transparency 87

How Bert Changed My Life

Bert is my new baby brother. He changed my life. I used to have my own room. Now Bert sleeps in my room in his crib. He likes to throw things on the floor. If I don't give them back to him, he cries. Now Bert can crawl. He knocks down my block castles! I know he is just a baby, so I build new castles. Things change when you are a big sister.

Writing Transparency 86   Writing Transparency 87

Day 3 Revise

REVISING CHECKLIST

Display **Transparency 87.** Have students use what they have learned to discuss how they can revise Danielle L's draft.

Display **Transparency 88** and discuss Danielle L.'s changes:

- She combined two short sentences.

- She added colorful, vivid details to make **Ideas and Content** stronger.

- She changed a statement to an exclamatory sentence to emphasize her feelings.

Have students revise their descriptive paragraphs, using a dictionary, thesaurus, or computer to select precise words.

Transparency 88

How Bert Changed My Life

Bert is my new baby brother. He changed my life. I used to have my own room. Now Bert sleeps in my room in his crib. He likes to throw things on the floor. If I don't give them back to him, he cries. Now Bert can crawl. He knocks down my block castles! I know he is just a baby, so I build new castles. Things change when you are a big sister.

Writing Transparency 88

Writing Transparency 88

Day 4 Proofread

REVIEW AND PROOFREAD

As students proofread their revisions, remind them to:

- Use classroom resources to check for correct spelling and end punctuation and use commas correctly.

- Use subject and object pronouns correctly to agree with the nouns they replace.

LOG ON   **Technology**

Students can try using a different color to make proofreading corrections. Have them select FONT and then COLOR from the FORMAT menu.

Day 5 Publish

PUBLISH AND PRESENT

To publish, students should make a neat, final copy.

Students can read their paragraphs aloud to a classmate and ask whether their partner can picture the details.

Review Speaking and Listening strategies with students.

EVALUATE

To evaluate student writing, use the 4-point Scoring Rubric. Since students learned about **Ideas and Content** this week, check carefully for that trait.

SCORING RUBRIC			
4 Excellent	**3** Good	**2** Fair	**1** Unsatisfactory
Ideas and Content Main idea is interesting and clear; supported by colorful and vivid examples	**Ideas and Content** Main idea is clear; supported by relevant descriptive details	**Ideas and Content** Main idea is clear, but includes few descriptive details	**Ideas and Content** Main idea is confusing; details seem irrelevant to topic
Organization Strong topic sentence; details in logical order	**Organization** Includes a topic sentence; details in logical order	**Organization** Weak topic sentence; details not entirely in logical order	**Organization** No topic sentence; details not in logical order
Voice Engaging and original; uses first person; expresses writer's personality and feelings	**Voice** First person; expresses writer's personality and feelings	**Voice** Does not clearly express writer's personality but includes feelings	**Voice** Flat; does not express writer's personality or feelings
Word Choice Excellent use of adjectives and descriptive words	**Word Choice** Uses accurate descriptive words	**Word Choice** Words vague or general; few precise descriptive words	**Word Choice** Uses words imprecisely or inaccurately
Sentence Fluency Good variety of sentence lengths and types	**Sentence Fluency** Uses long and short sentences	**Sentence Fluency** Sentences are short and fragmented	**Sentence Fluency** Incomplete or confusing sentences
Conventions Mostly free of errors in spelling, mechanics, and usage	**Conventions** Few errors in spelling, mechanics, and usage	**Conventions** Many errors in spelling, mechanics, and usage	**Conventions** Repeated errors in spelling, mechanics, and usage

Objectives

- Apply knowledge of word meanings and context clues
- Apply knowledge of word families

Materials

- Vocabulary Transparency 43
- Vocabulary Strategy Transparency 44
- Leveled Practice Books, p. 161

Vocabulary

gift (p. 194) something that is given to someone, such as a present

yearned (p. 193) wanted very much to have or do

tend (p. 193) to look after or take care of

produce (p. 198) to make or create

sturdy (p. 190) strong or solid

schoolhouse (p. 193) a building used as a school

kindhearted (p. 194) having a caring nature; helpful

ELL
Access for All

Draw Pictures/Write Sentences Have students choose two words, make a sentence for each one, and illustrate it. Then have students share their sentences in groups.

Review
Vocabulary

Words in Context

EXPLAIN/MODEL

Review the meanings of the vocabulary words. Display **Transparency 43.** Model how to use word meanings and context clues to fill in the first missing word.

> **Transparency 43**
>
> | gift | yearned | tend | produce |
> | sturdy | schoolhouse | kindhearted | |
>
> A (1) <u>kindhearted</u> person can find many ways to help people in need. For example, volunteers can help build a (2) <u>schoolhouse</u> in a community that does not have money for schools. They also can help families earn a living by giving them farm animals.
>
> Chickens can be a useful (3) <u>gift</u> for a family in need. The chickens (4) <u>produce</u> eggs, which the family can eat. The eggs can be sold, too.
>
> A family has to (5) <u>tend</u> to the chickens every day. Chickens need food and water. A (6) <u>sturdy</u> shelter can keep them safe.
>
> With the money they earn, families can buy food, medicine, clothing, and other things. They can get what they have always (7) <u>yearned</u> for.

Vocabulary Transparency 43

Think Aloud From the other words in the sentence I can tell that the missing word describes a person who helps people. A caring or kindhearted person would help others. The missing word is *kindhearted.*

PRACTICE

Help students complete item 2. Then have students use context clues to write missing words for items 3–7 on a separate piece of paper. Students can exchange papers, check answers, and explain context clues they used to figure out the missing words.

Remind students that they can use the Glossary to confirm word meanings.

STRATEGY
WORD PARTS: WORD FAMILIES

EXPLAIN/MODEL

- A word family is a group of related words that all contain the same base word, such as *school* in *schoolhouse* and *schooling*.

- Students can often use the meaning of the word and other word parts to figure out the meaning of an entire word.

Display **Transparency 44** and read the example sentence. Model using the word *kind* to help find the meaning of *kindhearted*. Point out that the words *kindly, unkind,* and *kindness* are related to *kindhearted* because they all have *kind* in them.

 Transparency 44

Word Parts: Word Families

Beatrice, some kindhearted people from far away have given us a lucky gift.

kindhearted	kindly	unkind	kindness

1. Anna was happy to eat <u>homemade</u> bread. (made by hand at home)

2. Jason did his <u>homework</u> after dinner. (school work that is done at home)

3. I felt <u>homesick</u> while I was on vacation. (sad because of being away from home)

4. Ted lives in Uganda, but his <u>homeland</u> is the United States. (country where someone was born)

Vocabulary Strategy Transparency 44

PRACTICE

 Have students read items 1–4 and identify the common word that appears in the underlined words. (home) Then have them write the meaning of the underlined words, using their knowledge of *home*.

Quick Check Can students choose the correct vocabulary word and apply knowledge of word families?

During **Small Group Instruction**

If No → **Approaching Level** Vocabulary, p. 217O

If Yes → **On Level** Options, pp. 217Q–217R

Beyond Level Options, pp. 217S–217T

Make an Analogy and Draw Relate word families to a real family. Draw a "family tree" with the words and say: *Water is the parent. The children are watering, waterfall, and waterway.* Use each "family member" in a sentence to help explain its meaning.

Vocabulary

Review last week's vocabulary words. Ask students to find two words in the compound word *sidewalks*. They can use each word to form the "trunk" of a "word tree." Have students then form the "branches" by naming words such as *sidelines* or *walkway* that are part of each word family.

On Level Practice Book O, page 161

Word families are groups of words that have the same main word part, or base word. Different parts, such as prefixes, suffixes, or another base word, may be added. For example, the base word *connect* becomes *connecting* when the suffix –*ing* is added. It becomes *disconnect* when the prefix *dis-* is added. When two base words are joined they form a compound word, like *sidewalk*.

A. For each word below, underline the base word. Sometimes this word part is the entire word. Then write another word in the same word family on the line. Possible responses provided.

1. dis<u>cover</u>ed   uncovered, recovered, recovery
2. dis<u>belief</u>   unbelief, believer, believable
3. <u>arrange</u>   rearrange, arrangement
4. <u>bookcase</u>   cookbook, bookkeeper
5. <u>carefree</u>   careless, careful
6. <u>handful</u>   handy, handed, handcraft

B. Look at the group of words and decide what the base word is. Underline the base word. Then come up with another word that contains the base word.

7. dog<u>house</u>, bird<u>house</u>, town<u>house</u>, <u>house</u>plant
   housework, housefly, household

8. <u>side</u>line, outside, <u>side</u>track, <u>side</u>burns
   sideways, sidewalk, inside

★ **Approaching Practice Book A,** page 161

◆ **Beyond Practice Book B,** page 161

Word Study

Objectives

- Segment and blend words with inflected endings
- Decode words with inflected endings

Materials

- Leveled Practice Books, p. 162

ELL

Provide Examples Write: *walks, walked, walking.* Write a sentence for each tense, but leave a line where the verb should go. Have students decide which verb form belongs in each sentence. Repeat the activity with other verbs. Be aware that inflected endings may be difficult for some students to hear and pronounce. Provide additional practice.

On Level Practice Book O, page 162

The **inflected endings** -s, -es, -ed, or -ing added to the end of a verb shows when action happens, as in: *He calls to his sister; He called his sister yesterday; He is calling his sister right now.* Some words drop the final e before adding -ed or -ing, as in *decided, deciding.* Words with the CVC pattern double the final consonant before adding -ed or -ing, as in *ripped, ripping.*

Add the inflected endings to the words below. Then choose one form of the word and write a sentence using the word.
Possible responses provided.

1. drop **drops, dropped, dropping**

   I kept dropping the frog because it was slippery.

2. wrap **wraps, wrapped, wrapping**

   My cat wraps its paws around the ball.

3. stomp **stomps, stomped, stomping**

   Our dog stomped on my foot as he ran after the cat.

4. clear **clears, cleared, clearing**

   We cleared the table so we could eat dinner.

5. name **names, named, naming**

   Naming my bird was very hard, I had so many ideas.

6. stop **stops, stopped, stopping**

   It finally stopped raining so we could play outside.

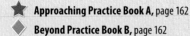 **Approaching Practice Book A, page 162**

◆ **Beyond Practice Book B, page 162**

Phonics

Decode Words with Inflected Endings

Access for All **EXPLAIN/MODEL**

- A base word does not have any word parts added to it. The endings *-s, -es, -ed,* and *-ing* can be added to base verbs.

- The *-s* or *-es* ending means that the action happens in the present.

- The *-ing* ending means that the action happens in the present.

- The *-ed* ending means the action happened in the past. This ending has the /t/ sound in *looked,* the /d/ sound in *entered,* or the /əd/ sound in *batted.*

- When a base verb ends in *e,* drop the final *e* before adding *-ed* or *-ing,* as in *dared, daring.* When a base verb ends with a vowel and consonant, such as *jog,* the final consonant is doubled before adding *-ed* or *-ing,* as in *jogged, jogging.*

Write: *Jan <u>hopped</u> on one foot.*

Think Aloud The underlined verb ends in *-ed,* so I know that the action took place in the past. I see that the letters *pp* comes before the *-ed* ending. When a base verb ends in a vowel and a consonant, the consonant doubles when *-ed* is added. If I cover up the final *p* and *-ed,* I see the base word *hop,* It has the CVC pattern and has the short *o* sound. I will try saying the /t/ sound at the end. /hopt/ That makes sense. I know that word, *hopped.*

PRACTICE/APPLY

Write *patted, liked, hoping,* and *wraps.* Have students circle the endings and identify the base words. Have students read the words aloud.

Decode Multisyllable Words Write *entering, affected, expanded, elaborated, fascinated,* and *refilling.* Model how to decode *entering.* Work with students to decode the remaining words.

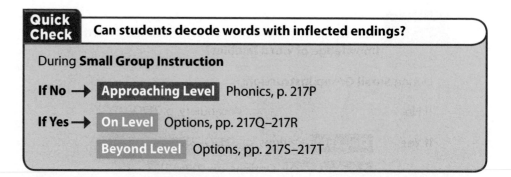

Quick Check **Can students decode words with inflected endings?**

During **Small Group Instruction**

If No → **Approaching Level** Phonics, p. 217P

If Yes → **On Level** Options, pp. 217Q–217R

Beyond Level Options, pp. 217S–217T

Vocabulary Building

Oral Language

Expand Vocabulary Work with students to brainstorm words about making a difference in the world. Write the words on a semantic web like the one below.

learn new things

give money

Making a Difference

yearn to help others

be kindhearted

volunteer

set goals

Apply Vocabulary

Write a Paragraph Have small groups of students use the vocabulary words *sturdy, yearned, produce, gift, tend, kindhearted,* and *schoolhouse* in a paragraph about helping others. Students can read their paragraphs aloud.

Vocabulary Building

Word History A word history tells how a word came into English. Explain the history of *breakfast* in *Beatrice's Goat*. Then have students look up the word histories of *fabric* and *structure* in the Student Book Glossary and record the word and its history. Review last week's vocabulary words. Have students choose one word, look up its history, and share it with the class.

breakfast	Word History
a morning meal	The word *breakfast* comes from an old English word that means "to break a fast." A fast is a time when people eat little or no food. Breakfast is the meal that "breaks" the "fast" between bedtime and waking up in the morning.

Spiral Review

Vocabulary Game

Have students play a game using the following words: *blossomed, community, determination, wailed, slogan, sturdy, grumbled.* List the words in one column on the board. Tape cards containing synonyms or brief definitions in random order in a second column.

- Divide the class into two teams. Have the teams take turns placing the meaning card next to the correct vocabulary word.

- Each team starts with 40 points. A correct match scores 10 points. An incorrect match reduces the team's score by 10 points. Continue until all the words and meanings are matched. The team with the most points wins.

Technology

Vocabulary PuzzleMaker

 For additional vocabulary and spelling games, go to
www.macmillanmh.com

5 Day Spelling

Words with Inflected Endings

Spelling Words

names	hoping	dropped
named	dances	dropping
naming	danced	wraps
hopes	dancing	wrapped
hoped	drops	wrapping

Review airplane, someone, newspaper

Challenge driving, traded

Dictation Sentences

1. She <u>names</u> her goats.
2. He **named** his dog Max.
3. She is <u>naming</u> the people in the band.
4. Alex <u>hopes</u> he can learn to ski.
5. Beatrice <u>hoped</u> that she could go to school.
6. People are <u>hoping</u> for peace.
7. Mimi <u>dances</u> in the show.
8. She <u>danced</u> with her friend.
9. <u>Dancing</u> together is fun.
10. The baby <u>drops</u> her toys.
11. I <u>dropped</u> my book.
12. I am always <u>dropping</u> my pen.
13. She <u>wraps</u> the food in foil.
14. He <u>wrapped</u> his arms around his pet.
15. Anna is <u>wrapping</u> a gift.

Review Words

1. The <u>airplane</u> will land in ten minutes.
2. <u>Someone</u> lost a shoe.
3. Our picture is in the <u>newspaper</u>.

Challenge Words

1. We are <u>driving</u> to the city.
2. Jon and Tess <u>traded</u> seats on the bus.

Note: The word in **bold** is from *Beatrice's Goat*.

Display the Spelling Words throughout the week.

Day 1 Pretest

ASSESS PRIOR KNOWLEDGE

Use the Dictation Sentences. Say the underlined word, read the sentence, and repeat the word. Have students write the words on **Spelling Practice Book** page 135. For a modified list, use the first 12 Spelling Words and the 3 Review Words. For a more challenging list, use Spelling Words 3–15 and the Challenge Words. Have students correct their own tests.

Have students cut apart the Spelling Word Cards BLM on **Teacher's Resource Book** page 87 and figure out a way to sort them. Have them save the cards for use throughout the week.

Students can use Spelling Practice Book page 136 for independent practice.

Day 2 Word Sorts

TEACHER AND STUDENT SORTS

- Review the Spelling Words, point out inflected endings, and discuss meanings.

- Use the cards on the Spelling Word Cards BLM. Attach the headings *-s, -es, -ed,* and *-ing* to a bulletin board.

- Model sorting words with inflected endings. Place the cards beneath the correct headings.

- Have students take turns sorting cards and explaining how they sorted them.

- Then have students use their own Spelling Word Cards. After placing the key headings on their desks, they can sort the Spelling Words three times. Have students write their last sort on Spelling Practice Book page 137.

Spelling Practice Book, 135–136

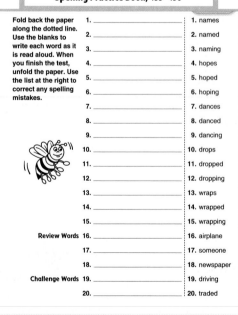

Fold back the paper along the dotted line. Use the blanks to write each word as it is read aloud. When you finish the test, unfold the paper. Use the list at the right to correct any spelling mistakes.

1. _____	1. names
2. _____	2. named
3. _____	3. naming
4. _____	4. hopes
5. _____	5. hoped
6. _____	6. hoping
7. _____	7. dances
8. _____	8. danced
9. _____	9. dancing
10. _____	10. drops
11. _____	11. dropped
12. _____	12. dropping
13. _____	13. wraps
14. _____	14. wrapped
15. _____	15. wrapping
Review Words 16. _____	16. airplane
17. _____	17. someone
18. _____	18. newspaper
Challenge Words 19. _____	19. driving
20. _____	20. traded

Spelling Practice Book, page 137

names	hopes	dances	drops	wraps
named	hoped	danced	dropped	wrapped
naming	hoping	dancing	dropping	wrapping

Pattern Power!

Write the spelling words that show what you do before adding *-ed* or *-ing*.

drop e and add -ed
1. danced
2. hoped
3. named

drop e and add -ing
6. dancing
7. hoping
8. naming

double final consonant and add -ed
4. dropped
5. wrapped

double final consonant and add -ing
9. dropping
10. wrapping

Rhyme Time

Write a spelling word that rhymes with each of these words.

11. stops ___ drops
12. ropes ___ hopes
13. maps ___ wraps
14. games ___ names
15. chances ___ dances

DEFINITIONS

Display the definitions below. Have students write the clues and the Spelling Words that go with them in a word study notebook.

1. wanted to get something very much (hoped)
2. jumping about quickly (dancing)
3. moved to music (danced)
4. caused to fall (dropped)
5. covers something with paper (wraps)

Challenge students to come up with clues for other Spelling Words, including Review Words and Challenge Words.

Have partners write a sentence for each Spelling Word, leaving a blank where the word should go. Then have them trade papers and write the missing word.

SPIRAL REVIEW

Review compound words. Write *airplane, someone,* and *newspaper* on the board. Have students identify the two smaller words in each compound word.

PROOFREAD AND WRITE

Write these sentences. Have students correct the errors.

1. Sam hopped he won. (hoped)
2. Ed wrappd the gift. (wrapped)

BLIND SORT

Partners use their Spelling Word Cards. They each write the headings *-s, -es, -ed, -ing* at the top of a sheet of paper. Then students take turns. One draws cards and says the words. The other writes them under the headings. After both have finished, they can check each other's papers.

POSTTEST

Use the Dictation Sentences on page 217G for the Posttest.

If students have difficulty with any of the words in the lesson, have them place them on a list called "Spelling Words I Want to Remember" in a word study notebook.

WORD STUDY NOTEBOOK

Challenge students to search for other words with inflected endings in their reading for the week and write them in a word study notebook under the heading "Other Words with Endings *-s, -es, -ed, -ing.*"

Spelling Practice Book, page 138

names	hopes	dances	drops	wraps
names	hoped	danced	dropped	wrapped
naming	hoping	dancing	dropping	wrapping

What's the Word?

Complete each sentence with a spelling word.

1. She was _____named_____ woman of the year for her good work.
2. The people _____danced_____ and sang for joy.
3. The mother was so happy that a tear _____dropped_____ from her eye.
4. The child _____hopes_____ to go to college in the future.
5. I _____hoped_____ to spend a year helping others.
6. My brother _____wraps_____ up sandwiches to give to the homeless.
7. The girl sings and _____dances_____ to get parts in musicals.
8. The group _____names_____ one winner of the service award each week.
9. When Dad _____drops_____ you off at school, go right inside.
10. We _____wrapped_____ the food up for the soup kitchen.

Find the Base Words

Write the base word of each -ing word.

11. naming _____name_____
12. wrapping _____wrap_____
13. dancing _____dance_____
14. dropping _____drop_____
15. hoping _____hope_____

Spelling Practice Book, page 139

There are six spelling mistakes in the speech below. Circle the misspelled words. Write the words correctly on the lines below.

Welcome, students, parents, and teachers, to this assembly!

This year our school is giving an award to the student who has done the most to help others. One student has shown us that it does not matter what you are naimmed or where you live. Everyone can find ways to help others.

She hoopes to be a role model for other students. Her actions prove that even small things can make a difference. Our winner spent time droping food off at a soup kitchen with her family and wraping small gifts for people in a nursing home. She has also shared her talents with others, danceing in performances at a local hospital.

For all these reasons and more, we are nameing Susan Harper our student of the year!

1. _____named_____
2. _____hopes_____
3. _____dropping_____
4. _____wrapping_____
5. _____dancing_____
6. _____naming_____

Writing Activity

Write a paragraph about how you could use your talents to help others. Use at least four spelling words in your description.

Spelling Practice Book, page 140

Look at the words in each set below. One word in each set is spelled correctly. Look at Sample A. The letter next to the correctly spelled word in Sample A has been shaded in. Do Sample B yourself. Shade the letter of the word that is spelled correctly. When you are sure you know what to do, go on with the rest of the page.

Sample A:
Ⓐ skips
Ⓑ skipse
Ⓒ skeps
Ⓓ skipce

Sample B:
Ⓔ hoppet
Ⓕ hopped
Ⓖ hoppt
Ⓗ haupped

1. Ⓐ naimes
   Ⓑ naimz
   Ⓒ namses
   Ⓓ names
2. Ⓔ named
   Ⓕ naimed
   Ⓖ naimd
   Ⓗ naymd
3. Ⓐ namin
   Ⓑ naiming
   Ⓒ nameing
   Ⓓ naming
4. Ⓔ haups
   Ⓕ haupes
   Ⓖ hopes
   Ⓗ hopps
5. Ⓐ haupt
   Ⓑ hoped
   Ⓒ hauped
   Ⓓ howpt

6. Ⓔ hauping
   Ⓕ hopin
   Ⓖ hoping
   Ⓗ hoppin
7. Ⓐ dances
   Ⓑ danses
   Ⓒ dancis
   Ⓓ dansis
8. Ⓔ dansed
   Ⓕ dancd
   Ⓖ danst
   Ⓗ danced
9. Ⓔ dancing
   Ⓕ dansing
   Ⓖ dancign
   Ⓗ dancin
10. Ⓐ drawps
    Ⓑ drops
    Ⓒ draups
    Ⓓ dropes

11. Ⓔ draupt
    Ⓕ drawpt
    Ⓖ dropped
    Ⓗ droped
12. Ⓐ draupin
    Ⓑ dropping
    Ⓒ droppin
    Ⓓ droppinge
13. Ⓐ rapse
    Ⓑ wrapse
    Ⓒ rapps
    Ⓓ wraps
14. Ⓔ rappt
    Ⓕ wrappt
    Ⓖ wrapt
    Ⓗ wrapped
15. Ⓐ wrapping
    Ⓑ rappin
    Ⓒ wrappin
    Ⓓ wrappen

5 Day Grammar

Subject and Object Pronouns

Use these activities to introduce each day's lesson. Write the day's activities on the board or use **Transparency 22.**

DAY 1

i plan to helpe at the food bank. We cant do it today. She will go next tuesday? (1: I; help; 2: can't; 3: Tuesday.)

DAY 2

it feels good too help them. Sam and i are going to wurk at the food bank. We will served soup to she. (1: It; to; 2: I; work; 3: serve; her)

DAY 3

Jack and grace helped we They picks up trash. then they droped it at the dump. (1: Grace; us.; 2: picked; 3: Then; dropped)

DAY 4

Her is the school nurse! me got hurt, and she took care of I. Then she called sumone to take me home, (1: She; nurse.; 2: I; me; 3: someone; home.)

DAY 5

diane gave he a new truk. Him was very excited John thanked she for the gift. (1: Diane; him; truck.; 2: He; excited.; 3: her)

ELL

Access for All

Group Work Write a few statements on the board using students' names: *Crisleyda and I like cats. Pat gave some books to Josue and Dave.* Underline the nouns. Put students in groups. Ask the groups to rewrite the sentences with subject and object pronouns.

Day 1 — Introduce the Concept

INTRODUCE SUBJECT PRONOUNS

Present the following:

- A **pronoun** is a word that takes the place of one or more nouns.

- A **subject pronoun** is used as the subject of a sentence.

- A subject pronoun must match the subject it replaces.

- Singular subject pronouns are *I, you, he, she,* and *it.*

- Plural subject pronouns are *we, you,* and *they.*

Examples:
Nan went to the beach.
She went to the beach.

Tom and Fred played soccer.
They played soccer.

 See Grammar Transparency 106 for modeling and guided practice.

Grammar Practice Book, page 135

- Use a **subject pronoun** as the subject of a sentence.
- *I, you, he she, it, we,* and *they* are subject pronouns.

Read the sentences. Choose the correct pronoun in parentheses to complete each sentence. Write the pronoun.

1. My brother, sister, and ____I____ visited our aunt's farm this summer. (me, I)
2. ____It____ was very different from where we live. (It, Them)
3. ____We____ each had our favorite animals. (Us, We)
4. ____He____ liked the roosters in the yard. (He, Him)
5. ____She____ preferred the little goats. (Her, She)
6. Have ____you____ ever seen a baby goat? (you, your)
7. ____They____ followed us around like puppies. (They, Them)
8. Could ____we____ have one as a pet? (we, us)
9. My aunt says ____they____ eat a lot. (they, them)
10. ____She____ feeds them three times a day. (Her, She)
11. "Why don't ____you____ ask Uncle Ben for help?" I asked. (your, you)
12. "____He____ is busy feeding the cows," she said. (He, Him)

Day 2 — Teach the Concept

REVIEW SUBJECT PRONOUNS

Review with students how to replace nouns with subject pronouns.

INTRODUCE OBJECT PRONOUNS

- An **object pronoun** can take the place of an object noun.

- Use an object pronoun after an action verb or words such as *for, at, of, with, in,* and *to.*

- Singular object pronouns are *me, you, him, her,* and *it.*

- Plural object pronouns are *us, you,* and *them.*

Examples:
Bill called **Jen.**   Bill called **her.**

He visited **Sue and Ed.**
He visited **them.**

 See Grammar Transparency 107 for modeling and guided practice.

Grammar Practice Book, page 136

- Use an **object pronoun** after an action verb or after a word such as *for, at, of, with,* or *to.*
- *Me, you, him, her, it, us,* and *them* are object pronouns.

Read the sentences. Choose the correct pronoun in parentheses to complete each sentence. Write the pronoun.

1. Ms. Robinson read ____us____ Beatrice's Goat. (us, we)
2. It is about a girl named Beatrice and the goat given to ____her____. (her, she)
3. The story showed how Beatrice's family took the goat's milk and sold ____it____ to raise money. (it, its)
4. Beatrice's family used the money to send ____her____ to school. (her, she)
5. Josh listened to the story with ____me____. (I, me)
6. I told ____him____ I had met some goats last summer at a farm. (he, him)
7. We played with ____them____ a lot while we were there. (they, them)
8. "I will show ____you____ a picture of a baby goat," I said. (you, your)

Day 3 | Review and Practice

REVIEW OBJECT PRONOUNS

Ask students what an object pronoun is.

MECHANICS AND USAGE: PRONOUN USAGE

- Use the subject pronouns *I, you, he, she, it, we,* and *they* as the subject of a sentence or to replace subject nouns.

- Use the object pronouns *me, you, him, her, it, us,* and *them* to replace object nouns.

- Be sure to use first-person singular pronouns correctly.

Right: Jim and I are friends.
Mom saw Jim and me.

Wrong: Jim and me are friends.
Mom saw Jim and I.

 See Grammar Transparency 108 for modeling and guided practice.

Grammar Practice Book, page 137

- Use a **subject pronoun** as the subject of a sentence.
- *I, you, he, she, it, we,* and *they* are subject pronouns.
- Use an **object pronoun** after an action verb or after a word such as *for, at, of, with,* or *to.*
- *Me, you, him, her, it, us,* and *them* are object pronouns.

Replace each underlined word or group of words in each sentence with the correct subject or object pronoun. Write the new sentences.

1. Mom and Dad took Tim and me to a petting zoo.
   They took us to a petting zoo.
2. A sign explained how to behave with the animals.
   It explained how to behave with them.
3. Tim petted a baby goat.
   He petted it.
4. Two other goats came along and poked at Tim and me.
   They came along and poked at us.
5. Mom told Tim that they were looking for food.
   She told him that they were looking for food.
6. Tim said to Mom and me, "I hope they don't think I'm lunch!"
   He said to us, "I hope they don't think I'm lunch!"
7. Dad took a picture of Tim and the goats.
   He took a picture of them.
8. Should I send you and Grandma a picture of the goats?
   Should I send you a picture of the goats?

Day 4 | Review and Proofread

REVIEW SUBJECT AND OBJECT PRONOUNS

Ask students to write a sentence using subject and object pronouns.

PROOFREAD

Have students correct errors in the following sentences.

1. My parents took we to camp. (us)

2. Them had a good time last summer. (They)

3. Jake took she a present. (her)

4. Us sing by the campfire (We)

5. Bill and me went to a movie. (I)

 See Grammar Transparency 109 for modeling and guided practice.

Grammar Practice Book, page 138

- Use a **subject pronoun** as the subject of a sentence.
- *I, you, he, she, it, we,* and *they* are subject pronouns.
- Use an **object pronoun** after an action verb or after a word such as *for, at, of, with,* or *to.*
- *Me, you, him, her, it, us,* and *them* are object pronouns.

Proofread the paragraphs below. Circle any pronouns that are used incorrectly.

My class read a book called *Beatrice's Goat.* Us learned how the gift of a goat from Heifer International helped Beatrice go to school. The book had an influence on we all. Everyone wanted to do something to help others.
We decided to make and sell farm animal pins. Everyone in town loved they Them helped the class raise a lot of money. We were glad to give the money to Heifer International. We felt good—we were helping they Maybe yous can help someone, too!

Rewrite the paragraph. Write the pronouns correctly.

My class read a book called *Beatrice's Goat.* We learned how the gift of a goat from Heifer International helped Beatrice go to school. The book had an influence on us all. Everyone wanted to do something to help others.
We decided to make and sell farm animal pins. Everyone in town loved them. They helped the class raise a lot of money. We were glad to give the money to Heifer International. We felt good—we were helping them. Maybe you can help someone too!

Day 5 | Assess and Reteach

ASSESS

Use the Daily Language Activity and page 139 of the **Grammar Practice Book** for assessment.

RETEACH

Have the class talk about *Beatrice's Goat.* Encourage students to use subject and object pronouns in sentences about characters, places, or events from the story. When common and proper nouns are used, ask students what pronouns could have been used in place of those nouns.

Use page 140 of the Grammar Practice Book for additional reteaching.

 See Grammar Transparency 110 for modeling and guided practice.

Grammar Practice Book, pages 139–140

Read the first sentence in each set. One of the four sentences that follow it correctly replaces the underlined words. Circle the correct sentence.

1. Our goat Annie lives in the small barn behind our house.
   A. They lives in the small barn behind our house.
   B. You lives in the small barn behind our house.
   C. Them lives in the small barn behind our house.
   D. It lives in the small barn behind our house.
2. Annie eats breakfast with my family every morning.
   A. She eats breakfast with us every morning.
   B. Her eats breakfast with us every morning.
   C. We eats breakfast with her every morning.
   D. They eats breakfast with us every morning.
3. Dad listens for Annie's hooves tapping on the porch.
   A. We listens for it tapping on the porch.
   B. He listens for them tapping on the porch.
   C. He listens for they tapping on the porch.
   D. I listens for her tapping on the porch.
4. My parents feed Annie a mix of different foods.
   A. Us feed them a mix of different foods.
   B. They feed him a mix of different foods.
   C. You feed us a mix of different foods.
   D. They feed her a mix of different foods.
5. Goats will eat anything you give them!
   A. We will eat anything you give them!
   B. She will eat anything you give them!
   C. It will eat anything we give them!
   D. They will eat anything you give them!

Administer the Test

Weekly Reading Assessment,
Passage and questions, pages 277–284

ASSESSED SKILLS

- Cause and Effect
- Vocabulary Words
- Word Parts/Word Families
- Words with Inflected Endings
- Subject and Object Pronouns

Macmillan/McGraw-Hill

Administer the **Weekly Assessment** from the CD-ROM or online.

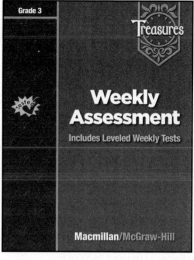

Weekly Assessment, 277–284

Fluency

Assess fluency for one group of students per week. Use the Oral Fluency Record Sheet to track the number of words read correctly. Fluency goal for all students: **97–117 words correct per minute (WCPM).**

Approaching Level	Weeks 1, 3, 5
On Level	Weeks 2, 4
Beyond Level	Week 6

Fluency Assessment

Alternative Assessments

- **ELL Assessment,** pages 140–141

ELL Assessment, 140–141

Diagnose		Prescribe
	IF . . .	**THEN . . .**
VOCABULARY WORDS **VOCABULARY STRATEGY** Word Parts: Word Families Items 1, 2, 3	0–1 items correct . . .	Reteach skills using the **Additional Lessons,** page T7 **LOG ON** Reteach skills: Go to www.macmillanmh.com **CD ROM** Vocabulary PuzzleMaker Evaluate for Intervention.
COMPREHENSION Skill: Cause and Effect Items 4, 5, 6,	0–1 items correct . . .	Reteach skills using the **Additional Lessons**, page T2 Evaluate for Intervention.
GRAMMAR Subject and Object Pronouns Items 7, 8, 9	0–1 items correct . . .	Reteach skills: **Grammar Practice Book,** page 140
SPELLING Words with Inflected Endings Items 10, 11, 12	0–1 items correct . . .	**LOG ON** Reteach skills: Go to www.macmillanmh.com
FLUENCY	89–96 WCPM 0–88 WCPM	**AUDIO CD** Fluency Solutions Evaluate for Intervention.

DIBELS LINK

PROGRESS MONITORING
Use Your DIBELS Results to Inform Instruction.
IF
DIBELS Oral **R**eading **F**luency   **(DORF)** 0–109

THEN
Use the Fluency Solutions Audio CD.

READING
Triumphs
AN INTERVENTION PROGRAM

To place students in the Intervention Program, use the **Diagnostic Assessment** in the Intervention Teacher's Edition.

Beatrice's Goat

Leveled Reader Lesson 1

Objective	Read to apply strategies and skills
Materials	• **Leveled Reader** *Henry Bergh and the ASPCA* • chart paper
	• **Approaching Practice Book A,** p. 159

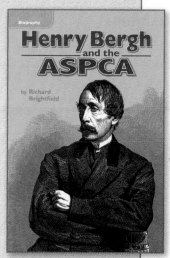

Leveled Reader

PREVIEW AND PREDICT

Read the title and table of contents. Check if any students know about the ASPCA. Have students preview the art, photos, and headings, make predictions about the book, and set their own reading purposes.

VOCABULARY WORDS

Display the **Vocabulary Cards.** As you read, have each student find one of the words in *Henry Bergh and the ASPCA: kindhearted*, p. 2; *schoolhouse*, p 3; *yearned*, p. 4; *gift, produce*, p. 5; *tend, sturdy*, p. 7. They should read the sentence aloud, explain what the word means, and name other words they could use in the sentence without changing the meaning.

STRATEGY
MAKE INFERENCES AND ANALYZE

Remind students that authors don't always tell a reader every detail. Readers often have to think carefully about the information in the story and then make inferences based on their own experience and the story clues.

Read pages 2–3 aloud. Model making inferences.

Think Aloud The first paragraph says that animals were often mistreated in the 1800s. Then it mentions Henry Bergh. I think Henry Bergh lived during the 1800s. The author doesn't say that exactly, but it seems like a reasonable guess. I'll keep reading to learn more.

SKILL
CAUSE AND EFFECT

Review cause and effect. Explain that to identify causes and effects, students should make inferences about what happened and why. Help students create a Cause and Effect Chart as they read.

READ AND RESPOND

Guide students' reading through Chapter 2. Discuss the "Ways to Keep Pets Healthy" feature. Does this seem like good advice for pet owners?

Fluency: REPEATED READING

Model reading the passage on **Practice Book** page 159 clearly, with a reading rate appropriate to the genre. Have the group echo-read. Then have partners practice reading it to each other. Circulate and provide feedback.

⭐ **Approaching Practice Book A,** page 159

As I read, I will pay attention to the genre of the passage.

	Bergh's behavior did not tend to make him well liked.
10	A cartoon showed him with a long nose, "butting it into
21	other people's business."
24	Bergh carried on. He had sturdy drinking fountains
32	made for the horses. He saw to it that clinics were built to
45	help animals who were sick.
50	Bergh had to convince people that the ASPCA was a
60	good idea. He gave talks whenever and wherever he could.
70	Soon people began to listen. The society spread to other
80	cities. Soon it reached all the way across the United States.
91	Bergh saw that some cats and dogs were abused too.
101	Dogs were forced to pull carts. They were made to fight
112	each other in shows. Stray dogs and cats were caught and
123	killed. 124

Comprehension Check

1. What kind of person was Henry Bergh? **Draw Conclusions** He was kind and dedicated to the proper treatment of animals.
2. How did Bergh try to improve things for horses? **Main Idea and Details** He had drinking fountains and clinics to take care of sick horses built.

	Words Read	−	Number of Errors	=	Words Correct Score
First Read		−		=	
Second Read		−		=	

Leveled Reader Library

Leveled Reader Lesson 2

Objective   Read to apply strategies and skills
Materials   • **Leveled Reader** *Henry Bergh and the ASPCA*

VOCABULARY WORDS

As necessary, clarify the meanings of the vocabulary words. Reinforce the meanings by helping students to demonstrate as many of the words as they can using pantomime, drawings, or other nonverbal clues. For example, they might draw a schoolhouse, point out items that are sturdy, and pantomime opening a gift.

SUMMARIZE AND PREDICT

Have students summarize Henry Bergh's work from Chapters 1 and 2. Then ask students to predict what else they will learn about Bergh's work.

SKILL

CAUSE AND EFFECT

Help students analyze causes and effects in Chapter 3 and the Conclusion. For example, discuss the effects of the Greyhound Protection League and the Society for the Prevention of Cruelty to Children. You may wish to help students extend their Cause and Effect Charts.

READ AND RESPOND

Have students read to the end of the selection. Discuss other problems Bergh found in society and the effect he had on solving those problems. Remind students to make inferences as they read and to analyze the text by asking questions to help them better understand the information. When they finish reading, have students paraphrase the main events. Discuss their personal responses. For example, ask students to explain if they think Henry Bergh made the world a better place, as he had hoped.

Leveled Reader

Fluency

Objective   Read with increasing fluency
Materials   • stopwatch   • **Approaching Practice Book A,** p. 159

TIMED READING

Have students do a final timed reading of the passage on **Practice Book** page 159. Students should begin reading the passage aloud when you say "Go" and stop reading after one minute when you say "Stop."

Pay attention to their miscues and remediate as necessary. Help students record and graph the number of words they read correctly.

Helping People Help Themselves

by Zoe Tomasi

Student Book

Comprehension

Objective	Identify cause and effect
Materials	• **Comprehension Transparencies 22a** and **22b**

SKILL
CAUSE AND EFFECT

Review that a cause is the reason something happens and an effect is the result of that cause. The effect often answers the question "What happened?" The cause often answers the question "Why?"

Display **Transparencies 22a** and **22b.** Read the first paragraph aloud.

Think Aloud The second sentence says that people were starving. The third sentence says that Dan West got an idea as he was helping people. I think there is a cause-effect relationship. The fact that people were starving was the cause. Dan West's idea to start Heifer International was the effect.

As they read on, have students underline each cause once and each effect twice. Discuss how causes can sometimes be traced after the fact, or how they sometimes lead directly and obviously to the consequence, or effect.

Vocabulary

Objective	Apply vocabulary word meanings and identify words in the same word families
Materials	• **Vocabulary Cards** • **Student Book** *Beatrice's Goat* • dictionary

VOCABULARY WORDS

Help students locate the vocabulary words in *Beatrice's Goat*. Read aloud the words in context and discuss meaning clues. Help students with words they do not know well. Then have students use each word in a sentence.

WORD PARTS: WORD FAMILIES

Write *schoolhouse* and *preschool*. Underline *school* in each. Explain that both words contain the same base word and are part of the same word family.

Challenge students to name other words that include the base word *school*. Suggest they use a dictionary. Have students write sentences with at least two words in the *school* family. Also brainstorm words that contain one of the word parts in *kindhearted*.

ELL

Access for All

Drawing Explain that illustrations often give clues to the meaning of a word. Write the following vocabulary words on the board: *gift, yearned, sturdy, schoolhouse,* and *kindhearted*. Divide children evenly into five groups. Give each group one of the words. Say: *First, talk about the illustration you could draw that would most clearly show the meaning of the word.* Have each group explain what it would draw and tell why.

| gift | yearned | tend | produce | sturdy | schoolhouse | kindhearted |

Phonics

Objective   Decode words with inflected endings

DECODE WORDS WITH INFLECTED ENDINGS

Review:

- An *-s* or *-ing* ending on a verb shows the action is happening in the present.

- An *-ed* ending on a verb shows the action happened in the past.

Show how to build the spelling word *hopes* from the base word and the *-s* ending. Underline the base word *hope*. Then show how to build *hoped*. Draw a slash through the *e* in *hope* and explain that it is necessary to drop the final *e* before adding the *-ed* ending. Repeat with *hoping*.

Have students build and say *dances, danced, dancing, names, named,* and *naming*, starting with the base words. They can refer to the models.

Additional Lessons

Use your **Quick Check** observations to help you identify students who might benefit from additional instruction. See page T2 for comprehension support and page T7 for vocabulary support.

Vocabulary

Objective   Apply vocabulary word meanings and identify words in the same word families
Materials   • **Vocabulary Cards**   • index cards   • dictionary

VOCABULARY WORDS

Read each word and review its meaning. As a group, brainstorm words in the same word families as the vocabulary words, such as *playhouse, kindness,* and *heartbeat*. Ask students to check the words in the dictionary.

Have students work in pairs to play a guessing game. In turn, each student makes up a meaning-based clue about a vocabulary word or a word in the same family, without saying any part of the word itself. The partner then tries to guess the word. For example: *This word means the same as "present."* (gift) Review the previous week's vocabulary words in the same way.

Make Connections Across Texts

Objective   Compare causes and effects across texts
Materials   • **Student Book** *Beatrice's Goat*   • **Leveled Reader** *Henry Bergh and the ASPCA*

SKILL
CAUSE AND EFFECT

Ask students to compare and contrast causes and effects in *Beatrice's Goat* and *Henry Bergh and the ASPCA*.

- Did Beatrice and Bergh have the same reasons for caring about animals? Explain.

- If Beatrice and Henry Bergh met, what might they talk about?

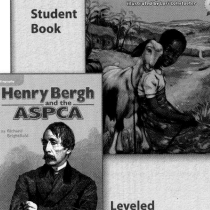

Student Book

Leveled Reader

Leveled Reader Lesson

Objective	Read to apply strategies and skills
Materials	• **Leveled Reader** *John Muir: Friend of Nature* • chart paper
	• **On Level Practice Book O,** p. 159

PREVIEW AND PREDICT

Show the cover and read the title. Ask students why they think John Muir is called a "friend of nature." Discuss how vocabulary words might be used.

STRATEGY
MAKE INFERENCES AND ANALYZE

Explain that good readers make inferences and analyze the text as they read by looking for story clues to fill in the gaps. Tell students to look for clues the author gives about John Muir and make inferences about what caused him to do the things he did. Read pages 2–3 aloud. Model how you make inferences and analyze.

Think Aloud On page 2, I learned that John Muir helped save Yosemite National Park. I'm going to keep reading to make inferences about how Muir was able to do this and what led to his taking action.

SKILL
CAUSE AND EFFECT

Review cause and effect. Discuss what caused John Muir to act on behalf of the environment. Ask what effect he had on state parks such as Yosemite. Students can create a Cause and Effect Chart on chart paper.

READ AND RESPOND

Have students read through Chapter 2. Remind them to ask questions that help them identify what John Muir did and why. Students should use their own experience and text clues to make inferences.

Later have students read to the end of the book. Once they have finished, have students paraphrase what they learned and discuss whether the environment would be the same without the efforts of John Muir and the Sierra Club. Ask if the book makes students want to help the environment.

Fluency: REPEATED READING

Model reading the passage on **Practice Book** page 159 at a rate appropriate to the genre. Have students echo-read.

Next have students work in pairs, taking turns reading the passage. Remind them to use a narrator's voice and show interest in the topic. Partners can continue practicing the passage for the rest of the week.

Leveled Reader

ELL
Leveled Reader
Go to pages
217U–217V.

On Level Practice Book O, page 159

As I read, I will pay attention to the genre of the passage.

	One man who came to the United States as a boy helped
12	to save Yosemite's natural wonders for you to enjoy. His
22	name was John Muir.
26	John Muir was born in a small town in Scotland in
37	1838. His family moved to the United States when he was
47	eleven. They moved to what is now Wisconsin and set up a
59	farm there. They were pioneers.
64	Muir went to school in a small schoolhouse. He liked
74	being a schoolboy. The rest of the time he worked on the
86	farm. He was busy from sunup until sundown. But Muir
96	yearned for more. He knew he didn't want to tend the farm
108	all his life. Muir liked to read and he read often. He also
121	liked to invent things. He made a special thermometer.
130	And he made something he called his "early-rising
138	machine." 139

Comprehension Check

1. What interests did John Muir have? **Main Idea and Details**
   John enjoyed school, reading, and inventing things.
2. What does the word pioneer mean? **Context Clues**
   A pioneer is someone who settles in land that is
   unknown or that has not been claimed.

	Words Read	−	Number of Errors	=	Words Correct Score
First Read		−		=	
Second Read		−		=	

Vocabulary

Objective   Apply vocabulary words and identify words from the same word family

Materials   • **Leveled Reader** *John Muir: Friend of Nature*   • **Vocabulary Cards**

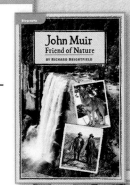

Leveled Reader

VOCABULARY WORDS

Show the **Vocabulary Cards** for *gift, yearned, tend, produce, sturdy, schoolhouse,* and *kindhearted.* Discuss how students might teach each word to a younger student. For example, have students use each word in a sentence that illustrates its meaning and identify familiar words within longer words.

WORD PARTS: WORD FAMILIES

Have students search page 4 of the Leveled Reader for three words with the base word *sun.* (*sunup, sundown, sunrise*) Have volunteers define these words. Then pose questions to help students name other words that belong to this word family, such as: *If the sun is shining, what kind of day is it?* (sunny) *What is the first day of the week?* (Sunday)

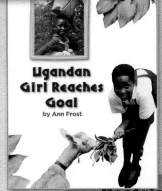

Student Book

Text Feature

Objective   Understand and analyze an editorial

Materials   • **Student Book** "Ugandan Girl Reaches Goal"   • newspapers or magazines

EDITORIAL

Discuss the information that the editorial on **Student Book** page 214 presents, as well as its persuasive elements. Ask students to identify the clues that reveal the opinion of the writer. Have students look at other editorials and letters to the editor in a newspaper or magazine. Discuss why editorials might be included in publications.

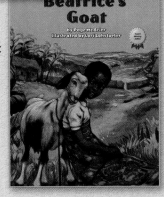

Student Book

Make Connections Across Texts

Objective   Make connections across texts and identify cause and effect

Materials   • **Student Book** *Beatrice's Goat*   • **Leveled Reader** *John Muir: Friend of Nature*

SKILL
CAUSE AND EFFECT

Discuss what happens in *Beatrice's Goat* and *John Muir: Friend of Nature* and what causes those things to happen. Ask how the actions of Beatrice and John Muir help others.

Review how good readers compare and contrast the articles they read. What connections can students make? What questions do they have?

Leveled Reader Lesson

Objective Read to apply strategies and skills

Materials
- **Leveled Reader** *Alexander Fleming and His Great Discovery*
- **Beyond Practice Book B,** p. 159

PREVIEW AND PREDICT

Show the cover and read the title of the book. Ask what students think Alexander Fleming's great discovery was based on the cover photo.

STRATEGY
MAKE INFERENCES AND ANALYZE

Remind students that making inferences and analyzing the text as they read can help them understand what happens in a story and why it happened.

SKILL
CAUSE AND EFFECT

Have a volunteer define cause and effect. During and after reading, discuss what happens to Fleming and why. Have students briefly state important events in Fleming's life. Discuss what caused him to pursue a medical career and what effect that had on the medical world. Students can create a Cause and Effect Chart to help them.

READ AND RESPOND

Have students read to the end of Chapter 2. Discuss how hard work and accidents led to Fleming becoming a doctor and to his important discovery.

After students finish reading, discuss how vocabulary words were used. Then ask:

- What would medicine be like if Fleming had not discovered penicillin?
- What were the most interesting facts about Fleming that you learned?
- Have you ever made a mistake or had an accident that led to an interesting discovery? What was it?

Fluency: REPEATED READING

Reread the fluency passage from *Alexander Fleming and His Great Discovery* to model expressive reading of nonfiction. Have students follow along and practice reading the passage using **Practice Book** page 159.

Have partners take turns reading the passage to each other and offering corrective feedback. Remind students to read at an even pace. Tell them that their voices should show interest in the subject.

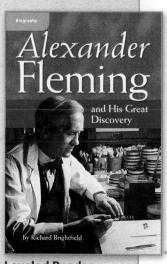

Leveled Reader

Beyond Practice Book B, page 159

As I read, I will pay attention to genre of the passage.

	Alexander Fleming was born in 1881. He grew up on
9	a farm in a remote part of Scotland. As a schoolboy, he
21	walked barefoot to a country schoolhouse miles away.
29	When not in school or tending sheep, he and his three
40	brothers would play outdoors.
44	When Fleming was in his teens, his family moved to
54	London. London was a crowded, noisy place. Fleming's
62	new home was over an underground railway. Every few
71	minutes the sturdy house would shake as a steam train
81	roared below.
83	Think about moving from a quiet, peaceful farm, to a
93	big city. Fleming and his brothers loved it. To them, it
104	probably felt like going from a desert island to the middle
115	of a fun fair.
119	Fleming left school at age 16 and went to work in an
130	office. He had to copy piles of letters and business forms
141	by hand. He did this for long hours, six days a week. He
154	yearned for another type of work. 160

Comprehension Check

1. What was Alexander Fleming's childhood like? **Summarize**
Alexander tended sheep, played outdoors with his brothers, and went to school.
2. How was Fleming's life different in London? **Compare and Contrast**
London was crowded and noisy, and his house shook every few minutes when steam trains roared below.

	Words Read	–	Number of Errors	=	Words Correct Score
First Read		–		=	
Second Read		–		=	

Vocabulary

Objective   Apply meanings of content vocabulary words
Materials   • **Student Book** "Ugandan Girl Reaches Goal"

CONTENT VOCABULARY

Review the content vocabulary words listed on **Student Book** page 212: *achieve, determined, encourages*. Ask students to write a paragraph that tells how they feel about Beatrice Biira's goal of encouraging all students to get a good education, and Alexander Fleming's goal of finding a medicine that destroyed bad bacteria. Have them use and underline the content vocabulary words.

Student Book

Text Feature

Objective   Analyze and write a persuasive editorial
Materials   • **Student Book** "Ugandan Girl Reaches Goal"

EDITORIAL

Ask students to review "Ugandan Girl Reaches Goal" on Student Book pages 212–215 and summarize the main ideas. Review and discuss the features of an editorial.

■ What opinion or judgment does the writer express? Do you agree? Explain.

■ What are some clues that tell you the writer is expressing an opinion?

■ Why do people write persuasive editorials?

Ask partners to write an editorial for the school newspaper to convince readers to help start a community garden. Tell them to give facts about getting tools and seeds. They should include opinions about why a community garden is a good idea. Have the group compare their work.

ELL   Access for All

Partnered Reading Have pairs read "Ugandan Girl Reaches Goal" as a partnered reading activity. Have one partner read a paragraph aloud, while the other reads along silently. Then have the partners switch roles. Continue for 10 minutes.

Self-Selected Reading

Objective   Read independently and identify cause and effect
Materials   • **Leveled Readers** or trade books at students' reading level

READ TO IDENTIFY CAUSE AND EFFECT

Invite students to choose a nonfiction book to read independently for enjoyment. For a list of theme-related titles, see pages T19–T20. As students read, have them note instances of cause and effect.

Afterward, partners who have read the same book should discuss how a change in events could have a different effect.

Academic Language

Throughout the week the English language learners will need help in building their understanding of the academic language used in daily instruction and assessment instruments. The following strategies will help to increase their language proficiency and comprehension of content and instructional words.

Oral Language For additional language support and oral vocabulary development, go to **www.macmillanmh.com**

Strategies to Reinforce Academic Language

- **Use Context** Academic Language (see chart below) should be explained in the context of the task during Whole Group. Use gestures, expressions, and visuals to support meaning.
- **Use Visuals** Use charts, transparencies, and graphic organizers to explain key labels to help students understand classroom language.
- **Model** Demonstrate the task using academic language in order for students to understand instruction.

Academic Language Used in Whole Group Instruction

Content/Theme Words	Skill/Strategy Words	Writing/Grammar Words
making a difference (p. 184)	word families (p. 187)	descriptive paragraph (p. 216)
achieve (p. 212)	make inferences and analyze (p. 187A)	vivid details (p. 216)
determined (p. 212)	cause and effect (p. 187A)	examples (p. 217)
encourages (p. 212)	newspaper article (p. 212)	topic sentence (p. 217A)
goal (p. 212)	editorial (p. 212)	ideas and content (p. 217)
nonprofit organization (p. 212)	opinion (p. 212)	subject pronoun (p. 217I)
		object pronoun (p. 217I)

ELL Leveled Reader Lesson

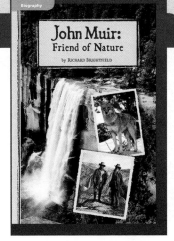

Before Reading

DEVELOP ORAL LANGUAGE

 Build Background Write the expression *Make a Difference* and discuss its meaning. Explain that natural resources, such as water and air, need to be protected. *How can we protect them?* Discuss.

Review Vocabulary Write the vocabulary and support words on the board and discuss their meanings. Ask students to use each one in a sentence. If necessary, start the sentence. *Paul takes care of abandoned animals, because he is _____.* (kindhearted)

PREVIEW AND PREDICT

Point to the cover photographs and read the title aloud. Show Yosemite on a map and explain that the photographs were taken there. *Look at the photograph of the two men. When do you think it was taken? What do you think we are going to read about?*

Set a Purpose for Reading Show the Cause and Effect Chart. Ask students to do a similar chart to help them identify examples of cause and effect.

During Reading

Choose from among the differentiated strategies below to support students' reading at all stages of language acquisition.

Beginning	**Intermediate**	**Advanced**
Shared Reading As you read, model how to make inferences. Use this information to identify examples of cause and effect and fill in the chart. Encourage students to help you.	**Read Together** Read Chapter 1. Model how to make inferences as you help students retell it. Identify examples of cause and effect and have students help fill in the chart. Ask them to take turns reading the rest and use the strategy.	**Independent Reading** Have students read the selection. Each day, ask them to discuss it with a partner and make inferences. Have them use this information to identify examples of cause and effect and fill in the chart.

After Reading

Remind students to use the vocabulary and story words in their whole group activities.

Objective
- **To apply vocabulary and comprehension skills**

Materials
- **ELL Leveled Reader**

ELL 5 Day Planner

DAY 1	• Academic Language • Oral Language and Vocabulary Review
DAY 2	• Academic Language • ELL Leveled Reader
DAY 3	• Academic Language • ELL Leveled Reader
DAY 4	• Academic Language • ELL Leveled Reader
DAY 5	• Academic Language • ELL Leveled Reader Comprehension Check and Literacy Activities

ELL Teacher's Guide for students who need additional instruction

Week At A Glance

Whole Group

 VOCABULARY
powered, declared, existed, artist's, pride

 Word Parts/Possessives

COMPREHENSION
Strategy: Make Inferences and Analyze
 Skill: Evaluate Fact and Opinion

 TEST STRATEGY
On My Own

 WRITING
Expository Writing

Social Studies Link

Science, Technology, and Society

Small Group Options

Differentiated Instruction for Tested Skills

 Tested Skills for the Week

Weekly Theme: In Motion

Real World Reading

Comprehension

Genre
A Nonfiction Article gives information about a real person, place, or event.

Make Inferences and Analyze
Fact and Opinion
A fact can be proved to be true. An opinion is a belief that does not have to be supported by facts.

A Carousel of Dreams

The creatures on the Children's Carousel at Riverbank State Park (above) were copied from kids' drawings, like the one below.

The carousel at Riverbank State Park in New York City is probably the most fantastic carousel in the country. It doesn't hold the usual herd of painted ponies. Instead, giant spiders pull a chariot, and a plaid zebra prances beside a two-headed octopus. These creatures were invented by kids. Milo Mottola, 32, is the artist who turned the kids' drawings into carousel critters.

AUDIO CD

Main Selection/Social Studies Link
Genre Nonfiction Article

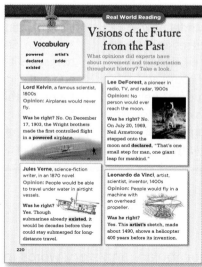

Real World Reading

Visions of the Future from the Past

Vocabulary
powered declared existed artist's pride

What opinions did experts have about movement and transportation throughout history? Take a look.

Lord Kelvin, a famous scientist, 1800s
Opinion: Airplanes would never fly.
Was he right? No. On December 17, 1903, the Wright brothers made the first controlled flight in a powered airplane.

Jules Verne, science-fiction writer, in an 1870 novel
Opinion: People would be able to travel under water in airtight vessels.
Was he right? Yes. Though submarines already existed, it would be decades before they could stay submerged for long-distance travel.

Lee DeForest, a pioneer in radio, TV, and radar, 1900s
Opinion: No person would ever reach the moon.
Was he right? No. On July 20, 1969, Neil Armstrong stepped onto the moon and declared, "That's one small step for man, one giant leap for mankind."

Leonardo da Vinci, artist, scientist, inventor, 1400s
Opinion: People would fly in a machine with an overhead propeller.
Was he right? Yes. This artist's sketch, made about 1490, shows a helicopter 400 years before its invention.

220

Vocabulary/ Comprehension

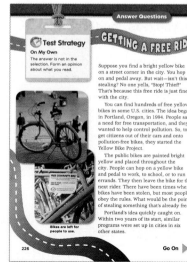

Answer Questions

Test Strategy
On My Own
The answer is not in the selection. Form an opinion about what you read.

GETTING A FREE RIDE

Suppose you find a bright yellow bike on a street corner in the city. You hop on and pedal away. But wait—isn't this stealing? No one yells, "Stop! Thief!" That's because this free ride is just fine with the city.

You can find hundreds of free yellow bikes in some U.S. cities. The idea began in Portland, Oregon, in 1994. People saw a need for free transportation, and they wanted to help control pollution. So, to get citizens out of their cars and onto pollution-free bikes, they started the Yellow Bike Project.

The public bikes are painted bright yellow and placed throughout the city. People can hop on a yellow bike and pedal to work, to school, or to run errands. They then leave the bike for the next rider. There have been times when bikes have been stolen, but most people obey the rules. What would be the point of stealing something that's already free?

Portland's idea quickly caught on. Within two years of its start, similar programs were set up in cities in six other states.

Bikes are left for people to use.

226

Go On

Test Strategy
On My Own

Leveled Readers

AUDIO CD

GR Levels N–R

Genre Informational Nonfiction

- Same Theme
- Same Vocabulary
- Same Comprehension Skills

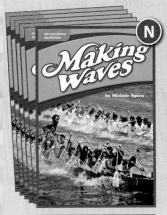
N

P

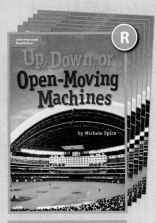
R

Approaching Level | **On Level** | **Beyond Level**

English Language Leveled Reader

On Level Reader sheltered for English Language Learner

ELL Teacher's Guide Available

Also Available
LEVELED READER PROGRAM

CLASSROOM LIBRARY

Genre Historical Fiction

Approaching | **On Level** | **Beyond**

Trade books to apply Comprehension Skills

INTERVENTION ANTHOLOGY

- Phonics and Decoding
- Comprehension
- Vocabulary

Reading Triumphs, Intervention Program also available

LEVELED PRACTICE

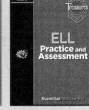

Practice Book A | Practice Book O | Practice Book B | ELL Practice and Assessment

Approaching | **On Level** | **Beyond** | **ELL**

Technology

www.macmillanmh.com

 LISTENING LIBRARY
- Main Selections
- Leveled Readers
- Intervention Anthology

FLUENCY SOLUTIONS

 VOCABULARY PuzzleMaker
NEW ADVENTURES WITH
BUGGLES AND BEEZY

 ONLINE INSTRUCTION
- Meet the Author/Illustrator
- Computer Literacy Lessons
- Research and Inquiry Activities
- Oral Language Activities
- Vocabulary and Spelling Activities

Suggested Lesson Plan

CD ROM
Instructional Navigator
Interactive Lesson Planner

A Carousel of Dreams, 222–225

Leveled Readers

Whole Group

ORAL LANGUAGE

- **Listening**
- **Speaking**
- **Viewing**

WORD STUDY

- **Vocabulary**
- **Phonics/Decoding**

READING

- **Develop Comprehension**

- **Fluency**

LANGUAGE ARTS

- **Writing**

- **Grammar**

- **Spelling**

ASSESSMENT

- **Informal/Formal**

Turn the Page for
Small Group Lesson Plan

218C

Day 1

Listening/Speaking/Viewing

❓ Focus Question How many different ways can you think of that people get from one place to another?

Build Background, 218

Read Aloud: "The Runner," 219

Vocabulary
 powered, declared, existed, artist's, pride, 220

Practice Book A-O-B, 163

 Strategy: Word Parts/Possessives, 221

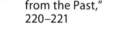

Read "Visions of the Future from the Past," 220–221

Comprehension, 221A–221B
  Strategy: Make Inferences and Analyze
  Skill: Fact and Opinion
  Practice Book A-O-B, 164

Student Book

Fluency Partner Reading, 218I
Model Fluency, 219

Writing

Daily Writing Prompt Walking on the moon, Neil Armstrong said, "One small step for man, one giant leap for mankind." What would you have said? Why?

Generate Questions: Brochure, 229A

Grammar Daily Language Activities, 229I
Possessive Pronouns, 229I
Grammar Practice Book, 141

Spelling Pretest, 229G
Spelling Practice Book, 141–142

Quick Check Vocabulary, 220
Comprehension, 221B

Differentiated Instruction 229M–229V

Day 2

Listening/Speaking

❓ Focus Question What makes a carousel in New York City so special?

Vocabulary
Review Vocabulary, 222

Phonics
Decode Words with Endings *y* to *i*, 229E

Practice Book A-O-B, 169

Read *A Carousel of Dreams,* 222–225

Comprehension, 222–225
  Strategy: Make Inferences and Analyze
  Skill: Fact and Opinion
  Practice Book A-O-B, 165

Student Book

Fluency Partner Reading, 218I

Writing

Daily Writing Prompt Write a radio or print advertisement for a new amusement park. Be sure to include descriptions of the most exciting rides and attractions.

Find Information: Brochure, 229A

Grammar Daily Language Activities, 229I
Possessive Pronouns, 229I
Grammar Practice Book, 142

Spelling Words with Endings *y* to *i*, 229G
Spelling Practice Book, 143

Quick Check Comprehension, 225
Phonics, 229E

Differentiated Instruction 229M–229V

Skills/Strategies

Vocabulary	Comprehension	Writing
Vocabulary Words	**Strategy:** Make Inferences and Analyze	Expository Writing
Word Parts: Possessives	**Skill:** Fact and Opinion	

Turn the Page for
Small Group Options

Day 3

Listening/Speaking

❓ Focus Question Compare the motion of Ham's space capsule with the motion of a carousel.
Summarize, 225

Vocabulary

Review Words in Context, 229C

Strategy: Word Parts/Possessives, 229D

Practice Book A-O-B, 168

Phonics

Decode Multisyllable Words, 229E

Read *A Carousel of Dreams,* 222–225

Comprehension

Comprehension Check, 225
Maintain Skill:
Summarize, 225A

Student Book

Fluency Practice Book A-O-B, 166
Partner Reading, 218I
Repeated Reading, 225A

Writing

Daily Writing Prompt Write a poem about what you see and hear on your way to school on a busy morning.

Organize Information: Brochure, 229B

Grammar Daily Language Activities, 229I
Possessive Pronouns, 229J
Grammar Practice Book, 143

Spelling Words with Endings *y* to *i*, 229H
Spelling Practice Book, 144

Quick Check Fluency, 225A

Day 4

Listening/Speaking

❓ Focus Question Why should cities have programs to cut down on air pollution?
Expand Vocabulary: Transportation, 229F

Vocabulary

Travel by Water, 229F

Apply Vocabulary to Writing, 229F

Read "Getting a Free Ride," 226–227
Test Strategy: On My Own

Research and Study Skills

Skim and Scan, 225B
Practice Book A-O-B, 167

Student Book

Fluency Partner Reading, 218I

Writing

Daily Writing Prompt Write an invitation asking friends to ride your new carousel. Be sure to include when and where the event will take place.

Synthesize and Write: Brochure, 229B

Grammar Daily Language Activities, 229I
Possessive Pronouns, 229J
Grammar Practice Book, 144

Spelling Words with Endings *y* to *i*, 229H
Spelling Practice Book, 145

Quick Check Vocabulary, 229D

Day 5
Review and Assess

Listening/Speaking

❓ Focus Question What are some facts about carousels? What are some opinions people have about riding carousels?
Speaking and Listening Strategies, 229A

Presentation of Expository Writing, 229B

Vocabulary

Spiral Review: Vocabulary Game, 229F

Read Self-Selected Reading, 218I

Comprehension

Strategy: Make Inferences and Analyze
Skill: Fact and Opinion, 225

Student Book

Fluency Partner Reading, 218I

Writing

Daily Writing Prompt Write a journal entry describing where in the universe you would like to be. How would you get to that place?

Share Information: Brochure, 229B

Grammar Daily Language Activities, 229I
Possessive Pronouns, 229J
Grammar Practice Book, 145–146

Spelling Posttest, 229H
Spelling Practice Book, 146

Weekly Assessment, 285–292

Differentiated Instruction 229M-229V **Differentiated Instruction 229M-229V** **Differentiated Instruction 229M-229V**

Small Group Options

What do I do in small groups?

Additional Instruction, Practice, and Extend Activities are provided for this week's tested skills.

Phonics	**Vocabulary**	**Comprehension**	**Fluency**
Decode Words with Endings *y* to *i*	**Words:** powered, declared, existed, artist's, pride **Strategy:** Word Parts/Possessives	**Strategy:** Make Inferences and Analyze **Skill:** Fact and Opinion	

Lesson Plan
TEACHER-LED SMALL GROUP

Instructional Navigator
Interactive Lesson Planner

	Day 1	**Day 2**
Approaching Level • **Additional Instruction/Practice** • **Tier 2 Instruction**	Leveled Reader Lesson 1, 229M • Vocabulary • Comprehension • Fluency	Leveled Reader Lesson 2, 229N • Vocabulary • Comprehension • Fluency **ELL** Name Possessives, 229O
On Level • **Practice**	Leveled Reader Lesson, 229Q • Vocabulary • Comprehension • Fluency **ELL** Leveled Reader, 229U–V	Leveled Reader Lesson, 229Q • Vocabulary • Comprehension • Fluency
Beyond Level • **Extend**	Leveled Reader Lesson, 229S • Vocabulary • Comprehension • Fluency	Leveled Reader Lesson, 229S • Vocabulary • Comprehension • Fluency

for Differentiated Instruction

Leveled Readers

GR Levels N–R
Matching students to text.

Also Available
LEVELED READER LIBRARY

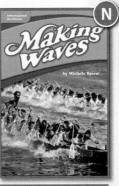

Approaching Level

- Benchmark 30
- Use other guided reading titles, N–P

On Level

- Benchmark 38
- Use other guided reading titles, P–R

Beyond Level

- Benchmark 40
- Use other guided reading titles, R–T

English Language Leveled Reader

On Level Reader sheltered for English Language Learner.

Leveled Reader Database
To search for additional Leveled Reader titles, go to **www.macmillanmh.com**

Day 3

Comprehension, 229O Vocabulary, 229O
Vocabulary, 229R
Self-Selected Reading, 229T

Day 4

Phonics, 229P Vocabulary, 229P
Study Skill, 229R
Vocabulary, 229T **ELL** Fact and Opinion, 229T

Day 5

Fluency, 229N Make Connections Across Texts, 229P
Make Connections Across Texts, 229R
Study Skill, 229T

Managing the Class

What do I do with the rest of my class?

Teacher-Led Small Groups

Cross-Curricular Workstations

Independent Activities

Leveled Reader Activities

Approaching

See inside back cover for activities

LEVELED PRACTICE

- Vocabulary, 163
- Comprehension: Fact and Opinion, 164
- Graphic Organizer, 165
- Fluency, 166
- Study Skill: Skim and Scan, 167
- Vocabulary Strategy: Possessives, 168
- Phonics, 169

⭐ **Approaching Practice Book A, 163–169**

A. Write the word from the box that can best replace the underlined word or words in each sentence.

powered	declared	artist's	existed	pride

1. Long ago some trains were <u>made to run</u> by steam engines.

    powered

2. The train conductor <u>said</u> that this was the last stop.

    declared

3. The workers who carefully repaired the antique cars feel great <u>honor</u> in the job they do.

    pride

4. Traffic signals were used even before cars <u>were invented</u>.

    existed

5. The painting of the train has the <u>creator's</u> signature in the corner.

    artist's

B. Choose one vocabulary word. Write a sentence that uses that word. Possible response provided.

6. I felt great <u>pride</u> when I won first place in the science

    contest.

Weekly Contract

| Name _____ | Date _____ |

My To-Do List

✓ Put a check next to the activities you complete.

📖 **Reading**
- ☐ Practice fluency
- ☐ Choose a book to read

🔤 **Word Study**
- ☐ Turn words into possessives
- ☐ Work with inflected endings

✏️ **Writing**
- ☐ Write a description
- ☐ Write about a ride

🔬 **Science**
- ☐ Research space satellites
- ☐ Organize note cards

🌐 **Social Studies**
- ☐ List ways of traveling
- ☐ Find pictures of vehicles

⚓ **Leveled Readers**
- ☐ Write About It!
- ☐ Content Connection

💻 **Technology**
- ☐ Vocabulary Puzzlemaker
- ☐ Fluency Solutions
- ☐ Listening Library
- ☐ www.macmillanmh.com

🖌 **Independent Practice**
- ☐ Practice Book, 163–169
- ☐ Grammar Practice Book, 141–146
- ☐ Spelling Practice Book, 141–146

Contracts   Unit 5 • A Carousel of Dreams 25

© Macmillan/McGraw-Hill

Teacher's Resource Book, page 25

• **Students use their Contracts to manage their time.**

HOME-SCHOOL CONNECTION

Pages 271–282

Independent Activities

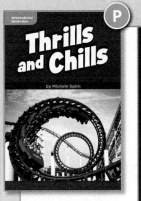

On Level

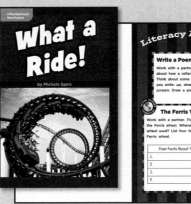

ELL

Beyond

On Level Practice Book O, 163–169

A. Fill in the blank in each sentence with the correct word from the box.

declared	artist's	existed	pride	powered

1. My computer is __powered__ by electricity.

2. "We will be landing in five minutes," __declared__ the pilot.

3. The pilot took great __pride__ in landing the plane smoothly.

4. It is hard to understand how people traveled long distances before trains __existed__.

5. This __artist's__ drawing of a carousel is very detailed.

B. Write a sentence using each vocabulary word. **Possible responses provided.**

6. pride __I have such pride in my work that I show all of my friends.__

7. artist's __The artist's work is on display at the museum.__

8. declared __The principal declared that we were having a fire-drill today.__

9. existed __Before computers existed people used typewriters to do their research papers.__

10. powered __In the future there may be cars that are powered by the sun.__

Beyond Practice Book B, 163–169

Do you like to travel by bike, car, train, airplane? Use all of the vocabulary words to write a paragraph describing your favorite way to travel. Include a title for your paragraph.
Possible response provided.

powered	declared	artist's	existed	pride

Traveling by Airplane

My favorite way to travel is by airplane. All over the wall of my room I have photographs and an artist's paintings of airplanes. It is hard to imagine going from the East Coast to the West Coast without airplanes. It must have taken a long time to go from Boston to Seattle before planes existed. Everytime I fly, I see airline employees taking pride in their airline. When I am buckled into my seat, I get excited when I hear the giant engines powered by thousands of gallons of fuel. And I am also thrilled after the pilot has declared our speed and altitude. I think traveling by plane is the best!

ELL Practice and Assessment, 142–143

Grade 3

Treasures

ELL Practice and Assessment

Macmillan/McGraw-Hill

Parent Letter

Take-Home Story

Turn the page for Cross-Curricular Activities.

Managing the Class

Cross-Curricular Activities

All activities reinforce this week's skills.

Reading

Objectives
- Read aloud with a partner.
- Write an opinion about a book.
- Select literature for daily reading enjoyment.

Word Study

Objectives
- Use an apostrophe (') and -s to make possessives.
- Make words with inflected endings.

Reading — Fluency
20 Minutes

- Choose a reading buddy. Take turns reading aloud page 166 of your Practice Book.
- Slow down when you come to hard words. Help each other pronounce hard words correctly.

Extension
- Read the page aloud again trying not to pause at hard words.
- Ask your partner how you did.
- Listen to the pronunciation of hard words on the audio disc.

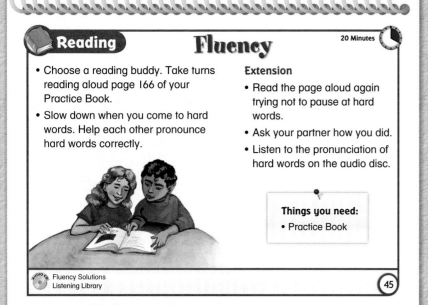

Things you need:
- Practice Book

Fluency Solutions
Listening Library

45

Word Study — Word Parts
20 Minutes

- Make a list of your favorite animals, such as cat, dog, horse, and elephant.
- Then add an apostrophe (') and -s to turn each word into a possessive noun.
- Use each possessive noun in a sentence.

Extension
- Suppose you lived on a farm. Write a short story about how your favorite animals would get along.

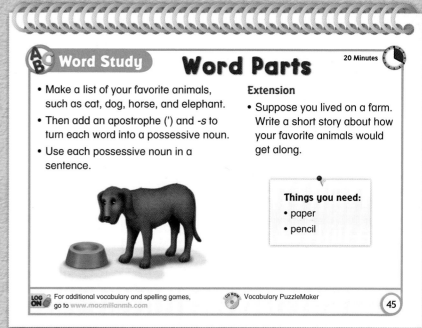

Things you need:
- paper
- pencil

For additional vocabulary and spelling games, go to www.macmillanmh.com

Vocabulary PuzzleMaker

45

Reading — Independent Reading
20 Minutes

- Choose a book you would like to read.
- Why did you choose it? List your reasons.
- Read the book.

Extension
- Write a paragraph in your response journal. Tell why you did or did not like the book.

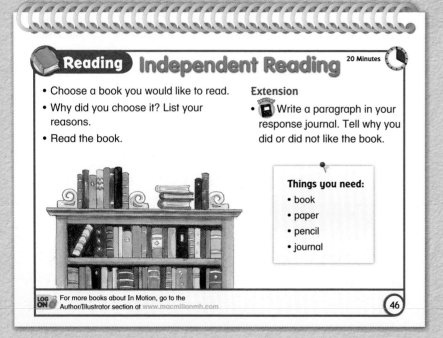

Things you need:
- book
- paper
- pencil
- journal

For more books about In Motion, go to the Author/Illustrator section at www.macmillanmh.com

46

Word Study — Inflected Endings
20 Minutes

- Write these words on note cards: try, trying, tries, and tried.
- Now make note cards for dry, drying, dries, and dried.
- Use the same spelling rules to add -ing, -es, and -ed to cry and fry. Make note cards for them.

Extension

Sort your cards into two piles. Make one pile for words with a -y and an ending. Make another pile for words with a -y changed to i and an ending.

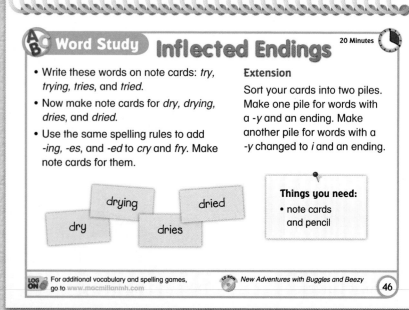

Things you need:
- note cards and pencil

For additional vocabulary and spelling games, go to www.macmillanmh.com

New Adventures with Buggles and Beezy

46

Independent Workstations

Writing

Objectives

- Write about traveling to a new place.
- Write a journal entry.

Science/Social Studies

Objectives

- Make lists of old and new kinds of transportation.
- Research information about satellites.

Writing — Descriptive Writing
20 Minutes

- Think about a time you traveled to a new place. How did you get there? Did you go by bus, car, train, boat, or plane?
- Write a paragraph. Tell about your trip.

Extension
- Read your paragraph to yourself. Add two or more descriptive details.

Things you need:
- paper
- pencil

45

Social Studies — Travel Through History
20 Minutes

- Talk with a partner about how people traveled long ago and how we travel now.
- Make a list of old kinds of transportation. Make a list of new kinds.

Extension
- Scan an encyclopedia or a history book. Find pictures of other vehicles.
- Add the vehicles you find to your lists.

Things you need:
- history book or encyclopedia
- paper and pencil

LOG ON Internet Research and Inquiry Activity
Students can find more facts at www.macmillanmh.com

45

Writing — What a Ride!
20 Minutes

- Think about a ride you have been on at a fair or fun park. Make believe you just got off it!
- Write a journal entry about your ride.

Extension
- Read your journal entry to some of your classmates.
- Ask if they could feel or picture what the ride was like.

Things you need:
- paper
- pencil

46

Science — Satellites
20 Minutes

- Do research in a science book or on the Internet. Find out how human-made satellites travel in space.
- Skim the articles. Find the most important information. Take notes on cards.

Extension
- Organize your note cards. Put the most important information on top.
- Give an oral summary of what you learned to a partner.

Things you need:
- science book or computer
- note cards and pencil

46

ORAL LANGUAGE
- Build Background
- Read Aloud
- Expand Vocabulary

 VOCABULARY
- Teach Words in Context
- Word Parts: Possessives

COMPREHENSION
- **Strategy:** Make Inferences and Analyze
- **Skill:** Fact and Opinion

SMALL GROUP OPTIONS
- Differentiated Instruction, pp. 229M–229V

Oral Language

Build Background

ACCESS PRIOR KNOWLEDGE

Present the following:

In Japan, many people take bullet trains that go about 180 miles per hour.

TALK ABOUT BEING IN MOTION

Discuss the weekly theme.

- What is your favorite way to travel?

- Do you like to move from place to place slowly or quickly? Why?

 FOCUS QUESTION Ask a volunteer to read aloud "Talk About It" on **Student Book** page 218 and describe the photograph.

- Why do you think someone might choose to travel by train instead of by car or airplane?

Talk About It

How many different ways can you think of that people get from one place to another?

 Find out more about movement and transportation at **www.macmillanmh.com**

IN MOTION

218

ENGLISH LANGUAGE LEARNERS

Access for All

Beginning **Activate Background Knowledge** Have students say what they can about the picture. Say: *This train is in motion.* Motion *means "movement."* Use gestures to show movement. Say: *We can travel by train. How else can we travel?* List the ways. Draw pictures to convey meaning. *Which way is your favorite?*

Intermediate **Generate Ideas** Have students describe the picture. Through discussion, generate ideas about other ways people can travel and write these on the board. Ask: *How have you traveled? Where have you traveled?*

Advanced **Make Comparisons** Complete the Intermediate task. Have students compare modes of transportation and give opinions about which is the "best" way to travel.

218

Read Aloud
Read "The Runner"

GENRE: Poetry
Review features of rhymed poetry:

- expresses a strong feeling or describes something
- is written in lines and often rhymes

LISTENING FOR A PURPOSE

Ask students to listen for comparative words and phrases about the runner in "The Runner" in the **Read-Aloud Anthology**. Choose from among the teaching suggestions.

Fluency Ask students to listen carefully as the poem is read aloud. Tell them to listen to your phrasing, expression, and tone of voice.

RESPOND TO THE POEM

Reread the poem line by line. Discuss the comparisons that the poet uses, such as *faster than the speed of light*. Ask students how these images help them picture the runner. Then ask them to make up more descriptions that compare the runner to other people and things.

Expand Vocabulary

Ask students to list several words or phrases that tell about being in motion, such as *speed of light, rocket*, and *spinning* and write a short poem that contains these words. Encourage students to use similes or other figurative language. Then have students present their poems to the class.

Picture Prompt

Tell students: Look at the picture. Write about what you see. You can write a poem, a story, a description, or use any other type of writing you like.

Technology

For an extended lesson plan and Web site activities for **oral language development,** go to **www.macmillanmh.com**

A Carousel of Dreams **219**

Vocabulary

TEACH WORDS IN CONTEXT

Use the following routine.

Routine

Define: Something that is **powered** is supplied with a source of energy.
Example: The car is powered by a hybrid engine.
Ask: What is something that is powered by batteries? EXAMPLE

- When a statement is **declared,** it is said firmly or with authority. "Humans will never live on Mars," she declared. What is a synonym for *declared*? (stated) SYNONYM

- Anything that once **existed** could be found. Large herds of buffalo once existed on the prairies. What are some things that once existed but are no longer around? PRIOR KNOWLEDGE

- An **artist's** paintbrush is a paintbrush that belongs to that artist. The artist's paintings are colorful. What are some other things that you might find in an artist's studio? DESCRIPTION

- **Pride** is a feeling of satisfaction in doing something well. I have pride in my ability to paint animals. What is something that you have pride in? COMPARE AND CONTRAST

Remind students they can find definitions of vocabulary words in the Student Book Glossary on pages 408–422.

Vocabulary

powered	artist's
declared	pride
existed	

Visions of the Future from the Past

What opinions did experts have about movement and transportation throughout history? Take a look.

Lord Kelvin, a famous scientist, 1800s

Opinion: Airplanes would never fly.

Was he right? No. On December 17, 1903, the Wright brothers made the first controlled flight in a **powered** airplane.

Jules Verne, science-fiction writer, in an 1870 novel

Opinion: People would be able to travel under water in airtight vessels.

Was he right?
Yes. Though submarines already **existed**, it would be decades before they could stay submerged for long-distance travel.

Lee DeForest, a pioneer in radio, TV, and radar, 1900s

Opinion: No person would ever reach the moon.

Was he right? No. On July 20, 1969, Neil Armstrong stepped onto the moon and **declared**, "That's one small step for man, one giant leap for mankind."

Leonardo da Vinci, artist, scientist, inventor, 1400s

Opinion: People would fly in a machine with an overhead propeller.

Was he right?
Yes. This **artist's** sketch, made about 1490, shows a helicopter 400 years before its invention.

220

Quick Check Do students understand word meanings?

During **Small Group Instruction**

If No → **Approaching Level** Vocabulary, p. 229P

If Yes → **On Level** Options, pp. 229Q–229R

Beyond Level Options, pp. 229S–229T

ELL   Access for All

Explain Talk about superheroes and what they do. Say: *Superheroes help people. They feel proud of what they do. They take pride in what they do. What do you take pride in?* Help students answer in complete sentences. Say: *What gives a car its energy to move? A car is powered by gasoline. What else is powered by gasoline?*

SMOOTH RIDING

This time line of inventions shows some real *movement!*

3800-3600 B.C.	The wheel
1783 A.D.	Hot air balloon Steamship
1831	Lawn mower
1885	Bicycle
1903	The Wright brothers' first flight
1908	Ford Model-T car
1939	Jet airplane
1980	In-line skates
1981	Space shuttle

LOG ON Find out more about transportation at **www.macmillanmh.com**

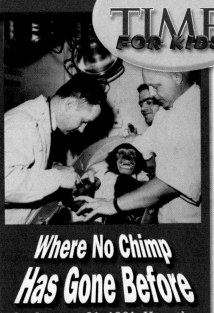

Where No Chimp Has Gone Before

On January 31, 1961, Ham the chimpanzee blasted off into space . . . and history books.

Ham's flight took him 156.5 miles into space at a speed of 5,800 miles per hour. The trip lasted 16.5 minutes. Then Ham's capsule splashed down into the Atlantic Ocean. Back on land, he gobbled up an apple and half an orange.

The U.S. space program took great **pride** in Ham. He paved the way for Alan Shepard to become the first American in space in May 1961.

After his space flight, Ham went on to live in a North Carolina zoo.

221

Vocabulary

eview last week's vocabulary words: **ift, yearned, tend, produce, sturdy, choolhouse,** and **kindhearted.**

On Level Practice Book O, page 163

A. Fill in the blank in each sentence with the correct word from the box.

declared	artist's	existed	pride	powered

1. My computer is ___powered___ by electricity.
2. "We will be landing in five minutes," ___declared___ the pilot.
3. The pilot took great ___pride___ in landing the plane smoothly.
4. It is hard to understand how people traveled long distances before trains ___existed___.
5. This ___artist's___ drawing of a carousel is very detailed.

B. Write a sentence using each vocabulary word.   Possible responses provided.

6. pride I have such pride in my work that I show all of my friends.
7. artist's The artist's work is on display at the museum.
8. declared The principal declared that we were having a fire-drill today.
9. existed Before computers existed people used typewriters to do their research papers.
10. powered In the future there may be cars that are powered by the sun.

⭐ **Approaching Practice Book A,** page 163

◆ **Beyond Practice Book B,** page 163

Vocabulary

Using the Strategies To figure out unfamiliar words, students can use phonics to decode words, look for word parts, look for context clues, or use a dictionary.

STRATEGY
WORD PARTS

Possessives Explain that possessives are nouns that show ownership. For example, "the boy's bicycle" is a bicycle that belongs to the boy.

■ When a singular noun shows ownership, it usually ends in an apostrophe (') and *s*, as in *boy's*.

■ For plural nouns that end in *s*, an apostrophe is added after the *s*, as in *boys'*.

Help students distinguish between possessives and contractions. In contractions, such as *isn't, he's,* and *won't,* the apostrophes stand for letters that are left out.

Point to the word *artist's* on **Student Book** page 220. Write *artist's* and *artists* on the board. Ask students to explain the difference between the two words. (*Artist's* is possessive. It ends in *'s* and it shows ownership; *artists* is plural and means "more than one artist.")

Read "Visions of the Future from the Past"

As students read "Visions of the Future from the Past," ask them to look for other possessives. (brothers', Ham's) Students will see more possessives in *A Carousel of Dreams.*

Objectives

- Make inferences and analyze
- Use academic language: *make inferences, analyze, fact, opinion*
- Identify facts and opinions

Materials

- Comprehension Transparency 23
- Leveled Practice Books, p. 164

Skills Trace

Fact and Opinion

Introduce	U2: 215A–B
Practice / Apply	U2: 216–219; Leveled Practice, 53–54
Reteach / Review	U2: 223M–T; U5: 221A–B, 222–227, 229M–T; Leveled Practice, 164–165
Assess	Weekly Tests; Unit 2, 5 Tests; Benchmark Tests A and B
Maintain	Unit 2: 249B; Unit 3: 347A

ELL

Give Examples Explain that a fact is something true and an opinion is how you feel about something. Say: *Every child has to go to school. Is this statement a fact or an opinion? School is easy. Is this statement a fact or an opinion?* Continue to give examples until students understand the difference.

Reread for
Comprehension

STRATEGY
MAKE INFERENCES AND ANALYZE

Authors don't always tell a reader every detail. Readers often have to **analyze,** or carefully look at, the information and then **make inferences** about it. To make inferences, good readers use what they know and clues in the selection to figure out details that the author did not include. When readers make inferences about information that is left out of a selection, they can better understand the events or people that the selection is about.

SKILL
FACT AND OPINION

EXPLAIN

- A **fact** is a statement that can be proved true.

- An **opinion** shows what a person or group believes, thinks, or feels about something or someone.

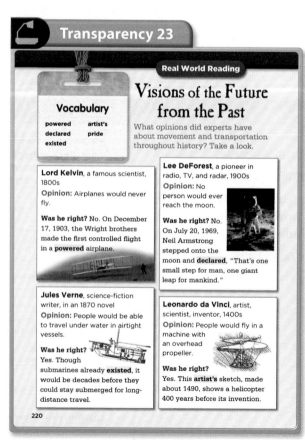

Transparency 23

Real World Reading

Visions of the Future from the Past

Vocabulary

powered   artist's
declared   pride
existed

What opinions did experts have about movement and transportation throughout history? Take a look.

Lord Kelvin, a famous scientist, 1800s
Opinion: Airplanes would never fly.

Was he right? No. On December 17, 1903, the Wright brothers made the first controlled flight in a **powered** airplane.

Jules Verne, science-fiction writer, in an 1870 novel
Opinion: People would be able to travel under water in airtight vessels.

Was he right? Yes. Though submarines already **existed**, it would be decades before they could stay submerged for long-distance travel.

Lee DeForest, a pioneer in radio, TV, and radar, 1900s
Opinion: No person would ever reach the moon.

Was he right? No. On July 20, 1969, Neil Armstrong stepped onto the moon and **declared**, "That's one small step for man, one giant leap for mankind."

Leonardo da Vinci, artist, scientist, inventor, 1400s
Opinion: People would fly in a machine with an overhead propeller.

Was he right? Yes. This **artist's** sketch, made about 1490, shows a helicopter 400 years before its invention.

220

Student Book page 220 available on Comprehension Transparency 23

- Some words that signal opinions are *I feel, I believe, the most, the best,* or *probably.*

MODEL

Reread the first information box in "Visions of the Future from the Past" on **Student Book** page 220.

Think Aloud I see that in the 1800s Lord Kelvin thought that airplanes would never fly. This is an opinion, not a fact. It could not be proved that airplanes would never fly. The clue word *opinion* in the fact box tells me this. In the same box, I see that the Wright brothers made the first flight in 1903. This is a fact. It can be proved true. As I read on, I will look for other facts and opinions.

GUIDED PRACTICE

Help students identify an opinion and a fact in the information box about Lee DeForest. (Opinion: No person would ever reach the moon. Fact: On July 20, 1969, Neil Armstrong stepped onto the moon.)

APPLY

Have students identify the opinion and the fact in the information box about Leonardo da Vinci. (Opinion: People would fly in a machine with an overhead propeller. Fact: The helicopter is a machine that flies with the help of an overhead propeller.)

RESEARCH
Why It Matters

English Language Learners Research indicates that to support second language readers' comprehension, teachers must develop the necessary background, vocabulary base, and the text content and structures to provide students with a solid foundation.

Josefina V. Tinajero

LOG ON Log on to
www.macmillanmh.com

On Level Practice Book O, page 164

A **fact** is something that can be proven to be true.
  Example: *The lawn mower was invented in 1831.*
An **opinion** is the writer's feelings or beliefs.
  Example: *The best summer job is mowing lawns.*

**Identify three facts and two opinions in the passage.
Then write each on the lines below.** **Possible responses provided.**

  Skateboarding is fun. It is also one of the fastest and best ways to get from place to place. Skateboarding began in the 1950s. Back then surfers wanted a way to get around when the weather and waves were not good for surfing. Surfers nailed the bases of roller skate wheels to the front and back of wooden boards. They used these boards to skateboard up and down the streets.
  In 1959 people could buy skateboards in stores. In 1963 the first skateboard contest was held in a school in Hermosa, California. The first outdoor skateboard park was built in Florida in 1976.
  Today skateboarding is still fun. I believe it is also one of the safest sports as long as you wear the right safety equipment.

1. Fact: Skateboarding began in the 1950s.
2. Fact: In 1959 skateboards went on sale.
3. Fact: The first outdoor skateboard park was built in Florida in 1976.
4. Opinion: Skateboarding is fun.
5. Opinion: I believe it is also one of the safest sports as long as you wear the right safety equipment.

Quick Check **Can students identify facts and opinions?**

During **Small Group Instruction**

If No → **Approaching Level** Comprehension, p. 229O

If Yes → **On Level** Options, pp. 229Q–229R

Beyond Level Options, pp. 229S–229T

 Approaching Practice Book A, page 164

◆ **Beyond Practice Book B,** page 164

Read

MAIN SELECTION

- *A Carousel of Dreams*
- **Skill:** Fact and Opinion

TEST PREP
- "Getting a Free Ride"
- **Test Strategy:** On My Own

WRITING
- **Tested Writing:** Personal Narrative
- **Writing Workshop:** Expository

SMALL GROUP OPTIONS

- Differentiated Instruction, pp. 229M–229V

Comprehension

GENRE: NONFICTION ARTICLE

Have a student read the definition of Nonfiction Article on **Student Book** page 222. Students should look for information about the topic of this informational nonfiction, carousels.

STRATEGY
MAKE INFERENCES AND ANALYZE

Good readers use their own experiences and clues in the article to figure out information the author has left out. This is called **making inferences and analyzing**. It helps the reader understand the article and make better predictions.

SKILL
FACT AND OPINION

Facts are statements that can be proved to be true. **Opinions** show what a person or group believes, thinks, or feels about something or someone.

Comprehension

Genre

A **Nonfiction Article** gives information about a real person, place, or event.

Make Inferences and Analyze

Fact and Opinion
A fact can be proved to be true. An opinion is a belief that does not have to be supported by facts.

A Carousel of Dreams

The creatures on the Children's Carousel at Riverbank State Park (above) were copied from kids' drawings, like the one below.

The carousel at Riverbank State Park in New York City is probably the most fantastic carousel in the country. It doesn't hold the usual herd of painted ponies. Instead, giant spiders pull a chariot, and a plaid zebra prances beside a two-headed octopus. These creatures were invented by kids. Milo Mottola, 32, is the artist who turned the kids' drawings into carousel critters.

222

Vocabulary

Vocabulary Words Review the tested vocabulary words: **powered, declared, existed, artist's,** and **pride**.

Selection Words Students may find these words difficult. Pronounce the words and present their meanings as necessary.

prefer (p. 223): to like someone or something more than someone or something else

craftspeople (p. 223): people who use special skills to make things

attraction (p. 224): something interesting or enjoyable for people to see or do

Mottola believed kids should be a big part of his carousel project, so he held drawing classes in Riverbank State Park. The kids created more than 1,000 drawings of creatures. It was tough to choose only 32 of them for the carousel. "They were all my favorites!" Mottola **declared**.

When 9-year-old Grover Austin heads to the carousel, he hops on the green lion. He thinks it's the best because he created it! The **artist's** signature is carved on the floor beneath each animal. The original drawing hangs above it.

The Children's Carousel at Riverbank State Park is one of only 200 major carousels that remain today. Amusement parks and fairs now have faster rides. People today seem to prefer rides that are scarier or more exciting than the gentle carousels. But during the early 1900s, carousels were very popular. About 6,000 of them **existed** in the United States.

History in the Round

At one time, carousels were considered rides for adults, not kids. Most carousels were created by craftspeople who came to the U.S. from other countries. They had a lot of **pride** in their designs of fancy horses and chariots. Chariots are the carousel seats that are like benches or little carriages. Most of these old-style carousels are gone. Some were destroyed by fires and other disasters. Many were simply not taken care of. Some originals, however, are still standing and most likely are still making people happy. One of them is in San Diego, California. Another one is in Memphis, Tennessee.

Milo Mottola with some of the carousel's kid artists and their creations

223

Read Together

If your students need support to read the Main Selection, use the prompts to guide comprehension and model how to complete the graphic organizer. Encourage students to read aloud.

Read Independently

If your students can read the Main Selection independently, have them read and complete the graphic organizer. Have students adjust their reading rate based on their purpose for reading.

If your students need an alternate selection, choose the **Leveled Readers** that match their instructional level.

Technology

Story available on **Listening Library Audio CD**

Preview and Predict

Ask students to read the title, preview the illustrations, and note questions and predictions about the article. What do they think they will learn about carousels?

Set Purposes

FOCUS QUESTION Ask: What is the most fantastic merry-go-round in the country? Point out the Fact and Opinion Chart on **Leveled Practice Book** page 165. Students will fill it in as they read.

Read *A Carousel of Dreams*

1 **STRATEGY**
MAKE INFERENCES AND ANALYZE

Teacher Think Aloud Only 32 drawings of creatures were chosen for the carousel. The author doesn't tell why. Use your own experiences and clues from the selection to make an inference about how Milo Mottola decided which creatures to use.

Encourage students to apply the strategy in a Think Aloud.

Student Think Aloud The text says that this is the country's most fantastic carousel and mentions several different kinds of unusual animals—a giant spider, a green lion, a plaid zebra, and a two-headed octopus. Using this information and what I know, I can make the inference that Mottola chose interesting and very different animals for the carousel. If I were building a carousel, that is what I would do.

Develop Comprehension

2 FACT AND OPINION

Is the first sentence on page 224 a fact or an opinion? How can you tell? (It is a fact. It tells when the Seaport Village carousel was built. This is a fact that I can prove.)

3 FACT AND OPINION

Read the fifth and sixth sentences in the first paragraph on page 224. Which is a fact? Which is an opinion? How can you tell? Let's place them on a Fact and Opinion chart. (The fifth sentence tells Brad Perron's opinion: The Seaport Village carousel is one of the two best in the nation. I see the signal word *best*. The sixth sentence tells that Perron owns a company that fixes carousels. This is a fact. It can be proved.)

Fact	Opinion
Perron owns a company that fixes carousels.	The carousel in Seaport Village is one of the two best in the nation.

---

2 The carousel that twirls in Seaport Village, San Diego, was built in 1895. The 41 hand-carved horses have natural horsehair tails. The 13 other animals include a giraffe, a dragon, a teddy bear, an elephant, a camel, a dog, and a lion. They were all made by hand, too. **3** "This is one of the two best carousels in the entire nation," says Brad Perron. He's the owner of a company that fixes old carousels so they are like new again. "They don't make them this way anymore," says Perron. He's talking about animals carved by hand from wood. Newer carousel animals are usually made out of material that is mostly plastic. Some people think the old carousels were better than newer ones.

Riders of the Grand Carousel in Memphis, Tennessee, can choose to ride one of the 48 wooden horses or two hand-carved chariots. Built in 1909, the carousel spun its magic in Chicago, Illinois, for about ten years. Now it is a famous attraction in Tennessee's Libertyland Amusement Park. This carousel is one of a kind. It is so important that it is listed in the National Register of Historic Places.

The Grand Carousel in Memphis, Tennessee

224

Comprehension

Fact and Opinion

Explain Tell students that **facts** are statements that can be proved to be true. **Opinions** show what a person or group believes, thinks, or feels about something or someone.

Discuss Write: *I believe that Milo Mottola is the best artist in New York.* Ask: *Is this a fact or opinion?* Help students see that this is an opinion because it cannot be proved. It also includes the clue word *best*.

Apply Ask students to read the first paragraph on page 223 and tell one fact and one opinion. Have them explain how they know. (Fact: Kids created more than 1000 drawings. Opinion: Motolla says, "They were all my favorites!" The first sentence is a fact because it can be proved. The second is an opinion because it shows what Mottola believes. It can't be proved.)

These and other historic carousels are **powered** by a motor in the center of the ride. The motor is covered up by panels with pretty drawings and carvings on them. Older carousels even have mirrors and special music that blares from nearby speakers. Blinking, bright lights call riders to come take a spin.

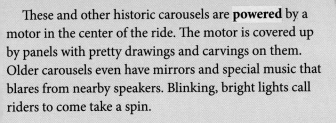

Did You Know?

* The earliest known carousel in the U.S. appeared in Salem, Massachusetts, in 1799.

* Some historic carousel horses were made with brass rings so that people could try to grab on for a free ride.

* Usually, the fanciest and most decorated horses on a carousel are the ones facing the outside.

* Many original carousel horses built in the early 1900s had real horsehair.

* What's the difference between a carousel and a merry-go-round? Traditionally, carousels had only horses, but merry-go-rounds included other animals.

* Original wooden carousel horses today cost between $200 and $80,000 each.

Think and Compare

1. Brad Perron says that the carousel at Seaport Village in San Diego is "one of the two best carousels in the entire nation." Is that a fact or an opinion? How do you know?

2. How were the creatures on the carousel at Riverbank State Park created?

3. If you could choose to ride a carousel or a faster, scarier ride at an amusement park, which would you choose? Why?

4. Compare the motion of the space capsule that Ham the chimpanzee rode with the motion of a carousel.

225

Quick Check
Can students identify facts and opinions?

During **Small Group Instruction**

If No → **Approaching Level** Leveled Reader Lessons, pp. 229M–229N

If Yes → **On Level** Options, pp. 229Q–229R

Beyond Level Options, pp. 229S–229T

PERSONAL RESPONSE

Have students write about their predictions and purposes. Were they correct? What did they learn about carousels? Have students write about ways they have experienced motion, choosing the writing mode that best suits their purpose.

Comprehension Check

SUMMARIZE

Have students give a summary of *A Carousel of Dreams* by paraphrasing the main ideas.

THINK AND COMPARE

Sample answers are given.

1. **Fact and Opinion:** This is an opinion. It has the signal word *best*. It tells how Brad Perron feels. It cannot be proved true.

2. **Details:** Children drew creatures. Then Milo Mottola chose 32 of them and made creatures for his carousel that looked like the drawings.

3. **Analyze/Text-To-Self:** Students may say they are nervous about fast, scary rides, or that such rides make them sick. They may also say faster, scarier rides are more exciting than carousels.

FOCUS QUESTION

4. **Evaluate/Text-To-Text:** Ham's ride was much faster than a carousel ride. His space capsule traveled at 5,800 miles per hour. The capsule also went straight up into the sky and then came back down. A carousel moves around in a circle.

Objectives

- Read fluently with echo-reading
- Review summarizing a nonfiction selection
- 97–117 WCPM

Materials

- Fluency Transparency 23
- Fluency Solutions Audio CD
- Leveled Practice Books, p. 166

 Transparency 23

Mottola believed kids should be a big part of his carousel project, so he held drawing classes in Riverbank State Park. The kids created more than 1,000 drawings of creatures. It was tough to choose only 32 of them for the carousel. "They were all my favorites!" Mottola declared.

When 9-year-old Grover Austin heads to the carousel, he hops on the green lion. He thinks it's the best because he created it! The artist's signature is carved on the floor beneath each animal. The original drawing hangs above it.

Fluency Transparency 23

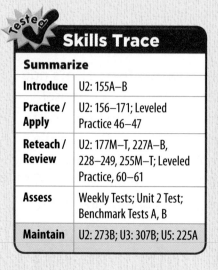 **Skills Trace**

Summarize	
Introduce	U2: 155A–B
Practice / Apply	U2: 156–171; Leveled Practice 46–47
Reteach / Review	U2: 177M–T, 227A–B, 228–249, 255M–T; Leveled Practice, 60–61
Assess	Weekly Tests; Unit 2 Test; Benchmark Tests A, B
Maintain	U2: 273B; U3: 307B; U5: 225A

Fluency

Repeated Reading: Punctuation

EXPLAIN/MODEL

Model reading aloud **Transparency 23.** Have students echo-read after you. Point out the punctuation used in the paragraphs: periods, commas, exclamation points, quotation marks, and an apostrophe. Discuss the function of each.

PRACTICE

Divide students into two groups. The first group reads the passage a sentence at a time. The second group echo-reads. Then groups switch roles. Remind students to come to a full stop when they see a period, pause when they see a comma, and read with strong feeling when they see an exclamation mark. For additional practice, have students use **Leveled Practice Book** page 166 or Fluency Solutions.

Comprehension

MAINTAIN SKILL
SUMMARIZE

EXPLAIN/MODEL

A summary is a short statement that tells the most important ideas in a paragraph, passage, or selection. Good readers **summarize** as they read so that they can keep track of the main idea.

Model how to summarize "Where No Chimp Has Gone Before" on page 221.

PRACTICE

Ask students: What is the topic of the article *A Carousel of Dreams?* How would you summarize the main idea on page 222? (The topic is carousels. The carousel in Riverbank State park has 32 unusual creatures that kids designed.)

Have students create idea webs about different kinds of carousels.

Research
Study Skills

 ## Skim and Scan a Nonfiction Article

EXPLAIN

Tell students that when they look for information to answer questions, they can skim and scan to find what they are looking for quickly. Discuss how to **skim** and **scan** a nonfiction article.

- To **skim,** quickly read each paragraph, looking for main ideas and important details.

- To find a key word or a fact, **scan** the article. To scan, move your eyes quickly over the text. When you locate a **key word,** stop scanning so you can carefully read information about it. Scan a book's table of contents and headings to locate sections that are worth skimming and scanning to find information.

- When skimming or scanning, check that the information answers the question. If it does not fit, skim or scan again, or find another source.

Display **Transparency 5.**

MODEL

Think Aloud I want to find out why the Model T was important. To find where the key word *Model T* is mentioned, I will scan the text. Then I will skim for main ideas. When I scan and skim the first paragraph, I find that the Model T was the first sturdy automobile. In the next paragraph I learn that 10,000 Model T's were sold in the first year they were made and that Ford opened a factory in Michigan. I do not see any information in the last paragraph about the Model T, so I will go back and read the first two paragraphs carefully to make sure I know why the Model T was important.

PRACTICE

Have students skim and scan Transparency 5 to answer these questions:

When was the first Model T sold? Did you skim or scan to find the answer? Why? (1908; I scanned until I found the key word *Model T* and the word *sold* in the second paragraph.) Which paragraph tells about automobile companies today? Did you skim or scan to find the answer? Why? (the third paragraph; I skimmed each paragraph looking for the main idea and details until I found this information.)

Objective

- Use skim and scan strategies to find information

Materials

- Study Skills Transparency 5
- Leveled Practice Books, p. 167

 Transparency 5

The Model T

When Henry Ford offered the Model T automobile for sale, he proudly showed off a car that was sturdy enough to travel over bumpy country roads without breaking down. Ford charged about $850 for the automobile, a price many working people could afford.

Ford sold the first Model T in 1908. One year later, he had sold 10,000 Model T's. Then he opened a big factory in Michigan. Some people did not think this was a good idea. They thought the automobile was just another fad and that people would stop buying them soon enough.

As you know, those predictions turned out to be incorrect. Today, many automobile companies make and sell many popular cars and trucks.

Study Skills Transparency 5

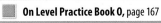 **On Level Practice Book O,** page 167

Skim means to read over a passage quickly to identify the main ideas. **Scan** means to search through a passage for key words or ideas.

Skim and scan the passage to help you answer the following questions. Possible responses provided.

Many people think of a motorcycle as a bicycle with a motor. In some ways they are right. Today's motorcycles run by gas engines. But that was not always the case.

The motorcycle was invented in 1867 by Sylvester Howard Roper. It was powered by a steam engine. Mr. Roper also invented a steam-engine car.

The first gas-powered motorcycle was invented in 1885 in Germany. Gottlieb Daimler built this motorcycle by attaching an engine to a wooden bicycle.

1. What is the main idea of this passage? The main idea is the history of motorcycles.

2. What did you do to figure out the main idea? I skimmed the passage for key words to find the main idea.

3. Draw a circle around the key words. How did they help you figure out the main idea? They are the important words in the passage.

4. When was the first motorcycle invented? It was invented in 1867.

 ★ **Approaching Practice Book A,** page 167

◆ **Beyond Practice Book B,** page 167

Answer Questions

Test Strategy: On My Own

REVIEW

Review with students the test strategies that they have learned in the previous units: **Right There, Author and Me,** and **Think and Search.** Have students use these strategies to answer questions 1–3 and identify the strategy they used. (Question 1: C, *Right There*; Question 2: B, *Think and Search*; Question 3: D, *Right There*)

EXPLAIN

- Good test takers know when a question is asking for an opinion. The answer will not be in the text, but information in the text will help you form an opinion.

- **Use what you know** Connect the ideas or events in the selection to your own thoughts, feelings, and experiences. Use your own ideas in your answer.

Tell students that good test takers know that when the answer cannot be found in the selection, they must use the **On My Own** strategy. To do this, they form their own ideas to answer a question.

MODEL

Question 4 Read question 4.

Think Aloud This question is asking me for an opinion based on what I know and the topic of the article. The answer will not be stated in the article, but information in it will help me form an opinion. I need to know why bike stealing is not a problem.

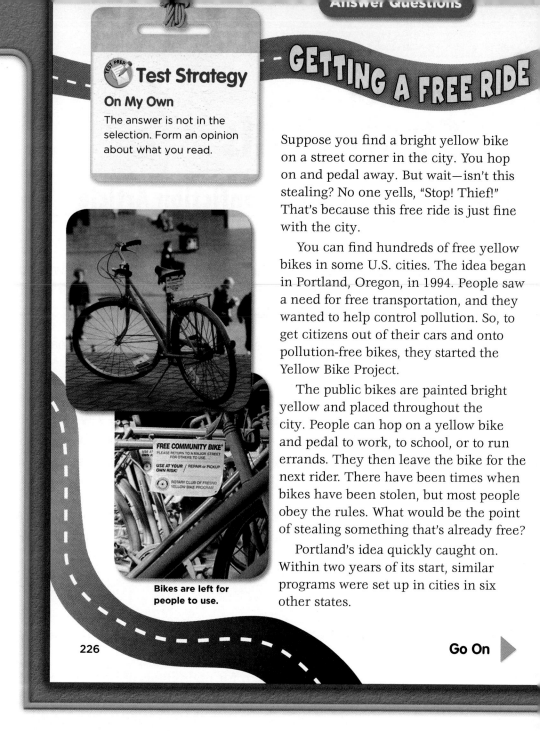

Test Strategy

On My Own

The answer is not in the selection. Form an opinion about what you read.

GETTING A FREE RIDE

Suppose you find a bright yellow bike on a street corner in the city. You hop on and pedal away. But wait—isn't this stealing? No one yells, "Stop! Thief!" That's because this free ride is just fine with the city.

You can find hundreds of free yellow bikes in some U.S. cities. The idea began in Portland, Oregon, in 1994. People saw a need for free transportation, and they wanted to help control pollution. So, to get citizens out of their cars and onto pollution-free bikes, they started the Yellow Bike Project.

The public bikes are painted bright yellow and placed throughout the city. People can hop on a yellow bike and pedal to work, to school, or to run errands. They then leave the bike for the next rider. There have been times when bikes have been stolen, but most people obey the rules. What would be the point of stealing something that's already free?

Portland's idea quickly caught on. Within two years of its start, similar programs were set up in cities in six other states.

Bikes are left for people to use.

226

Go On ▶

GUIDED PRACTICE

Which information in the selection talks about the bikes being stolen? (The third paragraph says some bikes are stolen but most people obey the rules. The bikes are bright yellow, and everyone can use them so there would be no point in stealing them.)

In order to form an opinion, what do you have to do? (Use what I know.) What do you know? (People don't usually steal items that can be easily identified, and they don't steal things that they can use any time they want.)

Directions: Answer the questions.

1. **Why was the Yellow Bike Project started?**

   A   to teach people who don't have a bike how to ride

   B   to teach bike safety and rules in cities

   C   to help control pollution by reducing the use of cars

   D   to sell more bicycles in cities

2. **Which of the following is a FACT about the Yellow Bike Project?**

   A   The bikes cause pollution.

   B   The idea began in Portland, Oregon.

   C   People need low-cost transportation.

   D   Yellow bikes are sold to the public.

3. **The photo caption helps explain that**

   A   yellow bike programs are found in many places.

   B   the bikes are painted bright yellow.

   C   the idea of free bikes caught on quickly.

   D   the bikes are left for the next rider.

4. **Why is stealing not a problem with the Yellow Bike Project?**

5. **Why should cities have programs to cut down on air pollution? Give your opinion and list several reasons why you feel this way.**

Tip

Form an opinion.

STOP   227

Sample Answer: Because the bikes are painted yellow, they are easy to recognize as public bikes, so people would not be so likely to steal them.

APPLY

Question 5 Read Question 5.

- Have students use the On My Own strategy to find an answer.

- After students have chosen an answer, ask: Which words in the question are key words? (programs to cut down on air pollution, opinion, reasons, why you feel this way)

- What does this question ask you to do? How do you know? (It asks me to state what I believe about programs that cut down on air pollution. I know this because the question asks for my opinion.)

- What do you know about the topic? (Cities are crowded and have a lot of cars and trucks that add to air pollution. Pollution makes it hard for people and animals to breathe. Because of pollution, they get sick more often. I also know that pollution makes buildings dirty.)

Possible answer: Cities should have programs to cut down on air pollution because many people and animals live and work there. There are many cars on the streets and factories that can pollute the air. People cannot get away from air pollution because they have to share small spaces. If there were more programs in cities to cut down on air pollution, people and animals would be healthier.

Writing Prompt

EXPLAIN

Before you begin to write, find the following information:

- What mode or type of writing is described in the prompt?

- What is the purpose for writing?

- Does the prompt tell the form or format for the writing?

- Who is the audience?

MODEL

Determine the writing mode Read aloud the prompt above the student model, emphasizing the words *you went* and *your experience*. What is the prompt asking this student to write? (a story about the student's own experience)

What clues tell the student to write a personal narrative? (you, your experience, write a story)

Determine the purpose Ask: What clues tell the student what his or her personal narrative should be about? (a first ride on a carousel or other ride)

Determine the form Ask: What clues tell the student the form of the personal narrative? (write a story in three paragraphs; your experience)

Determine the audience Does the prompt tell the student who to write to? (no) Who is the audience? (the teacher)

Write to a Prompt

In "A Carousel of Dreams" you read about old and new carousels. Rides such as carousels are entertaining and exciting. Tell about the first time you went on a carousel or another ride. Write a story in three paragraphs describing your experience.

I listed all my ideas before I started writing.

Giddyap, Horsey!

I gave my blue ticket to the man and ran to the horse I had chosen. I climbed up and held the gold pole with both hands. Loud music started, and the carousel began to turn.

My beautiful horse galloped up and down. The purple-gray mane looked like it was waving in the air. My saddle was painted bright red, blue, and yellow. The horse was grayish with smoky black spots. It was the best horse on the carousel!

When the ride stopped, I looked at the other people. A little kid about 2 years old had started to cry. A grandma sat on a bench with a baby on her lap. The baby's eyes were really big! Some big kids looked disappointed that the ride was over. This was my first carousel ride. I rode that same horse three more times that day!

228

SCORING RUBRIC

4 Points	**3** Points	**2** Points	**1** Point
Writing is on topic and interesting.	Writing is on topic.	Writing is generally on topic.	Writing may show little or no development of topic, but may contain meaningful vocabulary.
There is a clear beginning, middle, and end.	There is an attempt at sequence or development of thought.	There is an attempt to get sentences on paper.	There is an attempt to get words on paper.
Writing generally shows accuracy in punctuation and capitalization.	The writing holds the reader's attention.	Sentences may be simple or incomplete with limited vocabulary.	Written vocabulary is limited.
	May have errors that do not interfere with understanding.	Errors may make understanding difficult.	Writing shows no use of writing conventions.

Writing Prompt

In "A Carousel of Dreams" you read that carousels used to be very popular rides. In three paragraphs, write about your favorite ride at an amusement park or a fair. Tell about a time you rode on it, what you liked about it, and why it is your favorite ride. Make sure your story has a beginning, a middle, and an ending.

Writer's Checklist

☑ Ask yourself, who will read my story?
☑ Think about your purpose for writing.
☑ Plan your writing before beginning.
☑ Use details to support your story.
☑ Be sure your story has a beginning, a middle, and an ending.
☑ Use your best spelling, grammar, and punctuation.

229

Picture Prompt

For further timed writing practice, use the picture prompt on page 166 of the *Teacher's Resource Book.*

Teacher's Resource Book, page 166

Write to a picture prompt. Look at the photograph below. If you could go anywhere in the world, where would you go and how would you get there? Write a story about your trip.

 Writing Tips

• Use a graphic organizer to organize your thoughts.
• Write your story on lined paper.
• Proofread your story.

GUIDED PRACTICE

Read the sample narrative and help students use the Writer's Checklist to determine whether the narrative includes the correct mode, purpose, form, and audience stated in the prompt.

Mode: clues—your favorite, your story

Purpose: clues—write about your favorite ride at a fair or amusement park, what you liked about it, why it is your favorite

Form: clues—make sure your story has a beginning, a middle, and an ending

Audience: clues—no clues, write the story for the teacher

APPLY

Have students explain how clue words in the Writing Prompt on page 228 helped them determine that they should write a personal narrative. Be sure they mention the mode, purpose, form, and audience. Point out that no audience is listed, so they should write for the teacher.

TIMED WRITING PRACTICE

Have students practice writing to the prompt by simulating a test-taking situation. Tell students that after they have analyzed the prompt, they will have 45 minutes to write their personal narratives.

Tell students: You may use scrap paper to organize your thoughts on a story map before you begin writing. I will tell you when to begin, and I will tell you when you have 15 minutes left to finish the narrative. Use the writer's checklist to make sure that your writing is organized and error-free.

Writing Workshop

WRITING WORKSHOP
- Expository
- Research and Inquiry

WORD STUDY
- ✓ Words in Context
- ✓ **Word Parts:** Possessives
- **Phonics:** Endings *y* to *i*
- Vocabulary Building

SPELLING
- ✓ Endings *y* to *i*

GRAMMAR
- ✓ Possessive Pronouns

SMALL GROUP OPTIONS
- Differentiated Instruction, pp. 229M–229V

Speaking and Listening

Have students read their brochures aloud. Share these strategies.

SPEAKING STRATEGIES
- Practice your presentation beforehand.
- Use photos or drawings to engage the audience and gestures or facial expressions to emphasize key points.
- Speak at an appropriate rate and volume.

LISTENING STRATEGIES
- Look at the speaker.
- Tell how verbal and nonverbal clues help your understanding.
- Draw conclusions about the information you learn.

Expository Writing: Brochure

Day 1 | Generate Questions

DISCUSS THE TOPIC

Direct students to the time line on page 221 in the **Student Book.** Explain that they will research one form of transportation and then create an informative brochure. Show some examples of brochures. Tell students that their brochures should include a conclusion about the importance of that form of transportation. Point out the Internet Link at the end of the passage that will help them with their research.

Ask students what they would like to learn about different forms of transportation. Draw a KWL chart on the board and together fill in the first two columns.

What I Know	What I Want to Know	What I Learned
The first hot air balloon ride took place in 1753.	Who built the first hot air balloon? How do people use hot air balloons today?	

Have students create their own KWL chart to help them generate questions and narrow the focus of their topic. Have them reread their questions and think about the kind of information they will need to answer them. For example, will they need facts? Diagrams? Photographs? Ask students where they might find the information they need.

Day 2 | Find Information

SKIMMING AND SCANNING

Suggest that students use a variety of sources. Remind them that skimming and scanning can help them quickly find the best sources for their research project.

- Tell students that skimming helps readers get a general idea about the kind of information a source contains. To skim, read titles, headings, and key words. Look carefully at the table of contents for the best sections to skim.
- Skim the ending. Writers often summarize the most important ideas in the text at the end.
- To scan, have students look for specific information, such as key words from questions they placed on their KWL charts.

EVALUATE SOURCES

Remind students to evaluate the information by asking themselves questions about what they are reading.

- Is the information accurate?
- Is the information up to date?
- Who is the author? Is he or she an expert source?
- Will this information help me to write my brochure?
- Is this material too difficult to read? Do I need to find another source?

Day 3 Organize Information

TAKE NOTES

Have students take notes on their topic. Use **Transparency 89** to show students how to organize their research and keep track of the sources they used. For each source, they should include important information such as the author's name, the title of the book, article, or Web site, and other publishing information.

CREATE AN OUTLINE

Show **Transparency 90** and discuss with students how they can use their notes to create an outline. Remind students to list main ideas after Roman numerals and to list supporting details after capital letters. Explain that their outlines will help them draft their brochures.

Transparency 90

I. First hot air balloon flight
  A. Montgolfier brothers made balloon
  B. duck, sheep, rooster took ride
  C. France, 1783
II. Balloons today
  A. Go as high as 65,000 feet
  B. Cross oceans and around world
  C. U. S. Navy uses them to move things
  D. Quiet way to travel
  E. races

Writing Transparency 90   © Macmillan/McGraw-Hill

Writing Transparency 90

Day 4 Synthesize and Write

DRAFT

Have students use their outlines to carefully organize and write a draft of their brochure and include a title, main ideas, and details.

REVISE

Show **Transparency 91** and discuss the draft. Then display **Transparency 92** and discuss the changes. Have students revise their writing, exchange brochures, and review them.

PROOFREAD

Remind students to read their brochures carefully and to check spelling, punctuation, and grammar. Have them check all possessive pronouns.

Day 5 Share Information

PUBLISH

To publish their brochures, students should make a neat final copy, typing or using legible handwriting. They should use standard margins and proper spacing of words and sentences.

PRESENTATION IDEAS

Students can present the information by acting as tour guides at a museum, or they can role-play a museum employee who uses the brochures to answer visitors' questions.

EVALUATE

To evaluate student writing, use the 6-point scoring rubric. Check that facts are organized logically.

SCORING RUBRIC

Excellent	Good	Fair	Unsatisfactory
Ideas and Content Focused and to the point	**Ideas and Content** Fairly well focused	**Ideas and Content** Not clearly presented	**Ideas and Content** Does not have a clear focus
Organization Contains only information about the topic	**Organization** Contains some information that is not about the chosen topic	**Organization** Has information that does not relate to topic	**Organization** Contains information that is not about the topic
Voice Voice is natural and sounds as though the writer is talking with the reader	**Voice** Sometimes sounds more like the research than the writer	**Voice** Stilted and unnatural	**Voice** Like an entry in an encyclopedia
Word Choice Uses vivid words	**Word Choice** Accurate and descriptive	**Word Choice** Vague and uninteresting	**Word Choice** Words are used inaccurately
Sentence Fluency Has complete sentences of various lengths and types	**Sentence Fluency** Has complete sentences with some variety	**Sentence Fluency** Functional but little variety	**Sentence Fluency** Incomplete or confusing sentences
Conventions Mostly free of errors in usage, spelling, and mechanics	**Conventions** Few errors in usage, spelling, and mechanics	**Conventions** Errors in spelling, usage, and mechanics interfere with reading	**Conventions** Repeated errors in spelling, mechanics, and usage

Objectives

- Apply knowledge of word meanings and context clues
- Apply knowledge of possessive nouns
- Use academic language: *possessives*

Materials

- Vocabulary Transparency 45
- Vocabulary Strategy Transparency 46
- Leveled Practice Books, p. 168

Vocabulary

powered (p. 225) supplied with a source of energy

declared (p. 223) stated firmly

existed (p. 223) was real

artist's (p. 223) belonging to an artist

pride (p. 223) pleasure or satisfaction in one's work

ELL   Access for All

Practice Vocabulary
Give examples and ask questions to elicit the target vocabulary. Say: *Before electricity, candles existed to light our homes. What kinds of transportation existed before cars?*

Review
Vocabulary
 ## Words in Context

EXPLAIN/MODEL

Review the meaning of each vocabulary word. Display **Transparency 45.** Model how to complete the first sentence on the transparency by filling in the correct vocabulary word.

 Transparency 45

> powered   declared   existed
> artist's   pride
>
> 1. Susan <u>declared</u> that she wanted to go to the park.
> 2. The <u>artist's</u> paintings are very beautiful.
> 3. Some people take a lot of <u>pride</u> in their work.
> 4. Carousels <u>existed</u> before televisions or cars were invented.
> 5. Carousels are often <u>powered</u> by electric motors that make them turn.

Vocabulary Transparency 45

Think Aloud I think that the missing word is a verb. Susan would probably say or *state* what she wanted to do. I know that *declared* is another verb for *stated*. I think this is the missing verb. *Declared* makes sense in the sentence.

PRACTICE

 Have students complete items 2–5. Review students' answers as a class, or have partners check their answers together.

Remind students that they can use the Glossary on pages 408–422 to confirm word meanings.

STRATEGY
WORD PARTS: POSSESSIVES

EXPLAIN/MODEL

■ **Possessives** are nouns that show ownership. For example, "the artist's paintbrush" is a paintbrush that belongs to the artist.

■ When singular nouns show ownership, they usually end in an apostrophe (') and *s*, as in *artist's*. For plural nouns that end in *s*, an apostrophe is added after the *s*, as in *artists'*.

■ Help students distinguish between possessives and regular plural nouns ending in *s*. Remind students that contractions, such as *isn't, won't,* and *he's,* also include apostrophes.

 Display **Transparency 46.** Model how to identify the possessive noun and what it owns in the example.

Word Parts: Possessives

Tennessee's Libertyland Amusement Park is fun to visit.

1. Juan's bicycle isn't outside in the yard. (Juan's; bicycle)

2. The woman's car is parked in the street. It can't be far from her house. (woman's, car)

3. Mary's father flies airplanes. He's a good pilot. (Mary's, father)

4. If you see my sisters' skateboards, please tell me where they are. They aren't in the garage. (sisters', skateboards)

Vocabulary Strategy Transparency 46

PRACTICE

Help students identify the possessive noun and what it owns in item 1. Then have them complete items 2–4.

Quick Check

Can students use context clues to figure out word meanings and correctly identify possessive nouns?

During **Small Group Instruction**

If No ➞ **Approaching Level** Vocabulary, p. 229O

If Yes ➞ **On Level** Options, pp. 229Q–229R

Beyond Level Options, pp. 229S–229T

Vocabulary

Review last week's vocabulary words. Have students identify the two nouns. (gift, schoolhouse) Ask them to form sentences using the possessive forms of these two nouns.

◻ **On Level Practice Book O,** page 168

Possessives are nouns that show ownership. They show who or what another noun belongs to.
Marie's skates are very sharp.

A. Circle the possessive noun in each group of words. On the line at the right, write *correct* if the example is correct. If the example is incorrect write the correct possessive noun.

1. many (trains) windows _____ trains'
2. one (childs) bike _____ child's
3. a (skateboard's) wheels _____ correct
4. five (boats) steering wheels _____ correct
5. my only (sisters) shoes _____ sister's
6. a (man's) hat _____ correct
7. several (teammate's) uniforms _____ teammates'
8. two (brothers) bicycles _____ brothers'

B. Rewrite each phrase using a possessive noun.

Example: wheels of the car car's wheels

9. ship of the captain captain's ship
10. wings of two airplanes airplanes' wings
11. cars of the women women's cars
12. motorcycle of the officer officer's motorcycle

 Approaching Practice Book A, page 168

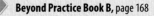 **Beyond Practice Book B,** page 168

Word Study

Objective

- Decode words with inflected endings with spelling change *y* to *i*

Materials

- Leveled Practice Books, p. 169

Mix and Match Write a list of base forms of regular verbs. Nearby, write the inflected endings (-s, -ed, -ing). Have individual students choose a verb from the list, match it with an inflected ending, pronounce the verb, and use it in a sentence.

On Level Practice Book O, page 169

The **inflected endings** -es and -ed can be added to the end of a verb to show when an action happens.
If the letter before the *y* is a consonant, change the *y* to *i* and add –es or –ed. Notice how the word *worry* changes to *worries* and *worried*.

| hurry | supply | study | dry | display | copy |

Fill in the blank in each sentence with the correct inflected form of a verb from the box. Think about when you need to change the *y* to *i* and add –es or –ed.

1. Club members _____ hurried _____ to catch the bus for their trip downtown.

2. Ana _____ studied _____ hard for the quiz on transportation.

3. Walt _____ copies _____ old photographs and uses them as guides when he draws antique cars.

4. Marla's grandmother _____ displayed _____ her teacup collection on a shelf in the living room.

5. I have to wait until my shirt _____ dries _____ before I can go outside and play again.

6. The conductor _____ supplied _____ all the passengers with blankets when the heat went off.

★ **Approaching Practice Book A,** page 169

◆ **Beyond Practice Book B,** page 169

Phonics

Decode Words with Endings *y* to *i*

 EXPLAIN/MODEL

- A base word is a word that does not have any word parts added to it. The endings *-s, -ed,* and *-ing* can be added to a base verb.

- The *-s* ending means that the action is happening in the present: *Ed jumps.* It is added to verbs that go with singular subjects. A present-tense form of *be* plus the *-ing* ending also means that the action is happening in the present: *Ed is jumping.* The *-ed* ending also means that the action happened in the past: *Ed jumped.*

- When a base verb ends in a consonant and *y,* change the *y* to *i* when *-es* or *-ed* is added, as in *tries* and *tried.* There is no change when *-ing* is added.

  Write: *Tina <u>dried</u> the dishes.*

Think Aloud The underlined verb ends in *-ed,* so I know that the action takes place in the past. When *-ed* is added to a verb that ends in a consonant and *y,* the *y* changes to *i* and *-ed* is added. So that means the base word for this word is probably the verb *dry* /drī/. I know the meaning of *dry,* so *dried* means "took away water from something that was wet." That meaning makes sense.

PRACTICE/APPLY

Write: *tries, hurried, studies,* and *playing.* For each have students circle the ending, tell what the base word is, and tell when the action of *tries, hurried,* and *studies* takes place. Have students segment and blend the sounds and read each word.

Decode Multisyllable Words Write these words: *copying, replied, displays, enjoying.* Model how to decode *copying.* Work with students to decode and read aloud the remaining words.

 Quick Check Can students decode words with inflected endings when the spelling changes from *y* to *i*?

During **Small Group Instruction**

If No → **Approaching Level** Phonics, p. 229P

If Yes → **On Level** Options, pp. 229Q–229R

Beyond Level Options, pp. 229S–229T

Vocabulary Building

Oral Language

Expand Vocabulary Work with students to brainstorm words related to transportation and write them on a word web like the one below.

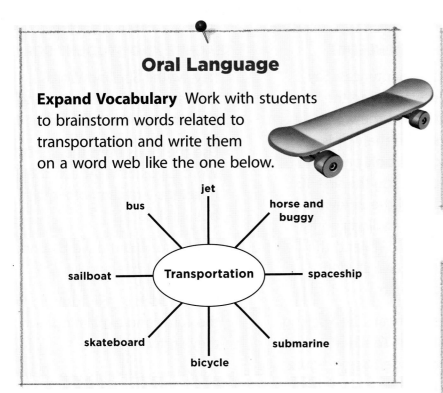

Vocabulary Building

Word Variety On a word web, have students name ways to travel on water.

Travel by Water: swimming, rowboat, kayak, freighter, canoe, dinghy, raft, ship, ocean liner, submarine

Do a similar semantic word web using one of last week's words, such as *Types of Gifts* or *People Who Are Kindhearted*.

Apply Vocabulary

Write a Paragraph Have students use the vocabulary words *powered, declared, existed, artist's,* and *pride* in a one-paragraph diary entry about taking a trip by land. Students can read their paragraphs to a partner.

Spiral Review

Vocabulary Game

■ Form two teams. Each team gets the **Vocabulary Cards** *declared, existed, yearned, sturdy, lonesome, traders, gift, tend.*

■ Each team writes sentences using each of their words, leaving a blank for the vocabulary word. The sentences must contain clear context clues.

■ Teams take turns reading the sentences aloud. The other team has to name the missing vocabulary word. If the word is correctly guessed, that team gets one point.

■ The team that has the most points wins the game.

gift   declared   existed   yearned

tend   sturdy   lonesome   traders

Technology

 Vocabulary PuzzleMaker

 For additional vocabulary and spelling games, go to www.macmillanmh.com

5 Day Spelling

Words with Endings *y* to *i*

Spelling Words

tries	drying	studied
tried	hurries	studying
trying	hurried	plays
dries	hurrying	played
dried	studies	playing

Review dances, hoping, wrapping

Challenge obeyed, worrying

Dictation Sentences

1. She always <u>tries</u> to win.
2. I <u>tried</u> to draw that picture.
3. We are <u>trying</u> to fix this.
4. It always <u>dries</u> faster in the sun.
5. Do you like <u>dried</u> cranberries?
6. The pictures are still <u>drying</u>.
7. Francine <u>hurries</u> home after school.
8. Justin <u>hurried</u> to finish his shopping.
9. We are <u>hurrying</u>.
10. The good student <u>studies</u> for all her tests.
11. We <u>studied</u> all afternoon.
12. I like <u>studying</u> artwork at the museum.
13. Who <u>plays</u> on your team?
14. My neighbor <u>played</u> basketball with the pros.
15. You are not <u>playing</u> that game again!

Review Words

1. No one <u>dances</u> like that anymore.
2. I was <u>hoping</u> you would come.
3. I am <u>wrapping</u> the present now.

Challenge Words

1. Martin <u>obeyed</u> the rules.
2. Stop <u>worrying</u> about that.

Display the Spelling Words throughout the week.

Day 1 Pretest

ASSESS PRIOR KNOWLEDGE

Use the Dictation Sentences. Say the underlined word, read the sentence, and repeat the word. Have students write the words on **Spelling Practice Book** page 141. For a modified list, use the first 12 Spelling Words and the 3 Review Words. For a more challenging list, use Spelling Words 3–15 and the Challenge Words. Have students correct their own tests.

Have students cut apart the Spelling Word Cards BLM on **Teacher's Resource Book** page 88 and figure out a way to sort them. Have them save the cards for use throughout the week.

Students can use Spelling Practice Book page 142 for independent practice.

Day 2 Word Sorts

TEACHER AND STUDENT SORTS

- Review the Spelling Words, discussing their meanings and pointing out the inflected endings.

- Use the cards from the Spelling Word Cards BLM. Attach the headings *y to i* and *other* to a bulletin board.

- Model sorting the words under the correct headings.

- Have students take turns sorting the cards and explaining how they sorted them.

- Then have students use their Spelling Word Cards. After placing the headings on their desks, they can sort the Spelling Words three times. Have students write their last sort on Spelling Practice Book page 143.

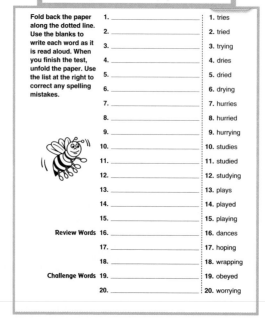

Spelling Practice Book, pages 141–142

Fold back the paper along the dotted line. Use the blanks to write each word as it is read aloud. When you finish the test, unfold the paper. Use the list at the right to correct any spelling mistakes.

1. _____	1. tries
2. _____	2. tried
3. _____	3. trying
4. _____	4. dries
5. _____	5. dried
6. _____	6. drying
7. _____	7. hurries
8. _____	8. hurried
9. _____	9. hurrying
10. _____	10. studies
11. _____	11. studied
12. _____	12. studying
13. _____	13. plays
14. _____	14. played
15. _____	15. playing
Review Words 16. _____	16. dances
17. _____	17. hoping
18. _____	18. wrapping
Challenge Words 19. _____	19. obeyed
20. _____	20. worrying

Spelling Practice Book, page 143

tries	dries	hurries	studies	plays
tried	dried	hurried	studied	played
trying	drying	hurrying	studying	playing

Pattern Power!

Write the spelling words that have one syllable.

1. tries 3. plays 5. dried
2. dries 4. tried 6. played

Write the spelling words that have two syllables.

7. hurries 10. studied 12. drying
8. studies 11. trying 13. playing
9. hurried

Write the spelling words that have three syllables.

14. studying
15. hurrying

Rhyme Time

Write a spelling word that rhymes with each of these words.

16. fries tries/dries
17. stayed played
18. praying playing
19. buddies studies
20. flying trying/drying

Day 3 — Word Meanings

DEFINITIONS

Display the definitions below. Have students write the clues and the Spelling Words that go with them in a word study notebook.

1. finding out if you can do something (trying)
2. made something not wet (dried)
3. moved fast (hurried)
4. reading and learning about something (studying)
5. doing something for fun (playing)

Challenge students to come up with clues for other Spelling Words, including Review Words and Challenge Words.

Have partners write a sentence for each Spelling Word, leaving a blank where the word should go. Then have them trade papers and write the missing word.

Day 4 — Review and Proofread

SPIRAL REVIEW

Review words with inflected endings. Write *dances, hoping, wrapping*. Have students tell why the *c* in *dances* and the *p* in *hoping* are not doubled.

PROOFREAD AND WRITE

Display this sentence. Have students correct the errors.

I hurryed to school after I dryed the dishes. (hurried, dried)

BLIND SORT

Partners use their Spelling Word Cards. They each write the headings *y to i* and *other* on a sheet of paper. Then they take turns. One draws cards and says the words. The other writes them under the correct headings. After both have finished, they can check each other's papers.

Day 5 — Assess and Reteach

POSTTEST

Use the Dictation Sentences on page 229G for the Posttest. If students have difficulty with any words in the lesson, have them place them on a list called "Spelling Words I Want to Remember" in a word study notebook.

WORD STUDY NOTEBOOK

Challenge students to search for other words with inflected endings of *y* to *i* in their reading for the week and write them in a word study notebook under the headings "Other Words with Endings That Change from *y* to *i*."

Spelling Practice Book, page 144

tries	dries	hurries	studies	plays
tried	dried	hurried	studied	played
trying	drying	hurrying	studying	playing

What's the Word?

Complete each sentence with a spelling word.

1. The baseball player **hurried** to get to first base.
2. After school she dances to music and **plays** volleyball with friends.
3. I **studied** hard for the test, so I hope I did well.
4. We were all **trying** to win the race.
5. The socks that were **drying** on the line were blowing in the wind.
6. The children **played** in the backyard after lunch.
7. The teacher was hoping that the students were **studying**.
8. The cat **tried** to climb the tree, but she could not do it.
9. Gretel was dropping crumbs while **hurrying** down the path.
10. The machine **dries** the clothes by blowing air on them.

Find the Base Words

Write the base word of each spelling word.

11. tries **try**
12. playing **play**
13. studies **study**
14. hurries **hurry**
15. dried **dry**

Spelling Practice Book, page 145

There are six spelling mistakes in this paragraph. Circle the misspelled words. Write the words correctly on the lines below.

Our class is (studieing) dances performed by people around the world. People dance for many reasons: to celebrate good things, to welcome visitors, or just to have fun.

We watched videos of children who were (plaing) and dancing with their friends. They (tryed) to jump as high and spin as fast as they could. It looked like fun!

I like to dance, too. I take ballet lessons. I am almost always late for class. Sometimes my tights have not (dryed) out from being washed. Other times I am (hurrieing) to finish my homework. My sister (studys) tap dancing. When I get older, I will learn other kinds of dancing, too.

I know why people all over the world dance. It's fun, and it's good exercise!

1. **studying**
2. **playing**
3. **tried**
4. **dried**
5. **hurrying**
6. **studies**

Writing Activity

Imagine that you are the coach of a soccer team. Write the speech that you would give your players before the big game. Use at least four spelling words in your description.

Spelling Practice Book, page 146

Look at the words in each set below. One word in each set is spelled correctly. Look at Sample A. The letter next to the correctly spelled word in Sample A has been shaded in. Do Sample B yourself. Shade the letter of the word that is spelled correctly. When you are sure you know what to do, go on with the rest of the page.

Sample A:
- Ⓐ cryed
- Ⓑ cried
- Ⓒ cride
- Ⓓ creid

Sample B:
- Ⓔ crys
- Ⓕ chries
- Ⓖ crise
- Ⓗ cries

1.
- Ⓐ trize
- Ⓑ tries
- Ⓒ trys
- Ⓓ treis

2.
- Ⓔ tryed
- Ⓕ tride
- Ⓖ tryd
- Ⓗ tried

3.
- Ⓐ trying
- Ⓑ trian
- Ⓒ treyeing
- Ⓓ triying

4.
- Ⓔ drys
- Ⓕ dryes
- Ⓖ drize
- Ⓗ dries

5.
- Ⓐ dryed
- Ⓑ dreid
- Ⓒ dried
- Ⓓ dride

6.
- Ⓔ driing
- Ⓕ drieing
- Ⓖ drying
- Ⓗ dring

7.
- Ⓐ hurrees
- Ⓑ hurrys
- Ⓒ hurries
- Ⓓ huries

8.
- Ⓔ hurried
- Ⓕ hureed
- Ⓖ hurryed
- Ⓗ huried

9.
- Ⓔ hurriing
- Ⓕ hurrying
- Ⓖ hurryin
- Ⓗ herrying

10.
- Ⓐ studies
- Ⓑ studyes
- Ⓒ studys
- Ⓓ studees

11.
- Ⓔ studyed
- Ⓕ studied
- Ⓖ studdied
- Ⓗ studeed

12.
- Ⓐ studing
- Ⓑ studieing
- Ⓒ studeeing
- Ⓓ studying

13.
- Ⓐ plaze
- Ⓑ plays
- Ⓒ plaise
- Ⓓ plais

14.
- Ⓔ plaide
- Ⓕ playde
- Ⓖ playd
- Ⓗ played

15.
- Ⓐ playing
- Ⓑ plaing
- Ⓒ plaeng
- Ⓓ playeing

Possessive Pronouns

Daily Language Activities

Use these activities to introduce each day's lesson. Write the day's activities on the board or use **Transparency 23.**

DAY 1
1. You friend are the best dancer. **2.** How long have your friend been Taking lessons. **3.** can he teach me he's dance moves (1: Your; is; 2: has; taking; lessons?; 3: Can; his; moves?)

DAY 2
1. "Those shoes are my," said Marie. **2.** She wanted to make sure no one taked her's shoes. **3.** "No one would take your" I said. (1: mine; 2: took her; 3: yours,")

DAY 3
1. I'm going to ride mine bike. **2.** Do yous want to ride your's **3.** We can ryde ours bikes together. (1: my; 2: you; yours?; 3: ride our)

DAY 4
1. That team always tryes to trick mine team, **2.** We know theirs moves. **3.** Ours coach used to be their. (1: tries; my team.; 2: their; 3: Our; theirs)

DAY 5
1. Manuel and jean hurryed to they school. **2.** Now they are studieing for theirs math test. **3.** Are you studying for your? (1: Jean; hurried; their; 2: studying; their; 3: yours)

Possessive Pronouns

Day 1 — Introduce the Concept

INTRODUCE POSSESSIVE PRONOUNS

Present the following:

- A **possessive pronoun** takes the place of a possessive noun.

- A possessive pronoun shows who or what owns something

- Use these possessive pronouns before nouns: *my, your, his, her, its, our, your,* and *their*.

Examples:
Al's book is black.
His book is black.

The book's cover is blue.
Its cover is blue.

Day 2 — Teach the Concept

REVIEW POSSESSIVE PRONOUNS

Ask what a possessive pronoun is. Review possessive pronouns that are used before nouns.

INTRODUCE POSSESSIVE PRONOUNS THAT STAND ALONE

Present the following:

- A possessive pronoun takes the place of a possessive noun.

- These possessive pronouns are used alone: *mine, yours, his, hers, its, ours,* and *theirs.*

Examples:
This book is **mine.**
These books are **yours.**
This books is **his.**
These books are **theirs.**

 See Grammar Transparency 111 for modeling and guided practice.

 See Grammar Transparency 112 for modeling and guided practice.

Grammar Practice Book, page 141

- A **possessive pronoun** takes the place of a possessive noun. It shows who or what owns something.
- Some possessive pronouns are used before nouns. These include *my, your, his, her, its, our,* and *their.*

Write the possessive pronoun on the line.

1. Riverbank State Park in New York City is famous for its carousel.
   its
2. Milo Mottola told people about his idea for the carousel.
   his
3. He asked his art students to draw animals for the carousel.
   his
4. Their designs were used to make the carousel. __Their__
5. Our class plans to take a trip to the park. __Our__
6. Lily wants to see the animal designed by her cousin. __her__
7. My mother told me to take a picture of the carousel. __My__
8. Will your class go on any trips this year? __your__
9. This is the first trip for our class this year. __our__
10. My father is going on the trip with us. __My__

Grammar Practice Book, page 142

- Some possessive pronouns can stand alone. These include *mine, yours, his, hers, its, ours, yours,* and *theirs.*

Read the sentences and the possessive pronouns in parentheses. Write the correct possessive pronoun.

1. The students in __our__ class are designing carousels. (our, ours)
2. I am almost finished with __mine__. (my, mine)
3. Did you finish __yours__? (your, yours)
4. Nina and Nick showed me __their__ designs. (their, theirs)
5. Nina used dinosaurs in __hers__. (her, hers)
6. Nick put only birds in __his__ carousel. (his, their)
7. I liked both of __theirs__. (their, theirs)
8. Each carousel had __its__ own style. (its, their)
9. __Your__ carousel would be different from anyone else's design. (Your, Yours)
10. All of __ours__ are different. (our, ours)
11. I hope the teacher likes __mine__! (my, mine)
12. __Our__ class has worked really hard. (Our, Ours)

Day 3 — Review and Practice

REVIEW POSSESSIVE PRONOUNS

Review using possessive pronouns before nouns and without nouns.

MECHANICS AND USAGE: POSSESSIVE PRONOUNS

- A possessive pronoun can replace a possessive noun.

- Use these possessive pronouns before nouns: *my, your, his, her, its, our, their.*

- Use these possessive pronouns alone: *mine, yours, his, hers, its, ours, theirs.*

Examples:
Jan's dog barks a lot.
Her dog barks a lot.

That book is **Jan's.**
That book is **hers.**

See Grammar Transparency 113 for modeling and guided practice.

Grammar Practice Book, page 143

- A possessive pronoun can replace a possessive noun.
- Use these possessive pronouns before nouns: *my, your, his, her, its, our, their.*
- Use these possessive pronouns alone: *mine, yours, his, hers, its, ours, theirs.*

Circle the correct possessive pronoun in the parentheses.

1. Mrs. Parker asked (her) hers) students to design a carousel.
2. The students are all drawing (their) theirs) favorite animals.
3. Mario said (his) his's) is the elephant.
4. Tomas and Kwan said (their, (theirs) is the crocodile.
5. Some of us are using (our) ours) imaginations to create interesting animals.
6. (My) Mine) animal is a green tiger with wings.
7. I colored (its) it's) wings purple.
8. David says (your) yours) drawing is the best.
9. We like (your, (yours) a lot, too.
10. I told Sola (her, (hers) is very colorful.

Day 4 — Review and Proofread

REVIEW POSSESSIVE PRONOUNS

Review with students how to use possessive pronouns with and without nouns.

PROOFREAD

Have students correct errors in the following sentences.

1. Try a piece of ours pizza. (our)
2. Is that bicycle your? (yours)
3. Which skateboard is mines? (mine)
4. This is ours school. (our)
5. Hers towel is the pink one. (Her)

See Grammar Transparency 114 for modeling and guided practice.

Grammar Practice Book, page 144

- A **possessive pronoun** takes the place of a possessive noun. It shows who or what owns something.
- Some possessive pronouns are used before nouns. These include *my, your, his, her, its, our, your, and their.*
- Some possessive pronouns can stand alone. These include *mine, yours, his, hers, its, ours, and theirs.*

Rewrite this journal entry. Be sure to correct the pronouns and nouns.

We visited ours relatives in New York City this summer. Mine cousin Tracy took we to Riverbank State Park, along the Hudson River. Her showed us an unusual carousel in the park. The octopus had two heads. The zebra was plaid. The lion was green. She explained that the carousels animals were all designed by local kids. Tracy pointed out how the artists signature is engraved beneath each animal.

We visited our relatives in New York City this summer. My cousin Tracy took us to Riverbank State Park, along the Hudson River. She showed us an unusual carousel in the park. The octopus had two heads. The zebra was plaid. The lion was green. She explained that the carousel's animals were all designed by local kids. Tracy pointed out how the artist's signature is engraved beneath each animal.

Day 5 — Assess and Reteach

ASSESS

Use the Daily Language Activity and page 145 of the **Grammar Practice Book** for assessment.

RETEACH

Help students create a set of flash cards with the possessive pronouns *my, mine, her, hers, your,* and *yours* on them. With a partner, each student pulls a possessive pronoun from the deck. The partner makes up a sentence using the pronoun. Have students correct each other when necessary.

Use page 146 of the Grammar Practice Book for additional reteaching.

See Grammar Transparency 115 for modeling and guided practice.

Grammar Practice Book, pages 145–146

A. Write *yes* if the underlined word is a possessive pronoun. Write *no* if the underlined word is not a possessive pronoun.

1. Milo Mottola asked kids in his neighborhood to design the carousel. **yes**
2. The kids became Mottola's art students. **no**
3. He chose 32 of their drawings for the actual carousel. **yes**
4. All the students hoped that one of theirs would be chosen. **yes**
5. The artist's signature was engraved beneath each of the animals. **no**

B. Write *yes* if the underlined word is the correct possessive pronoun. Write *no* if the underlined word is not the correct possessive pronoun.

6. Our class took a trip to an amusement park. **yes**
7. Mine favorite ride is the roller coaster. **no**
8. Cara said that hers is the waterslide. **yes**
9. George said his's is the carousel. **no**
10. I said I would try their favorites if they would try mine. **yes**

Administer the Test

Weekly Reading Assessment,

Passage and questions, pages 285–292

ASSESSED SKILLS

- Fact and Opinion
- Vocabulary Words
- Word Parts/Possessives
- Words with Endings *y* to *i*
- Possessive Pronouns

Macmillan/McGraw-Hill

Administer the **Weekly Assessment** from the CD-ROM or online.

Weekly Assessment, 285–292

Fluency

Assess fluency for one group of students per week. Use the Oral Fluency Record Sheet to track the number of words read correctly. Fluency goal for all students: **97–117 words correct per minute (WCPM).**

Approaching Level	Weeks 1, 3, 5
On Level	Weeks 2, 4
Beyond Level	Week 6

Fluency Assessment

Alternative Assessments

- **Leveled Weekly Assessment,** for Approaching Level, pages 293–299
- **ELL Assessment,** pages 144–145

ELL Assessment, 144–145

Tested

End-of-Week Assessment

Diagnose		Prescribe
	IF . . .	**THEN . . .**
VOCABULARY WORDS **VOCABULARY STRATEGY** Word Parts: Possessives Items 1, 2, 3	0–1 items correct . . .	Reteach skills using the **Additional Lessons,** page T9 LOG ON Reteach skills: Go to **www.macmillanmh.com** CD ROM Vocabulary PuzzleMaker Evaluate for Intervention.
COMPREHENSION Skill: Fact and Opinion Items 4, 5, 6,	0–1 items correct . . .	Reteach skills using the **Additional Lessons**, page T3 Evaluate for Intervention.
GRAMMAR Possessive Pronouns Items 7, 8, 9	0–1 items correct . . .	Reteach skills: **Grammar Practice Book,** page 146
SPELLING Words with Endings *y* to *i* Items 10, 11, 12	0–1 items correct . . .	LOG ON Reteach skills: Go to **www.macmillanmh.com**
FLUENCY	89–96 WCPM 0–88 WCPM	AUDIO CD Fluency Solutions Evaluate for Intervention.

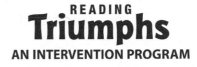

READING
Triumphs
AN INTERVENTION PROGRAM

Also Available

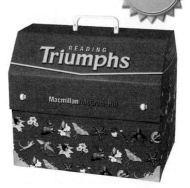

To place students in the Intervention Program, use the **Diagnostic Assessment** in the Intervention Teacher's Edition.

Leveled Reader Lesson 1

Objective Read to apply strategies and skills

Materials • **Leveled Reader** *Making Waves* • **Approaching Practice Book A**, p. 166

Leveled Reader

PREVIEW AND PREDICT

Show the cover and read the title. Have students skim the text and preview the photos and headings. What do they think "dragon boats" and "ice boats" might be? What questions do they have?

VOCABULARY WORDS

As students preview and read, discuss the five vocabulary words as they appear in the context of the book: *artist's*, p. 4; *declared*, p. 6; *existed*, p. 8; *powered*, p. 9; *pride*, p. 11. Reinforce the word meanings and ask students to give an example of when they might use each word. Can they name a synonym or antonym for any of the words?

STRATEGY
MAKE INFERENCES AND ANALYZE

Discuss why making inferences can deepen students' understanding of what they read. Remind them that their inferences should be based on the text and what they already know. Read page 2 aloud and model the strategy.

Think Aloud The text says that people race ice boats in cold places. The author doesn't say exactly how ice boats work. But, based on what I already know, I would expect that the ice boats glide across the ice, like skates. I'll keep reading to find out if my inference is correct.

SKILL
FACT AND OPINION

Remind students that facts are statements that can be proven true and opinions are statements of how a person feels or what a person believes. Point out words that signal opinions: *feel, believe, most, best, probably*. Encourage students to look for facts and opinions as they read.

READ AND RESPOND

Have students read the first chapter. Monitor their comprehension by asking questions and having them summarize the main ideas. Discuss facts and opinions about dragon boats.

Fluency: REPEATED READING

Model reading the passage on **Practice Book** page 166. Review how to pronounce any difficult vocabulary. Have the group echo-read the passage. Then have partners practice reading it to each other. Circulate and provide corrective feedback.

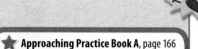

Approaching Practice Book A, page 166

As I read, I will pay attention to my pronunciation of vocabulary words and other difficult words.

	Ice boating has **existed** for more than 4,000 years. It is
10	one of the fastest winter sports. Racers in boats with sails
21	glide over an area of ice to see who can go the fastest.
34	Ice boating began in Europe in the mid-1600s. When
43	their canals froze, the Dutch used ice boats to move their
54	goods. In the 1800s, ice boats were used on the Great
64	Lakes to transport lumber and food during the winter.
73	Today ice boat racing is just a fun sport.
82	Ice boats are **powered** by the wind. How? Ice boaters
92	turn the sails to catch the wind. The wind then moves the
104	boat. Ice boaters also use the speed of the wind and the
116	direction in which it is blowing to help steer their
126	boats. 127

Comprehension Check

1. What is ice boating? **Summarize** Ice boating is when a boat with sails glides over the ice with the help of the wind.

2. How did ice boating begin? **Main Idea and Details** The Dutch used iceboats in the mid-1600s to move goods across the frozen canals.

	Words Read	−	Number of Errors	=	Words Correct Score
First Read		−		=	
Second Read		−		=	

Leveled Reader Lesson 2

Objective Read to apply strategies and skills

Materials • **Leveled Reader** *Making Waves* • chart paper • **Vocabulary Cards**

VOCABULARY WORDS

Use the **Vocabulary Cards** to review the words. Discuss meanings if necessary and help students identify context clues for the words within *Making Waves*. For example, help them identify clues to the meaning of *powered* on page 9, such as the words "wind then moves the boat."

SUMMARIZE AND PREDICT

Have students summarize what they learned in the first chapter and confirm or revise the predictions they made before reading. Ask students to note any additional questions they have. How might snake boats differ from dragon boats?

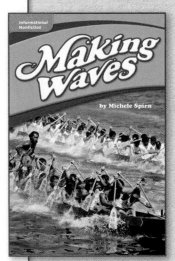

Leveled Reader

SKILL

FACT AND OPINION

Begin Chapter 2. Discuss if these statements are facts or opinions:

- Today ice boat racing is just a fun sport. (page 8)
- Ice boating began in Europe in the mid-1600s. (page 8)

During and after reading, help students to create a Fact and Opinion Chart.

READ AND RESPOND

Students should read the rest of the book. Remind students to make inferences to help them evaluate what the author says about the topic. They should also try to distinguish statements of fact from statements of opinion.

Once they have read the whole book, have them share personal responses. Do they think ice boat or snake boat racing would be fun?

Fluency

Objective Read with increasing fluency

Materials • stopwatch • **Approaching Practice Book A,** p. 166

TIMED READING

At the end of the week, have students do a timed reading. They should

- begin reading the passage aloud when you say "Go."
- stop reading the passage after one minute when you say "Stop."

Keep track of students' miscues and provide corrective feedback. Help students graph the number of words they read correctly.

Student Book

Comprehension

Objective Evaluate fact and opinion

Materials • **Comprehension Transparency 23** • **Student Book** "Visions of the Future from the Past," "Smooth Riding," and "Where No Chimp Has Gone Before"

SKILL
FACT AND OPINION

Remind students that facts are statements that can be proved to be true. Some articles tell opinions about what people think or believe. Display **Transparency 23.** Read the first section about Lord Kelvin.

Think Aloud Lord Kelvin thought that airplanes would never fly. That was his opinion. In fact, we all know now that airplanes can fly. This was proved to be true on December 17, 1903, by the Wright brothers.

Have students identify the facts (often accompanied by dates) and opinions in the three articles on **Student Book** pages 220–221.

ELL
Access for All

Name Possessives Write the vocabulary word *artist's* on the board. Explain that this is the possessive form of the word *artist.* Use the word in a sentence. Ask: *What is the possessive form of your name?* As students volunteer the possessive forms of their names, write them on the board. Reinforce by saying, _____'s book is on the desk. Or, _____'s shoes are brown. Continue until each student has had a turn.

Vocabulary

Objective Apply vocabulary word meanings and use possessives

Materials • **Vocabulary Cards** • **Student Book** *A Carousel of Dreams*

VOCABULARY WORDS

Review the words using the **Vocabulary Cards.** Help students locate and read the vocabulary words in the main selection, *A Carousel of Dreams,* and compare how the words are used in the articles on pages 220–221. Ask students to write a cloze sentence for each vocabulary word, exchange sentences with a partner, and complete each other's sentences.

> powered   declared   existed   artist's   pride

WORD PARTS: POSSESSIVES

Write the word *artist's* on the board. Remind students that possessives show ownership; most use an apostrophe.

Write these phrases on the board: *secrets of a racer, eyes that belong to a dragon, the final touch of an artist, speed of the boat, paddle that belongs to a rower.* Have students reword each phrase using a possessive. (*a racer's secrets; a dragon's eyes; an artist's final touch; the boat's speed; a rower's paddle*)

Phonics

Objective Decode words with inflected endings *y* to *i*

DECODE WORDS WITH ENDINGS *y* TO *i*

Write *cries, cried,* and *crying* on the board. Segment and blend each word, and have students echo you. Show how each word is formed from the base word *cry*. Explain that if a base word ends with a consonant + *y,* you change the *y* to an *i* before adding *-es* or *-ed* but not before adding *-ing.*

Have students name the base word for the spelling words *dries, dried,* and *drying* and for *hurries, hurried,* and *hurrying.* Ask volunteers to say each spelling word and show how it is formed from the base word.

Additional Lessons

Use your **Quick Check** observations to help you identify students who might benefit from additional instruction. See page T3 for comprehension support and page T9 for vocabulary support.

Vocabulary

Objective Identify and apply vocabulary word meanings
Materials • **Vocabulary Cards**

VOCABULARY WORDS

Read each vocabulary word from this week and last and its definition. Then play a guessing game. Provide students with clues like these:

- This word is a verb. It means "lived." (existed)

- This word is a noun. People feel it when they do something well. (pride)

- I might use this word instead of *said* or *announced.* (declared)

- This word is a verb. I might use it when I talk about how a machine gets its energy. (powered)

- This word describes someone who may be a volunteer. (kindhearted)

Make Connections Across Texts

Objective Compare facts and opinions across texts
Materials • **Student Book** *A Carousel of Dreams* • **Leveled Reader:** *Making Waves*

SKILL
FACT AND OPINION

Have students discuss *A Carousel of Dreams* and *Making Waves.* Ask students to paraphrase the main ideas and compare the selections.

- How were the facts and opinions similar and different?

- What clues in both selections helped you tell if a statement was fact or opinion?

- Which selection did you enjoy reading more? Why?

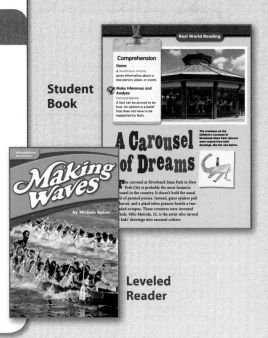

Student Book

Leveled Reader

Leveled Reader Lesson

Objective   Read to apply strategies and skills

Materials   • **Leveled Reader** *Thrills and Chills*   • **On Level Practice Book O,** p. 166

PREVIEW AND PREDICT

Show the cover and read the title of the book. Ask students what they think of when they hear the words *chills* and *thrills*. Have students skim the text and note questions and predictions.

STRATEGY
MAKE INFERENCES AND ANALYZE

Remind students that making inferences and analyzing as they read can help them find clues that tell which statements are facts and which are opinions. Read page 2 aloud. Model how to make inferences and analyze.

Think Aloud I can use personal experience to guess what this selection is about. The first paragraph describes a roller coaster ride. The author doesn't say so, but I know because I've been on a roller coaster before.

SKILL
FACT AND OPINION

Discuss the facts and opinions about the origins of roller coasters from the book. Remind students that facts can be verified, while opinions cannot.

- Where were the first roller coasters built?
- Was Catherine's summer slide, built in 1784, the first real roller coaster? Can it be proved?

Students can create a Fact and Opinion Chart to help them.

READ AND RESPOND

Have students read to the end of Chapter 1. They should look for important facts about the first roller coasters and see if the author gives any opinions. They should notice how the vocabulary words are used.

Then have students finish reading the book. Ask if the title *Thrills and Chills* was appropriate. Ask students to share their favorite fact or opinion.

Fluency: REPEATED READING

Read the passage on **Practice Book** page 166. Have students echo-read.

Then have partners alternate reading the passage and following along. Remind readers to sound out difficult words or use context clues to help them. Students should practice the passage throughout the week. At the end of the week, have partners time each other and note how many words they read correctly in one minute.

Leveled Reader

ELL
Leveled Reader
Go to pages
229U–229V.

On Level Practice Book O, page 166

As I read, I will pay attention to my pronunciation of vocabulary words and other difficult words.

	Around the time the Pilgrims were landing in the New
10	World, the Russians were building the first roller coaster.
19	They built huge wooden slides. Then they poured water
28	on them. In the cold winter, the water turned to ice. Large
40	sleds would race down these icy slides.
47	Over one hundred years later, Empress Catherine the
55	Great of Russia asked workmen to build her a special slide.
66	She wanted one that could be used in the summer. In 1784,
77	they built one that could be ridden on by a cart on wheels.
90	Many people think this was the first real roller coaster.
100	An **artist** painted Empress Catherine's slide. People
107	said that the **artist's** work was fit for a queen.
117	The first American roller coaster was built in the
126	mountains of Pennsylvania. It was called the Mauch Chunk
135	Switchback Railway. 137

Comprehension Check

1. Compare and contrast the first roller coaster in Russia and the roller coaster built for Empress Catherine the Great. **Compare and Contrast** Compare: Both roller coasters were built of wood. Contrast: first coaster used in winter and other coaster used in summer
2. List one fact and one opinion about Empress Catherine's slide. **Fact and Opinion** Fact: An artist painted the slide. Opinion: The artist's work was fit for a queen.

	Words Read	−	Number of Errors	=	Words Correct Score
First Read		−		=	
Second Read		−		=	

Vocabulary

Objective	Apply vocabulary words and identify and use possessives
Materials	• **Leveled Reader** *Thrills and Chills* • dictionary

Leveled Reader

VOCABULARY WORDS

Write the words *powered, declared, existed, artist's,* and *pride.* Review how to form possessives such as *artist's* and how they differ from plurals. Have students work in pairs, taking turns giving sentence clues for each word as the partner guesses which word fits the clues. Give them an example, such as: *The judge announced the name of the winner. The judge _____ it.* (declared)

WORD PARTS: POSSESSIVES

Student Book

Have students look through *Thrills and Chills* and locate possessives: *Catherine's* (p. 5), *Thompson's* (p. 7), *world's* (p. 8), *Japan's* (p. 9), and *mouth's* (p. 9). Students can work in pairs to write new sentences using each word.

Study Skill

Objective	Skim and scan articles to locate information
Materials	• Newspaper or magazine articles

SKIM AND SCAN

Discuss how to skim and scan articles and books for research. Remind students that to **skim,** they should quickly read each paragraph, looking for main ideas and important details; to **scan** an article for a key word, they should move their eyes quickly over the text. If they find a key word, they should stop and read closely.

Tell students to look at tables of contents and headings in newspapers and magazines for key words. Ask students what key words or clues they would skim for if they wanted to write about old roller coasters.

Make Connections Across Texts

Objective	Make connections across texts and distinguish fact from opinion
Materials	• **Student Book** *A Carousel of Dreams* • **Leveled Reader** *Thrills and Chills*

SKILL
FACT AND OPINION

Discuss the facts and opinions in *A Carousel of Dreams* and *Thrills and Chills.* Ask students if *A Carousel of Dreams* presents similar information to *Thrills and Chills.* If so, what information is similar?

Leveled Reader Lesson

Objective	Read to apply strategies and skills
Materials	• **Leveled Reader** *Up, Down, or Open-Moving Machines* • chart paper
	• **Beyond Practice Book B,** p. 166

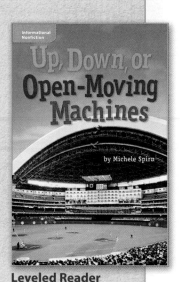

Leveled Reader

PREVIEW AND PREDICT

Show the cover and read the title. Ask students what kind of machines they will learn about in this book. What questions do they have?

STRATEGY
MAKE INFERENCES AND ANALYZE

Remind students to make inferences using text clues and their own experience to evaluate the facts and opinions in the text. Read pages 2–3 aloud. Model how you make inferences and analyze information.

Think Aloud The picture on page 3 shows some machines with moving parts. I think these are examples of complex machines. I wonder if the author will explain how they work. I'll keep reading to find out.

SKILL
FACT AND OPINION

Remind students that provable statements are facts, and statements telling what people believe are opinions. Discuss how the invention of drawbridges and escalators made life easier. Students can create a Fact and Opinion Chart to help them separate facts from opinion statements.

READ AND RESPOND

Have students read to the end of Chapter 2 and identify statements of fact and opinion. Discuss vocabulary words as they appear.

After students finish reading the book, discuss how the original machines mentioned in this book are similar to and different from their modern counterparts. Ask if students agree with the author's opinion that modern machines make our lives more pleasant and why.

Fluency: REPEATED READING

Reread the fluency passage from *Up, Down, or Open-Moving Machines* and have students follow along on **Practice Book** page 166. Then have students read with a partner and offer corrective feedback on paying attention to punctuation and help with difficult words.

Have students continue practicing the passage during independent time. At the end of the week, partners should do a timed reading of the passage to check how many words they each read correctly in one minute.

◆ Beyond Practice Book B, page 166

As I read, I will pay attention to my pronunciation of vocabulary words and other difficult words.

	Drawbridges came into use when castles were first built in England
11	after 1066. This was about thirty years before the time of knights in
23	shining armor. People who lived in these castles owned the land around
35	them for many miles. Castles **existed** as forts to protect this land. From
48	the highest part of the castle, they could see if someone was trying to
62	invade their land.
65	If attacked, those who lived in the castle could defend themselves in
77	several ways. Standing at the top of the castle, they could shoot arrows at
91	their enemies. They could also use a drawbridge. Moats surrounded many
102	castles, and the only way to cross them was to use the drawbridge. When
116	the castle was threatened, someone inside would turn a winch that worked
128	a pulley. This pulley pulled a chain attached to the drawbridge. The
140	drawbridge would turn on a pivot and lift up.
149	In our time, drawbridges let tall ships pass through a waterway. Modern
161	drawbridges use a light sensor to tell when a ship or boat is near. 175

Comprehension Check

1. How did moats and drawbridges protect castles? **Summarize** Moats surrounded the castle, and the drawbridge was the only way to cross the moat.

2. How are the first drawbridges different from drawbridges today? **Compare and Contrast** The first drawbridges were used to defend castles, today they are used to let tall ships pass through a waterway.

	Words Read	–	Number of Errors	=	Words Correct Score
First Read		–		=	
Second Read		–		=	

Vocabulary

Objective   Apply vocabulary word meanings
Materials   • **Student Book** *A Carousel of Dreams*

EXTEND VOCABULARY

Have students review the vocabulary words shown on **Student Book** page 220: *powered, declared, existed, artist's* and *pride.* Ask them to think of the inventions they read about in *A Carousel of Dreams* and *Up, Down, or Open-Moving Machines* and to write original descriptive sentences about the inventions using the vocabulary words.

Study Skill

Objective   Skim and scan to find information
Materials   • **Study Skills Transparency 5**

SKIM AND SCAN

Review **Transparency 5.** Ask students to skim through the information in one minute. Tell them that skimming an article means that they do not have to read each word, but they should look for key words that tell them what the passage is about. Discuss what they have been able to glean from skimming the article. Then ask them to scan the information for specific details, such as who invented the Model T, how much it cost, and what invention led to it being mass-produced.

Have students list and share with the group five things they learned from skimming and scanning the passage.

Self-Selected Reading

Objective   Read independently and identify facts and opinions
Materials   • Leveled Readers or trade books at students' reading level

READ TO FIND FACTS AND OPINIONS

Invite students to select a nonfiction book to read independently for enjoyment based on their interests, favorite authors, and reading preferences. For a list of theme-related titles, see pages T19–T20. Remind students to make inferences and analyze information as they read. It will assist them in distinguishing fact from opinion.

Afterward, have students share and compare what they have learned in a literature circle. They should identify three facts and opinions they read.

ELL   Access for All

Fact and Opinion Review the difference between fact and opinion. On the board, write two columns labeled **Fact** and **Opinion**. Begin the **Fact** column by writing: *Our school's name is* _____. Have students take turns completing the fact. In the **Opinion** column, write: *The best thing about my school is* _____. Have students take turns completing the opinion. Add to the list as students volunteer other facts and opinions.

Academic Language

Throughout the week the English language learners will need help in building their understanding of the academic language used in daily instruction and assessment instruments. The following strategies will help to increase their language proficiency and comprehension of content and instructional words.

 **Technology**

Oral Language For additional language support and oral vocabulary development, go to
www. macmillanmh.com

Strategies to Reinforce Academic Language

- **Use Context** Academic Language (see chart below) should be explained in the context of the task during Whole Group. Use gestures, expressions, and visuals to support meaning.

- **Use Visuals** Use charts, transparencies, and graphic organizers to explain key labels to help students understand classroom language.

- **Model** Demonstrate the task using academic language in order for students to understand instruction.

Academic Language Used in Whole Group Instruction

Content/Theme Words	Skill/Strategy Words	Writing/Grammar Words
movement (p. 218)	make inferences and analyze (p. 222)	expository (p. 229A)
transportation (p. 218)	fact (p. 222)	generate questions (p. 229A)
high-speed trains (p. 218)	opinion (p. 222)	skim and scan (p. 229A)
bicycling (p. 218)	summarize (p. 225A)	evaluate sources (p. 229A)
airplanes (p. 220)		informative brochure (p. 229A)
carousel (p. 222)		possessive pronouns (p. 229I)

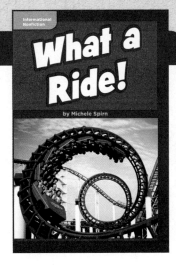

ELL Leveled Reader Lesson

Before Reading

DEVELOP ORAL LANGUAGE

Build Background Say this simple riddle: *Think of something that goes up (motion up) and down (motion down) very fast, and makes people scream "Aaaah." What is it?* Help students guess a rollercoaster. *Have you ever been on a rollercoaster?*

Review Vocabulary Write the vocabulary and support words on the board and discuss their meanings. When possible, use the pictures in the book to help explain the words. Use the picture on pages 2–3 to introduce *amusement park*. Ask students to use each word in a sentence.

PREVIEW AND PREDICT

Point to the cover photo. Explain that many people enjoy the thrills of a roller coaster ride. Discuss the word *thrills. What things give you "thrills"? For me, it's concerts. I get very excited!*

Set a Purpose for Reading Show the Fact and Opinion Chart. Ask students to do a similar chart to record facts and opinions. Encourage them to ask: *Is this a fact—something that can be proven, or an opinion—someone's belief?*

During Reading

Choose from among the differentiated strategies below to support students' reading at all stages of language acquisition.

Beginning	**Intermediate**	**Advanced**
Shared Reading As you read, model how to find facts and opinions. Ask yourself questions and answer them. *Is this something that happened? Can I prove it?* Record the information in the chart.	**Read Together** Read Chapter 1. Help students retell it and model asking questions to identify facts and opinions. Encourage students to answer. As you continue taking turns reading, ask them to use the strategy.	**Independent Reading** Have students read the story. Each day, ask them to discuss it with a partner and identify facts and opinions. Have them use the strategy to fill in the chart. Encourage them to use the information on the pages to prove facts.

After Reading

Remind students to use the vocabulary and story words in their whole group activities.

Objective
- To apply vocabulary and comprehension skills

Materials
- ELL Leveled Reader

ELL 5 Day Planner

DAY 1	• Academic Language • Oral Language and Vocabulary Review
DAY 2	• Academic Language • ELL Leveled Reader
DAY 3	• Academic Language • ELL Leveled Reader
DAY 4	• Academic Language • ELL Leveled Reader
DAY 5	• Academic Language • ELL Leveled Reader Comprehension Check and Literacy Activities

ELL Teacher's Guide for students who need additional instruction

Week At A Glance

Whole Group

 VOCABULARY
escape, fled, image, newspaper, numb, screamed, shuddered

 Context Clues/Figurative Language

 COMPREHENSION
Strategy: Make Inferences and Analyze
Skill: Make and Confirm Predictions

 WRITING
Descriptive

 Social Studies Link

Culture

Small Group Options

Differentiated Instruction for Tested Skills

 Tested Skills for the Week

Weekly Theme: Heroes

THE PRINTER

by Myron Uhlberg
illustrated by Henri Sørensen

AUDIO CD

Main Selection
Genre Realistic Fiction

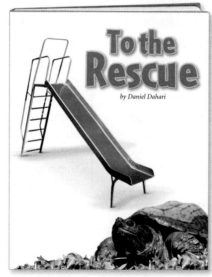

To the Rescue
by Daniel Dahari

Vocabulary/ Comprehension

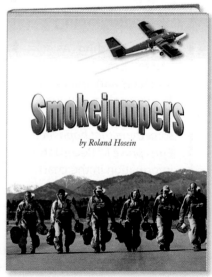

Smokejumpers
by Roland Hosein

 **Social Studies Link**
Genre Nonfiction Article

Resources for Differentiated Instruction

Leveled Readers

AUDIO CD

GR Levels N–R

Genre Informational Nonfiction

- Same Theme
- Same Vocabulary
- Same Comprehension Skills

N · Blizzard Heroes by Marc Gave

P · Hurricane HEROES by Marc Gave

R · EARTHQUAKE HEROES by Susan Blackaby

Approaching Level

On Level

Beyond Level

Keeping Us Safe by Marc Gave

English Language Leveled Reader

On Level Reader sheltered for English Language Learner

ELL Teacher's Guide Available

Also Available
LEVELED READER PROGRAM

CLASSROOM LIBRARY

Genre Historical Fiction

The Babe & I

The Year of Miss Agnes

AMELIA AND ELEANOR GO FOR A RIDE

Approaching

On Level

Beyond

Trade books to apply Comprehension Skills

INTERVENTION ANTHOLOGY

- Phonics and Decoding
- Comprehension
- Vocabulary

Reading Triumphs, Intervention Program also available

READING Triumphs
AUDIO CD

LEVELED PRACTICE

Practice Book A

Practice Book O

Practice Book B

ELL Practice and Assessment

Approaching

On Level

Beyond

ELL

Technology

www.macmillanmh.com

AUDIO CD
LISTENING LIBRARY
- Main Selections
- Leveled Readers
- Intervention Anthology

FLUENCY SOLUTIONS

CD ROM
VOCABULARY PuzzleMaker

NEW ADVENTURES WITH
BUGGLES AND BEEZY

LOG ON
ONLINE INSTRUCTION
- Meet the Author/Illustrator
- Computer Literacy Lessons
- Research and Inquiry Activities
- Oral Language Activities
- Vocabulary and Spelling Activities

Suggested Lesson Plan

CD ROM
Instructional Navigator
Interactive Lesson Planner

Integrated **ELL** Support Every Day

The Printer, 234–251

Leveled Readers

Whole Group

ORAL LANGUAGE
- **Listening**
- **Speaking**
- **Viewing**

WORD STUDY
- **Vocabulary**
- **Phonics/Decoding**

READING
- **Develop Comprehension**

- **Fluency**

LANGUAGE ARTS
- **Writing**

- **Grammar**

- **Spelling**

ASSESSMENT
- **Informal/Formal**

Turn the Page for
Small Group Lesson Plan

230C

Day 1

Listening/Speaking/Viewing
❓ Focus Question A hero is a person who helps others. What qualities do all heroes have?
Build Background, 230
Read Aloud: "The Name of the Tree," 231

Vocabulary
 screamed, numb, escape, fled, shuddered, image, newspaper, 232
Practice Book A-O-B, 170
 Strategy: Context Clues: Figurative Language

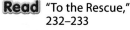
Read "To the Rescue," 232–233

Comprehension, 233A–233B
Strategy: Make Inferences and Analyze
Student Book
 Skill: Make and Confirm Predictions
Practice Book A-O-B, 171
Fluency Partner Reading, 230I
Model Fluency, 231

Writing
Daily Writing Prompt Write about a hero you know of and why you think he or she is a hero. Explain what the person did to be heroic.
Prewrite a Speech, 259A

Grammar Daily Language Activities, 259I
 Pronoun-Verb Agreement, 259I
Grammar Practice Book, 147
 Spelling Pretest, 259G
Spelling Practice Book, 147–148

Quick Check Vocabulary, 232
Comprehension, 233B

Differentiated Instruction 259M–259V

Day 2

Listening/Speaking
❓ Focus Question Will the printer become friends with everyone at the plant?

Vocabulary
Review Vocabulary, 234
Phonics
Decode Words with Inflected Endings *y* to *i*, 259E
Practice Book A-O-B, 176

Read *The Printer,* 234–251

Comprehension, 234–253
Strategy: Make Inferences and Analyze
Student Book
 Skill: Make and Confirm Predictions
Practice Book A-O-B, 172
Fluency Partner Reading, 230I
Expression, 242

Writing
Daily Writing Prompt Write a description of the firefighter on pages 230–231. Tell what you think the firefighter did to win a heroism award.
Draft a Speech, 259A

Grammar Daily Language Activities, 259I
Pronoun-Verb Agreement, 259I
Grammar Practice Book, 148
Spelling The VC/CV Pattern, 259G
Spelling Practice Book, 149

Quick Check Comprehension, 243, 251
Phonics, 259E

Differentiated Instruction 259M–259V

Skills/Strategies

Vocabulary
Vocabulary Words
Context Clues:
   Figurative Language

Comprehension
Strategy: Make Inferences
and Analyze
Skill: Make and Confirm
   Predictions

Writing
Descriptive
Paragraph/
Introductory
Speech

Turn the Page for
Small Group
Options

Day 3

Listening/Speaking

❷ Focus Question How are the warning and rescue in "To the Rescue" different from the warning and rescue in *The Printer*?

Summarize, 253

Vocabulary

Review Words in Context, 259C

Strategy: Context Clues: Figurative Language, 259D

Practice Book A-O-B, 175

Read *The Printer*, 234–251

Comprehension

Comprehension Check, 253

Maintain Skill: Sequence, 253B

Student Book

Fluency Partner Reading, 230I

Practice Book A-O-B, 173

Repeated Reading, 253A

Writing

Daily Writing Prompt Pretend you are a firefighter and did something heroic. Write an entry in your journal telling what you did and how you felt.

Writing Trait: Voice, 259
Revise a Speech, 259B

Grammar Daily Language Activities, 259I
Mechanics and Usage, 259J
Grammar Practice Book, 149

Spelling The VC/CV Pattern, 259H
Spelling Practice Book, 150

Quick Check Fluency, 253A

Differentiated Instruction 259M-259V

Day 4

Listening/Speaking

❷ Focus Question How was the boy's father in *The Printer* like the smokejumpers? How was he different?

Expand Vocabulary: Heroes, 259F

Vocabulary

Content Vocabulary: *remote, smokejumpers, physical, retreat,* 254

Related Words, 259F

Apply Vocabulary to Writing, 259F

Phonics

VCCV Game, 259E

Read "Smokejumpers," 254–257

Comprehension

Social Studies: Nonfiction Article

Text Feature: Map, 254
Practice Book A-O-B, 174

Student Book

Fluency Partner Reading, 230I

Writing

Daily Writing Prompt Imagine that you are a smokejumper. Write a diary entry for a day on the job. Describe what you see, hear, smell, touch, and do.

Proofread a Speech, 259B

Grammar Daily Language Activities, 259I
Pronoun-Verb Agreement, 259J
Grammar Practice Book, 150

Spelling The VC/CV Pattern, 259H
Spelling Practice Book, 151

Quick Check Vocabulary, 259D

Differentiated Instruction 259M-259V

Day 5
Review and Assess

Listening/Speaking

❷ Focus Question Think about the heroes we have read about. Who would be most helpful in a forest fire? In an accident in a noisy factory? How do you know?

Speaking and Listening Strategies, 259A

Presentation of a Descriptive Paragraph, 259B

Vocabulary

Spiral Review: Crossword Puzzles, 259F

Read Self-Selected Reading, 230I

Comprehension

Connect and Compare, 257

Student Book

Fluency Partner Reading, 230I

Writing

Daily Writing Prompt Write a persuasive paragraph explaining why sign language should or should not be taught to everyone at school.

Publish a Speech, 259B

Grammar Daily Language Activities, 259I
Pronoun-Verb Agreement, 259J
Grammar Practice Book, 151–152

Spelling Posttest, 259H
Spelling Practice Book, 152

Weekly Assessment, 301–308

Differentiated Instruction 259M-259V

Small Group Options

What do I do in small groups?

Use your Quick Checks to inform instruction.

Additional Instruction, Practice, and Extend Activities are provided for this week's tested skills.

Phonics	Vocabulary	Comprehension	Fluency
Decode Words with the VC/CV Pattern	**Words:** screamed, numb, escape, fled, shuddered, image, newspaper **Strategy:** Context Clues: Figurative Language	**Strategy:** Make Inferences and Analyze **Skill:** Make and Confirm Predictions	

Lesson Plan
TEACHER-LED SMALL GROUP

 CD ROM

Instructional Navigator
Interactive Lesson Planner

Day 1

Day 2

Approaching Level

- **Additional Instruction/Practice**
- **Tier 2 Instruction**

Day 1
Leveled Reader Lesson 1, 259M
- Vocabulary
- Comprehension
- Fluency

Day 2
Leveled Reader Lesson 2, 259N
- Vocabulary
- Comprehension
- Fluency

ELL Practice Using Vocabulary, 259O

On Level

- **Practice**

Leveled Reader Lesson, 259Q
- Vocabulary
- Comprehension
- Fluency

ELL Leveled Reader, 259U–V

Leveled Reader Lesson, 259Q
- Vocabulary
- Comprehension
- Fluency

Beyond Level

- **Extend**

Leveled Reader Lesson, 259S
- Vocabulary
- Comprehension
- Fluency

Leveled Reader Lesson, 259S
- Vocabulary
- Comprehension
- Fluency

for Differentiated Instruction

Leveled Readers

GR Levels N–R
Matching students to text.

Also Available
LEVELED READER LIBRARY

LOG ON
Leveled Reader Database
To search for additional Leveled Reader titles, go to www.macmillanmh.com

Approaching Level
- Benchmark 30
- Use other guided reading titles, N–P

On Level
- Benchmark 38
- Use other guided reading titles, P–R

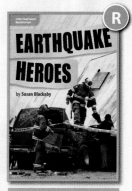

Beyond Level
- Benchmark 40
- Use other guided reading titles, R–T

English Language Leveled Reader

On Level Reader sheltered for English Language Learner

Day 3

Comprehension, 259O
Vocabulary, 259O

Vocabulary, 259R

Self-Selected Reading, 259T

Day 4

Phonics, 259P
Vocabulary, 259P

Text Feature, 259R

Vocabulary, 259T

Day 5

Fluency, 259N
Make Connections Across Texts, 259P

Make Connections Across Texts, 259R

Text Feature, 259T
ELL Description, 259T

The Printer **230F**

Managing the Class

What do I do with the rest of my class?

Teacher-Led Small Groups

Cross-Curricular Workstations

Independent Activities

Weekly Contract

Name _____ **Date** _____

My To-Do List

✔ Put a check next to the activities you complete.

📖 **Reading**
- ☐ Practice fluency
- ☐ Read the first part of story

🔤 **Word Study**
- ☐ Discuss figurative language
- ☐ Work with VC/CV words

✏️ **Writing**
- ☐ Write a description
- ☐ Describe a historical person

🔬 **Science**
- ☐ Research how fires start
- ☐ Create a Sequence Chart

🌎 **Social Studies**
- ☐ Research firehouses
- ☐ Write about firehouses

📖 **Leveled Readers**
- ☐ Write About It!
- ☐ Content Connection

🍎 **Technology**
- ☐ Vocabulary Puzzlemaker
- ☐ Fluency Solutions
- ☐ Listening Library
- ☐ www.macmillanmh.com

🖌️ **Independent Practice**
- ☐ Practice Book, 170–176
- ☐ Grammar Practice Book, 147–152
- ☐ Spelling Practice Book, 147–152

26 Unit 5 • The Printer   Contracts

© Macmillan/McGraw-Hill

Teacher's Resource Book, page 26

• Students use their Contracts to manage their time.

Leveled Reader Activities

Approaching

See inside back cover for activities

LEVELED PRACTICE

- Vocabulary, 170
- Comprehension: Make and Confirm Predictions, 171
- Graphic Organizer, 172
- Fluency, 173
- Text Feature: Maps, 174
- Vocabulary Strategy: Figurative Language, 175
- Phonics, 176

⭐ Approaching Practice Book A, 170–176

A. Draw a line matching the vocabulary words with the correct definitions.

1. fled — b. ran away
2. screamed — a. a picture in one's mind or a likeness
3. numb — c. a set of printed pages with news
4. escape — d. unable to move or feel anything
5. shuddered — e. to get free
6. image — f. made a loud cry from fear or surprise
7. newspaper — g. shook or trembled

B. Circle the correct vocabulary word to complete each sentence.

8. My father was reading about yesterday's basketball game in the sports section of the _____.
   a. newspaper   b. image

9. Everybody _____ from the park when the bad thunderstorms began.
   a. shuddered   **b. fled**

10. My little brother and sister _____ with fright during the scary part of the movie.
    a. escape   **b. screamed**

11. I had an _____ in my mind of the kind of shoes I wanted to buy.
    a. image   b. escape

12. The racoon tried very hard to _____ from the cage that it was trapped in.
    a. escape   b. shuddered

HOME-SCHOOL CONNECTION

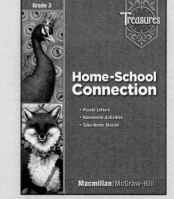

Pages 283–294

230G

Independent Activities

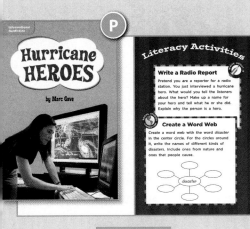

On Level

ELL

Beyond

On Level Practice Book O, 170–176

A. Read the paragraph. Then fill in each blank with the word from the box that makes the most sense.

> fled screamed numb escape shuddered image newspaper

Julio read an article in the **newspaper** about a dog whose name used to be Rover.

Rover Saves the Day!

Rover had **fled** from her owner's living room after she saw a huge ball bouncing toward a playground where children were playing. She made her **escape** through the front door which had been left open. Mr. Greene, her owner, **screamed** at Rover to stop the ball before it hit the children. Mr. Greene said he couldn't move. He felt **numb** when he saw the ball bouncing toward three children who were playing at the playground. Rover dashed over and hit the ball with her nose. Luckily, the ball bounced away from the children. Rover's owner was shaking. He **shuddered** when he thought about how the ball might have hurt the children. Rover saved the day and got a new name, too. It was Hero!

Julio smiled when he saw the **image** of Hero with the three children.

B. Write a sentence or two using as many vocabulary words as possible. Possible responses provided.

I was so afraid during the movie that I sat <u>numb</u> in my seat with fear. Then I <u>screamed</u> and <u>fled</u> from the movie theater and hid my face under a <u>newspaper</u>.

Beyond Practice Book B, 170–176

Write a short newspaper article that describes a heroes actions. Use all the words from the box in your article. Possible response provided.

> fled   screamed   numb   escape
> shuddered   image   newspaper

The hero who saved three dogs from a burning house early yesterday is Sean Williams. The family was able to <u>escape</u> from the house. After they <u>fled</u> their home, someone <u>screamed</u> that their three dogs were still upstairs. Williams was riding by on his bicycle when he heard the screams, and rushed to the scene. Onlookers were <u>numb</u> with fear watching the fire race through the house. Williams acted fast and climbed up onto the roof and through a window. "When I heard the children screaming I shuddered at the <u>image</u> of my own dogs in that situation, and that is why I acted," said Williams. He grabbed the three dogs and carried them to the roof. He climbed down to the waiting arms of the owners. The fire department quickly arrived and brought the fire under control. <u>Newspaper</u> reporters showed up and interviewed the hero of the day.

ELL Practice and Assessment, 146–147

Grade 3

Treasures

ELL Practice and Assessment

Macmillan/McGraw-Hill

Parent Letter

Take-Home Story

Turn the page for Cross-Curricular Activities.

Managing the Class

Cross-Curricular Activities

All activities reinforce this week's skills.

Reading

Objectives

- Read aloud with a partner.
- Make predictions about what will happen in a story.
- Select literature for daily reading enjoyment.

Word Study

Objectives

- Use context clues to find a word's meaning.
- Identify the number of syllables in words.

 Reading — **Fluency** — 20 Minutes

- Choose a reading buddy. Take turns reading aloud page 173 of your Practice Book.
- Read with strong feeling when you see an exclamation point.

Extension

- Read page 173 aloud to your partner.
- Ask your partner to raise a hand when he or she hears you read an exclamation.
- Listen to the responses to end punctuation on the audio disc.

Things you need:
- Practice Book

Fluency Solutions Listening Library

47

Word Study — **Figurative Language** — 20 Minutes

- Read this sentence: *The wind screamed through the windows and woke me up.*
- Is the wind really screaming? Talk with a partner about the meaning of the word *screamed* in this sentence.

Extension

- Look up the word *sigh*. Write a sentence that begins with these words: *The wind sighed.*
- Write context clues in your sentence to show the meaning of *sighed.*

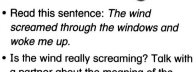

Things you need:
- paper
- pencil

For additional vocabulary and spelling games, go to www.macmillanmh.com Vocabulary PuzzleMaker

47

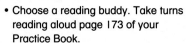 **Reading** — **Independent Reading** — 20 Minutes

- Work with a partner. Choose a story that is new to both of you.
- Have your partner read the first part of the story aloud to you. Tell your partner what you think will happen. Tell why.
- Then switch roles.

Extension

- Read the rest of the story with your partner. Were your predictions correct?

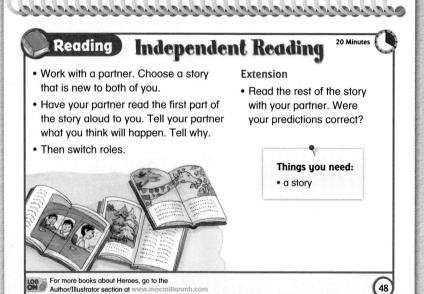

Things you need:
- a story

For more books about Heroes, go to the Author/Illustrator section at www.macmillanmh.com

48

Word Study — **The VC/CV Pattern** — 20 Minutes

- Write these words on note cards: *mammal, basket, rabbit, number, letter,* and *problem.*
- Read each word aloud. Clap your hands to show the number of syllables.

Extension

- Cut each card apart to separate the syllables.
- Mix up all the pieces. Then put all the words back together again.

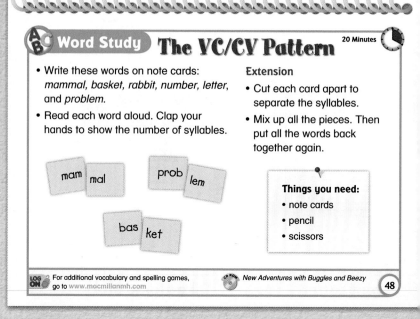

Things you need:
- note cards
- pencil
- scissors

For additional vocabulary and spelling games, go to www.macmillanmh.com New Adventures with Buggles and Beezy

48

Independent Workstations

Writing

Objectives

- Write a descriptive paragraph about an admirable person.
- Write a paragraph about a historical figure.

Writing — Descriptive Writing
20 Minutes

- Think about someone you admire. This person can be someone you know or someone you have read about.
- Write a descriptive paragraph. Tell who this person is. Tell why you admire him or her.

Grandpa

He helps sick people at the hospital. He plays baseball with me.

Extension

- Draw an award to give this person. Write two sentences. Tell why he or she deserves it.

Things you need:
- paper
- pencil
- crayons or markers

47

Writing — Get the Scoop!
20 Minutes

- Think about a person you admire in history.
- Use an encyclopedia, a history book, or the Internet. Learn more about this person.
- Write a descriptive paragraph. Tell why you admire this person.

George Washington   Rosa Parks

Extension

- Pretend this person is still alive. Write three questions you would ask him or her.

Things you need:
- computer, history book, or encyclopedia
- paper
- pencil

48

Science/Social Studies

Objectives

- Research information about firehouses.
- Research information about the causes of fire.

Social Studies — At the Firehouse
20 Minutes

- Firefighters stay at the firehouse until a call comes in.
- What does the inside of a firehouse look like? Look in books, in an encyclopedia, or on the Internet to find pictures of firehouses. Take notes.

Extension

- Write five things you learned about the history of fire houses.

Things you need:
- books, encyclopedia, or computer
- paper
- pencil

Internet Research and Inquiry Activity
Students can find more facts at www.macmillanmh.com

47

Science — Fires
20 Minutes

- What causes a fire to start? Do research in an encyclopedia or on the Internet to find out.
- Take notes on the information you find.

Sequence Chart

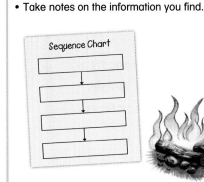

Extension

- Create a Sequence Chart. Tell how fires begin. Tell what happens first, next, then, and last.

Things you need:
- computer or encyclopedia
- paper
- pencil

48

Prepare

ORAL LANGUAGE
- Build Background
- Read Aloud
- Expand Vocabulary

 VOCABULARY
- Teach Words in Context
- Context Clues: Figurative Language

COMPREHENSION
- **Strategy:** Make Inferences and Analyze
- **Skill:** Make and Confirm Predictions

SMALL GROUP OPTIONS

- Differentiated Instruction, pp. 259M–259V

230

Oral Language

Build Background

ACCESS PRIOR KNOWLEDGE

Share the following information.

A hero is someone who shows great courage or strength. People who take risks or put themselves in danger so they can help others are heroes.

TALK ABOUT HEROES

Discuss students' knowledge of heroes.

- Do you know any real-life heroes? What makes them heroes?

 FOCUS QUESTION Ask a volunteer to read "Talk About It" on **Student Book** page 231 and describe the photograph.

- Why do you think firefighters are considered heroes?

ENGLISH LANGUAGE LEARNERS

Access for All

Beginning Activate Background Knowledge Help students say what they can about the photo. Say: *This firefighter is a hero. A hero helps people in danger. A police officer is a hero, too. What heroes do you know about?*

Intermediate Make Comparisons Have students talk about the picture. Then mention superheroes. Have students compare and contrast superheroes to real-life heroes. Write their statements on the board. Introduce words such as *courage/courageous, risk, strong,* and *danger/dangerous.*

Advanced Discuss Do the same task as at the Intermediate level. Ask: *Do we need heroes? Why? What stories have we read in which someone was a hero?* Encourage students to use more complex language. Model this by restating what they say.

Talk About It

A hero is any person who helps others. What qualities do all heroes have?

LOG ON Find out more about heroes at **www.macmillanmh.com**

HEROES

231

Picture Prompt

Tell students: Look at the picture. Write about what you see. You can write a poem, a story, a description, or use any other type of writing you like.

LOG ON Technology

For an extended lesson plan and Web site activities for **oral language development,** go to www.macmillanmh.com

Read Aloud
Read "The Name of the Tree"

GENRE: Folk Tale
Review features of folk tales:

- stories based on customs and traditions of a people or a region

- are handed down orally from one generation to the next

LISTENING FOR A PURPOSE

Ask students to listen to find out who is a hero as they listen to "The Name of the Tree" in the **Read-Aloud Anthology.** Choose from among the teaching suggestions.

Fluency Ask students to listen carefully as you read aloud. Tell students to listen to your phrasing, expression, and tone of voice and to watch your facial expressions.

RESPOND TO THE FOLK TALE

Ask: Who was the hero in this tale? Why was this character the hero? What did he do?

Expand Vocabulary

Ask students to choose three or more words from the folk tale that relate to the theme of heroes, such as *climb, fastest, kindly, thanked,* and *grateful.*

Have students use these words to make up a story about a hero. Ask them to write a newspaper article about what this hero did to help someone else. Ask students to share their articles with a partner.

Vocabulary

TEACH WORDS IN CONTEXT

Use the following routine.

Routine

__Define:__ If you **screamed,** you cried out loudly from fear or excitement.

__Example:__ Chris screamed when the bat flew into the house.

__Ask:__ Were you ever so scared that you screamed? PRIOR EXPERIENCE

- Someone who is **numb** is unable to move or feel. I was numb with fear. What else can make you numb? EXAMPLE

- To **escape** is to get away. The cat chased the mouse, but the mouse was able to escape. Why would an animal try to escape from something? EXPLANATION

- If you **fled,** you ran away. People fled from the burning building. What word means the opposite of *fled*? (stayed) ANTONYM

- If people **shuddered,** they shook or trembled from fear. The boy in the fairy tale shuddered when he saw the giant. When have you shuddered? Why? EXAMPLE

- An **image** is a picture in your mind. An image can also be a likeness or a copy of a real thing, such as a photograph. What image comes to mind when you hear the word *smile*? DESCRIPTION

- A **newspaper** is a set of pages that has the news printed on them. A city newspaper is usually printed every day. What is the difference between a newspaper and a magazine? COMPARE AND CONTRAST

Vocabulary

screamed	shuddered
numb	image
escape	newspaper
fled	

Context Clues

Figurative Language makes unexpected comparisons between people or things.

The van *shuddered* to a stop.

To the Rescue

by Daniel Dahari

It was recess time. It was a perfect spring day, and Ms. Clark's class hurried outdoors.

Erica headed straight for the slide. There was nothing better than a climb and a slide. Especially on a day like this! She was just about to place her foot on the ladder when she stopped and **screamed** with fear. Everyone ran over to find out what had happened. Erica stood there, **numb**. She couldn't move an inch. Under the ladder's first rung was a turtle, a big turtle—and it was stuck!

"Stand clear," warned Ms. Clark. "It's trying to **escape**, but it can't get out. Poor thing."

Several boys and girls **fled** across the yard. That turtle looked mean.

232

Quick Check

Do students understand word meanings?

During **Small Group Instruction**

If No → **Approaching Level** Vocabulary, p. 259P

If Yes → **On Level** Options, pp. 259Q–259R

Beyond Level Options, pp. 259S–259T

"That's a snapping turtle," said Jeff. "Snappers have really strong jaws. That thing can really bite! I wonder how it got here."

The turtle tried to dig with its feet but remained stuck.

"I'll call the police," said Ms. Clark. "They'll send over Animal Control. They'll know what to do."

An Animal Control van pulled up and **shuddered** to a stop. The officer said, "That's a snapping turtle, all right. It must have come up from the marsh. We'd better get him back where he belongs."

She got a small shovel and carefully removed the sand beneath the turtle. Then the officer gently wrapped the turtle in a towel. She said, "You did the right thing by calling me. It's very dangerous to try to free a trapped animal yourselves."

Ms. Clark took a picture. "This **image** will go on the front page of the school **newspaper** next week," she said. "It's not every day that we get a snapshot of a snapping turtle!"

Reread for **Comprehension**

Make Inferences and Analyze
Make and Confirm Predictions
When you make predictions, you are making an inference about what you think might happen in the story based on the story clues.

A Predictions Chart can help you analyze clues to make good predictions. Reread the story to confirm what you predicted.

What I Predict	What Happens

233

Vocabulary

eview last week's vocabulary words: **owered, declared, existed, artist's** nd **pride.**

■ **On Level Practice Book O,** page 170

A. Read the paragraph. Then fill in each blank with the word from the box that makes the most sense.

fled screamed numb escape shuddered image newspaper

Julio read an article in the ___newspaper___ about a dog whose name used to be Rover.

Rover Saves the Day!

Rover had ___fled___ from her owner's living room after she saw a huge ball bouncing toward a playground where children were playing. She made her ___escape___ through the front door which had been left open. Mr. Greene, her owner, ___screamed___ at Rover to stop the ball before it hit the children. Mr. Greene said he couldn't move. He felt ___numb___ when he saw the ball bouncing toward three children who were playing at the playground. Rover dashed over and hit the ball with her nose. Luckily, the ball bounced away from the children. Rover's owner was shaking. He ___shuddered___ when he thought about how the ball might have hurt the children. Rover saved the day and got a new name, too. It was Hero! Julio smiled when he saw the ___image___ of Hero with the three children.

B. Write a sentence or two using as many vocabulary words as possible. Possible responses provided.

I was so afraid during the movie that I sat numb in my seat with fear. Then I screamed and fled from the movie theater and hid my face under a newspaper.

★ **Approaching Practice Book A,** page 170
◆ **Beyond Practice Book B,** page 170

Vocabulary

Using the Strategies To figure out unfamiliar words, students can use phonics to decode words, look for word parts, look for context clues, or use a dictionary.

STRATEGY
USE CONTEXT CLUES

Figurative Language Writers sometimes use a word in a way different from the word's literal or dictionary meaning. This unusual use of words is a kind of **figurative language.** For example, *growled* is used in an unusual way in this sentence: *The car's engine growled loudly.* The word *growled* usually describes a deep rumbling sound an animal makes in its throat. Here it describes the sound a car makes. To figure out the meaning of *growled*, readers use context clues.

Point to the word *shuddered* on **Student Book** page 233. It usually means "trembled from fear" and tells about a person or living thing. In this case, the word describes the van, so the word *shuddered* is being used in a different way from the meaning in the dictionary. To figure out the meaning, a reader has to look at the meaning of the rest of the sentence. Here *shuddered* means "shook."

Read "To the Rescue"

As students read "To the Rescue," ask them to identify clues that reveal the meanings of the highlighted words. Tell students they will read these words again in *The Printer.*

Objectives

- Make inferences about a story
- Analyze a story
- Make and confirm predictions about a story
- Use academic language: *inferences, analyze, predictions*

Materials

- Comprehension Transparencies 24a and 24b
- Graphic Organizer Transparency 24
- Leveled Practice Books, p. 171

Skills Trace

Make and Confirm Predictions	
Introduce	U4: 115A–B
Practice / Apply	U4: 116–139; Practice Book, 141–142
Reteach / Review	U4: 145M–T; U5: 233A–B; 234–253; 259M–T; Leveled Practice, 171–172
Assess	Weekly Tests; Unit 4, 5 Tests; Benchmark Tests A, B
Maintain	U6: 379B

ELL   Access for All

Use an Analogy Ask: *What's the weather going to be like tomorrow?* Elicit predictions and write them on the board. Say: *We don't know for sure what kind of weather we're going to have, but we know the weather today and what season this is. We can use those clues to make a prediction. You can make predictions when you read a story, too.*

Reread for
Comprehension

STRATEGY
MAKE INFERENCES AND ANALYZE

Authors don't always tell a reader every detail in a story. Readers often have to **analyze,** or carefully look at, the information in the story and then **make inferences** about it. They can also make inferences to predict what will happen in the story. To make inferences, good readers use what they know and story clues to figure out what is missing. When readers make inferences they can better understand the characters and events.

SKILL
MAKE AND CONFIRM PREDICTIONS

EXPLAIN

 When readers **make predictions,** they make inferences using story clues and what they know to tell what they think will happen next.

Tell students:

- To make a prediction, look for story clues that hint at what might happen in the story. Use your own knowledge and experience.

 Transparency 24a

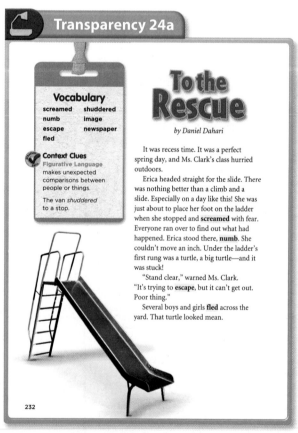

Vocabulary

screamed	shuddered
numb	image
escape	newspaper
fled	

Context Clues
Figurative Language makes unexpected comparisons between people or things.

The van *shuddered* to a stop.

To the Rescue

by Daniel Dahari

It was recess time. It was a perfect spring day, and Ms. Clark's class hurried outdoors.

Erica headed straight for the slide. There was nothing better than a climb and a slide. Especially on a day like this! She was just about to place her foot on the ladder when she stopped and **screamed** with fear. Everyone ran over to find out what had happened. Erica stood there, **numb.** She couldn't move an inch. Under the ladder's first rung was a turtle, a big turtle—and it was stuck!

"Stand clear," warned Ms. Clark. "It's trying to **escape**, but it can't get out. Poor thing."

Several boys and girls **fled** across the yard. That turtle looked mean.

232

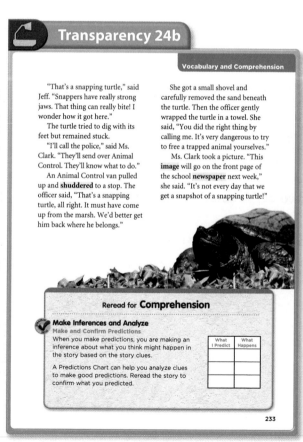 **Transparency 24b**

Vocabulary and Comprehension

"That's a snapping turtle," said Jeff. "Snappers have really strong jaws. That thing can really bite! I wonder how it got here."

The turtle tried to dig with its feet but remained stuck.

"I'll call the police," said Ms. Clark. "They'll send over Animal Control. They'll know what to do."

An Animal Control van pulled up and **shuddered** to a stop. The officer said, "That's a snapping turtle, all right. It must have come up from the marsh. We'd better get him back where he belongs."

She got a small shovel and carefully removed the sand beneath the turtle. Then the officer gently wrapped the turtle in a towel. She said, "You did the right thing by calling me. It's very dangerous to try to free a trapped animal yourselves."

Ms. Clark took a picture. "This **image** will go on the front page of the school **newspaper** next week," she said. "It's not every day that we get a snapshot of a snapping turtle!"

Reread for Comprehension

Make Inferences and Analyze
Make and Confirm Predictions
When you make predictions, you are making an inference about what you think might happen in the story based on the story clues.

A Predictions Chart can help you analyze clues to make good predictions. Reread the story to confirm what you predicted.

What I Predict	What Happens

233

Student Book pages 232–233 available on Comprehension Transparencies 24a and 24b

■ Read on to see if the prediction is correct. If you find new information, you may need to revise your prediction.

MODEL

Read aloud the title and first two paragraphs of "To the Rescue" from **Student Book** page 232.

Think Aloud I know that the title of a story often gives a clue about what will happen. "To the Rescue" tells me that the story will be about helping someone or something in trouble. Then I read that Erica finds a turtle stuck under the ladder of the slide. If I saw a stuck turtle, I would try to help it. Using the clue in the story title and what I know, I predict that the class will free the turtle. As I continue to read, I will check to see if my prediction was correct. If not, I will revise my prediction.

GUIDED PRACTICE

Display **Transparency 24.** On the chart under "What I Predict," write the first prediction: "The class will rescue the turtle."

■ Have students read the rest of page 232 and predict what the turtle will do. Have them tell why they made this prediction. (It will bite someone. Clues: the turtle looks mean, wild animals can be dangerous) After they read the first column on page 233, help them confirm or revise the first prediction and write what happens on the chart under "What Happens." (The class does not rescue the turtle. They call the police.)

■ To help students make a third prediction, ask: *Will the officer from Animal Control be able to rescue the turtle?* Have students add this prediction to their charts.

APPLY

Have students confirm or revise their other predictions and complete the "What Happens" column of the chart as they read the rest of the story.

 Transparency 24

Predictions Chart

What I Predict	What Happens
The class will rescue the turtle.	The class does not rescue the turtle. They call the police to help the turtle.
The turtle will bite someone.	The turtle does not bite anyone.
The animal control officer will rescue the turtle.	The animal control officer rescues the turtle.

Graphic Organizer Transparency 24

On Level Practice Book O, page 171

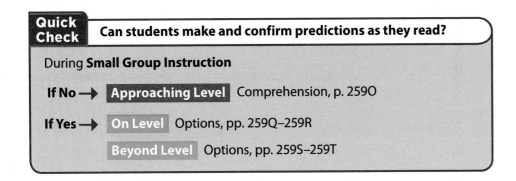

What you learn in a story can help you **predict** what will happen next. As you read on, **confirm** your prediction, or find out if you were right.

There are four predictions in the box. Choose a prediction for each paragraph. Then write it on the line.

> She will go see the movie. She will work on the project.
> He will go to the competition. He will stay home and find something else to do.

1. Juanita's hero is her teacher. She wants to make her teacher proud of her. Juanita has a project due tomorrow. Her friend has just invited her to see a movie that Juanita has yearned to see. There is not enough time to finish the project and see the movie.

   She will work on the project.

2. Pedro has been an in-line skater for two years. He has been practicing for a big competition. Heavy rain has been falling all day. The competition has been delayed until the rain stops. Pedro is disappointed.

   He will stay home and find something else to do.

3. Lily's heroes are actors. She has just learned that she might get a role in a movie. She wants to watch a lot of movies to learn more about acting. Lily's friend has invited her to see a new movie in town.

   She will go see the movie.

4. Carl wants to learn more about bike racing. He knows that a good way to learn is by watching others race. There's a big competition in town.

   He will go to the competition.

★ **Approaching Practice Book A,** page 171

◆ **Beyond Practice Book B,** page 171

Quick Check — **Can students make and confirm predictions as they read?**

During **Small Group Instruction**

If No → **Approaching Level** Comprehension, p. 259O

If Yes → **On Level** Options, pp. 259Q–259R

Beyond Level Options, pp. 259S–259T

Read

Comprehension

GENRE: REALISTIC FICTION

Have a student read the definition of Realistic Fiction on **Student Book** page 234. Students should look for events that might happen in real life and characters who seem like real people.

STRATEGY
MAKE INFERENCES AND ANALYZE

Good readers use their own experiences and clues in the story to figure out information the author has left out to make predictions about what will happen next. This is called **making inferences.**

SKILL
MAKE AND CONFIRM PREDICTIONS

When readers **make predictions,** they make inferences using story clues and their own experiences to tell what they think will happen next. As they read, they will confirm or revise the predictions.

234

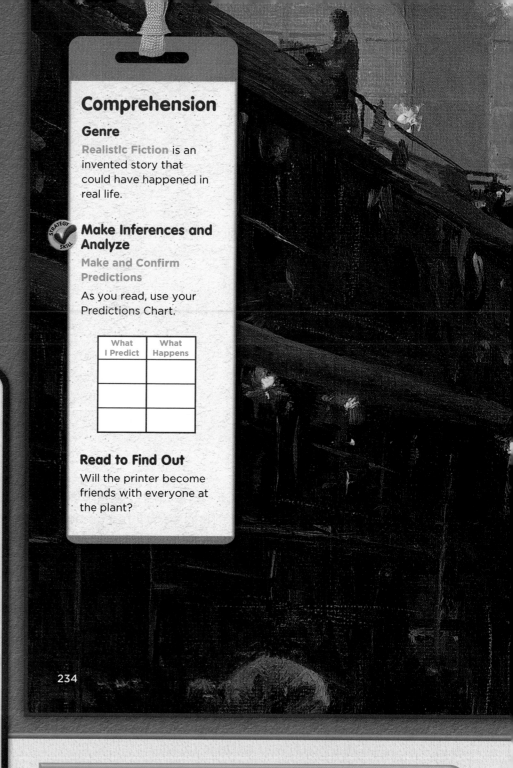

Comprehension

Genre

Realistic Fiction is an invented story that could have happened in real life.

Make Inferences and Analyze

Make and Confirm Predictions

As you read, use your Predictions Chart.

What I Predict	What Happens

Read to Find Out

Will the printer become friends with everyone at the plant?

234

Vocabulary

Vocabulary Words Review the tested vocabulary words: **screamed, numb, escape, fled, shuddered, image,** and **newspaper.**

Story Words Students might find this word difficult.

lead-type (p. 239): small metal blocks with raised letters for use on a printing press

THE PRINTER

by Myron Uhlberg
illustrated by Henri Sørensen

235

Main Selection Student pages 234–235

Preview and Predict

Ask students to read the title, preview the illustrations, note questions and make predictions about the story. Have students write their predictions and anything else they want to know about the story.

Set Purposes

FOCUS QUESTION Discuss the "Read to Find Out" question. Remind students to look for the answer as they read.

Point out the Predictions Chart in the **Student Book** and on **Leveled Practice Book** page 172. Explain that students will fill in Predictions Charts as they read the story.

Read *The Printer*

Use the questions and Think Alouds for additional instruction to support the comprehension strategy and skill.

Read Together	Read Independently
If your students need support to read the Main Selection, use the prompts to guide comprehension and model how to complete the graphic organizer.	If your students can read the Main Selection independently, have them read and complete the graphic organizer. Have students set and modify their purposes and reading rates.

If your students need an alternate selection, choose the **Leveled Readers** that match their instructional level.

Technology

Story available on **Listening Library Audio CD**

On Level Practice Book O, page 172

As you read *The Printer*, fill in the Predictions Chart.

Predictions Chart

What I Predict	What Happens

How does the information you wrote in this Predictions Chart help you make inferences and analyze *The Printer*?

⭐ **Approaching Practice Book A,** page 172

◆ **Beyond Practice Book B,** page 172

Develop Comprehension

1 MAINTAIN
SEQUENCE

What happens each day after the narrator's father gets home from work but before the narrator goes to bed? (The narrator's father reads the newspaper he brings home with him. When he is finished, he uses one of the pages to make a hat for the narrator. At bedtime, the narrator takes off the hat.)

236

My father was a printer. He wore a printer's four-cornered **newspaper** hat. Every day after work, he brought home the next day's paper. After reading it, he always folded a page into a small hat and gently placed it on my head.

I would not take off my newspaper hat until bedtime.

My father was deaf. Though he could not hear, he felt through the soles of his shoes the pounding and rumbling of the giant printing presses that daily spat out the newspaper he helped create.

237

Develop Comprehension

2 **STRATEGY**
USE CONTEXT CLUES

The phrase *spat out* is **figurative language.** What do you think it means? How can you figure out the meaning for sure? (I think it might mean "rejected," but I will use context clues to help me judge the meaning better. I know that the newspaper presses don't really spit out paper. "Spitting out" is something that a baby does, not a machine. By using context clues, I understand that this phrase means the presses are quickly pushing out sheets of paper.)

Develop Comprehension

3 **NARRATOR'S POINT OF VIEW**

Who is telling the story? How do you know? (The narrator is a character in the story. He is the printer's son. He calls the printer "my father" and he calls himself "me" and "I." This shows that the narrator is also one of the story's characters. An illustration on page 237 shows the son watching his father make him a newspaper hat, an event the narrator describes in the story.)

238

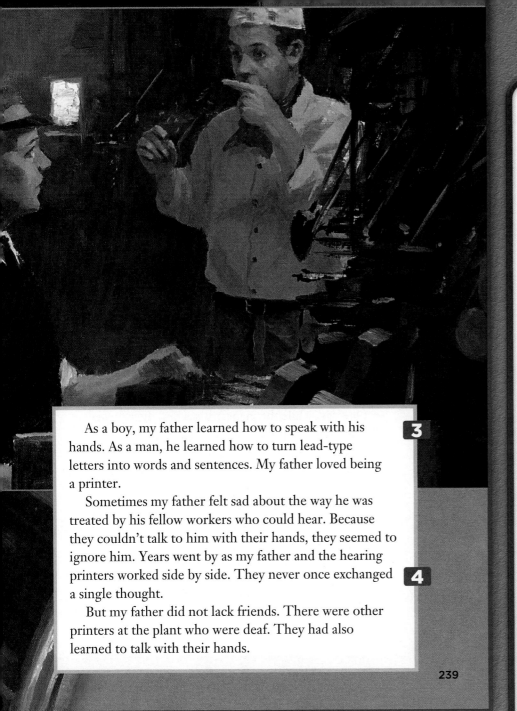

As a boy, my father learned how to speak with his hands. As a man, he learned how to turn lead-type letters into words and sentences. My father loved being a printer.

3

Sometimes my father felt sad about the way he was treated by his fellow workers who could hear. Because they couldn't talk to him with their hands, they seemed to ignore him. Years went by as my father and the hearing printers worked side by side. They never once exchanged a single thought.

4

But my father did not lack friends. There were other printers at the plant who were deaf. They had also learned to talk with their hands.

239

Cross-Curricular Connection

AMERICAN SIGN LANGUAGE

The father in the story speaks with his hands. Explain that many hearing-impaired people communicate by using American Sign Language (ASL), a language that uses the hands, face, and body to form letters, words, and phrases.

Have students locate books about ASL in the library. Encourage them to learn to sign statements, such as "good morning" and "thank you," and learn the Sign Language alphabet so they can sign their names. Have students present what they have learned in a class demonstration. Encourage them to write a brief summary and to make a poster or illustration.

Develop Comprehension

4 STRATEGY
MAKE INFERENCES AND ANALYZE

Teacher Think Aloud The boy's father, who is deaf, seems to be the main character in the story. I can make inferences about what will happen to him by using clues in the story. The son says that the father was sad sometimes because he was ignored by fellow workers who could hear. They never ever spoke to one another. I know if I were the boy's father, I would want to do something about this. Using this information, I can infer, or make a prediction, that later in the story the boy's father will make friends with the other workers. As I read, I will see if my prediction is correct.

RESEARCH
Why It Matters

Comprehension *Contemporary Educational Psychology* states that: "It is helpful for students to think about *when* and *where* they might use a reading strategy again. This assists students in taking a strategy they learned and applying that strategy to their own personal reading. The application of the strategy to real reading can often make a difference in whether or not students will use the strategy on their own when they do not have the support or assistance of a teacher."

Janice A. Dole

LOG ON   Log on to
www.macmillanmh.com

Develop Comprehension

5 MAKE PREDICTIONS

How will the printer tell people about the fire? Place your prediction on a Predictions Chart. (The printer speaks with his hands. There are other deaf printers who work in the pressroom, so he will probably use his hands to tell them there is a fire. That is what I would do.)

What I Predict	What Happens
He will use his hands to tell the other deaf printers about the fire.	

One day, while the giant presses ran, their noises shutting out all other sound, my father spotted a fire flickering in a far corner of the pressroom.

The fire was spreading quickly, silently. Suddenly, the wood floor burst into flames.

My father knew he had to tell everyone. He couldn't speak to shout a warning. Even if he could, no one would hear him over the loud roar of the presses.

5 But he could speak with his hands.

 Make and Confirm Predictions
How will the printer tell people about the fire?

240

Comprehension

Make and Confirm Predictions

Explain To make predictions, readers use clues in the story and personal experiences to tell what will happen next. As they continue to read, they see if the prediction was correct. If their predictions are incorrect, they can revise them, using new information from the story.

Discuss Ask students: What happens during fire drills at school? (When the alarm rings, everyone walks out of the building calmly but quickly. Teachers check that everyone has left.) What do you think the printer will do? (He will tell the other deaf printers. Together, they will act like teachers at a fire drill, lead everyone out, and check that no one is left behind.)

Apply Have students confirm or revise their predictions about what the printer will do as they continue reading. Have them continue making and confirming predictions as they read.

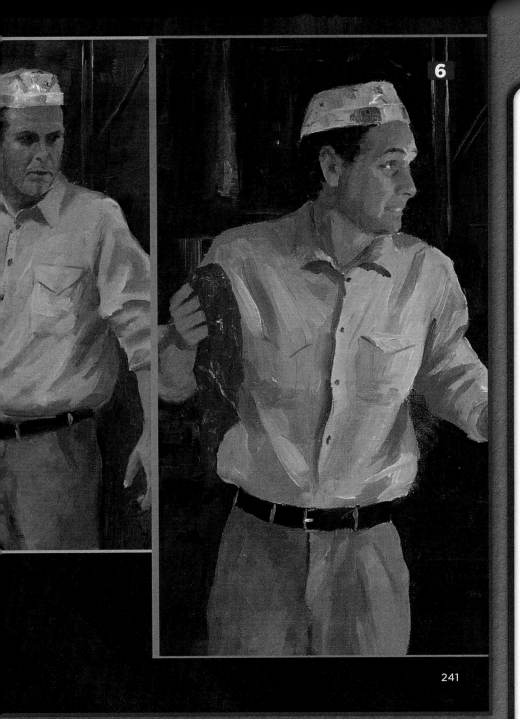

241

Develop Comprehension

6 **GENRE: REALISTIC FICTION**

How do the actions and events described on page 240 show that this story is realistic fiction? Which details in the art add to the realism of the characters or setting? (The fire in the story puts people in danger, just as fires do in real life. The printer needs to find a way to tell the others, just as people in real life do when they face problems that need to be solved quickly. The characters in the story act just like people do in real life. The printer's changing facial expressions in the art make him seem more realistic.)

Develop Comprehension

MAKE INFERENCES AND ANALYZE

Teacher Think Aloud The author doesn't tell us how the printers feel about the fire. Use what you know and story clues to make this inference.

Encourage students to apply the strategy in a Think Aloud.

Student Think Aloud I know that most people are very frightened of fire. I see that the father is waving his arms and shouting with his hands and that another printer's fingers screamed to the other deaf workers. I see that words the deaf people "say" are in capital letters, showing they are really trying to tell everyone to get out. Using what I know and the actions of characters in the story, I think that the printers are all very frightened of the fire.

8 **STRATEGY**
USE CONTEXT CLUES

Is it possible for hands to shout? Why or why not? What does *shout* mean here? Is this use of *shout* an example of **figurative language**? (Hands can't really shout, because *shout* means that someone cries out with his or her voice. Here *shout* means that the narrator's father is using his hands wildly to tell the other deaf printers there is a fire. It is like shouting to them. Yes, *shout* is an example of figurative language.)

242

Fluency

Expression

Explain Tell students: When you read a part of a story that is suspenseful or exciting, your voice shows emotion. This helps listeners understand the importance of what is taking place.

Model Point out that when you read the beginning of the passage on **Student Book** page 240, and available on **Transparency 24,** your voice shows concern for the printers. Tell students that as you continue reading page 243, where the passage continues, you read more quickly to show the suspense of the events taking place. Your voice has the most emotion when you read the words the printer signs to the others. Encourage students to look for nonverbal ways you express the emotions, too.

Apply Have students take turns reading the passage, showing emotion while making sure their words can be clearly understood.

He did not hesitate. He jumped onto an ink drum and **7** waved his arms excitedly until, clear across the room, he caught the attention of a fellow printer who also couldn't hear a sound.

My father's hands shouted through the terrible noise **8** of the printing presses, **9**

FIRE! FIRE!

TELL EVERYONE TO GET OUT!

TELL THE HEARING ONES!

His friend climbed onto a huge roll of newsprint. His fingers **screamed** to the other deaf workers,

FIRE! FIRE!

TELL THE HEARING ONES!

All the printers who couldn't hear ran to fellow workers who could. They pointed to the fire, which had now spread to the wall next to the only exit.

Not one of my father's friends left until everyone knew of the danger. My father was the last to **escape**.

243

Extra Support

Monitor Comprehension

Help students see that to confirm or revise a prediction, they have to think about their original prediction and then figure out if what happens in the story matches it. Ask: *How does the printer talk to other people?* (He is deaf so he uses his hands.) *How did you think he would warn everyone about the fire?* (with his hands) *On page 243, How does the printer warn everyone?* (He uses his hands.) *Is this what you thought would happen?*

If students have difficulty making and confirming predictions, review the definitions on **Student Book** page 233A. Ask them to recall the prediction they made when they read page 240 and tell whether or not their prediction was correct according to the information on page 243. They should see that the narrator's father uses his hands to warn the other workers.

Develop Comprehension

9 CONFIRM PREDICTIONS

How does the printer tell the people about the fire? Was your prediction correct? If not, how did you revise your prediction? Place the information about what happens in the chart. (Yes, my prediction was correct. I thought the printer would use his hands to tell the people about the fire, and that is exactly what happened. OR No, my prediction was not correct. I thought that the printer would write a message. So I had to revise my prediction.)

What I Predict	What Happens
He will use his hands to tell the other deaf printers about the fire.	He uses his hands to tell the other printers about the fire.

PERSONAL RESPONSE

Have students respond to the story by confirming or revising their predictions and forming new questions.

Quick Check   **Can students make and confirm predictions about the story? If not, see the Extra Support on this page.**

Stop here if you wish to read this selection over two days.   **STOP**

Develop Comprehension

10 SUMMARIZE

What has happened so far in the story? Retell the story emphasizing the plot. (The printer is the first to see that the plant where he works has caught fire. He alerts another deaf printer, and together they work to let everyone know that they must escape. Everyone gets out of the plant safely. Fire engines arrive.)

10

By the time everyone had **fled**, the fire—feeding on huge quantities of paper—had engulfed the enormous plant. The giant presses, some still spewing out burning sheets of newspaper, had fallen partly through the floor. Great shafts of flame shot out of the bursting windows.

The printers stood in the street, broken glass at their feet. They embraced one another as the fire engines arrived. They were happy to be alive.

11

244

ELL   Access for All

Visualize Help students visualize the fire. Reread aloud page 244. Show by your voice and gestures how the author vividly pictures the massiveness of the plant by the use of words such as *huge* (quantities of paper), *enormous* (plant), and *giant* (presses). Use gestures and restate in simpler terms the meaning of words such as *engulfed, spewing, fallen,* and *shot out.* Explain the meaning of the word *embraced.*

Vocabulary

Read the sentence that contains the word **fled**. What does *fled* mean? (left a place very quickly)

Develop Comprehension

11 **WRITING TRAIT: VOICE**

How does the author add suspense and excitement to the scene? (The description of burning newspapers "spewing" out of the presses, the presses falling partly through the floor, and the "great shafts of flame" shooting through the broken windows show the dangers the printers face as they escape. It is clear that the printers were frightened because when they are safely outside of the building, the narrator says that they were happy to be alive.)

245

Comprehension

Ways to Confirm Meaning

Syntactic/Structural Cues

Explain Tell students that good readers sometimes use context clues and grammar to help them understand a difficult word.

Model Read the word *engulfed* in context. Begin by sounding it out.

Think Aloud I see the word has an *ed* ending. The base word has *ul* in it and reminds me of other words I know like *dull* and *gull*. I know from the sentence that it is a verb because it is something the fire has done. I know that the printing press has fallen partly through the floor and huge flames have shot out of the windows. So, I think that *engulfed* means "completely covered."

Apply Have students predict what other difficult words mean and use phonics and grammatical clues to help them check their guesses. For example, is the word a noun, adjective, or verb?

Develop Comprehension

12 STRATEGY
MONITOR AND CLARIFY: REREAD TO CLARIFY

What strategy can you use to figure out what kind of repairs were needed while the printing plant was closed? (Rereading pages 244 and 247 helps me understand details about the damage to the plant. The presses had fallen partly through the floor, so the floor needs to be fixed. The windows were broken so the glass must be replaced. The presses themselves were destroyed so new ones must be put in place.)

246

Vocabulary

Read the sentence that contains the vocabulary words **numb** and **image.** Put this sentence into your own words. (My father stood by himself and felt nothing because he still saw the awful picture of the burning presses in his mind.)

My father stood alone, struck **numb** by the last **image** of the burning presses.

The fire destroyed the printing presses. The plant had to close for repairs. But not one printer had been hurt. **12**

When the printing plant finally reopened, my father went back to the work he loved. The new presses were switched on and roared into life. **13**

STRATEGY SKILL

Make and Confirm Predictions
How will the hearing printers treat the narrator's father now that the plant has reopened?

247

Develop Comprehension

13 MAKE PREDICTIONS

How will the hearing printers treat the narrator's father now that the plant has reopened? Why do you think this? Place your prediction on a Predictions Chart. (The printers know that the narrator's father and the other deaf printers saved everyone's lives by alerting them to the fire. I think they feel grateful, so they will now be more friendly to the narrator's father. I think this because it is what I would do. When someone does something for me, I show how grateful I am.)

What I Predict	What Happens
He will use his hands to tell the other deaf printers about the fire.	He uses his hands to tell the other printers about the fire.
The hearing printers will treat the narrator's father in a friendlier way.	

ELL

Access for All

STRATEGIES FOR EXTRA SUPPORT:

Question 13 MAKE PREDICTIONS
Explain that *treat* refers to how the hearing printers will act towards the father. *Will they be kinder, friendlier, nicer, more respectful, or mean and unfriendly?* Ask for specific examples: *How will they show their feelings?* Help students express their ideas. Help students figure out the meaning of *reopened* from context clues and its root word.

Develop Comprehension

14 STRATEGY

MAKE INFERENCES AND ANALYZE

The hearing printers tell the narrator's father "thank you" with their hands. Use story clues and your experience to explain why they do this.

Student Think Aloud I know that before the fire, the other printers seemed to ignore the narrator's father. They never talked to him because they did not bother to learn any sign language. After the fire, the other printers wanted to show how thankful they were because he saved their lives. That's what I would have done, too. The only way they could really talk to the narrator's father was with their hands. That's why they learned to sign "thank you."

When the day's newspaper had been printed, the presses **shuddered** to a stop. Now there was silence.

In the midst of the stillness, my father's co-workers gathered around him. They presented him with a hat made of the freshly printed newspaper.

And as my father put the hat on his head, all the printers who could hear did something surprising.

14 15   They told him THANK YOU with their hands.

248

Develop Comprehension

15 **CONFIRM PREDICTIONS**

How do the hearing printers treat the narrator's father when the plant reopens? Was your prediction correct? Use this information to complete your Predictions Chart. (The hearing printers give the narrator's father the hat they had made for him and tell him "thank you" with their hands. Yes, my prediction was correct. I thought the other printers would act friendlier than before because they were grateful to the narrator's father.)

What I Predict	What Happens
He will use his hands to tell the other deaf printers about the fire.	He uses his hands to tell the other printers about the fire.
The hearing printers will treat the narrator's father in a friendlier way.	The hearing printers give the narrator's father the hat they had made for him and tell him "thank you" with their hands.

249

Develop Comprehension

16 DRAW CONCLUSIONS

How does the narrator feel about his father? How do you know? (The narrator loves his father and wants to grow up to be like him. He tells this story about how brave his father was. He goes to sleep still wearing the hat and thinks about working beside his father at the printing plant.)

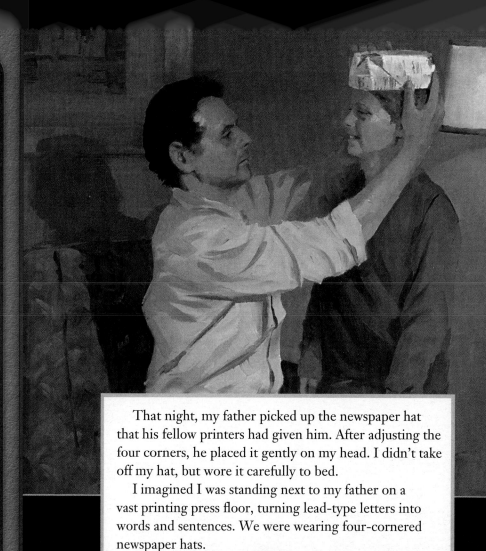

That night, my father picked up the newspaper hat that his fellow printers had given him. After adjusting the four corners, he placed it gently on my head. I didn't take off my hat, but wore it carefully to bed.

I imagined I was standing next to my father on a vast printing press floor, turning lead-type letters into words and sentences. We were wearing four-cornered newspaper hats.

We were printers.   **16**

250

251

Develop Comprehension

RETURN TO PREDICTIONS AND PURPOSES

Review students' predictions and purposes. Were they correct? Were students able to make and confirm predictions about characters and events in the story? Discuss any questions students have about the story and strategies for answering them.

REVIEW READING STRATEGIES

Ask students: How did making inferences help you to understand the story? What strategies did you use when you came to difficult words?

PERSONAL RESPONSE

Ask students to share their responses and opinions about the story. Then have them write a new ending by telling how the deaf and hearing printers can get to know each other better now that they have returned to work. Examples might include writing messages or learning sign language during their lunch break. Challenge students to replicate the author's style.

Quick Check   **Can students make and confirm predictions as they read realistic fiction?**

During **Small Group Instruction**

If No → **Approaching Level** Leveled Reader Lessons, pp. 259M–259N

If Yes → **On Level** Options, pp. 259Q–259R

         Beyond Level Options, pp. 259S–259T

Author and Illustrator

SAVE THE DAY WITH MYRON AND HENRI

Have students read the author and illustrator biographies.

DISCUSS

- Why do you think Myron Uhlberg created a character who was like his father? He titled his book after his father's job. Can you think of another title he could have used? Base your answer on details in the story.

- What feelings do you think Henri Sørensen had when he made his illustrations? Why?

Write About It

Call on a volunteer to read aloud the directions for the writing activity. Discuss with students their experiences with being thanked for something they have done. Suggest that they include why the incident they chose was memorable. Look for specific details when you evaluate their work.

LOG ON **Technology**

Students can find more information about Myron Uhlberg and Henri Sørensen at www.macmillanmh.com

---

SAVE THE DAY WITH MYRON AND HENRI

Author

Myron Uhlberg used memories of his father to write his story. Myron's father was born deaf. He worked as a newspaper printer just like the father in the story. When Myron was young, he would visit his father at work. Even today, Myron still remembers how noisy the pressroom was. He also remembers the hats his father made out of newspaper for him.

Other books by Myron Uhlberg: *Flying Over Brooklyn* and *Mad Dog McGraw*

Illustrator

Henri Sørensen grew up in Denmark and spent much of his childhood in a quiet museum. Every week he visited the museum to look at paintings. When Henri illustrates a story, he thinks about how the words make him feel. Then he tries to show the feeling in his pictures.

LOG ON Find out more about Myron Uhlberg and Henri Sørensen at www.macmillanmh.com

Write About It

The father in this story is rewarded with a hat and a "thank you," said in sign language. What was the best "thank you" you've ever received?

252

Author's Craft
Sensory Images

Myron Uhlberg uses sensory details and images in *The Printer* to help readers feel like they are a part of the story.

- **Sensory images** are words that appeal to the five senses: sight, touch, hearing, smell, and taste. For example: *Though he could not hear, he felt through the soles of his shoes the pounding and rumbling of the giant printing presses that daily spat out the newspaper he helped create.* (p. 237)

- Readers can imagine what it feels like to stand in a printing plant as the presses run.

Have students look for and discuss other examples of sensory details and images, such as "My father's hands shouted through the terrible noise of the printing presses."

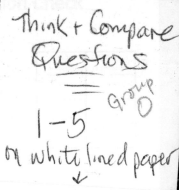

Comprehens[ion Check]

Summarize

Use the Predictions Chart to help you summarize what happens in *The Pri[nter].* Tell what you thought would happe[n] and what really happened at the en[d of] the story.

[Handwritten note:] Think + Compare Questions = 1-5 Group O on white lined paper ↓

Think and Compare

1. When the deaf printer noticed the fire in the **newspaper** plant, what did you predict would happen next? Were you right? Explain. **Make Inferences and Analyze: Make and Confirm Predictions**

2. Reread page 248. What is the importance of the hearing printers learning how to say "thank you" in sign language? **Evaluate**

3. If you did not know sign language, how would you tell a friend who is deaf something important? Explain. **Synthesize**

4. Before the fire, the hearing printers seemed to ignore the deaf printer. Why? **Analyze**

5. Read "To the Rescue" on pages 232-233. How are the warning and rescue in this story different from the warning and rescue in *The Printer?* Use details from both selections in your answer. **Reading/Writing Across Texts**

253

Strategies for Answering Questions

Author and Me

Model the Author and Me strategy with question 1.

The answers to Author and Me questions are not directly stated in the selection. Students will have to think about what they already know and link it to what they learned from the text.

Think Aloud Question 1: The question asks about my prediction, so the answer is not in the story. When I read that the deaf printer noticed the fire, I thought about what I would do to tell everyone about the fire so that no one would get hurt. I knew that the printer could only talk with his hands. Using my own experience and this clue from the story, I predicted that he would talk with his hands. I was correct because that is exactly what he did.

Comprehension Check

SUMMARIZE

Have partners summarize *The Printer* in their own words by retelling the main events. Remind students to use their Predictions Charts to help them organize their summaries.

THINK AND COMPARE

Sample answers are given.

1. **Make and Confirm Predictions:** I predicted the father would do something to let the other workers know about the fire. I was right. USE AUTHOR AND ME

2. **Evaluate:** The hearing printers had never tried to speak with the deaf printers in sign language before the fire. When they said "thank you" in sign language, it showed that they were very thankful.

3. **Text-to-Self:** Students might say that they would write the important message down so their friend could read it.

4. **Text-to-World:** Students may say the hearing printers probably didn't realize that learning some sign language would have made the deaf printers feel more welcome.

FOCUS QUESTION

5. **Text-to-Text:** In both stories, a character warned others about danger, but the rescues were different. In "To the Rescue," an officer warns students that snapping turtles are dangerous and then rescues the turtle. In *The Printer*, the deaf printer warns his fellow workers about a fire and makes sure everyone gets to safety.

Objective
- Read fluently with choral reading
- 97–117 WCPM

Materials
- Fluency Transparency 24
- Fluency Solutions Audio CD
- Leveled Practice Books, p. 173

ELL | **Access for All**

Partner Read Review the meaning of the passage. Echo-read the passage a few times. Then have students take turns reading sentences with a partner until the last three sentences. Have them read those lines together.

On Level Practice Book O, page 173

As I read, I will pay attention to punctuation.

	Winds scream. Rain pelts down. Buildings shudder.
7	Trees sway back and forth. Branches break and fall to the
18	ground. It's a hurricane!
22	You've probably seen pictures or images of hurricanes
30	in a newspaper or on TV. What makes a storm a hurricane?
42	A hurricane is a storm with very strong winds and
52	heavy rain. It starts over warm waters in an ocean. The
63	storm might take the shape of a circle or an oval. It can be
77	up to 400 miles (640 km) wide.
82	How do people prepare for hurricanes? How do
90	"hurricane heroes" do their work? They do their jobs in
100	offices and shelters. They are important before, during, and
109	after a big storm. They help save lives.
117	How do people find out if a bad storm is coming?
128	Air Force pilots called hurricane hunters fly into the
137	eye of the storm. 141

Comprehension Check

1. What is a hurricane? **Main Idea and Details** a storm with very strong winds and heavy rain
2. Who are hurricane hunters? **Main Idea and Details** Hurricane hunters are Air Force pilots who fly into the eye of the hurricane.

	Words Read	–	Number of Errors	=	Words Correct Score
First Read		–		=	
Second Read		–		=	

  ★ **Approaching Practice Book A, page 173**

◆ **Beyond Practice Book B, page 173**

253A

Fluency
Repeated Reading: Punctuation in Dialogue

EXPLAIN/MODEL Tell students that they will be reading this passage chorally. Model reading the last three lines on **Transparency 24,** demonstrating the vocal emotion shown in the capitalized exclamatory words and sentences.

 Transparency 24

My father knew he had to tell everyone. He couldn't speak to shout a warning. Even if he could, no one would hear him over the loud roar of the presses.

But he could speak with his hands.

He did not hesitate. He jumped onto an ink drum and waved his arms excitedly until, clear across the room, he caught the attention of a fellow printer who also couldn't hear a sound.

My father's hands shouted through the terrible noise of the printing presses,

FIRE! FIRE!

TELL EVERYONE TO GET OUT!

TELL THE HEARING ONES!

Fluency Transparency 24
from *The Printer*, pages 240–243

 PRACTICE Divide the class into two groups. Have the groups alternate reading the sentences from the passage. Remind students that the last three lines are exclamatory and should be read with strong emotion. For additional practice, have students use **Leveled Practice Book** page 173 or Fluency Solutions.

Quick Check Can students read fluently with choral reading?

During **Small Group Instruction**

If No → **Approaching Level** Fluency, pp. 259M–259N

If Yes → **On Level** Options, pp. 259Q–259R

Beyond Level Options, pp. 259S–259T

Comprehension

 **MAINTAIN SKILL**
SEQUENCE

EXPLAIN/MODEL

- In a fiction story, **sequence** is the order in which events happen.

- Sometimes the author uses signal words such as *first, then, next, last, later,* and *after* to help a reader figure out when events take place.

- Understanding the sequence of events can help a reader identify and remember the main events in a story. Good readers summarize stories using sequence.

Model how to identify the sequence of events on page 232 of "To the Rescue."

PRACTICE

Ask students:

- In *The Printer,* what did the narrator's father do every day after work? (He returned to his home with a copy of the next day's newspaper. He read the paper and used one page to make a hat for his son. He placed the hat on his son's head.)

- What did the narrator's father do after he saw the fire at the printing plant? (As the fire spread, he jumped onto an ink drum, got another deaf printer's attention, and signed to him to get everyone out. Then he and the other printers who could not hear ran to everyone else and pointed to the fire. Once he was sure everyone had gotten out of the building safely, the narrator's father escaped.)

- What happened first, next, and last at the printing plant on the day it reopened? (First, the new presses were switched on so the printers could work. Next, the other printers gathered around the narrator's father and gave him a hat they had made out of a newspaper page. Last, they signed "thank you" as he put on the hat.)

Have students compare *The Printer* with other stories they have read. Ask why the stories are worthwhile and relevant.

Objectives

- Describe events in a story in the correct sequence
- Use academic language: *sequence*
- Identify sequence signal words

Skills Trace

Sequence	
Introduce	U3: 387A–B
Practice / Apply	U3: 388–411; Leveled Practice, 104–105
Reteach / Review	U3: 417M–T; U5: 153A–B; 154–177, 183M–T; Leveled Practice, 150–151
Assess	Weekly Tests; Unit 3, 5 Tests; Benchmark Tests A, B
Maintain	U4: 107B; U5: 253B

Informational Text: Social Studies

GENRE: NONFICTION ARTICLE

Have students read the bookmark on **Student Book** page 254. Explain that a nonfiction article

- gives information about real people, places, or events;

- usually has headings that tell the subtopic of the text under them;

- often contains graphic aids, such as photographs, maps, and charts, that make information easy to understand.

Text Feature: Map

EXPLAIN Point out the map on page 255. Explain that this map shows the fire danger levels in different parts of California.

- A **map** is a flat drawing of a place, such as a city, state, or country.

- Maps use symbols that stand for things, such as colors or drawings, to show features of the place. Symbols might stand for towns, parks, and so on.

- Most maps include keys that explain what the symbols or colors mean.

- Most maps have a compass rose that shows the cardinal directions North, South, East, and West.

APPLY Have students locate the title of the map and the area that it gives information about. (Title: California Fire Danger; Area: California) Discuss who this map might help. (It could be helpful for people living in California or people thinking about moving there.)

Social Studies

Genre

Nonfiction Articles give information about real people, places, or things.

Text Feature

A **Map** is a drawing that shows the surface features of an area.

Content Vocabulary

remote
smokejumpers
physical
retreat

Smokejumpers

by Roland Hosein

Some wildfires start in places so **remote** that there are no roads or open spaces for a helicopter to land. When this happens, it is time to call in the **smokejumpers**. They are firefighters trained to parachute close to remote wildfires and put them out.

Smokejumpers need to move fast. They need to get to fires while they are still small.

254

Content Vocabulary

Review the spelling and meaning of each content vocabulary word for "Smokejumpers" on Student Book page 254: *remote, smokejumpers, physical, retreat.*

- When we say a place is **remote,** we mean it is hidden or out of the way. What is the most remote place you have ever visited?

- **Smokejumpers** are firefighters trained to jump out of airplanes near remote fires and put them out. Why might it be scary to be a smokejumper?

- **Physical** means related to the body. Why is it important to have physical education class?

- **Retreat** means to step or move back. Why might you have to retreat from a fire?

There are nine smokejumper bases in the United States. One of these is in California. During the summer, the danger of fire in California can be very high. The map below shows the fire danger in different parts of the state. Let's take a look at what it's like to be a smokejumper in California.

Smokejumper Training

It takes six and a half weeks of training to become a California smokejumper. Only those with experience fighting fires in the wild are chosen for this training.

California Fire Danger

Reading a Map

This map uses different colors to show the fire danger levels in different parts of the state.

MAP KEY
- Moderate
- High
- Very High
- Water

The map key shows what the colors mean.

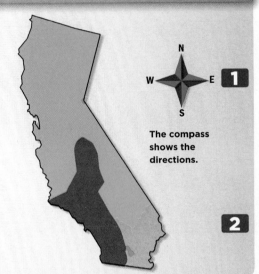

1

The compass shows the directions.

2

255

Paired Selection   Student page 255

Informational Text

Read "Smokejumpers"

Access for All As you read, remind students to apply what they have learned about reading a map. Also have them identify clues to the meanings of the highlighted words and use headings to identify the subtopics.

1 TEXT FEATURE: MAP

Tested What does the compass rose on the map show? (It shows the directions: north, east, south, west.)

2 TEXT FEATURE: MAP

Tested On the map, what does blue mean? What does red mean? How can you tell? (Blue shows where there is water. Red means that the fire danger is very high. I can tell what the colors mean by looking at the key.)

ENGLISH LANGUAGE LEARNERS

Access for All

Beginning Build Concepts Explain what smokejumpers are. Ask: *Are smokejumpers heroes?* Show the map, explain the map key, and have students match the color key with places on the map.

Intermediate Understand a Map Complete the Beginning task. Point out the compass and review the names of the directions. Ask questions such as: *Where in California is danger of a fire the highest?* Help students answer using the directions.

Advanced Give an Explanation Complete the Intermediate task. Ask: *Would you like to be a smokejumper? Why or why not?*

Informational Text

3 **DRAW CONCLUSIONS**

Can people who are not strong be smokejumpers? Why or why not? (No, they can not. Smokejumpers need a great deal of body strength because they must parachute out of planes and climb trees while carrying heavy equipment. Someone who does not have a lot of physical strength would not be able to do all of these things.)

4 **SEQUENCE**

After the crew leader decides on a safe spot where the smokejumpers can retreat, what do the smokejumpers do? (First, they clear the area around the edge of the fire to keep it from spreading. Then they radio for water or chemicals to be dropped onto the blaze. After they put out the fire, they are picked up by a helicopter or they hike to the nearest road.)

3 It takes a great deal of **physical**, or body, strength to be a smokejumper. Much time is spent stretching, running, and carrying heavy gear. All smokejumpers must be able to parachute from a plane, steer around trees, and climb at least 150 feet up a tree with all their equipment.

The Fire Call

As soon as a request for help comes in, the smokejumpers move quickly. They put on padded jump jackets and pants. They also wear a helmet with a wire-mesh face mask. Each jumper carries a small gear bag. It contains water, fire shelter, a hard hat, and gloves. They need to be on the plane within 10 minutes.

After the jumpers have landed, firefighting gear is dropped from the plane. The crew leader decides on a safe spot where the smokejumpers can **retreat**, or move back to, if the fire comes too close. Once this spot is chosen, it's time to fight the fire!

256

On Level Practice Book O, page 174

A **map** is a drawing that shows the surface features of an area. Maps have a compass rose that shows directions and a map key that tells what the pictures on the map stand for.

There were many heroes in the Old West. Help one hero find her way to the campground. Then help her follow directions by answering the questions below.

Map to Campground

1. The hero begins her trip on the trail from the hills. She is traveling to the campground. In which direction should she travel?

   north *or* **northwest**

2. Will traveling through the forest be a problem for the hero as she heads for the campground? Why or why not?

   No, because the hero does not need to travel

   through the forest to get to the campground.

3. Why is the bridge important to the hero as she travels to the campground?

   She must use the bridge to cross the lake.

4. Is the campground north or south of the town? _____ north

Map Key
Trail
Lake
Forest
Campground
Hills
Bridge
Town

⭐ **Approaching Practice Book A,** page 174

◆ **Beyond Practice Book B,** page 174

First, the smokejumpers clear around the edge of the fire to keep it from spreading. Then they might radio for water or chemicals to be dropped onto the blaze. When the fire is under control, the smokejumpers put it out with water. Before they leave, smokejumpers make sure that the whole area is completely cool.

After they finish putting out a fire, smokejumpers are often picked up by a helicopter, but sometimes they must hike out to the nearest road while carrying all their tools and gear!

Once they return to their base, they rest … until the next fire call comes in.

4

Connect and Compare

1. Look at the map on page 255. What is the fire danger level for most of California? How can you tell? **Reading a Map**

2. What are some personality traits that smokejumpers are likely to have? **Analyze**

3. How is the boy's father in *The Printer* like the smokejumpers you just read about? How is he different? **Reading/Writing Across Texts**

Social Studies Activity
Use the library to do research on firefighters. Find out what kind of special clothing and equipment they use. Draw a firefighter wearing the equipment. Label and explain what each piece is for.

 Find out more about firefighters at **www.macmillanmh.com**

257

 Technology

Internet Research and Inquiry Activity Students can find more facts at **www.macmillanmh.com**

Informational Text

Connect and Compare

SUGGESTED ANSWERS

1. The fire danger for most of California is moderate. Most of the state is light green on the map. Light green stands for moderate danger. READING A MAP

2. Answers will vary. Smokejumpers probably care about the environment and enjoy working outdoors. They are also brave. ANALYZE

FOCUS QUESTION

3. The father is like a smokejumper because when he faced danger, he was brave and quick. The article "Smokejumpers" doesn't say it directly, but I don't think any smokejumpers are deaf, like the father in the story. READING/WRITING ACROSS TEXTS

Social Studies Activity
Have volunteers present their drawings and discuss their research sources, as well as the purpose of each piece of clothing and equipment. Have them write an invitation with an addressed envelope (including appropriate return and recipient addresses) to ask local firefighters to speak to the class and show equipment.

Writing

Descriptive Writing

OPTIONS FOR STUDENT WRITING

- Use these two pages for a short writing lesson focused on the features of an introductory speech and on the writing trait from **Student Book** pages 258–259.

- For a more detailed five-step writing process lesson, use the **Writing Workshop** on pages 259A–259B.

- Use the Daily Writing Prompts found in the Weekly Planner for brief writing assignments.

FEATURES

Present and discuss these features of an introductory speech with students.

- It introduces someone to an audience.

- It describes who that person is and the important things he or she does or has done, using precise and descriptive language.

- It is enthusiastic.

- It includes the writer's opinions.

- It has a clear and controlling idea.

- It ends with a concluding sentence that gives a clear sense of closure.

Have students read "Meet Mrs. Adorno" on Student Book page 258. Ask volunteers to point out examples of the features of an introductory speech in Edward M.'s paragraph.

Writing

Voice

One way writers express their voice is to share opinions, or how they feel about something. Introductory speeches often include the writers' opinions.

I wrote a short speech to introduce the best teacher in the school.

I included personal opinions to tell how I feel.

Write an Introductory Speech

Meet Mrs. Adorno

by Edward M.

Today we are giving the award for favorite teacher to Mrs. Adorno. She is the nicest, funniest teacher I have ever had. A lot of you must think so too, because you voted for her. She is the only person who can make science seem like fun. She always makes us laugh, and she is our softball team's biggest fan. Now say hello to our favorite teacher, Mrs. Adorno!

258

Your Turn

Pretend that someone is getting an award and you have to give a speech to introduce that person. It might be a famous person or someone you know. Write your speech in one paragraph. Be sure to describe this person and tell why he or she is important to you. Use the Writer's Checklist to check your writing.

Writer's Checklist

 Ideas and Content: Have I clearly explained why this person is receiving an award?

 Organization: Did I include a topic sentence?

 Voice: Does my introduction show enthusiasm?

 Word Choice: Did I choose words that describe the person and show how I feel about them?

 Sentence Fluency: Does my speech flow smoothly when I read it out loud?

 Conventions: Did I make sure that pronouns and verbs agree? Did I check my spelling?

259

WRITING TRAIT: VOICE

- Have a student read the bookmark on **Student Book** page 258. Discuss the Voice trait.

- Voice is the way writers communicate their personality through writing.

- One way writers express voice in a speech is by sharing opinions and feelings.

- To show voice in an introductory speech, writers use enthusiastic and lively language.

Have students reread "Meet Mrs. Adorno" on Student Book page 258. Discuss the callouts on the left. Does Edward M.'s speech tell his feelings?

Use **Transparency 93** to help students understand how a writer can express voice in a speech by showing feelings and opinions. Work with students to help them understand how the revision better shows voice.

YOUR TURN

Read the "Your Turn" prompt on Student Book page 259 with students. Talk about people whom students admire. Remind students to share their opinions and feelings in their speech.

WRITER'S CHECKLIST

Review the six Good Writing Traits on the Writer's Checklist. Have students give an example of Word Choice or Voice in Edward M.'s speech. Then discuss how students can apply the traits to help them draft, revise, and proofread their introductory speech.

Transparency 93

Voice in an Introductory Speech

Mr. Smith is the person to receive this year's Favorite Teacher Award. Kids agree he is a good reading teacher. Everyone is happy to give him this award. He always meets with students after school to help them. He chooses interesting books. Here he is, Mr. Smith.

Possible Revision: Who's the winner of this year's Favorite Teacher Award? I'm thrilled to tell you that it's Mr. Smith. If you've taken his class, you know he's a great reading teacher. He chooses really interesting books for us to read. Plus, he always meets with students after school. He's there to help us out. Now, here he is, our Mr. Smith!

Writing Transparency 93

Writing Workshop

Connect Language Arts

WRITING WORKSHOP
- **Descriptive Writing:** Speech

WORD STUDY
- Words in Context
- Figurative Language
- **Phonics:** VC/CV Pattern
- Vocabulary Building

SPELLING
- VC/CV Pattern

GRAMMAR
- Pronoun-Verb Agreement

SMALL GROUP OPTIONS
- Differentiated Instruction, pp. 259M–259V

Speaking and Listening

Share these strategies.

SPEAKING STRATEGIES
- Speak clearly and enthusiastically.
- Vary the rise and fall of your voice.
- Use appropriate gestures.

LISTENING STRATEGIES
- Make eye contact with the speaker.
- Listen for enjoyment and reasons that the person is getting an award.
- Look at the speaker to show your interest.
- Think about the person being introduced.

Descriptive Writing: Speech

Day 1 Prewrite

PURPOSE AND AUDIENCE

- The purpose of an introductory speech is to describe a person and explain why that person is important.

- The audience is the teacher and classmates.

Display **Transparency 94.** Discuss Edward M.'s Question and Answer Chart. Tell students that they will use a Chart to plan their introductory speech.

Prompt *Write a paragraph to introduce someone who is getting an award.*

CHOOSE A TOPIC

Students can write about a real or fictional person or select another appropriate topic.

Transparency 94

Question and Answer Chart

Questions	Answers
Purpose?	Introduce Mrs. Adorno.
Audience?	Kids and Teachers
WHO?	Science Teacher
WHAT?	Favorite Teacher Award
WHY?	Nice
	Makes Science fun
	Softball fan

Writing Transparency 94

Writing Transparency 94

Day 2 Draft

DRAFTING CHECKLIST

Display **Transparency 95.** Review Edward M.'s draft of "Meet Mrs. Adorno." Discuss how the Question and Answer Chart was used. As students write their drafts:

- Encourage them to keep their purpose and audience in mind.

- Review the features of an introductory speech.

- Remind them to express their feelings and opinions.

- Suggest that they end with a concluding sentence that clearly closes their speech.

- Have students refer to their Question and Answer Chart and to the Good Writing Traits on the Writer's Checklist.

Transparency 95

Meet Mrs. Adorno

Today we are giving the award to Mrs. Adorno. She is the nicest teacher I have ever had. A lot of you must think so too. She is the only person who can make science seem like fun. She always makes us laugh, and she is our softball team's biggest fan.

Writing Transparency 95

Writing Transparency 95

Day 3 Revise

REVISING CHECKLIST

Display **Transparency 95.** Have students use what they have learned to discuss how they can revise Edward M.'s draft.

Display **Transparency 96** and discuss Edward M.'s changes:

- He made his topic sentence clear.

- He explained how the person won the award.

- To improve **Voice,** he added a descriptive word and an enthusiastic final exclamatory sentence.

Have students revise their introductory speeches and give them effective titles.

Day 4 Proofread

REVIEW AND PROOFREAD

Tell students that they are now ready to proofread their revisions.

Remind students to:

- Check all capitalization and punctuation in declarative, imperative, interrogative, and exclamatory sentences.

- Use classroom resources and dictionaries to check spelling, including spelling of simple compounds, homophones, contractions, and words with affixes.

- Check for sentence fragments.

- Check that pronouns agree with verbs.

Day 5 Publish

PUBLISH AND PRESENT

To publish their speech, students should make a neat, final copy using a computer or their best handwriting. Remind them to pay attention to correct letter formation, spacing between words and sentences, and use of standard margins.

Students might want to deliver their speech to their classmates. Review Speaking and Listening strategies with students.

EVALUATE

To evaluate student writing, use the 4-point Scoring Rubric. Since students learned about **Voice** this week, check carefully for that trait.

Transparency 96

Meet Mrs. Adorno

Today we are giving the award for favorite teacher to Mrs. Adorno. She is the nicest funniest teacher I have ever had. A lot of you must think so too. She is the only person because you voted for her who can make science seem like fun. She always makes us laugh, and she is our softball team's biggest fan. Now say hello to our favorite teacher, Mrs. Adorno.

Writing Transparency 96   © Macmillan McGraw-Hill

Writing Transparency 96

SCORING RUBRIC

4 Excellent	3 Good	2 Fair	1 Unsatisfactory
Ideas & Content Clear, lively introduction	**Ideas & Content** Clear introduction	**Ideas & Content** Introduction not always clear	**Ideas & Content** Confusing introduction
Organization Strong topic sentence, supported with details and examples	**Organization** Has a topic sentence, supported with some details	**Organization** Weak topic sentence, few details	**Organization** No topic, details out of order
Voice Expresses enthusiastic writer's voice	**Voice** Expresses writer's voice	**Voice** Somewhat flat and ordinary; few opinions or feelings	**Voice** Flat and does not express writer's opinions
Word Choice Uses strong, lively, descriptive, and expressive words	**Word Choice** Adequate use of descriptive and expressive words	**Word Choice** Few descriptive or expressive words used	**Word Choice** Few or no descriptive or expressive words
Sentence Fluency Good flow of sentences, easy to follow when read aloud	**Sentence Fluency** Uses long and short sentences, relatively easy to follow	**Sentence Fluency** Sentences choppy or overlong	**Sentence Fluency** Incomplete or confusing sentences
Conventions Mostly free of errors in spelling, mechanics, and usage	**Conventions** Few errors in spelling, mechanics, and usage	**Conventions** Many errors in spelling, mechanics, and usage	**Conventions** Repeated errors in spelling, mechanics, and usage

Word Study

Objectives

- Apply knowledge of word meanings and context clues
- Use context clues to figure out figurative language

Materials

- Vocabulary Transparency 47
- Vocabulary Strategy Transparency 48
- Leveled Practice Books, p. 175

Vocabulary

screamed (p. 243) made a loud cry or sound

numb (p. 247) unable to feel or move

escape (p. 243) to become free

fled (p. 244) ran away from something

shuddered (p. 248) shook or trembled suddenly

image (p. 247) a picture of a person or thing

newspaper (p. 237) a set of pages that contain news

ELL

Access for All

Demonstrate Have students demonstrate *screamed, shuddered,* and *fled.* Write the present and past tense forms of the words on the board and co-construct sentences with them.

Review
Vocabulary

 ## Words in Context

EXPLAIN/MODEL

Review the meanings of the vocabulary words. Ask students to describe a made-up newspaper story using three of the words.

Display **Transparency 47.** Model how to use word meanings and context clues to fill in the first missing word.

 Transparency 47

escape	fled	image	newspaper
numb	screamed	shuddered	

My mother was reading the (1) <u>newspaper</u>. "I see a news story about a fire," she said. "Luckily, everyone was able to (2) <u>escape</u> before the building burned down. The people (3) <u>fled</u> quickly down the stairs."

In my mind, I could see an (4) <u>image</u> of a huge fire. I pictured the flames and the smoke. I imagined the whole building as it (5) <u>shuddered</u> and then fell apart.

Later that night, Aunt Pat came to visit. She told us that she had seen the fire. She heard people as they (6) <u>screamed</u> with fear. When they got out, most of them stood in the street and stared. They were too (7) <u>numb</u> to move.

Vocabulary Transparency 47

Think Aloud The first sentence tells me that the mother was reading something, so I know the missing word is something to read. The next sentence tells me she is reading a news story. Together those two clues tell me that *newspaper* must be the missing word.

PRACTICE

 Help students complete item 2. Then have students use context clues to write missing words for items 3–7 on a separate piece of paper. Students can exchange papers, check answers, and explain context clues they used to figure out the missing words.

Remind students that they can use the Glossary on pages 408–422 to confirm word meanings.

STRATEGY
CONTEXT CLUES: FIGURATIVE LANGUAGE

EXPLAIN/MODEL

Sometimes writers use **figurative language,** or use words in a way that is different from the literal, or dictionary, meaning. Readers can use context clues to help them figure out the meaning of these words.

 Display **Transparency 48**. Model how to figure out the meaning of *screamed* in the example sentence using the context clue "Fire."

 Transparency 48

Figurative Language

His fingers screamed FIRE! to the other deaf workers. (screamed; moved fingers in large quick motions)

1. The fast-spreading fire gobbled up the paper. (gobbled; quickly burned up)

2. The new presses roared to life when we switched the power on. (roared; made a lot of noise)

3. The floor groaned under the weight of the water from the fire hoses. (groaned; made loud noises)

4. The newspapers were so popular that they were flying off the shelves. (were flying off the shelves; were selling very fast)

Vocabulary Strategy Transparency 48

PRACTICE

Help students complete item 1. Then have them identify the figurative language words or phrases in items 2–4 and use context clues to tell what they mean.

Quick Check Can students choose the correct meaning of a word and use context clues to figure out figurative language?

During **Small Group Instruction**

If No → **Approaching Level** Vocabulary, p. 259O

If Yes → **On Level** Options, pp. 259Q–259R

Beyond Level Options, pp. 259S–259T

ELL Access for All

Monitor Understanding

Students may need help with the literal meanings of *gobbled, roared, groaned,* and other vocabulary words before they can understand the figurative meanings. Tell students to ask themselves: *Can fingers really scream or fires gobble? If the answer is no, then the meaning is figurative.*

Vocabulary

Review last week's vocabulary words. Then have students discuss what it might mean to have an *artist's eye,* or to *swallow one's pride.*

■ **On Level Practice Book O,** page 175

Figurative language makes unexpected comparisons between people or things.
Example: Her eyes *screamed* with terror.

Read each sentence. Underline the figurative language. Then write a sentence of your own that includes the underlined words. Possible responses provided.
1. My hero is an inventor who was <u>as smart as a whip</u>.
   The scientist was as smart as a whip and created three inventions in one year.

2. He was <u>a hurricane of action</u>, rushing from one task to another.
   The professor was a hurricane of action and was conducting three experiments at the same time.

3. He was <u>as busy as a bee</u> as he worked to create his inventions.
   Shelly was as busy as a bee as she did research on several different inventions she was working on.

4. He must have been <u>as happy as a lark</u> when he invented the light bulb.
   My father was as happy as a lark when the television remote control was invented.

5. His eyes were <u>shining diamonds</u> when he created the light bulb.
   His teeth were shining diamonds after he used the new invention, an electric toothbrush.

★ **Approaching Practice Book A,** page 175

◆ **Beyond Practice Book B,** page 175

Word Study

Objectives

- Recognize closed syllables
- Segment and blend syllables in two-syllable words
- Decode two-syllable words with the VC/CV pattern

Materials

- Leveled Practice Books, p. 176

ELL   **Access for All**

Distinguish Syllables

Say: *A syllable is a short word or part of a word with one vowel sound. Cat is one word, one syllable. Catnip is two syllables and two vowel sounds.* Write familiar words on the board and have students clap out the syllables.

On Level Practice Book O, page 176

Some words have the **VC/CV** pattern: Vowel, Consonant, Consonant, Vowel. A word with this pattern usually divides into syllables between the two consonants, as in *bet/ter*.

Divide a word into syllables by dividing the word between the consonants.

r	a	b		b	i	t
	V	C		C	V	
	vowel	consonant		consonant	vowel	

A. Write the six words from the box that have the VCCV pattern on a line. Draw a line to divide it into syllables. Then write the letters VCCV below the letters that form the pattern.

lemon	fifteen	baths	pepper	tender	friends
cotton	hero	spinal	market	writer	winter

1. fif|teen
   VCCV
2. pep|per
   VCCV
3. ten|der
   VCCV
4. mar|ket
   VCCV
5. cot|ton
   VCCV
6. win|ter
   VCCV

B. Write two sentences each using two words from above with the VCCV pattern.

7. At the market we bought some pepper.

8. My coach bought fifteen pairs of cotton socks for the team.

★ **Approaching Practice Book A,** page 176

◆ **Beyond Practice Book B,** page 176

Phonics

Decode Words with the VC/CV Pattern

 EXPLAIN/MODEL

- A syllable is a word part that has one vowel sound. Dividing a word into syllables can help in pronouncing it. When the syllable ends in a consonant, the vowel sound is usually short, as in *cat*.

- When the first syllable of a word has a short vowel sound, the word usually has the VC/CV (vowel-consonant-consonant-vowel) pattern and divides between the two consonants, as in *bet/ter* or *nap/kin*. When the first syllable ends in a consonant, it is closed.

- The two consonants in the VC/CV pattern may be the same, as *pp* in *pepper*. The consonants may be different, as *pt* in *chapter*.

Write: basket

Think Aloud I know that a syllable has only one vowel sound. *Basket* has two vowel sounds and two syllables. It has the VC/CV pattern. I can divide *basket* into two syllables by drawing a line between the consonants *s* and *k*. (Write V-C-C-V under the letters *a–s–k–e* and draw a line between the consonants.) Listen as I say each syllable slowly. /bas/ /kət/. The first syllable is *bas*. It ends in the consonant *s*. The vowel *a* has the short *a* /a/ sound.

PRACTICE/APPLY

Write: *ladder, Sunday, rabbit, chicken, sandwich*. Have students write the VC/CV pattern under the correct letters and draw a line between the consonants to show the syllable breaks. Have them decode each word syllable by syllable and then blend the syllables.

VC/CV Game Have students work in groups. Announce a letter, such as *B*, and give each group two minutes to think of as many two-syllable VC/CV words they can that begin with that letter. Words can have the same or different consonants. (bar/ter, big/ger) Groups can get points based on the amount they have correct or unique.

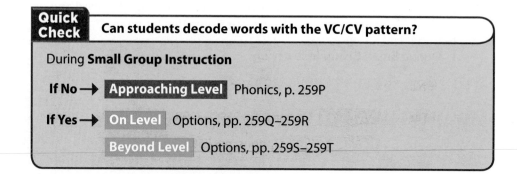

Quick Check   Can students decode words with the VC/CV pattern?

During **Small Group Instruction**

If No → **Approaching Level**   Phonics, p. 259P

If Yes → **On Level**   Options, pp. 259Q–259R

Beyond Level   Options, pp. 259S–259T

Vocabulary Building

Oral Language

Expand Vocabulary Write "Heroes" in the center of a word web. Using the selection, print or electronic dictionaries, thesauruses, or encyclopedias, have students find words that relate to this week's topic.

police —— **Heroes** —— forest rangers

firefighters

courageous   doctors   danger

Vocabulary Building

Related Words In *The Printer* there is a huge fire. Have students brainstorm words with *fire* and place them on a word family web.

firefighter

fire escape   campfire

bonfire   **Words with Fire**   firewood

firefly   fireworks

fireplace   fireproof

Have students create a word family web for one of last week's words, such as *powered* or *existed*.

Apply Vocabulary

Write a Paragraph Have small groups of students use the vocabulary words *newspaper, escape, fled, numb, image, shuddered,* and *screamed* in a paragraph about a heroic adventure or a self-selected topic. Students can read their paragraphs aloud to the class.

Spiral Review

Crossword Puzzles

- Divide the class into small groups. Give each group a set of the **Vocabulary Cards** *lonesome, numb, pride, produce, tend, wailed, powered, declared.*

- Have each group create a crossword puzzle for these words. Provide each group with large-grid graph paper, or have students use a crossword-puzzle generator on the computer. Make sure students know how to number the words across and down. After the group members have generated their puzzle, they can write definition-style word clues.

- Make copies of the students' blank puzzles with clues. Then have the groups exchange their puzzles and solve them.

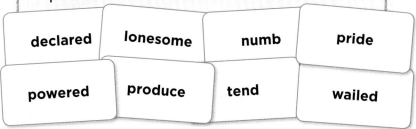

declared   lonesome   numb   pride

powered   produce   tend   wailed

Technology

 Vocabulary PuzzleMaker

 For additional vocabulary and spelling games, go to www.macmillanmh.com

5 Day Spelling

The VC/CV Pattern

Spelling Words

basket	bedtime	follow
rabbit	mammal	problem
napkin	number	chicken
letter	fellow	butter
invite	chapter	Sunday

Review tried, studies, drying

Challenge splendid, complete

Dictation Sentences

1. The <u>basket</u> is full of paper.
2. Our pet is a <u>rabbit</u>.
3. Please pass me a <u>napkin</u>.
4. The <u>letter</u> needs a stamp.
5. I will <u>invite</u> my friends to the party.
6. My <u>bedtime</u> is nine o'clock.
7. A whale is a <u>mammal</u>.
8. What is your telephone <u>number</u>?
9. Who is that **<u>fellow</u>** with a hat?
10. This <u>chapter</u> is about heroes.
11. <u>Follow</u> the signs to the exit.
12. The boy solved the <u>problem</u>.
13. The <u>chicken</u> laid an egg.
14. Do you like bread and <u>butter</u>?
15. We will be home on <u>Sunday</u>.

Review Words

1. I <u>tried</u> to open the jar.
2. David <u>studies</u> in the library.
3. The clothes are <u>drying</u> in the sun.

Challenge Words

1. The fireworks were <u>splendid</u>.
2. I must <u>complete</u> my homework.

Note: The word in **bold** type is from *The Printer*.

Display the Spelling Words throughout the week.

Day 1 Pretest

ASSESS PRIOR KNOWLEDGE

Use the Dictation Sentences. Say the underlined word, read the sentence, and repeat the word. Have students write the words on **Spelling Practice Book** page 147. For a modified list, use the first 12 Spelling Words and the 3 Review Words. For a more challenging list, use Spelling Words 3–15 and the Challenge Words. Have students correct their own tests.

Have students cut apart the Spelling Word Cards BLM on **Teacher's Resource Book** page 89 and figure out a way to sort them. Have them save the cards for use throughout the week.

Students can use Spelling Practice Book page 148 for independent practice.

Day 2 Word Sorts

TEACHER AND STUDENT SORTS

- Review the Spelling Words, point out the VC/CV syllable patterns, and discuss meanings.

- Use the cards on the Spelling Word Cards BLM. Attach the headings *matter* and *pencil* to a bulletin board.

- Model sorting words with the two VC/CV patterns, using *basket* and *rabbit*.

- Have students take turns sorting the remaining cards and explaining how they sorted them.

- Then have students sort their own Spelling Word Cards. They can sort the Spelling Words three times. Have students write their last sort on Spelling Practice Book page 149.

Spelling Practice Book, pages 147–148

Fold back the paper along the dotted line. Use the blanks to write each word as it is read aloud. When you finish the test, unfold the paper. Use the list at the right to correct any spelling mistakes.

1. _____
2. _____
3. _____
4. _____
5. _____
6. _____
7. _____
8. _____
9. _____
10. _____
11. _____
12. _____
13. _____
14. _____
15. _____

Review Words
16. _____
17. _____
18. _____

Challenge Words
19. _____
20. _____

1. basket
2. rabbit
3. napkin
4. letter
5. invite
6. bedtime
7. mammal
8. number
9. fellow
10. chapter
11. follow
12. problem
13. chicken
14. butter
15. Sunday
16. tried
17. studies
18. drying
19. splendid
20. complete

Spelling Practice Book, page 149

basket	letter	mammal	chapter	chicken
rabbit	invite	number	follow	butter
napkin	bedtime	fellow	problem	Sunday

Pattern Power!

Write the spelling words with these spelling patterns.

ll
1. follow
2. fellow

mm
3. mammal

tt
4. letter
5. butter

bb
6. rabbit

Order Please!

Write each group of spelling words in alphabetical order.

basket, chapter, chicken, bedtime
7. basket
8. bedtime
9. chapter
10. chicken

invite, napkin, Sunday, number, problem
11. invite
12. napkin
13. number
14. problem
15. Sunday

Day 3 — Word Meanings

DEFINITIONS

- Display the definitions. Have students write the clues and the Spelling Words in a word study notebook.

1. used to hold things (basket)
2. furry animal with long ears that hops (rabbit)
3. a mailed message (letter)
4. yellow food made from milk (butter)
5. the day after Saturday (Sunday)

- Challenge students to come up with clues for other Spelling Words, including Review Words and Challenge Words.

- Have partners write a sentence for each Spelling Word, leave a blank for the word, and then trade papers and write the missing word.

Day 4 — Review and Proofread

SPIRAL REVIEW

Review inflected endings with *y* to *i*. Write *tied, studies,* and *drying* on the board. Have students identify the letters that spell the endings.

PROOFREAD AND WRITE

Write these sentences. Have students correct the errors.

1. A rabit hid in a baskket. (rabbit, basket)
2. That felow wants a nappkin. (fellow, napkin)

BLIND SORT

Partners use their Spelling Word Cards. Each writes key words *matter* and *pencil* at the top of a sheet of paper. Then students take turns. One draws cards and says the words while the other writes them. After both have finished, they can check each other's papers.

Day 5 — Assess and Reteach

POSTTEST

Use the Dictation Sentences on page 259G for the Posttest.

If students have difficulty with any of the words in the lesson, have them place them on a list called "Spelling Words I Want to Remember" in a word study notebook.

WORD STUDY NOTEBOOK

Challenge students to search for other words with the final VC/CV spelling patterns in their reading for the week and write them in a word study notebook under the heading "Other Words Like *Basket* and *Rabbit*."

Spelling Practice Book, page 150

basket	letter	mammal	chapter	chicken
rabbit	invite	number	follow	butter
napkin	bedtime	fellow	problem	Sunday

What's the Word?

Complete each sentence with a spelling word.

1. The nurse brought the sick man soup and bread with **butter**.
2. The police officers' awards dinner will be on **Sunday** night.
3. The next **chapter** of the book is about firefighters.
4. My mom rescued my pet **rabbit** from a neighborhood dog.
5. Officer Dan is a wonderful father and a good **fellow**.
6. When you have a **problem**, ask your parents for help.
7. Will you **invite** your friend to the firehouse fundraiser?
8. **Follow** the police officer to safety.
9. They delivered a **basket** of fruit to the firefighters who saved them.
10. I wrote a **letter** to her because she is my hero.

It Takes Three

Write a spelling word that goes with the other two words.

11. reptile, bird, **mammal**
12. fork, placemat, **napkin**
13. letter, symbol, **number**
14. pig, cow, **chicken**
15. lunchtime, daytime, **bedtime**

Spelling Practice Book, page 151

There are six spelling mistakes in this story. Circle the misspelled words. Write the words correctly on the lines below.

The Great Rescue

One (Sonday) afternoon my family went on a picnic. My mother packed our lunch in a big (bascett.) We found a shady spot under a tree and ate fried (chikin) and bread with (bauter.)

After lunch my sister and I took a canoe out on the lake. We were drifting along when suddenly my sister screamed. I looked over to see what the (problime) was. There was a hole in the bottom of the boat. The canoe was filling up with water.

Luckily our parents saw us and ran for help. Another person said he would help. This fine (fello) swam out to the canoe. He held out a rope for us to grab onto, and then he dragged us to shore. He was our hero!

It was an exciting end to an almost peaceful picnic.

1. **Sunday**   4. **butter**
2. **basket**   5. **problem**
3. **chicken**   6. **fellow**

Writing Activity

Imagine that you are on a picnic and something unexpected happens. Write a short story about it, using at least four spelling words.

_____
_____
_____
_____

Spelling Practice Book, page 152

Look at the words in each set below. One word in each set is spelled correctly. Look at Sample A. The letter next to the correctly spelled word in Sample A has been shaded in. Do Sample B yourself. Shade the letter of the word that is spelled correctly. When you are sure you know what to do, go on with the rest of the page.

Sample A:
- Ⓐ ento
- Ⓑ intoo
- Ⓒ into
- Ⓓ intue

Sample B:
- Ⓔ daddy
- Ⓕ daddie
- Ⓖ dady
- Ⓗ dadie

1.
- Ⓐ basket
- Ⓑ bakset
- Ⓒ baseket
- Ⓓ basskit

2.
- Ⓐ rabbit
- Ⓑ rabit
- Ⓒ rabbet
- Ⓓ rabet

3.
- Ⓐ nappkin
- Ⓑ napkin
- Ⓒ napekin
- Ⓓ napkine

4.
- Ⓔ leter
- Ⓕ lettar
- Ⓖ letar
- Ⓗ letter

5.
- Ⓐ invite
- Ⓑ envite
- Ⓒ invit
- Ⓓ inevite

6.
- Ⓔ bedtim
- Ⓕ bedtime
- Ⓖ beddtime
- Ⓗ beadtime

7.
- Ⓐ mamal
- Ⓑ mammel
- Ⓒ mammal
- Ⓓ mamul

8.
- Ⓔ nummer
- Ⓕ numer
- Ⓖ numbur
- Ⓗ number

9.
- Ⓔ felow
- Ⓕ fellow
- Ⓖ felou
- Ⓗ felloou

10.
- Ⓐ chapper
- Ⓑ chapter
- Ⓒ chatper
- Ⓓ chappter

11.
- Ⓔ folow
- Ⓕ follo
- Ⓖ follow
- Ⓗ falow

12.
- Ⓐ probem
- Ⓑ problum
- Ⓒ problem
- Ⓓ prolbem

13.
- Ⓐ chicken
- Ⓑ chiken
- Ⓒ chiccen
- Ⓓ chickn

14.
- Ⓔ buter
- Ⓕ butter
- Ⓖ buttar
- Ⓗ butor

15.
- Ⓐ Senday
- Ⓑ Sundai
- Ⓒ Sudnay
- Ⓓ Sunday

Pronoun-Verb Agreement

DAY 1

My father are my hero. Him is kind and careing. i feel safe with him (1: is; 2: He; caring.; 3: I; him.)

DAY 2

the firefighters keep we safe. They also solves problms. We is lucky to have they? (1: The; us; 2: solve problems.; 3: are; them.)

DAY 3

the hero gives a speech. Thenn she get a medal. Many newspapers rite about she. (1: The; 2: Then; gets; 3: write; her.)

DAY 4

many dog saves people. them barks at fires. Me mother say they be wonderful. (1: Many dogs save; 2: They bark; 3: My; says; are)

DAY 5

Doctors helps we feel better. Them give us medicine I takes it right away. (1: help us; 2: They; medicine.; 3: take)

Day 1 | Introduce the Concept

INTRODUCE PRONOUN-VERB AGREEMENT

Present the following:

- A present-tense verb must agree with its subject pronoun.

- Add *-s* or *-es* to most present-tense action verbs when using singular pronouns *he, she,* and *it.*

- Do not add *-s* or *-es* to a present-tense action verb when using plural pronouns *we, you,* and *they,* or singular pronouns *I* and *you.*

Examples:
He wears a hat.
I wear a hat.
You wear a hat.
They wear hats.
We wear hats.

See Grammar Transparency 116 for modeling and guided practice.

Grammar Practice Book, page 147

- A **present-tense** verb must agree with its **subject pronoun.**
- Add -s or -es to most action verbs when you use the pronouns *he, she,* and *it.*
- Do not add -s or -es to an action verb in the present tense when you use the pronouns *I, we, you,* and *they.*

Choose the correct verb to complete each sentence. Write the verb.

1. I (deliver, delivers) newspapers every day with my brother.
   ___**deliver**___

2. Some days it (rain, rains). ___**rains**___

3. Then we (get, gets) a ride from Mom. ___**get**___

4. She (drive, drives) from house to house. ___**drives**___

5. I (open, opens) the window of the car. ___**open**___

6. He (throw, throws) the newspapers onto the driveways.
   ___**throws**___

7. It (take, takes) less time on sunny days. ___**takes**___

8. Then we (walk, walks) down the streets and see our customers.
   ___**walk**___

9. They (wave, waves) to us. ___**wave**___

10. Do you (read, reads) a newspaper every day? ___**read**___

Day 2 | Teach the Concept

REVIEW PRONOUN-VERB AGREEMENT

Remind students that pronouns and verbs must agree in a sentence. Ask students the rules for making pronouns and verbs agree.

MORE PRONOUN-VERB AGREEMENT

- A present-tense verb must agree with its subject pronoun.

Examples:
She reads the newspaper.
I watch TV news.
You watch the firefighters.
We want to be printers.
They fight fires.

See Grammar Transparency 117 for modeling and guided practice.

Grammar Practice Book, page 148

- A present-tense verb must agree with its subject pronoun.
- Add -s or -es to most present-tense action verbs when using the pronouns *he, she,* and *it.*
- Do not add -s or -es to most present-tense action verbs when using the pronouns *I, we, you,* and *they.*

Circle the correct present-tense verb to complete each sentence.

1. I (work, works) on our school newspaper.

2. It (discuss, discusses) important issues in our community.

3. We (write, writes) many stories for our newspaper.

4. He (write, writes) the funniest stories each week.

5. You (learn, learns) many things when you work on a newspaper.

6. She (help, helps) us to improve our writing.

7. They (know, knows) people who work at real newspapers.

8. We (take, takes) photographs with a camera.

9. They (read, reads) newspapers every day.

10. You (like, likes) to read our interviews.

Day 3 — Review and Practice

REVIEW PRONOUN-VERB AGREEMENT

Ask students to state the rules for pronoun-verb agreement.

MECHANICS AND USAGE: PRONOUN-VERB AGREEMENT

- A present-tense verb must agree with its subject pronoun.

- Add -s or -es to most present-tense action verbs when using the singular pronouns *he, she,* and *it.*

- Do not add -s or -es to a present-tense action verb when you use the plural pronouns *we, you,* and *they,* or the singular pronouns *I* and *you.*

 See Grammar Transparency 118 for modeling and guided practice.

Grammar Practice Book, page 149

- A present-tense verb must agree with its subject pronoun.
- Add -s to most action verbs when you use the pronouns *he, she,* and *it.*
- Do not add -s to an action verb in the present tense when you use the pronouns *I, we, you,* and *they.*

Write the correct present-tense verb to complete each sentence.

1. We **buy** the newspaper at the store. (buy, buys)
2. I **look** at the sports section first. (look, looks)
3. She **reads** the news section in the morning. (read, reads)
4. It **tells** readers what is happening in the city. (tell, tells)
5. We **trade** sections when we are done reading. (trade, trades)
6. They **work** hard at the newspaper. (work, works)
7. He **circles** vocabulary words he does not know. (circle, circles)
8. You **get** information from newspapers and magazines. (get, gets)
9. They **like** to talk about the news stories. (like, likes)
10. She **uses** a computer when she writes. (use, uses)

Day 4 — Review and Proofread

REVIEW PRONOUN-VERB AGREEMENT

Review pronouns with students. Remind them to check the rules they have learned to make sure that their pronouns agree with their verbs.

PROOFREAD

Have students correct errors in the following sentences.

1. We helps our city. (help)
2. He like books about heroes. (likes)
3. They fights fires. (fight)
4. You plants the flowers. (plant)
5. I teaches the children. (teach)

 See Grammar Transparency 119 for modeling and guided practice.

Grammar Practice Book, page 150

- A **present-tense** verb must agree with its **subject pronoun**.
- Add -s or -es to most action verbs when you use the pronouns *he, she,* and *it.*
- Do not add -s or -es to an action verb in the present tense when you use the pronouns *I, we, you,* and *they.*

Proofread the paragraph. Circle any verbs that do not agree with their pronouns.

This summer my's best friend and I are doing something new. We puts out our own newspaper every week. It be only four pages long, but it take a lot of time to do it well. I are in charge of the stories. Curt takes all the pictures. Each week, we has to find new stories for our paper. I talk to people in town. I looks for interesting things. He take his camera everywhere. We has more pictures than pages!

Writing Activity

Rewrite the paragraph. Make sure the verbs agree with their pronouns. Fix any incorrect possessive pronouns.

This summer my best friend and I are doing something new. We put out our own newspaper every week. It is only four pages long, but it takes a lot of time to do it well. I am in charge of the stories. Curt takes all the pictures. Each week, we have to find new stories for our paper. I talk to people in town. I look for interesting things. He takes his camera everywhere. We have more pictures than pages!

Day 5 — Assess and Reteach

ASSESS

Use the Daily Language Activity and page 151 of the **Grammar Practice Book** for assessment.

RETEACH

Help students write the rules about pronoun-verb agreement on an index card.

Have them write sentences with the subject pronouns *I, he, it, you, we, they* and action verbs. Remind them to make sure that the pronouns and verbs agree. The sentences should tell about actions in *The Printer.* Have students illustrate their sentences. Use sentences as a part of a bulletin board display.

Use page 152 of the Grammar Practice Book for additional reteaching.

 See Grammar Transparency 120 for modeling and guided practice.

Grammar Practice Book, pages 151–152

A. Read each group of sentences. Circle the one with the subject pronoun that does not agree with the action verb.

1. A. We deliver the newspaper every day.
   B. He folds the newspapers.
   C. I toss the papers onto the porches.
   D. They brings them inside.
2. A. We read different sections of the newspaper.
   B. I likes the movie reviews.
   C. She enjoys the crossword puzzles.
   D. On Sunday it takes all morning to read the paper.
3. A. They read the newspaper.
   B. It gives me information.
   C. We learns about our community.
   D. You get more knowledge about events.

B. Read the sentences. Choose the correct verb form to complete each sentence. Write the correct verb on the line.

4. I _____ the editor of our school newspaper.
   A. know
   B. likes
   C. visits
   D. are
5. We _____ new stories every week.
   A. has
   B. shows
   C. creates
   D. write
6. They _____ news about our school.
   A. says
   B. is
   C. give
   D. presents

End-of-Week Assessment

Administer the Test

Weekly Reading Assessment,
Passage and questions, pages 301–308

ASSESSED SKILLS

- Make and Confirm Predictions
- Vocabulary Words
- Context Clues/Figurative Language
- Words with VC/CV Pattern
- Pronoun-Verb Agreement

Progress Reporter
Macmillan/McGraw-Hill

Administer the **Weekly Assessment** from the CD-ROM or online.

Fluency

Assess fluency for one group of students per week. Use the Oral Fluency Record Sheet to track the number of words read correctly. Fluency goal for all students: **97–117 words correct per minute (WCPM).**

Approaching Level	Weeks 1, 3, 5
On Level	Weeks 2, 4
Beyond Level	Week 6

Alternative Assessments

- **ELL Assessment,** pages 148–149

Weekly Assessment, 301–308

Fluency Assessment

ELL Assessment, 148–149

Diagnose | ## Prescribe

Diagnose	IF . . .	THEN . . .
VOCABULARY WORDS **VOCABULARY STRATEGY** Context Clues: Figurative Language Items 1, 2, 3	0–1 items correct . . .	Reteach skills using the **Additional Lessons,** page T8 **LOG ON** Reteach skills: Go to www.macmillanmh.com **CD ROM** Vocabulary PuzzleMaker Evaluate for Intervention.
COMPREHENSION Skill: Make and Confirm Predictions Items 4, 5, 6,	0–1 items correct . . .	Reteach skills using the **Additional Lessons,** page T4 Evaluate for Intervention.
GRAMMAR Pronoun-Verb Agreement Items 7, 8, 9	0–1 items correct . . .	Reteach skills: **Grammar Practice Book,** page 152
SPELLING Words with VC/CV Pattern Items 10, 11, 12	0–1 items correct . . .	**LOG ON** Reteach skills: Go to www.macmillanmh.com
FLUENCY	89–96 WCPM 0–88 WCPM	**AUDIO CD** Fluency Solutions Evaluate for Intervention.

DIBELS LINK

PROGRESS MONITORING
Use Your DIBELS Results to Inform Instruction.
IF
DIBELS Oral **R**eading **F**luency   **(DORF)** 0–109

THEN
Use the Fluency Solutions Audio CD.

READING
Triumphs
AN INTERVENTION PROGRAM

Also Available

To place students
in the Intervention
Program, use
the **Diagnostic**
Assessment in the
Intervention Teacher's
Edition.

Leveled Reader Lesson 1

Objective Read to apply strategies and skills
Materials • **Leveled Reader** *Blizzard Heroes*   • chart paper
 • **Approaching Practice Book A,** p. 173

Informational Nonfiction

BLIZZARD Heroes
by Marc Gave

Leveled Reader

PREVIEW AND PREDICT

Have students preview the book. Show the cover. Read the title and table of contents. Ask what they think this book will be about. Make sure they understand the word *blizzard*.

VOCABULARY WORDS

As they read, help students locate and read the words: *screams,* p. 2; *images, newspaper,* p. 4; *fled, escape, shuddering, numb,* p. 10. Help students to confirm or determine meanings based on context. Then ask students to use each word in a sentence.

STRATEGY
MAKE INFERENCES AND ANALYZE

Explain that making inferences and analyzing the text as they read will increase students' understanding. Read the Introduction (pages 2–3) aloud.

Think Aloud The second paragraph on page 3 says that many people "spring into action" to warn, help, and rescue others during a storm. It sounds like these might be the people who become the "blizzard heroes."

SKILL
MAKE AND CONFIRM PREDICTIONS

Remind students that predictions are guesses about what will happen. Before they read Chapter 1, have students predict what heroes help people before a storm. Then read the chapter. Before they read Chapter 2, have students predict who the heroes are during a blizzard. Then have them read and look for information that confirms their predictions.

Have students create their own Predictions Charts. As they read further, discuss which predictions they needed to change as they learned more.

READ AND RESPOND

Have students read through Chapter 2 orally. Encourage them to ask questions. Discuss their personal responses to the selection.

Fluency: REPEATED READING

Model reading the passage on **Practice Book** page 173. Have the group echo-read it. Then have partners practice reading to each other, paying close attention to punctuation. Provide corrective feedback.

★ Approaching Practice Book A, page 173

As I read, I will pay attention to punctuation.

	Some people are in real danger during a storm. How
10	are they helped? Friends and neighbors can be blizzard
19	heroes. They shovel walks and scrape ice from cars. They
29	bring food and medicine to people who are ill.
38	During a blizzard several feet of snow can fall within a
49	very short time. If the wind is blowing too hard, the
60	snowplows may not be able to do their job. The wind
71	could blow the snow right back to where it was.
81	Sheriffs or state troopers must close off roads.
89	Even with warnings, some people drive their cars or
98	stay outdoors longer than they should. Often they get
107	stuck. The police or the National Guard may help them. 117

Comprehension Check

1. How can friends and neighbors be blizzard heroes? **Main Idea and Details** by shoveling walks, scraping ice from cars, and bringing medicine and food to sick people
2. Who are some people who have important roles during a blizzard? **Main Idea and Details** sheriffs, state troopers, the police, the National Guard, and people who operate snow plows

	Words Read	−	Number of Errors	=	Words Correct Score
First Read		−		=	
Second Read		−		=	

Leveled Reader Lesson 2

Objective   Read to apply strategies and skills
Materials   • **Leveled Reader** *Blizzard Heroes*   • **Vocabulary Cards**

VOCABULARY WORDS

Display the **Vocabulary Cards.** Review the definition of each word, and ask students to identify its part of speech. Discuss words that have more than one meaning, such as *images*. Remind students to notice how the words are used in *Blizzard Heroes*.

SUMMARIZE AND PREDICT

Have students describe the heroes who help people before and during blizzards. Ask students to predict what they will learn in the rest of the selection. Who do they think will be the heroes after a blizzard?

SKILL
MAKE AND CONFIRM PREDICTIONS

Have students review their Predictions Chart from the previous day. Were their predictions correct? What information, if any, did they find surprising?

READ AND RESPOND

Have students restate their predictions about who will be the heroes after a blizzard. Then have them read to the end of the selection. Remind students to make inferences and analyze the text as they read to understand what happens in the selection and why.

Afterward, have them share their ideas and opinions about the selection. How do they feel about the people who help others during dangerous storms? Can they ever imagine being "blizzard heroes"?

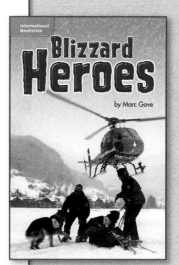

Leveled Reader

Fluency

Objective   Read with increasing fluency
Materials   • stopwatch   • **Approaching Practice Book A,** page 173

TIMED READING

Have students do a final timed reading of the passage from *Blizzard Heroes*. Students should

- begin reading the passage aloud when you say "Go."

- stop reading the passage after one minute when you say "Stop."

Pay attention to where students make mistakes or struggle with words. Offer feedback and support. Students should graph the number of words they read correctly.

Student Book

Practice Using Vocabulary Write the following words on the board as headings: *escape, fled, image, screamed,* and *shuddered.* Say: *Think of a word that could be a synonym for each of these words. For example, one synonym for* image *could be* picture. *What synonyms can you think of?* As students volunteer synonyms, write the words under the appropriate headings.

Comprehension

Objective	Make and confirm predictions about a story
Materials	• **Comprehension Transparencies 24a** and **24b**

SKILL

MAKE AND CONFIRM PREDICTIONS

Explain that as students read, they should try to predict what will happen and then reflect back on their predictions as they get further. Ask what students would predict just based on the title "To the Rescue." As they reread, they should look for clues to what will happen.

Display **Transparencies 24a** and **24b.** Read the fifth paragraph.

Think Aloud In this paragraph, Jeff warns that a snapping turtle might bite. I'm going to predict that someone might be bitten. I won't know until the end if I predicted correctly, though. I'll check back to confirm.

Have students underline words and phrases that help them predict what will happen. Discuss which predictions proved accurate.

Vocabulary

Objective	Apply vocabulary word meanings and analyze figurative language
Materials	• **Student Book** *The Printer*

VOCABULARY WORDS

Help students locate and read the vocabulary words in *The Printer*. For words they do not know, help students to determine the meanings based on how the words are used in context. Then compare the definitions of each word in the Glossary of the **Student Book.** Ask students to write statements about the selection using at least three of the words.

CONTEXT CLUES: FIGURATIVE LANGUAGE

Write *screamed.* Remind students that *screamed* as used in the statement "His fingers screamed to the other deaf workers" (from *The Printer*) is an example of figurative language.

Have students work in pairs to write two sentences with *fled* or *escape*: one sentence using the word in the usual manner and the other sentence showing an example of figurative language. Share examples: *The fire fled from one room to another. Close the door or the heat will escape.*

escape | fled | image | newspaper | numb | screamed | shuddered

Phonics

Objective   Decode two-syllable words with the VC/CV pattern

DECODE WORDS WITH THE VC/CV PATTERN

Write *invite* and *napkin*. Label the VC/CV pattern. Segment and blend each word and point out the short vowel sound in the first syllable. Explain that when a two-syllable word has a short vowel sound at the beginning and a VC/CV pattern, the syllables break between the consonants. Say each word aloud and clap the syllables. Have students echo you.

Write *follow* and *Sunday*. Have students say each word and clap the syllables. Then have them underline the short vowel in the first syllable, label the VC/CV pattern, and draw a slash to show where the syllables break. Ask a volunteer to explain why the *S* is capitalized in *Sunday*.

Additional Lessons

Use your **Quick Check** observations to help you identify students who might benefit from additional instruction. See page T4 for comprehension support and page T8 for vocabulary support.

Vocabulary

Objective   Apply vocabulary word meanings
Materials   • **Vocabulary Cards**

VOCABULARY WORDS

Read this week and last week's vocabulary words and definitions. Play a vocabulary guessing game. Provide clues such as these.

- I'm thinking of a compound word. It names something that is black and white and read all over. What is it? (newspaper)

- I'm thinking of a verb that names an action in the past. It's something you do with your voice when you are afraid. (screamed)

Invite students to make up clues for the other words.

Make Connections Across Texts

Objective   Make and confirm predictions across texts
Materials   • **Student Book** *The Printer*   • **Leveled Reader** *Blizzard Heroes*

SKILL

MAKE AND CONFIRM PREDICTIONS

Summarize and discuss *The Printer* and *Blizzard Heroes*. Ask students to compare and contrast predictions they made about the people in each.

- Was it easier to make predictions about *The Printer* or *Blizzard Heroes*? Why?

- What does the main character in *The Printer* have in common with the people described in *Blizzard Heroes*?

Student Book

Leveled Reader

Leveled Reader Lesson

Objective Read to apply strategies and skills
Materials • **Leveled Reader** *Hurricane Heroes* • **On Level Practice Book O,** p. 173

Leveled Reader

PREVIEW AND PREDICT

Show the cover and read the title. Ask students if they know what a hurricane is. Ask who they think a "hurricane hero" might be.

STRATEGY
MAKE INFERENCES AND ANALYZE

Remind students that by looking for text clues and using prior knowledge, they can make inferences and analyze the text. As they read this book, they should try to figure out what happens to people who are affected by hurricanes. Read pages 2–3 aloud.

Think Aloud In the last paragraph on page 3, the author says that "hurricane heroes" help save lives. I'm going to keep reading, looking for clues, and using what I already know to figure out who "hurricane heroes" are and how they save lives.

SKILL

MAKE AND CONFIRM PREDICTIONS

Ask students to think about what professionals such as weather forecasters or emergency workers might do before, during, and after a hurricane. As they read, students should check to see if their predictions were accurate. Students can create a Predictions Chart to help them.

READ AND RESPOND

Have students read to the end of Chapter 1. Ask them to make inferences about people who help out in a hurricane and why the author considers them to be "heroes." Also discuss how vocabulary words are used.

Have students read to the end of the book. Ask what they feel is the most essential job that people do before, during, or after a hurricane.

Fluency: REPEATED READING

Model expressive reading using the fluency passage from *Hurricane Heroes*. Students should follow along on **Practice Book** page 173. Then have the group read the passage chorally.

Students should practice rereading with partners. Ask students to increase expression when reading sentences that end in exclamation marks. Remind listeners to wait until the reader finishes a sentence before offering corrections. Circulate and observe as students read.

ELL
Leveled Reader
Go to pages
259U–259V.

Tested

On Level Practice Book O, page 173

As I read, I will pay attention to punctuation.

Winds scream. Rain pelts down. Buildings shudder.
7 Trees sway back and forth. Branches break and fall to the
18 ground. It's a hurricane!
22   You've probably seen pictures or images of hurricanes
30 in a newspaper or on TV. What makes a storm a hurricane?
42   A hurricane is a storm with very strong winds and
52 heavy rain. It starts over warm waters in an ocean. The
63 storm might take the shape of a circle or an oval. It can be
77 up to 400 miles (640 km) wide.
82   How do people prepare for hurricanes? How do
90 "hurricane heroes" do their work? They do their jobs in
100 offices and shelters. They are important before, during, and
109 after a big storm. They help save lives.
117   How do people find out if a bad storm is coming?
128   Air Force pilots called hurricane hunters fly into the
137 eye of the storm. 141

Comprehension Check

1. What is a hurricane? **Main Idea and Details** a storm with very strong winds and heavy rain
2. Who are hurricane hunters? **Main Idea and Details** Hurricane hunters are Air Force pilots who fly into the eye of the hurricane.

	Words Read	−	Number of Errors	=	Words Correct Score
First Read		−		=	
Second Read		−		=	

Vocabulary

Objective Apply vocabulary word meanings and analyze figurative language

Materials • **Leveled Reader** *Hurricane Heroes*

Leveled Reader

VOCABULARY WORDS

Review the words *screamed, numb, escape, fled, shuddered, image,* and *newspaper.* Give students a list of scrambled vocabulary words, with definitions for each word. Have students unscramble the words and write sentences for each. Invite students to read their sentences aloud.

CONTEXT CLUES: FIGURATIVE LANGUAGE

Explain that figurative language uses words in an unexpected way to create a strong image. Have students locate *scream* on page 2 of *Hurricane Heroes.* Discuss how it is used figuratively. Ask: *How can winds scream if they don't have voices?* Discuss other examples of figurative language.

Student Book

Text Feature

Objective Read and use a map

Materials • **Student Book** "Smokejumpers" • social studies textbook

MAPS

Discuss the information presented in the map on **Student Book** page 255. Point out how the map key explains the colors on the map. Have students discuss how to use this to predict where fires might occur.

Then have students find a map in their social studies textbook and compare the features of both maps. When would they use a map?

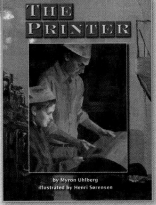

Student Book

Make Connections Across Texts

Objective Make connections across texts and make and confirm predictions

Materials • **Student Book** *The Printer* • **Leveled Reader** *Hurricane Heroes*

SKILL
MAKE AND CONFIRM PREDICTIONS

Review the idea that good readers make connections and compare the stories they read. Discuss whether the predictions students made about the heroes in *The Printer* and *Hurricane Heroes* were correct and why. Ask what the father in *The Printer* and the people in *Hurricane Heroes* have in common and how they are different.

Leveled Reader Lesson

Objective Read to apply strategies and skills

Materials • **Leveled Reader** *Earthquake Heroes* • **Beyond Practice Book B,** p. 173

PREVIEW AND PREDICT

Have students preview the book. Show the cover and read the title and chapter headings. Have them skim the text and note questions. Ask students what they think earthquake heroes do.

STRATEGY
MAKE INFERENCES AND ANALYZE

Remind students that analyzing story clues and making inferences as they read will help them to make accurate predictions.

SKILL
MAKE AND CONFIRM PREDICTIONS

After reading the Introduction, discuss who would help prepare people for earthquakes. As students read, ask them to make predictions about why these professionals are considered heroes. They can create a Predictions Chart. Afterward, students can check their charts to see if their predictions were accurate.

READ AND RESPOND

Have students make predictions about how people prepare for earthquakes. Then have them read to the end of Chapter 2 and reflect on their predictions. Encourage students to notice the vocabulary words.

After reading, have students discuss how many people are involved in earthquake preparation and emergency work. Ask students what they think is the most important thing to understand about earthquakes and why.

Fluency: REPEATED READING

Model reading nonfiction expressively. Use the passage from *Earthquake Heroes* that is reproduced on **Practice Book** page 173.

Then have students take turns reading the passage to a partner and offering feedback. Remind them to read smoothly, with seriousness and interest. Ask students to listen to their partner and be ready when it is their turn to read. Remind them to tell their partner when his or her reading has been good. Listen as each student reads and offer support as needed. Encourage partners to continue practicing the passage throughout the week.

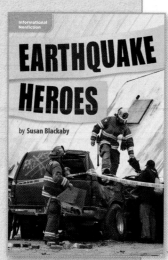

Leveled Reader

◆ **Beyond Practice Book B,** page 173

As I read, I will pay attention to punctuation.

	We know a lot of things about earthquakes. We know
10	what causes them and where they are likely to happen. We
21	know what to do to be prepared.
28	However, we cannot tell when an earthquake will hit or
38	how big it will be. We have to be ready for anything. We
51	must rely on earthquake heroes to help us.
59	Earthquake heroes work before, during, and after
66	an earthquake. They try to make sure that people are safe
77	and property is protected.
81	Some earthquake heroes are on the job even before an
91	earthquake strikes. A scientist who studies earthquakes
98	is called a seismologist. Seismologists are part of a team
108	of earthquake heroes. They work in labs and in the field
119	to learn how energy moves through rock. They watch
128	how Earth's crust moves. They keep track of where
137	and when quakes occur. They measure how strong the
146	quakes are. 148

Comprehension Check

1. What do we know about earthquakes? **Main Idea and Details** We know where and why they happen, but not when or how strong they will be.

2. What are seismologists and what do they do? **Summarize** scientists who study earthquakes. They study Earth's crust and how energy moves through rock.

	Words Read	–	Number of Errors	=	Words Correct Score
First Read		–		=	
Second Read		–		=	

Vocabulary

Objective Write a paragraph using content vocabulary words
Materials • **Student Book** "Smokejumpers"

CONTENT VOCABULARY

Discuss the content vocabulary words *remote, smokejumpers, physical,* and *retreat* found on **Student Book** page 254. Have students work in pairs or independently to write a paragraph about what they imagine it would be like to be a smokejumper. Encourage them to use the content vocabulary words. Invite them to read their writing to the group.

Student Book

Text Feature

Objective Read and use a map
Materials • **Student Book** "Smokejumpers"

MAPS

Ask students to review "Smokejumpers" on Student Book pages 254–257 and summarize the main ideas. Discuss the map and its features.

- What information does the map show? What details does it include?
- What features do maps usually have?
- How do maps help readers?

Have several students work together to create a neighborhood map. They should include streets, parks, rivers, and any important landmarks. Remind them to label the items on the map and to use color meaningfully. They should include a map key and compass rose.

ELL **Access for All**

Description Explain that a good description uses very specific words to help set the scene for the reader. Have students look at the cover of "Smokejumpers." Ask them to brainstorm descriptive words to describe what the people on the cover are wearing. Write the words on the board. Then ask students to create one-sentence descriptions using those words.

Self-Selected Reading

Objective Read independently and make and confirm predictions
Materials • Leveled Readers or trade books at students' reading level

READ TO MAKE AND CONFIRM PREDICTIONS

Invite students to choose a fiction book to read independently for enjoyment. For a list of theme-related titles, see pages T19–T20. Remind students to make inferences and analyze information so they can make good predictions.

After reading, students can hold a literature circle to share the kinds of clues they used to make their predictions and whether or not they were accurate. Have them share opinions and recommendations.

Academic Language

Throughout the week the English language learners will need help in building their understanding of the academic language used in daily instruction and assessment instruments. The following strategies will help to increase their language proficiency and comprehension of content and instructional words.

Oral Language For additional language support and oral vocabulary development, go to www.macmillanmh.com

Strategies to Reinforce Academic Language

- **Use Context** Academic Language (see chart below) should be explained in the context of the task during Whole Group. Use gestures, expressions, and visuals to support meaning.

- **Use Visuals** Use charts, transparencies, and graphic organizers to explain key labels to help students understand classroom language.

- **Model** Demonstrate the task using academic language in order for students to understand instruction.

Academic Language Used in Whole Group Instruction

Content/Theme Words	Skill/Strategy Words	Writing/Grammar Words
heroes (p. 230)	context clues (p. 232)	descriptive paragraph (p. 258)
courageous (230)	figurative language (p. 232)	introductory speech (p. 258)
rescue (p. 230)	making inferences (p. 233)	audience (p. 258)
remote (p. 254)	make/confirm predictions (p. 233)	voice (p. 258)
physical (p. 254)	sequence (p. 253B)	opinion (p. 258)
retreat (p. 254)	reading a map (p. 254)	pronoun–verb agreement (p. 259I)
training (p. 255)		singular and plural pronouns (p. 259J)

ELL Leveled Reader Lesson

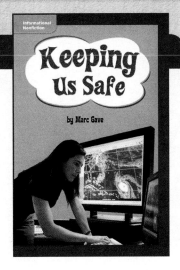

Informational Nonfiction

Keeping Us Safe

by Marc Gave

Before Reading

DEVELOP ORAL LANGUAGE

 Build Background Ask students to share stories about when they or someone they know helped people. Then say: *Sometimes people do brave things to help people. We call these people "heroes." Do you know any heroes?*

 Review Vocabulary Write the definitions of the words on sentence strips. Write the vocabulary and support words on the board. Read each definition and have students match it to its word. Use each word in a sentence and involve students. *I read the* newspaper *everyday. Can you make a sentence with the word* newspaper?

PREVIEW AND PREDICT

Point to the cover photo and read the title. *What kind of people help to keep us safe?* Do a book walk to help students answer.

 Set a Purpose for Reading Show the Predictions Chart. Ask students to do a similar chart to record and check predictions. Tell them to stop after each chapter to predict: *What will I learn about in the next chapter?*

During Reading

Choose from among the differentiated strategies below to support students' reading at all stages of language acquisition.

Beginning	Intermediate	Advanced
Shared Reading As you read, model using the text and picture clues to make predictions about the next chapter. Then check your predictions and fill in the chart.	**Read Together** Read Chapter 1. Model using text and picture clues to make predictions about the next chapter. Have students take turns reading and continue using the strategy. Ask them to help you fill in the chart.	**Independent Reading** Have students read the selection. Ask them to discuss each chapter with a partner and predict what they will read about next using text and picture clues. Have them fill in the chart.

After Reading

Remind students to use the vocabulary and story words in their whole group activities.

Objective

- To apply vocabulary and comprehension skills

Materials

- ELL Leveled Reader

ELL 5 Day Planner

DAY 1	• Academic Language • Oral Language and Vocabulary Review
DAY 2	• Academic Language • ELL Leveled Reader
DAY 3	• Academic Language • ELL Leveled Reader
DAY 4	• Academic Language • ELL Leveled Reader
DAY 5	• Academic Language • ELL Leveled Reader Comprehension Check and Literacy Activities

ELL Teacher's Guide for students who need additional instruction

Student Book Selections

Weekly Theme: Animal Architects

Week At A Glance

Whole Group

VOCABULARY
architects, contain, hives, retreats, shallow, shelter, structures

Analogies

COMPREHENSION
Strategy: Summarize
Skill: Identify Text Structure: Description

WRITING
Descriptive Poem

Science Link

Life Science
Ecosystems in Balance

Small Group Options

Differentiated Instruction for Tested Skills

Animal Homes
by Ann O. Squire

AUDIO CD

Main Selection/Science Link
Genre Infomational Nonfiction

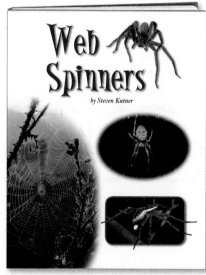

Web Spinners
by Steven Kutner

Vocabulary/Comprehension

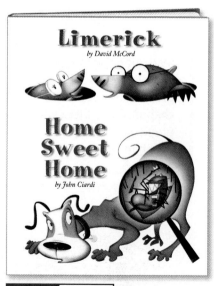

Limerick
by David McCord

Home Sweet Home
by John Ciardi

Genre Poetry

Resources for **Differentiated Instruction**

Leveled Readers

AUDIO CD

GR Levels N–R

Genre Informational Nonfiction

- Same Theme
- Same Vocabulary
- Same Comprehension Skills

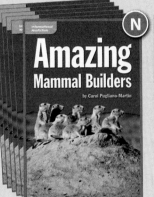
(N)
Amazing Mammal Builders
by Carol Pugliano-Martin

Approaching Level

(P)
Amazing Bird Builders
by Carol Pugliano-Martin

On Level

Bird Builders
by Carol Pugliano-Martin

English Language Leveled Reader

(R)
Amazing Insect and Spider Builders
by Carol Pugliano-Martin

Beyond Level

On Level Reader sheltered for English Language Learner

ELL Teacher's Guide Available

Also Available
LEVELED READER PROGRAM

CLASSROOM LIBRARY

Genre Historical Fiction

The Babe & I
Approaching

The Year of Miss Agnes
Kirkpatrick Hill
On Level

AMELIA AND ELEANOR GO FOR A RIDE
Beyond

Trade books to apply Comprehension Skills

INTERVENTION ANTHOLOGY

- Phonics and Decoding
- Comprehension
- Vocabulary

Reading Triumphs, Intervention Program also available

Reading Triumphs
AUDIO CD
Macmillan/McGraw-Hill

LEVELED PRACTICE

Practice Book A
Macmillan/McGraw-Hill
Approaching

Practice Book O
Macmillan/McGraw-Hill
On Level

Practice Book B
Macmillan/McGraw-Hill
Beyond

ELL Practice and Assessment
Macmillan/McGraw-Hill
ELL

Technology

www.macmillanmh.com

AUDIO CD
LISTENING LIBRARY
- Main Selections
- Leveled Readers
- Intervention Anthology

FLUENCY SOLUTIONS

CD ROM
VOCABULARY PuzzleMaker

NEW ADVENTURES WITH BUGGLES AND BEEZY

LOG ON
ONLINE INSTRUCTION
- Meet the Author/Illustrator
- Computer Literacy Lessons
- Research and Inquiry Activities
- Oral Language Activities
- Vocabulary and Spelling Activities

Suggested Lesson Plan

 CD ROM **Instructional Navigator**
Interactive Lesson Planner

Animal Homes, 264–279

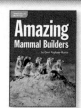    

Leveled Readers

Integrated **ELL** Support Every Day

Whole Group

ORAL LANGUAGE

- **Listening**
- **Speaking**
- **Viewing**

WORD STUDY

- **Vocabulary**
- **Phonics/Decoding**

READING

- **Develop Comprehension**
- **Fluency**

LANGUAGE ARTS

- **Writing**
- **Grammar**
- **Spelling**

ASSESSMENT

- **Informal/Formal**

Day 1

Listening/Speaking/Viewing

❓**Focus Question** How are animals' homes similar to people's homes?
Build Background, 260

Read Aloud: "Nests and How They Are Built," 261

Vocabulary

hives, architects, structures, contain, retreats, shallow, shelter, 262

Practice Book A-O-B, 177

Strategy: Analogies, 263

Read "Web Spinners," 262–263

Comprehension, 263A–263B
Strategy: Summarize
Skill: Description
Practice Book A-O-B, 178

Fluency Partner Reading, 260I
Model Fluency, 261

Student Book

Writing

Daily Writing Prompt Pretend you are a web spinner you have learned about. Write a classified ad to sell your home.

Prewrite a Descriptive Poem, 285A

Grammar Daily Language Activities, 285I
Pronoun-Verb Contractions, 285I
Grammar Practice Book, 153

Spelling Pretest, 285G
Spelling Practice Book, 153–154

Quick Check Vocabulary, 262
Comprehension, 263B

Differentiated Instruction 285M–285V

Day 2

Listening/Speaking

❓**Focus Question** How are some animal homes similar to your home?

Vocabulary
Review Vocabulary, 264

Phonics
Decode Words with the V/CV and VC/V Pattern, 285E
Practice Book A-O-B, 183

Read *Animal Homes,* 264–279

Comprehension, 264–281
Strategy: Summarize
Skill: Description
Practice Book A-O-B, 179

Fluency Partner Reading, 260I
Phrase-Cued Text, 272

Student Book

Writing

Daily Writing Prompt Pretend you could be any size. Write a paragraph describing your home and tell why you would want to live there.

Draft a Descriptive Poem, 285A

Grammar Daily Language Activities, 285I
Pronoun-Verb Contractions, 285I
Grammar Practice Book, 154

Spelling The V/CV and VC/V Patterns, 285G
Spelling Practice Book, 155

Quick Check Comprehension, 273, 279
Phonics, 229E

Differentiated Instruction 285M–285V

Turn the Page for
Small Group Lesson Plan

Skills/Strategies

Vocabulary	Comprehension	Writing
Vocabulary Words	**Strategy:** Summarize	Descriptive Poem
Analogies	**Skill:** Description	

Turn the Page for
Small Group Options

Day 3

Listening/Speaking

❓ Focus Question Compare the structures on pages 262–263 of "Web Spinners" with the structure of another animal home.

Summarize, 281

Vocabulary

Review Words in Context, 285C

Strategy: Analogies, 285D

Practice Book A-O-B, 182

Phonics

Decode Multisyllable Words, 285E

Read *Animal Homes*, 264–279

Student Book

Comprehension

Comprehension Check, 281

Maintain Skill: Summarize, 281B

Fluency Practice Book A-O-B, 180
Partner Reading, 260I
Repeated Reading, 281A

Writing

Daily Writing Prompt Describe an animal home that you would like to build for a pet. List the materials you will use and write steps to build the home.

Writing Trait: Word Choice, 285
Revise a Descriptive Poem, 285B

Grammar Daily Language Activities, 285I
Mechanics and Usage, 285J
Grammar Practice Book, 155

Spelling The V/CV and VC/V Patterns, 285H
Spelling Practice Book, 156

Quick Check Fluency, 281A

Differentiated Instruction 285M-285V

Day 4

Listening/Speaking

❓ Focus Question Do the mole and the flea both like their homes? Explain.

Expand Vocabulary: Animal Architects, 285F

Vocabulary

Onomatopoeia, 285F

Apply Vocabulary to Writing, 285F

Read "Home Sweet Home," "Limerick," 282–283

Student Book

Comprehension

Poetry: Limerick

Literary Elements: Simile and Rhythmic Pattern, 282
Practice Book A-O-B, 181

Fluency Partner Reading, 260I

Writing

Daily Writing Prompt Write a limerick about an animal's home. Remember to follow the pattern of rhythm and rhyme of limericks.

Proofread a Descriptive Poem, 285B

Grammar Daily Language Activities, 285I
Pronoun-Verb Contractions, 285J
Grammar Practice Book, 156

Spelling The V/CV and VC/V Patterns, 285H
Spelling Practice Book, 157

Quick Check Vocabulary, 285D

Differentiated Instruction 285M-285V

Day 5

Review and Assess

Listening/Speaking

❓ Focus Question Based on *Animal Homes*, "Web Spinners," and the poems in "Home Sweet Home," describe some of the many different animal homes.

Speaking and Listening Strategies, 285A

Presentation of the Descriptive Poem, 285B

Vocabulary

Spiral Review: Vocabulary Game, 285F

Read Self-Selected Reading, 260I

Student Book

Comprehension

Connect and Compare, 283

Fluency Partner Reading, 260I

Writing

Daily Writing Prompt Imagine you are an animal. Write a description of your home from the animal's point of view.

Publish a Descriptive Poem, 285B

Grammar Daily Language Activities, 285I
Pronoun-Verb Contractions, 285J
Grammar Practice Book, 157–158

Spelling Posttest, 285H
Spelling Practice Book, 158

Weekly Assessment, 309–316

Differentiated Instruction 285M-285V

Small Group Options

What do I do in small groups?

Quick Check
Use your Quick Checks to inform instruction.

Additional Instruction, Practice, and Extend Activities are provided for this week's tested skills.

Phonics
Decode the V/CV and VC/V Pattern

Vocabulary
Words: hives, architects, structures, contain, retreats, shallow, shelter
Skill: Analogies

Comprehension
Strategy: Summarize
Skill: Description

Fluency

Lesson Plan
TEACHER-LED SMALL GROUP

 CD ROM
Instructional Navigator
Interactive Lesson Planner

	Day 1	**Day 2**
Approaching Level • **Additional Instruction/Practice** • **Tier 2 Instruction**	Leveled Reader Lesson 1, 285M • Vocabulary • Comprehension • Fluency	Leveled Reader Lesson 2, 285N • Vocabulary • Comprehension • Fluency **ELL** Analogies, 285O
On Level • **Practice**	Leveled Reader Lesson, 285Q • Vocabulary • Comprehension • Fluency **ELL** Leveled Reader, 285U–V	Leveled Reader Lesson, 285Q • Vocabulary • Comprehension • Fluency
Beyond Level • **Extend**	Leveled Reader Lesson, 285S • Vocabulary • Comprehension • Fluency	Leveled Reader Lesson, 285S • Vocabulary • Comprehension • Fluency

Leveled Readers

AUDIO CD

GR Levels N–R
Matching students to text.

Also Available
LEVELED READER LIBRARY

LOG ON
Leveled Reader Database
To search for additional Leveled Reader titles, go to www.macmillanmh.com

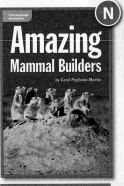

N

Approaching Level

- Benchmark 30
- Use other guided reading titles, N–P

P

On Level

- Benchmark 38
- Use other guided reading titles, P–R

R

Beyond Level

- Benchmark 40
- Use other guided reading titles, R–T

English Language Leveled Reader

On Level Reader sheltered for English Language Learner

Day 3

Comprehension, 285O Vocabulary, 285O
Vocabulary, 285R
Self-Selected Reading, 285T

Day 4

Phonics, 285P Vocabulary, 285P
Literary Elements, 285R
Vocabulary, 285T **ELL** Poetic Language, 285T

Day 5

Fluency, 285N Make Connections Across Texts, 285P
Make Connections Across Texts, 285R
Literary Elements, 285T

Managing the Class

What do I do with the rest of my class?

Teacher-Led Small Groups

Cross-Curricular Workstations

Independent Activities

Weekly Contract

Name _____ Date _____

My To-Do List

✔ Put a check next to the activities you complete.

📖 **Reading**
- [ ] Practice fluency
- [ ] Choose a book to read

🔤 **Word Study**
- [ ] Work with analogies
- [ ] Analyze V/CV and VC/V patterns

✏️ **Writing**
- [ ] Write a descriptive poem
- [ ] Write a descriptive paragraph

🔬 **Science**
- [ ] Research an animal's home
- [ ] Write a poem about its home

🌎 **Social Studies**
- [ ] Research kinds of homes
- [ ] Write facts about homes

⚓ **Leveled Readers**
- [ ] Write About It!
- [ ] Content Connection

💻 **Technology**
- [ ] Vocabulary Puzzlemaker
- [ ] Fluency Solutions
- [ ] Listening Library
- [ ] www.macmillanmh.com

✒️ **Independent Practice**
- [ ] Practice Book, 177–183
- [ ] Grammar Practice Book, 153–158
- [ ] Spelling Practice Book, 153–158

Contracts   Unit 5 • Animal Homes (27)

© Macmillan/McGraw-Hill

Teacher's Resource Book, page 27

• **Students use their Contracts to manage their time.**

Leveled Reader Activities

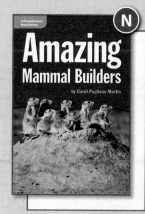

Approaching

See inside back cover for activities

LEVELED PRACTICE

- Vocabulary, 177
- Comprehension: Description, 178
- Graphic Organizer, 179
- Fluency, 180
- Literary Elements: Simile and Rhythmic Pattern, 181
- Vocabulary Strategy: Analogies, 182
- Phonics, 183

★ **Approaching Practice Book A,** 177–183

A. Draw a line to connect each vocabulary word with the correct definition.

1. architects — a. any things that are built
2. shallow — b. something that covers or protects
3. structures — c. to draw or move back
4. contain — d. boxes or houses for bees to live in
5. retreats — e. not deep
6. shelter — f. to hold
7. hives — g. people who design buildings

B. Choose a vocabulary word from above that has the same or almost the same meaning as the underlined word or words in each sentence.

8. Do not go too close to the bees' homes or you may get stung!
   (a) hives   b. shelters   _____hives_____

9. The building designers came to our class and explained how they design buildings.
   a. retreats   (b) architects   _____architects_____

10. The river was not deep so we decided to wade across it.
    a. structures   (b) shallow   _____shallow_____

11. It was difficult to hold my pet dog when we wanted to give him a bath.
    (a) contain   b. retreats   _____contain_____

12. My pet cat moves back everytime a stranger approaches her.
    (a) retreats   b. contain   _____retreats_____

HOME-SCHOOL CONNECTION

Pages 295–306

Independent Activities

On Level

ELL

Beyond

On Level Practice Book O, 177–183

Fill in the blank with the correct word from the box.
Some words will be used more than once.

architects	shallow	structures	contain
retreats	shelter	hives	

1. Animals are like __architects__ because they build their own homes.

2. Termites build tall __structures__.

3. Some __architects__ study animal homes for ideas about solving problems with buildings.

4. Honeybees build __hives__ made of waxy honeycombs.

5. The tortoise builds a __shallow__ hole to keep cool.

6. A polar bear, however, needs a very different type of __shelter__.

7. Bears may get stung if they poke around in honeybees' __hives__.

8. If you come across a spider's web, be careful because it may __contain__ an insect.

9. A turtle __retreats__ into its shell when it senses danger.

10. A hermit crab finds __shelter__ in an empty shell.

Beyond Practice Book B, 177–183

Look at the crossword puzzle. Some of the answers have been given. Some clues have been provided. Complete the crossword and fill in the missing clues. Possible responses provided.

Crossword answers: architects, contain, shallow, structures, shelter, hives

Across
1. people who plan and design houses and other buildings
6. a structure that protects
7. where bees live

Down
2. draws back
3. to hold
4. not deep
5. things that are built

ELL Practice and Assessment, 150–151

Grade 3

Treasures

ELL Practice and Assessment

Macmillan/McGraw-Hill

Parent Letter

Take-Home Story

Turn the page for Cross-Curricular Activities.

Managing the Class

Cross-Curricular Activities

All activities reinforce this week's skills.

Reading

Objectives

- Read aloud with a partner, using voice to stress important facts.
- Summarize important facts from a book or encyclopedia entry.

 Word Study

Objectives

- Use word cards to write analogy sentences.
- Sort words with long and short vowels.

📖 Reading — Fluency
20 Minutes ⏱

- Choose a paragraph from the fluency passage on page 180 of your Practice Book. Take turns reading the sentences aloud with a partner.
- Practice using your voice to stress important facts.

Extension
- Read the paragraph aloud to your partner. Slow down on sentences with important information.
- Ask your partner to tell you the most important facts in the paragraph.

> **Things you need:**
> - Practice Book

 Fluency Solutions Listening Library

49

🔤 Word Study — Analogy Action
20 Minutes ⏱

- Write the following words on cards: *honeybee, hive, polar bear, den, alligator, swamp, bird,* and *nest.* Match up the cards. Put each animal with its home.

alligator
polar bear
swamp
den

Extension
- Use your card pairs to write analogy sentences like this one: *A honeybee is to a hive as a polar bear is to a den.* Make as many analogies as you can.

> **Things you need:**
> - note cards and paper
> - pencil

LOG ON For additional vocabulary and spelling games, go to www.macmillanmh.com   Vocabulary PuzzleMaker

49

📖 Reading — Independent Reading
20 Minutes ⏱

- Find a book or an encyclopedia entry about your favorite animal. Make a list of at least five facts that describe the animal, including where it makes its home.

Extension
- Write sentences describing the animal without using its name. Share your sentences with a partner. Can your partner guess the animal?

> **Things you need:**
> - book or encyclopedia
> - paper and pencil

LOG ON For more books about Animal Architects, go to the Author/Illustrator section at www.macmillanmh.com

50

🔤 Word Study — The V/CV and VC/V Patterns
20 Minutes ⏱

- Write these words on cards: *pilot, diner, tiger, favor, lemon, planet, model,* and *melon.*
- On each card, underline the letter that makes the first vowel sound in the word.

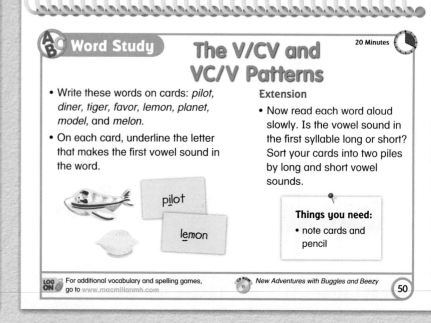

pilot
lemon

Extension
- Now read each word aloud slowly. Is the vowel sound in the first syllable long or short? Sort your cards into two piles by long and short vowel sounds.

> **Things you need:**
> - note cards and pencil

LOG ON For additional vocabulary and spelling games, go to www.macmillanmh.com   New Adventures with Buggles and Beezy

50

260I

Independent Workstations

Writing

Objectives

- Write a poem about a favorite place at home.
- Write a descriptive title and a paragraph for a magazine article.

Science/Social Studies

Objectives

- Research information about different kinds of homes.
- Research and write facts about animal homes.

Writing — Writing a Poem
20 Minutes

- Where is your favorite place at home? It might be your bedroom, the kitchen, or a spot by a window. Write a poem. Describe your special place. Your poem doesn't have to rhyme.

My Red Bench
I love to sit
On the little red bench
In our garden.
In winter, the weather is cold.
I can watch the snow fall.
In summer, the weather is warm.
I can smell the flowers and watch them grow.

Extension

- Draw a picture of your special place at home. Include as many details as you can.
- Then reread your poem. Does it describe all the details? Add or change words as needed.

Things you need:
- paper and pencil
- crayons or markers

49

Science — Animals at Home
20 Minutes

- Choose an animal that interests you. Do research. Use books or an encyclopedia to find out about where it lives.
- Write three fact cards on what you find.

Extension

- Use your notes to write a poem about the animal's home. Your poem does not need to rhyme, but try to give it a special rhythm.

Things you need:
- books or encyclopedia
- paper and pencil
- note cards

49

Writing — Unusual Homes
20 Minutes

- Think about a special place to live, such as a treehouse or an igloo. Pretend you are a magazine writer reporting on the people who live there. Write a descriptive title and the first paragraph of an article. Do research if you need to.

Extension

- Draw a picture of the unusual home. Include a caption.

Things you need:
- paper and pencil
- crayons or markers

Internet Research and Inquiry Activity
Students can find more facts at www.macmillanmh.com

50

Social Studies — Homes Around the World
20 Minutes

- People around the world live in all kinds of homes, from apartments and houses to mud huts. Do research in books or an encyclopedia to find out about different kinds of homes.

Extension

- Write three interesting facts about homes around the world.

Things you need:
- books or encyclopedia
- paper and pencil

50

260

Prepare

ORAL LANGUAGE
- Build Background
- Read Aloud
- Expand Vocabulary

VOCABULARY
- Teach Words in Context
- Analogies

COMPREHENSION
- **Strategy:** Summarize
- **Skill:** Description

SMALL GROUP OPTIONS
- Differentiated Instruction, pp. 285M–285V

Oral Language

Build Background

ACCESS PRIOR KNOWLEDGE

Share the following information.

An architect designs buildings and makes sure they are built correctly.

TALK ABOUT ANIMAL ARCHITECTS

Discuss the weekly theme.

- What do you think an *animal architect* is?

- What wild animals have you seen in your neighborhood? What types of homes do the animals have?

 FOCUS QUESTION Ask a volunteer to read aloud "Talk About It" on **Student Book** page 261 and describe the photograph.

- What kind of home do bees build?

ENGLISH LANGUAGE LEARNERS

Access for All

Beginning **Ask Questions** Say as you draw a house: *People live in houses.* Point as you say: *A bee lives in a hive. Who builds the hive? Where does a [bird] live?* Help students answer. Ask about other animals to find out how much students can say in English. Draw items as necessary.

Intermediate **Webbing** Make a Word Web about animals and their homes. Encourage students to describe each animal and where it lives. Restate what they say using more descriptive language. Draw pictures when possible to convey meaning. Explain the word *architect* and discuss how animals are like architects.

Advanced **Relate to Personal Experience** Do the Intermediate task. Have students describe animal homes they have seen.

Talk About It

How are animals' homes similar to people's homes?

LOG ON Find out more about animal homes at www.macmillanmh.com

ANiMAL ARCHITECTS

261

Picture Prompt

Tell students: Look at the picture. Write about what you see. You can write a poem, a story, a description, or use any other type of writing.

LOG ON   Technology

For an extended lesson plan and Web site activities for **oral language development,** go to www.macmillanmh.com

Read Aloud
Read "Nests and How They Are Built"

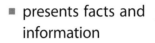
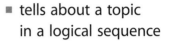

GENRE: Informational Nonfiction
Review features of nonfiction:

- presents facts and information

- tells about a topic in a logical sequence

LISTENING FOR A PURPOSE

Ask students to listen for the steps in building a nest as they listen to "Nests and How They Are Built" in the **Read-Aloud Anthology.** Choose from among the teaching suggestions.

Fluency Ask students to listen carefully as you read the article aloud. Tell students to listen to your phrasing, expression, and tone of voice.

RESPOND TO THE ARTICLE

Ask students if any words or wording gave them trouble. Then have them retell the main idea of the article.

Expand Vocabulary

Ask students to choose three or more words from the article that relate to the weekly theme, such as *build, nest, habitat, home,* and *weaves.* Have students take turns using these and other related words in oral instructions on how to build a bird's nest. Students can describe how to build different kinds of nests. Then have volunteers paraphrase the directions.

Vocabulary

TEACH WORDS IN CONTEXT

Use the following routine.

Routine

Define: Honeybees live in **hives**.

Example: Beekeepers make hives for their bees.

Ask: What else do you know about bees and their hives? PRIOR KNOWLEDGE

- **Architects** are people who plan and design houses and other buildings. The architects drew up plans for the new library downtown. What skills do you think architects need for their jobs? EXPLANATION

- Another word for *buildings* is **structures**. Bridges, towers, and monuments are also structures. What are some structures in your neighborhood? EXAMPLE

- To **contain** means "to hold." A bottle might contain milk. What might a box contain? EXAMPLE

- If something **retreats**, it turns back, usually because of danger or a difficult situation ahead. The cat quickly retreats to safety when it sees a dog. What word or phrase means about the same as *retreats*? (leaves, moves back) SYNONYM

- If something is **shallow**, it is not deep. Most lakes are shallow near the shore. What is an antonym for *shallow*? ANTONYM

- A **shelter** is something that protects or covers. People can stand under a shelter while waiting for a bus. What is the difference between a shelter and a house? COMPARE AND CONTRAST

Vocabulary

hives	retreats
architects	shallow
structures	shelter
contain	

Analogies

An **analogy** shows how two pairs of words are alike. The analogy below compares the homes of two animals.

bee is to *hive* as *spider* is to *web*

262

Web Spinners

by Steven Kutner

Just as bees build **hives** to live in, spiders spin webs. Spiders are talented **architects**. They design and build **structures** to live in that are works of art. These structures are also traps for other insects.

Spinning Silk

Spider webs are made from silk. Spiders make silk in their bellies. Their silk-making gland has many tiny holes. The silk goes through the holes to get outside the spider's body. When it meets the air, the silk forms a thread. The thread is very thin but very strong.

Spiders can make different kinds of silk. Some **contain** a material that makes the silk sticky. Other silks do not have this material.

A spider spins a thread behind itself everywhere it goes. This thread is called a dragline. If an enemy comes near, the spider **retreats** on its dragline. Being able to go backwards on its own line is like having a self-made escape route!

Quick Check   Do students understand word meanings?

During **Small Group Instruction**

If No → **Approaching Level** Vocabulary, p. 285P

If Yes → **On Level** Options, pp. 285Q–285R

Beyond Level Options, pp. 285S–285T

ELL   **Access for All**

Draw/Demonstrate For *structures*, draw a building. Say: *A building is a structure.* Draw other examples (bridge, tower). Ask: *What does the structure of the school look like?* Have students draw it and show others. For *retreats*, demonstrate the action as you say: *I see a dog. I'm afraid. I'm going to retreat. If you were walking and saw a dog, would you retreat?*

Tangled Webs

Different spiders build different kinds of webs. The simplest web is called a tangled web. It is just a mess of threads that are attached to something. A cobweb is a dusty, old, tangled web.

Cellar Spiders

Some spiders are called cellar spiders. This is because they usually build tangled webs in cellars or other dark places.

Orb Weavers

The most common webs are shaped like wheels. They are built by orb weavers. You can find these webs in open areas, such as the spaces between branches.

Water Spiders

The water spider builds its web in tiny ponds and other places with **shallow** water. The web looks like a small air-filled balloon. The water spider feeds and raises its family inside this cozy **shelter**.

Reread for **Comprehension**

Summarize

Description

In an article an author will describe each part of a topic to organize information. Use the description of each part of the topic to summarize what you have read.

A Description Web helps you remember details so that you can summarize the topic. Reread "Web Spinners" and record the details of one description.

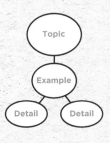

Topic → Example → Detail, Detail

263

Vocabulary

Review last week's vocabulary words: **creamed, numb, escape, fled, huddered, image,** and **newspaper.**

On Level Practice Book O, page 177

Fill in the blank with the correct word from the box. Some words will be used more than once.

| architects | shallow | structures | contain |
| retreats | shelter | hives | |

1. Animals are like ___architects___ because they build their own homes.

2. Termites build tall ___structures___.

3. Some ___architects___ study animal homes for ideas about solving problems with buildings.

4. Honeybees build ___hives___ made of waxy honeycombs.

5. The tortoise builds a ___shallow___ hole to keep cool.

6. A polar bear, however, needs a very different type of ___shelter___.

7. Bears may get stung if they poke around in honeybees' ___hives___.

8. If you come across a spider's web, be careful because it may ___contain___ an insect.

9. A turtle ___retreats___ into its shell when it senses danger.

10. A hermit crab finds ___shelter___ in an empty shell.

⭐ **Approaching Practice Book A,** page 177

◆ **Beyond Practice Book B,** page 177

Vocabulary

Using the Strategies To figure out unfamiliar words, students can

- decode words using phonics principles;
- look for word parts;
- look for context clues;
- use a dictionary.

SKILL

ANALOGIES

An **analogy** shows the relationship between words or how they go together. Display the following analogy: *black is to white as top is to bottom.* Point out that both pairs of words (*black/white* and *top/bottom*) have the same relationship. They are antonyms.

Point to *hives* on **Student Book** page 262 and write this analogy: *hives are to bees as webs are to spiders.* Help students identify the relationship between *hives* and *bees* and *webs* and *spiders.* Each pair of words shows an animal and its home. Tell students that sometimes they will have to complete analogies for tests.

Have students complete this analogy and explain the relationship between words: *big is to small as tall is to _____* (short; antonyms)

Read *"Web Spinners"*

As students read "Web Spinners," ask them to identify clues that reveal the meanings of the highlighted words. Tell students they will read these words again in *Animal Homes.*

Objectives

- Summarize information
- Use academic language: *summarize, description*
- Identify the description text structure

Materials

- Comprehension Transparencies 25a and 25b
- Graphic Organizer Transparency 25
- Leveled Practice Books, p. 178

Skills Trace

Description

Introduce	U5: 263A–B
Practice / Apply	U5: 264–281; Leveled Practice, 178–179
Reteach / Review	U5: 285M–T
Assess	Weekly Tests; Unit 5 Test
Maintain	Grade 4, Unit 6: 761A–B; 762–777; 783M–T

ELL / Access for All

Clarify Explain description and summarizing by describing the classroom and then asking for details of what you said. List the details on the board. Then say: *I gave you a description, or examples and details, about our classroom. When we put the most important details together about a topic, we are summarizing.* Tell students what signal words to look for.

Reread for Comprehension

STRATEGY
SUMMARIZE

 Access for All

To **summarize** nonfiction, readers identify the main ideas and important details in a passage, an article, a chapter, or a book, and then state these ideas in their own words. Summarizing can help readers understand and remember text that has the description text structure.

SKILL
DESCRIPTION

EXPLAIN

Nonfiction articles that give information about a topic often have a text structure called **description**. In description, the author uses examples and details to identify characteristics or qualities that describe the topic. Look for signal words and phrases, such as *most important, for example, to begin with, first,* and *in fact,* that tell the reader a list, or set, of characteristics is coming up.

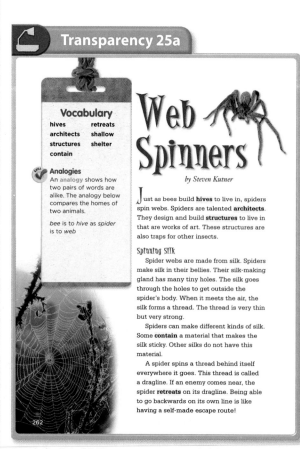

Transparency 25a

Vocabulary

hives	retreats
architects	shallow
structures	shelter
contain	

Analogies
An *analogy* shows how two pairs of words are alike. The analogy below compares the homes of two animals.

bee is to *hive* as *spider* is to *web*

Web Spinners
by Steven Kutner

Just as bees build **hives** to live in, spiders spin webs. Spiders are talented **architects**. They design and build **structures** to live in that are works of art. These structures are also traps for other insects.

Spinning Silk

Spider webs are made from silk. Spiders make silk in their bellies. Their silk-making gland has many tiny holes. The silk goes through the holes to get outside the spider's body. When it meets the air, the silk forms a thread. The thread is very thin but very strong.

Spiders can make different kinds of silk. Some **contain** a material that makes the silk sticky. Other silks do not have this material.

A spider spins a thread behind itself everywhere it goes. This thread is called a dragline. If an enemy comes near, the spider **retreats** on its dragline. Being able to go backwards on its own line is like having a self-made escape route!

262

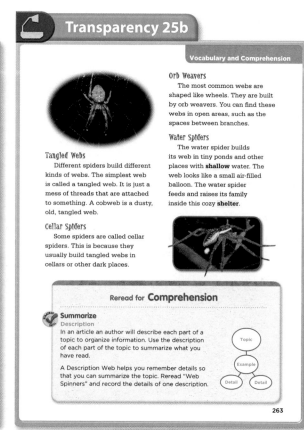

Transparency 25b

Vocabulary and Comprehension

Orb Weavers

The most common webs are shaped like wheels. They are built by orb weavers. You can find these webs in open areas, such as the spaces between branches.

Water Spiders

The water spider builds its web in tiny ponds and other places with **shallow** water. The web looks like a small air-filled balloon. The water spider feeds and raises its family inside this cozy **shelter**.

Tangled Webs

Different spiders build different kinds of webs. The simplest web is called a tangled web. It is just a mess of threads that are attached to something. A cobweb is a dusty, old, tangled web.

Cellar Spiders

Some spiders are called cellar spiders. This is because they usually build tangled webs in cellars or other dark places.

Reread for Comprehension

Summarize
Description
In an article an author will describe each part of a topic to organize information. Use the description of each part of the topic to summarize what you have read.

A Description Web helps you remember details so that you can summarize the topic. Reread "Web Spinners" and record the details of one description.

Topic → Example → Detail, Detail

263

Student Book pages 262–263 available on Comprehension Transparencies 25a and 25b

MODEL

Write the following:

Spiders use the silk thread they spin in different ways. For example, they spin it behind them everywhere they go. When spiders see an enemy, they retreat on this silk thread, or dragline. They also use the silk to spin webs.

Think Aloud The topic of this paragraph is how spiders use the silk they spin. In the second sentence, I see the signal words *for example*. These signal words tell me that the author is using the description text structure to describe ways that the spiders use their silk. By identifying this text structure, I will remember important details about the topic in the article.

GUIDED PRACTICE

- Display the Description Web on **Transparency 25.** Remind students that a Description Web organizes information found in a nonfiction article.

- Write "Spider Webs" in the top circle of the Description Web.

- Help students see that the first two paragraphs on page 263 are about tangled webs. Then write "tangled webs" as the example in the second circle on the web.

- Ask students to reread the paragraphs and state two details that describe types of tangled webs. (Cobwebs are tangled webs. Cellar spiders make tangled webs.) Have students add these details to the web.

APPLY

Have students look at the last two paragraphs in the article. Help them identify the topic: Other kinds of spider webs. Then help them identify details about other types of spider webs that are listed in these paragraphs. (Other types of spider webs include wheel-shaped webs and air-filled, balloon-shaped webs that are found in shallow ponds.)

Quick Check Can students use information in expository text to complete a description web?

During **Small Group Instruction**

If No → **Approaching Level** Comprehension, p. 285O

If Yes → **On Level** Options, pp. 285Q–285R

Beyond Level Options, pp. 285S–285T

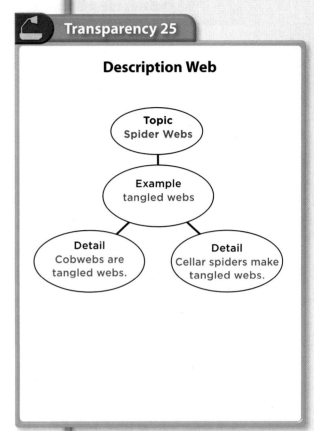

Transparency 25

Description Web

Topic
Spider Webs

Example
tangled webs

Detail
Cobwebs are
tangled webs.

Detail
Cellar spiders make
tangled webs.

Graphic Organizer Transparency 25

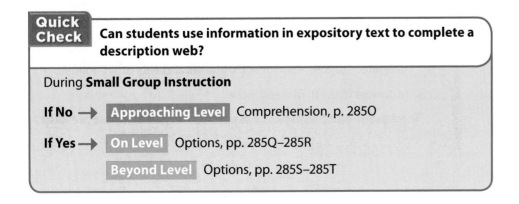

On Level Practice Book O, page 178

Nonfiction articles that have information about a topic often use **description.** In this description, the author uses examples and details to identify characteristics or qualities that help you understand the topic. These examples and details also help you remember what you read.

Read the passage below. Summarize it by writing the main topic, the example, and any supporting details on the lines.
Possible responses provided.

Trees are important habitats for gray squirrels. The young are raised in holes in the trees while the older squirrels usually nest in piles of leaves near the trees. The trees provide many sources of food for the gray squirrels, such as acorns, hickory nuts, insects, flower buds, bark, and roots. Trees are very important to the gray squirrel.

Topic: "Gray Squirrels and their Habitat"

Example: how trees help squirrels

Detail: There are holes to raise their young.

Detail: The leaves provide nests.

Detail: Trees provide all kinds of food, such as nuts, acorns, insects, buds, bark, and roots.

 Approaching Practice Book A, page 178

Beyond Practice Book B, page 178

Animal Homes 263B

MAIN SELECTION
- *Animal Homes*
- **Skill:** Description

PAIRED SELECTION
- "Home Sweet Home," "Limerick"
- **Literary Elements:** Simile and Rhythmic Pattern

WRITING
- Descriptive Poem
- **Writing Trait:** Word Choice

SMALL GROUP OPTIONS

- Differentiated Instruction, pp. 285M–285V

Comprehension

GENRE: INFORMATIONAL NONFICTION

Have a student read the definition of Informational Nonfiction on **Student Book** page 264. Students should look for facts and illustrations that give information about a variety of animal homes.

STRATEGY
SUMMARIZE

A **summary** is a short statement of the most important ideas in a selection. Summarizing helps readers understand and remember what they read.

SKILL
DESCRIPTION

Description is a nonfiction text structure in which the author introduces a topic and gives a list of characteristics or qualities that describe the topic.

Comprehension

Genre
Informational Nonfiction is a detailed explanation of real things using facts.

Summarize
Description

As you read, use your Description Web.

```
        ( Topic )
           |
       ( Example )
        /      \
  ( Detail )  ( Detail )
```

Read to Find Out
How are some animal homes similar to your home?

264

Vocabulary

Vocabulary Words Review the tested vocabulary words: **hives, architects, structures, contain, retreats, shallow,** and **shelter.**

Selection Words Students may find these words difficult. Pronounce the words and present the meanings as necessary.

hibernating (p. 268): sleeping for the winter

predator (p. 269): an animal that hunts and eats other animals

lodgings (p. 274): places to stay

Animal Homes

by Ann O. Squire

265

Preview and Predict

Ask students to read the title, preview the illustrations, and note questions and predictions about the selection. Ask: Will this selection be about real animals and their homes? Have students write their predictions and any questions they have about the selection.

Set Purposes

FOCUS QUESTION Discuss the "Read to Find Out" question and how students can look for the answer as they read.

Point out the Description Web in the **Student Book** and on **Leveled Practice Book** page 179. Explain that students will fill it in as they read.

Read *Animal Homes*

Use the questions and Think Alouds for additional instruction to support the comprehension strategy and skill.

Read Together	Read Independently
If your students need support to read the Main Selection, use the prompts to guide comprehension and model how to complete the graphic organizer.	If your students can read the Main Selection independently, have them read and complete the graphic organizer. Suggest that students set purposes and choose reading strategies based on the purpose.

If your students need an alternate selection, choose the **Leveled Readers** that match their instructional level.

Technology

Selection available on **Listening Library Audio CD**

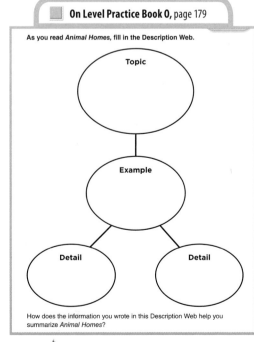

On Level Practice Book O, page 179

As you read *Animal Homes*, fill in the Description Web.

Topic

Example

Detail   Detail

How does the information you wrote in this Description Web help you summarize *Animal Homes*?

⭐ **Approaching Practice Book A,** page 179

◆ **Beyond Practice Book B,** page 179

Develop Comprehension

1 SKILL

ANALOGIES

Nests are to birds as hives are to _____. Which word from the selection fits in the blank to complete this **analogy**? How can you figure it out? (An analogy shows how ideas go together. I read that a nest is a bird home and that a hive is a honeybee home. So *nests* goes with *birds* like *hives* goes with *honeybees*. The missing word is *honeybees*.)

Why Do Animals Need Homes?

Animals need homes for many of the same reasons that people do. What are some of those reasons? Start by thinking about your own home, and the kinds of things you do there.

Some kinds of penguins build nests to protect their chicks.

266

ELL

Access for All

Build Background Knowledge Preview the photos with students to find out what the students know about the animals and their homes. As students describe the pictures, introduce and write key words (the names of the animals, *hive, burrow, nest, dirt, ground, shell*) on the board with short descriptions. For example, hive = home for honeybees.

Eating is one very important thing you do every day. Your house has a kitchen where you store and prepare food. Some animals also keep food in their homes. Honeybees, for example, live in **hives** made up of waxy honeycombs. Each honeycomb has many six-sided cubbies, or cells, where the bees store their honey.

The cells of the honeycomb are also used as nurseries for young bees. And that may remind you of another reason people and animals need homes. They need a safe place to raise their young. Birds' nests, alligator mounds, and the dens of polar bears are other kinds of homes made for raising a family.

> **Description**
> What are two ways honey bees use their hives?

▲ Other cells are used as nurseries for bee larvae.

▶ Bees store honey in some of the cells of their hive.

267

Cross-Curricular Connection

HEXAGONS

Cells in honeycombs store honey or hold young bees. Each cell has six equal sides. This shape is called a hexagon. Point out the photograph on **Student Book** page 267. Tell students that the hexagon shape allows many cells to fit, with very little wasted space between them. It also allows all the cells to be the same size.

Have students draw hexagons and write notes for their uses in a math journal. They can brainstorm other uses for the hexagon shape and reasons for and against using it. For example, if students' desks were shaped like hexagons, more desks would fit in the room but without rows, it would be harder to walk around the room.

Develop Comprehension

2 DESCRIPTION

What are two ways honeybees use their hives? What signal words help you? Place this information on a Description Web. (Honeybees store their honey inside their hives in honeycombs. Honeycombs are nurseries for young bees. The signal words are *for example*.)

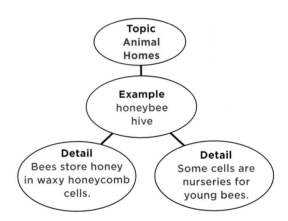

Topic
Animal Homes

Example
honeybee hive

Detail
Bees store honey in waxy honeycomb cells.

Detail
Some cells are nurseries for young bees.

3 STRATEGY
SUMMARIZE

Teacher Think Aloud To understand and remember what I read in informational nonfiction, I will summarize it. Headings tell me what I will read about so I will read them first. Then I'll look for the main idea of each paragraph. In the first paragraph on page 266, the main idea is stated: Animals need homes for many reasons. In the second and third paragraphs, the main idea is not stated. I think the main ideas are: Some animals keep food in their homes, and animals need a place to raise their young. Identifying main ideas can help me summarize as I read.

Develop Comprehension

4 STRATEGY
MONITOR AND CLARIFY: ADJUST READING RATE

Why might you change your reading speed when you begin the section that includes facts about the desert tortoise? (When I begin to read a section that contains a lot of facts, I need to slow down. Slowing down and reading more carefully helps me understand what I am reading.)

5 ASK ESSENTIAL QUESTIONS

Think about the questions *Who?, What?, Why?, Where?, When?,* and *How?* How can asking yourself these questions during and after reading help you understand this selection? How can you find the answers? (Asking these questions will help me understand the text better. I will have to read carefully and look for the answers. After I finish reading, I can ask myself the questions again, using my own experiences and knowledge and information from the text to see if I understood what I read.)

Vocabulary

Read the sentence with the word **shallow**. What word or phrase can you substitute for *shallow* to mean something similar? (not deep)

A desert tortoise in its burrow

Doesn't it feel good to come indoors on a cold winter day or turn up the air conditioner on a hot and humid summer night? That's another reason we need a home—to protect us from bad weather.

4 The desert tortoise lives in dry parts of the southwestern United States, where summer temperatures often go above 100 degrees Fahrenheit (38 degrees Celsius). To escape the heat, the tortoise digs a **shallow** burrow, or hole, where it can rest during the hottest part of the day.

In the winter, when temperatures fall below freezing, the tortoise digs a much deeper burrow. Then it climbs in and spends the winter there, **5** hibernating with other tortoises.

268

Comprehension

Nonfiction Text Structure: Description

Explain Description is one kind of nonfiction text structure. The author introduces a topic and gives a list or set of characteristics that describe the topic. The author may use signal words, such as *for instance* or *for example*, to show that a list of characteristics will follow.

Discuss The text on page 269 describes a prairie dog burrow. Ask: *What signal words do you see in the second sentence?* (for example) *What are the characteristics of a prairie dog burrow?* (long winding burrows; many different rooms and tunnels; several openings for easy escape)

Apply Have students identify the characteristics of a termite tower on page 272. (It is tall, made of dirt and saliva, has air shafts and many special rooms, and may last for a century.)

Underground burrows also give animals a place to hide from their enemies. Prairie dogs, for example, dig long, winding burrows with many different rooms and tunnels.

Many peoples' homes have a front door, a back door and maybe even a side door. A prairie-dog burrow has several openings, too. If a hungry predator invades the burrow through the main entrance, the prairie dogs can escape out the back way.

 Description
How would you describe a burrow? **6**

A prairie dog standing near its burrow entrance

A coyote trying to invade a prairie-dog burrow

269

Develop Comprehension

6 DESCRIPTION

 How would you describe a burrow? (The author compares prairie dog burrows to people's homes. Prairie dog burrows have several openings, just like people's homes often have several doors. Prairie dog burrows have many different rooms and tunnels. The author also says the burrows are long and winding.)

ELL

Access for All

STRATEGIES FOR EXTRA SUPPORT

Question 6 DESCRIPTION
Use analogies to explain vocabulary such as *winding, tunnel, openings,* and *main entrance.* Talk about winding streets and trails, train tunnels, doors and windows as openings, and the front door of the school being the main entrance.

Develop Comprehension

7 STRATEGY
SUMMARIZE

Teacher Think Aloud Page 270 is the last page of this section. Before we start a new section, we need to be sure we understand what we just read. To do this, we can stop here and summarize the information on pages 266–270. Tell how you would summarize these pages and then explain how summarizing helped you.

Encourage students to apply the strategy in a Think Aloud.

Student Think Aloud The heading for this section is the question "Why Do Animals Need Homes?" It tells me the topic. To summarize, I can look for main ideas in each paragraph that answer this question. This is how I would summarize the section: Animals need homes to store food and to raise families. They need homes to protect them from bad weather, to keep them safe from predators, and to trap prey. Summarizing helped me understand why animals need homes. Now I am ready to continue reading.

Some animals build homes for more tricky reasons. Many spiders spin webs mainly to trap unlucky insects.

7 Now that you know some of the reasons animals need homes, let's find out about some unusual animal homes.

270

Media Literacy

Finding the Main Idea

Explain Students can better understand electronic media—videos, movies, DVDs, TV,—about nonfiction topics, by identifying the main idea or central theme and any opinions that might be presented. Identifying the main idea helps them understand what the media is about. Identifying facts and opinions helps them evaluate the information.

Discuss Show students a short nonfiction video about one of the animals named in *Animal Homes*. Then discuss the main idea, or central theme, of the video and any opinions presented.

Apply Show students another short video. Have them take notes to identify the main idea and opinions and use them to write a summary later. Then provide a nonfiction print article or book on the same topic, have students identify the main idea and any opinions presented in both, and then compare the print and video.

A weaverbird building its nest

Building a Home

Many animals build their own homes. These animal **architects** can be birds, mammals, insects, and even fish.

The African weaverbird's name is a clue to the way this bird builds its nest. The male weaverbird gathers long blades of grass, which he knots and weaves into a sturdy ring. Then he adds grass to the ring, making a hollow ball. To keep out tree snakes, the ball is open only at the bottom. When the nest is finished, the weaverbird calls to attract nearby females. If a female likes the nest, she moves in, and the two raise a family.

◀ A spider trapping prey in its web

8

9

271

Develop Comprehension

8 **STRATEGY**
MONITOR AND CLARIFY: ADJUST READING RATE

How can adjusting your reading rate help you understand how the weaverbird builds its nest? (If I read more slowly, I can picture what the nest looks like and what the bird does at each step. This helps me better understand what the weaverbird does to make a home.)

9 **SEQUENCE**

What does the weaverbird do after he knots and weaves grass into a ring? How do you know this? (He adds grass to the ring to make a hollow ball. The signal word *then* helps me figure this out.)

Vocabulary

Read the sentence with the word **architects**. Who else can be architects? What do they do? (People can also be architects. They design many structures, such as houses, office buildings, and schools. Then architects make sure the structures are built correctly.)

Develop Comprehension

10 DESCRIPTION

What words and phrases does the author use to describe the special features of a termite tower? How is this description helpful to readers? (She says that a termite tower can be as tall as a giraffe. It has rock-hard walls made of dirt and saliva. It has air shafts inside that keep the tower cool. It has many special rooms, including an underground garden. This description helps readers understand what a termite tower is and how it is used.)

RESEARCH
Why It Matters

Fluency
Research indicates that partners will do a better job if they are prepared to be partners. Showing students how to respond to their partners' oral reading miscues can make fluency practice more beneficial for everybody.

Timothy Shanahan

LOG ON Log on to
www.macmillanmh.com

Termite towers have many rooms.

Some insects build homes, too. One of the largest and most complicated **structures** in the animal world is created by tiny African termites.

10 A termite tower may be as tall as a giraffe and **contain** millions of termites. The walls of the tower are made of a rock-hard mixture of dirt and saliva. They contain air shafts that keep the inside of the tower cool, even in the blazing sun.

The tower has many special rooms. It has a royal chamber, where the termite king and queen live, nurseries for the young, rooms for storing food, and even an underground garden. Most termites live for only a few years, but a termite tower may last for close to a century.

A termite tower in Ghana, Africa

272

Fluency

Phrase-Cued Text

Explain Punctuation helps readers know when to pause: for a short time after a comma and for a slightly longer time after a period or other end punctuation.

Model Read aloud the passage on **Student Book** page 273, available on **Transparency 25**. Ask: *When did I pause for a short time?* (after a comma) *When did I pause for longer to show I finished a sentence?* (after a period, question mark, or exclamation point) Point out that on the transparency pauses after commas are marked with one slash. Pauses after periods are marked with two slashes.

Apply Have students reread the passage chorally and then with a partner. Students should take turns reading aloud, listening attentively, and providing corrective feedback. They should focus on pausing correctly for different punctuation marks.

Beavers use sticks and mud to build a dam. Then they build their lodge in the middle of the pond formed by the dam.

Have you ever heard people say someone is as "busy as a beaver"? You'd know what they mean if you saw how much work goes into building a beaver lodge.

First, the beavers use sticks and mud to make a dam across a stream. Then water backs up behind the dam to form a pond. In the center of the pond, the beavers build their lodge. It looks like nothing more than a pile of sticks, but the lodge has a room inside that is reached by underwater tunnels. The beavers can come and go easily, but it's almost impossible for wolves and other predators to find a way in.

11

12

273

Develop Comprehension

11 DESCRIPTION

How does the author describe a beaver lodge? (Beavers use sticks and mud to make a dam across a stream so that the water forms a pond. Then they build their lodge in the center of the pond. The lodge looks like a pile of sticks, but it has a room inside that is reached by underwater tunnels.)

12 MAKE INFERENCES

Why is a beaver lodge a safe place for beavers to live? (Wolves and other predators would have to travel through the underwater tunnels, which are very narrow. Many predators may not be able to swim well enough to get to the lodge. Also, the beaver lodge looks like a pile of sticks, so predators might not know beavers are living inside.)

Have students respond to the selection by confirming or revising their predictions and purposes and noting any additional questions.

Quick Check Can students find descriptions in the selection? If not, see the **Extra Support** on this page.

Extra Support

Monitor Comprehension

Discuss how authors use description to help readers better understand a topic. Ask: *What did the description of a beaver lodge tell you about animal homes?* (Animals such as beavers work hard to build their homes. They make sure their homes are safe from predators.) *Why do you think the author included this description?* (It is an example of why homes are important for animals.)

If students have difficulty recognizing description, have them reread the second paragraph on page 271. Ask: *What does the male African weaverbird need to build a nest?* (long blades of grass) *How does he build it?* (He knots and weaves the grass into a ring. Then he adds more grass to the ring. This makes a hollow ball that becomes his nest.) *Why is the nest only open on the bottom?* (to keep out tree snakes) Discuss how this paragraph helps the reader understand what the nest is made of and what it looks like.

Stop here if you wish to read this selection over two days.

Develop Comprehension

13 **MAINTAIN**
SUMMARIZE

What have you learned so far about animals' homes? How would you summarize the main ideas and supporting details for pages 266–273? (Animals need homes for many of the same reasons that people need homes. They use their homes to store food, raise families, and protect them from bad weather. Other reasons to have homes include keeping the animals safe from predators and trapping prey. Some animals build their own homes. For example, the male African weaverbird knots and weaves grass to make a nest, termites build towers from dirt and saliva, and beavers build lodges in streams from sticks and mud.)

14 **GENRE: INFORMATIONAL NONFICTION**

Headings tell readers how information is organized. What is the heading on page 274? What do you think this part of the **informational nonfiction** article will be about? (The heading is "Finding a Home." It tells readers that this section will be about how animals find their homes.)

The hermit crab makes its home in an empty seashell.

13

14 # Finding a Home

Bees, weaverbirds, termites, and beavers all work long and hard to build their homes. But some animals take the easy way out. They look around for ready-made lodgings.

Unlike most other crabs, the hermit crab does not have a hard shell to protect it. It needs a safe place to live, so the hermit crab searches for an empty snail shell. When it finds a shell that fits, the hermit crab squeezes inside. It stays there until it grows too big for that shell. Then it must look for a larger shell.

274

STRATEGIES FOR EXTRA SUPPORT

Question 13 SUMMARIZE
Have students call out the animals they read about in the text. Then have them reread to look for examples and details about those animals. Remind students that headings can help them identify the topics in the selection. Guide students to identify the main idea through questions: *What's the first topic?* Help students use the heading to create a topic sentence. You may want to write this on the board: *What's the main idea of the first paragraph? Give me one example of the main idea.* Continue to do this with the other paragraphs. Help students as necessary. Then guide them to create a summary using the main ideas.

The pea crab doesn't even wait until a shell is empty. This tiny crab moves in with the original owner! It squeezes into the shell of a mussel, clam, or oyster while that animal is still alive. The shellfish isn't even bothered by the pea crab sharing its home. As the shellfish filters food through its gills, the pea crab catches tiny bits of food as they float past. **15**

A pea crab

275

Develop Comprehension

15 **COMPARE AND CONTRAST**

Hermit crabs and pea crabs both look for ready-made homes. What is the difference between the kinds of homes these animals look for? (Hermit crabs look for empty shells to live in until they grow too large. Then they find a new shell. Pea crabs squeeze into shells with shellfish that are still alive, but the crabs are so small that the shellfish are not bothered by them.)

Develop Comprehension

16 DESCRIPTION

What does the mother cowbird do to find a nest for her egg? (First she searches for another nesting bird. Then she waits for the nesting bird to leave so she can throw out one of the eggs. She lays her own egg in its place before the nesting bird returns.)

A white cowbird egg in a nest containing blue wood thrush eggs

A cowbird chick being raised by a yellow warbler

The cowbird is even more daring. Instead of building its own nest, the female cowbird searches the forest for other nesting birds. When she sees a likely couple, she settles down to wait.

16 As soon as the unsuspecting birds leave their nest, the cowbird darts in and throws out one of their eggs. Then she quickly lays one of her own. The nesting birds never know the difference! They raise the cowbird chick as if it were one of their own.

Burrowing owls ▶

276

Birds don't usually live underground, but **17** one that does is the burrowing owl. These long-legged owls sometimes move into abandoned prairie-dog burrows. The birds come out in the cool of the evening to hunt small rodents, frogs, and insects.

277

Develop Comprehension

17 **MAIN IDEA AND DETAILS**

What is the main idea of the paragraph on page 277? Is it stated or unstated? What details tell about, or support, the main idea? Are any details unimportant? (The main idea is stated in the first sentence: "Birds don't usually live underground, but one that does is the burrowing owl." Details tell that these owls move into abandoned prairie-dog holes and they come out in the evening to hunt for food. All the details are important.)

Develop Comprehension

18 WRITING TRAIT: WORD CHOICE

What word does the author use to describe the homes of snails, turtles, and bagworms? Why is this word a good choice? (The author says their homes are *mobile* homes. This word was a good choice because it describes how these animals' homes go wherever the animal goes.)

19 STRATEGY
SUMMARIZE

Explain how would you summarize page 278. Tell why it helps you to summarize what you have read.

Student Think Aloud First I will look at the heading. It tells me that this section is about mobile homes. Because the topic of this selection is animals' homes, I know this section is about animals' mobile homes. As I summarize I will look for the main ideas in the two paragraphs. The first main idea is: Some animals live in mobile homes. The main idea of the second paragraph is: Turtles' and tortoises' shells are mobile homes because they carry them on their backs. Summarizing helps me understand what I have just read. It helps me figure out that the rest of this section will also be about animals that have mobile homes.

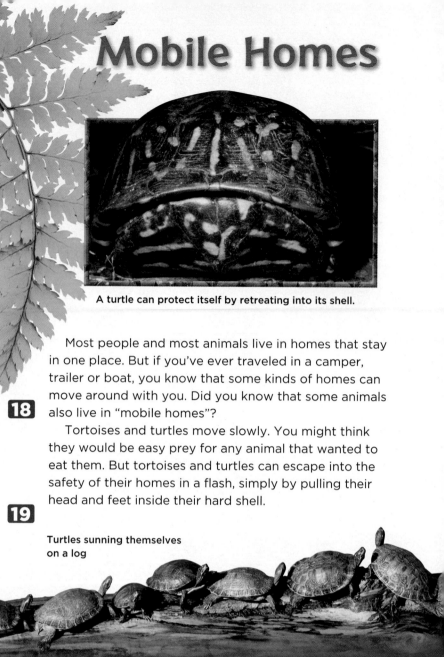

Mobile Homes

A turtle can protect itself by retreating into its shell.

Most people and most animals live in homes that stay in one place. But if you've ever traveled in a camper, trailer or boat, you know that some kinds of homes can move around with you. Did you know that some animals also live in "mobile homes"?

18

Tortoises and turtles move slowly. You might think they would be easy prey for any animal that wanted to eat them. But tortoises and turtles can escape into the safety of their homes in a flash, simply by pulling their head and feet inside their hard shell.

19

Turtles sunning themselves on a log

278

Comprehension

Main Idea and Details

Explain The main idea is what a paragraph is about. It may be stated in a topic sentence or it may be unstated. When the main idea is unstated, the reader uses supporting details to figure out the main idea.

Discuss In the second paragraph on page 278, the main idea is unstated. Point out the section topic "Mobile Homes" and the paragraph details: Turtles move slowly; they seem to be easy prey; when in danger, they pull their head and feet into their hard shell. Help students see that the main idea is: A turtle's shell is a mobile home that offers protection.

Apply Have students identify the main ideas of the paragraphs on page 279. Are they stated or unstated? (Both main ideas are stated in a topic sentence at the beginning of each paragraph.)

The snail is another animal that carries its house on its back. Snails need damp conditions in order to survive. In cold or dry weather, the snail **retreats** into its spiral shell to avoid drying out.

Like turtles, snails can retreat into their shells.

A kind of caterpillar called the bagworm makes its home out of twigs woven together with silk. The bagworm lives inside this silken case and drags its **shelter** along as it moves from branch to branch feeding on leaves.

A bagworm hanging from a spruce tree

279

Develop Comprehension

RETURN TO PREDICTIONS AND PURPOSES

Review students' predictions and purposes. Were they correct? Can students describe different animal homes? What questions for further study do they have now that they have finished the selection?

REVIEW READING STRATEGIES

How did identifying descriptions help students to summarize the story?

PERSONAL RESPONSE

Ask students to pretend they are animals, such as prairie dogs or weaverbirds, whose home is described in the selection. Have them use an index card to write a postcard to a friend, describing their new home. Students can draw a picture of the animal home on the other side of the postcard. When they are finished, ask them to reflect on themselves as writers.

Quick Check Can students identify descriptions in the text?

During **Small Group Instruction**

If No → **Approaching Level** Leveled Reader Lessons, pp. 285M–285N

If Yes → **On Level** Options, pp. 285Q–285R

Beyond Level Options, pp. 285S–285T

Author and Illustrator

AT HOME WITH ANN

Have students read the biography of Ann O. Squire.

DISCUSS

- How can you tell that Ann O. Squire has studied animals for a long time?

- Do you think Ann O. Squire chose the photographs for this selection well? How do the photographs help explain the information that appears under each heading?

Write About It

Call on a volunteer to read aloud the directions for the writing activity. Discuss with students ways in which some animals' homes are similar to their own. When you evaluate students' work, check that the writing includes comparisons.

LOG ON Technology

Tell students they can find more information about Ann O. Squire at www.macmillanmh.com

At Home with Ann

AUTHOR
Ann O. Squire
is an expert on how animals behave. Before Ann began to write books for children, she studied many different kinds of animals. She has studied everything from rats to the African electric fish.

Other books by Ann O. Squire: *Growing Crystals* and *Seashells*

LOG ON Find out more about Ann O. Squire at **www.macmillanmh.com**

Write About It

Many animal homes look very different from each other. Explain which animals' homes are similar to yours and how they are similar.

280

Author's Craft
Text Feature: Headings, Photos, and Captions

Ann O. Squire uses headings, photos, and captions in *Animal Homes* to present and organize information. Photos and captions give more information about the text. Each **heading** signals a new topic in a nonfiction article. For example, here is the first heading in *Animal Homes: Why Do Animals Need Homes?* The information that follows this heading is divided into paragraphs that describe and give examples of why animals need homes.

Help students identify the other headings in the selection: "Building a Home," "Finding a Home," and "Mobile Homes." Discuss what readers will likely read about under each heading. Next have students skim the text to check that the heading matches the information that comes after it. Then have students tell what extra information photos and captions give.

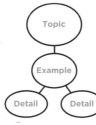

Comprehension Check

SUMMARIZE

Have students write a summary of *Animal Homes* in their own words. Remind students that their Description Webs can help them identify the relationship between main ideas and details and organize their summaries.

THINK AND COMPARE

Sample answers are given.

1. **Description:** Answers will depend on the animal chosen. For example: The hermit crab carries a snail shell as its shelter. It needs the shell for protection from predators. When the hermit crab gets too big for the shell, it looks for a bigger one.

2. **Analyze:** The most useful thing about mobile homes is protection from predators.

3. **Text-to-Self:** I'd like to see a termite tower because it is so large.
   USE ON MY OWN

4. **Text-to-World:** It's important for people to learn about animal homes so that they respect the animals and their homes and take care not to harm them.

FOCUS QUESTION

5. **Text-to-Text:** Accept reasonable responses that compare animal structures using details.

Comprehension Check

Summarize

Use the Description Web to help you summarize facts about *Animal Homes*. Create a topic sentence about animal homes, and then describe important information about different kinds of animal homes.

Topic

Example

Detail   Detail

Think and Compare

1. Choose an animal that carries its **shelter** around. Using details from the text and your Description Web, describe that animal and its home. **Summarize: Description**

2. Reread pages 278-279 of *Animal Homes*. What do you think is the most useful thing about having a mobile home? **Analyze**

3. Which animal home in this story would you choose to see in person? Explain your answer. **Synthesize**

4. Is it important for people to learn about animal homes? Why or why not? **Evaluate**

5. Read "Web Spinners" on pages 262-263. Look at the photographs in the two selections you have read. Compare the structures of the spider webs to the structure of another animal home. Use details from both selections in your answer. **Reading/Writing Across Texts**

281

Strategies for Answering Questions

On My Own

Model the On My Own strategy with question 3.

Students will not find the answers to On My Own questions in the selection. Sometimes they will be asked to form an opinion based on what they have read. Other times they will answer the question using information they already know.

Think Aloud Question 3: I won't find the answer in the selection because it asks about something that I would like to see. I will think about this selection and then form my opinion. I learned about many animal homes. I like tall structures. I'd like to see a termite tower because it's one of the largest structures in the animal world and can also last for almost a century. Thinking about what I read and what I like helped me form an opinion.

Objective
- Read fluently with proper phrasing and tempo
- 97–117 WCPM

Materials
- Fluency Transparency 25
- Fluency Solutions Audio CD
- Leveled Practice Books, p. 180

ELL   **Access for All**

Partner Reading
Group students in pairs. Direct one student to read the passage slowly, word by word, pointing to each word as he or she pronounces it. Their partners should echo-read. For a second reading, students should read faster, phrase by phrase.

On Level Practice Book O, page 180

As I read, I will pay attention to the genre of the passage.

	Many different kinds of animals build their own
8	homes. Their homes are structures that shelter them
16	from the cold and the rain. They are also places where
27	they can retreat from danger. Beavers build lodges, bees
36	build **hives**, and birds build incredible nests where they
45	hatch their eggs and raise their babies.
52	Have you ever seen a bird's nest? Some are made of
63	twigs and are round and shallow. Others are made of
73	grass and are long and deep. Still others are made from
84	mud and look like small cups. There are even birds that
95	use their own saliva, or spit, when they build a nest.
106	Many birds' nests contain feathers and hair. This makes the
116	nest a soft place for their babies, or chicks, to sleep. Birds
128	are some of the most amazing **architects** in the animal
138	world! 139

Comprehension Check
1. Compare and contrast different birds' nests? **Compare and Contrast**
   Compare: Many nests contain feathers and hair.
   Contrast: Nests are different sizes and shapes, and are made with different materials.
2. What does the word saliva mean? **Context Clues**
   Saliva is spit.

	Words Read	−	Number of Errors	=	Words Correct Score
First Read		−		=	
Second Read		−		=	

⭐ **Approaching Practice Book A,** page 180

◆ **Beyond Practice Book B,** page 180

Fluency
Repeated Reading: Tempo and Genre

EXPLAIN/MODEL Tell students that good readers learn to read groups of words together in phrases, paying special attention to slower tempos when they read expository nonfiction. Explain that the text on **Transparency 25** has been marked with slashes that indicate pauses and stops. A single slash indicates a pause. A double slash indicates a full stop. Have the class listen carefully for pauses, stops, and use of tempo.

Transparency 25

Have you ever heard people say someone is as "busy as a beaver"?// You'd know what they mean if you saw how much work goes into building a beaver lodge.//

First,/ the beavers use sticks and mud to make a dam across a stream.// Then water backs up behind the dam to form a pond.// In the center of the pond,/ the beavers build their lodge.// It looks like nothing more than a pile of sticks,/ but the lodge has a room inside that is reached by underwater tunnels.// The beavers can come and go easily,/ but it's almost impossible for wolves and other predators to find a way in.//

Fluency Transparency 25
from *Animal Homes*, page 273

PRACTICE Read the first two sentences of the passage with students. Model the slower pace you use when reading expository nonfiction. Then have students do a choral reading. First, one student reads a sentence. Then the next student joins in, then a third. Repeat until all students are reading together. When students reach the end of the passage, they should go back to the beginning until everyone has been included in the reading. For additional practice, have students use **Leveled Practice Book** page 180 or Fluency Solutions.

Access for All

Quick Check   **Can students read fluently, with proper phrasing and tempo?**

During **Small Group Instruction**

If No → **Approaching Level**   Fluency, pp. 285M–285N

If Yes → **On Level**   Options, pp. 285Q–285R

         Beyond Level   Options, pp. 285S–285T

Comprehension

MAINTAIN SKILL
SUMMARIZE

EXPLAIN/MODEL

■ A **summary** is a short statement of the main ideas and most important supporting details in a nonfiction passage, an article, or a book. It shows the relationship between the main ideas and supporting details.

■ When readers summarize, they should only include important details, or essential information, that tells about the topic.

■ When there are headings in an article, readers find the main idea of each section so that they can include it in their summaries. To summarize, readers use their own words. Summaries should not include feelings or opinions.

Model how to summarize using "Web Spinners" on pages 262–263.

PRACTICE

Ask the following questions about *Animal Homes*:

■ What is the topic of the section that begins on page 266? How do you know? (The topic is reasons why animals need homes. This topic is stated in the heading, "Why Do Animals Need Homes?")

■ How would you summarize the two paragraphs on page 267? (Some animals keep food in their homes. Bees store honey in cells in their hives. Animals also use their homes to raise their young. Bees use their hives as nurseries, birds use nests, alligators use mounds, and polar bears use dens.)

Have students form literature circles and discuss types of animal homes they have learned about. Remind students to use **Discussion and Conversation Guidelines** on page 150I.

Objectives

- Summarize nonfiction passages
- Distinguish between important and unimportant details
- Use academic language: *summarize, important details, unimportant details*

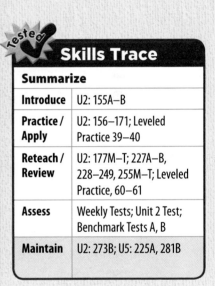

Skills Trace

Summarize	
Introduce	U2: 155A–B
Practice / Apply	U2: 156–171; Leveled Practice 39–40
Reteach / Review	U2: 177M–T; 227A–B, 228–249, 255M–T; Leveled Practice, 60–61
Assess	Weekly Tests; Unit 2 Test; Benchmark Tests A, B
Maintain	U2: 273B; U5: 225A, 281B

Poetry

GENRE: LIMERICK

Have students read the bookmark on **Student Book** page 282. Explain that a limerick

- is a humorous five-line poem;

- rhymes the end words of its first, second, and fifth lines;

- has shorter third and fourth lines which rhyme.

Literary Elements:
Simile and Rhythmic Pattern

EXPLAIN Poets use special language, such as similes, and special rhythms to make their poems interesting.

- A **simile** is a kind of figurative language that uses the words *like* or *as* to compare two things that are not alike. An example of a simile is: *The wind howled like a wolf.*

- A **rhythmic pattern** is a series of stressed and unstressed syllables that create a beat, or rhythm.

- Similes and rhythmic patterns are literary elements that poets use to help a reader picture or visualize what is described in the poem. They also make poetry interesting and memorable.

APPLY Have students identify the rhythmic pattern in "Home Sweet Home" on page 282. Ask: Why do you think the poet used a rhythmic pattern in his poem? (Answers will vary. Students may say the poet used a rhythmic pattern to make his poem fun for people to read.)

Home Sweet Home

Poetry

A **Limerick** is a short funny poem. It has five lines. Usually the last words in the first, second, and fifth lines rhyme. The third and fourth lines usually rhyme with each other.

Literary Elements

A **Simile** compares two different things by using the words *like* or *as*.

A **Rhythmic Pattern** is a series of stressed and unstressed syllables that create a beat.

 A flea on a pooch doesn't care
Which part it is crossing to where.
    Like mud to a frog
    Any part of a dog
Suits a flea, and it's glad to be there.

— *John Ciardi*

The rhythmic pattern of these two lines creates the beat: da DAH da da DAH da da DAH.

282

Limerick

Think of darkness. Then think of the mole
In his tunnel: black, black as coal.
But the traffic is light, ←
And the weather's all right,
And the tunnel is free—there's no toll.

— *David McCord*

This simile compares two unlike things; the darkness of the tunnel and coal.

Connect and Compare

1. In the second limerick, what picture comes to mind when you read the simile "black as coal"? **Simile**

2. Reread the first two lines of "Home Sweet Home." Do these two lines have the same rhythmic pattern? **Evaluate**

3. Do the mole and the flea both like their homes? Explain your answer. **Reading/Writing Across Texts**

 Find out more about limericks at **www.macmillanmh.com**

283

LOG ON Technology

Internet Research and Inquiry Activity
Students can find more facts at **www.macmillanmh.com**

Read "Home Sweet Home" and "Limerick"

 As you read, remind students to apply what they have learned about similes and rhythmic patterns.

1 **LITERARY ELEMENT: RHYTHMIC PATTERN**

 Which words or syllables should you stress in the first two lines of "Home Sweet Home"? (flea, pooch, care, part, cross-, where)

2 **LITERARY ELEMENT: SIMILE**

 What is the simile in "Limerick"? What two things does the simile compare? (The mole's tunnel is "black as coal." The poet compares the darkness of the tunnel to coal, which is black.)

Connect and Compare

SUGGESTED ANSWERS

1. I think of something that is so dark that I can't see through it. SIMILE

2. Yes. Each line has eight syllables and follows this pattern: da DAH da da DAH da da DAH. EVALUATE

FOCUS QUESTION

3. Yes. The poet says that the flea is "glad to be there," so the flea likes its home. The mole seems to like his home, too. There is little traffic, the weather is fine, and he can travel in the tunnel for free. READING/WRITING ACROSS TEXTS

Writing

Descriptive Writing

OPTIONS FOR STUDENT WRITING

- Use these two pages for a short writing lesson focused on the features of a descriptive poem and on the writing trait from **Student Book** pages 284–285.

- For a more detailed five-step writing process lesson, use the **Writing Workshop** on pages 285A-285B.

- Use the Daily Writing Prompts in the Weekly Planner for brief writing assignments.

FEATURES

Present and discuss these features of a descriptive poem with students.

- It is divided into lines, and it is sometimes organized into groups of lines called *stanzas*.

- It uses precise, descriptive language that helps paint a picture for the reader.

- It contains a pleasing rhythm when the lines are read aloud, and it may rhyme.

Have students read "Desert Tortoise" on Student Book page 284. Ask volunteers to point out the features of a descriptive poem in Sam C.'s writing.

Write a Descriptive Poem

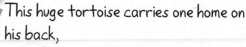

Writing

Word Choice

In poetry, it is important to paint pictures with words. Use colorful words. For example, the word *huge* is stronger and more precise than the word *big*.

I wrote a poem about a desert tortoise's two homes.

I used strong words so the reader can picture the tortoise by reading the poem.

Desert Tortoise

by Sam C.

This huge tortoise carries one home on his back,
And he lives in another home the same time as that.
His other home is so hot and dry there are cracks on the ground,
But his shell makes a solid, safe cover as he crawls in the sun.
He can dig a shallow hole to get shade from the heat,
Or dig even deeper to warm up on cold nights.
The desert is the tortoise's other home.
He's lucky to have two. I only have one.

284

Your Turn

Write a descriptive poem that is about six to ten lines long. Your poem could be about any animal that makes its own home. Use strong, precise words that create a "picture" for the reader. Use the Writer's Checklist to check your writing.

Poem

Writer's Checklist

✓ **Ideas and Content:** Will the topic of my poem interest my reader?

✓ **Organization:** Is my writing structured like a poem rather than a paragraph?

✓ **Voice:** Does my personality come through?

☐ **Word Choice:** Did I use strong words that paint a picture?

✓ **Sentence Fluency:** Does my poem make sense?

✓ **Conventions:** Did I use pronoun contractions such as *I've* and *he's* correctly? Did I check my spelling?

285

WRITING TRAIT: WORD CHOICE

Have a student read the bookmark on **Student Book** page 284. Discuss the Word Choice trait.

- A writer uses strong, precise, and colorful words in a poem to paint a picture in readers' minds.

- Descriptive words, such as vivid adjectives, help readers use sight, hearing, touch, taste, or smell to experience what the writer is describing.

Have students reread "Desert Tortoise" on Student Book page 284. Discuss the callouts. Ask students to identify the colorful words used to paint a memorable picture of the tortoise.

Use **Transparency 97** to help students understand how words can create pictures for readers. Have students substitute words or phrases that are more precise and colorful than the underlined words and phrases.

YOUR TURN

Read the "Your Turn" prompt on Student Book page 285 with the class. Students may choose to describe an animal, bird, or insect that makes its own home such as a beaver, robin, or bee. Remind students to make every word count as they write their poems. They should pay attention to rhythm and use rhyme if they wish.

WRITER'S CHECKLIST

Review the six Good Writing Traits on the Writer's Checklist. Have students give an example of Word Choice or Voice in Sam C.'s writing. Then discuss how students can apply the traits to help them draft, revise, and proofread their own poems.

◆ Transparency 97

Word Choice
Watching a Frog

It <u>jumped</u> across the pond.
Its shiny, green back looked like <u>bright things</u>,
Against the <u>pretty</u> water.
Then the rain came.
The frog <u>went</u>
Into the bushes on the shore.
I couldn't see anything except <u>big</u> weeds.

(Answers will vary. Possible answers include: 1. leaped; hopped; sprang 2. emeralds; jewels; stars 3. calm; shimmering; glistening 4. disappeared; fled; vanished 5. gigantic; huge bunches of; clumps of)

Writing Transparency 97

Writing Workshop

Connect
Language Arts

WRITING WORKSHOP
- **Descriptive:** Poem

WORD STUDY
- Words in Context
- Analogies
- **Phonics:** V/CV and VC/V Pattern
- Vocabulary Building

SPELLING
- The V/CV and VC/V Pattern

GRAMMAR
- Pronoun-Verb Contractions

SMALL GROUP OPTIONS
- Differentiated Instruction, pp. 285M–285V

Speaking and Listening

Have students read their descriptive poems aloud. Share these strategies.

SPEAKING STRATEGIES
- Use facial expressions and gestures to convey feelings.
- Speak slowly, clearly, and with expression.
- Make frequent eye contact with your audience.

LISTENING STRATEGIES
- Listen carefully for descriptive words and phrases.
- Set your own purpose for listening.
- Picture the scene being described.

Descriptive: Poem

Day 1 Prewrite

PURPOSE AND AUDIENCE

Tell students:
The purpose of writing a descriptive poem is to paint a picture with words for readers. The audience is your classmates.

Display **Transparency 98.** Review Sam C.'s Word Web with the class. Tell students that they will use a Word Web to plan their poems.

Prompt *Write a descriptive poem that is six to ten lines long about an animal that makes its own home.*

Choose a Topic Students can write about a pet or a wild animal. Students can also self-select a topic that interests them and write about it.

Day 2 Draft

DRAFTING CHECKLIST

Display **Transparency 99.** Review Sam C.'s draft. Discuss how Sam used his Word Web to organize information. As students begin to draft:

- Remind them to keep their purpose and audience in mind.
- Review the features of a descriptive poem. Emphasize the importance of colorful and vivid words, especially adjectives.
- Have them think about rhythm and rhyme for their poem.
- Have students refer to their Word Web and to the Good Writing Traits on the Writer's Checklist.

Transparency 98

Word Web

- desert home is hot and dry
- cracks on ground
- digs hole to get shade
- carries one on his back
- **Topic** Tortoise has two homes
- digs deep to stay warm at night
- covers him when he is in the sun
- makes a safe cover

Writing Transparency 98

Writing Transparency 98

Transparency 99

Desert Tortoise

This tortoise carries a home on his back,

And he lives in another home at the same time.

His other home is hot and dry. There are cracks on the ground.

But his shell covers him as he crawls in the sun.

He can dig a hole to get shade from the heat,

Or dig even deeper to warm up on cold nights.

The desert is the tortoise's other home.

He's lucky he's got two. I only have one.

Writing Transparency 99

Writing Transparency 99

Day 3 Revise

REVISING CHECKLIST

Display **Transparency 99.** Ask students to use what they have learned to discuss how they would revise Sam C.'s draft.

Display **Transparency 100** and discuss Sam's changes.

- He added details.

- He combined two sentences to improve the poem's rhythm.

- He improved **Word Choice** by replacing dull words with more, colorful descriptive words and phrases.

Have students revise their descriptive poems using the Writer's Checklist and a dictionary or thesaurus. Have partners review each other's work.

Day 4 Proofread

REVIEW AND PROOFREAD

Tell students they are now ready to proofread their revisions. Remind students to:

- Structure their writing like a poem, giving it a title.

- Check spelling, using word walls.

- Check for correct use of apostrophes in contractions.

LOG ON Technology

Remind students that as they draft, revise, and proofread, they can copy one line that they want to work on and paste it at the bottom of the poem. When they have revised the line, they can cut and paste it back where it belongs in the poem.

Day 5 Publish

PUBLISH AND PRESENT

To prepare to publish, remind students to use appropriate spacing between words and sentences and make standard margins. Suggest that students read their poems aloud to the class. Review Speaking and Listening strategies.

Handwriting Remind students to write legibly to meet school or district standards.

For cursive models, see **Teacher's Resource Book,** pages 168–173.

EVALUATE

To evaluate student writing, use the 4-point Scoring Rubric. Check the **Word Choice** trait carefully.

Transparency 100

Desert Tortoise

This tortoise carries a home on his back,
And he lives in another home at the same time.
His other home is hot and dry. There
are cracks on the ground.
But his shell covers him as he crawls in the sun.
He can dig a hole to get shade from the heat,
Or dig even deeper to warm up on cold nights.
The desert is the tortoise's other home.
He's lucky he's got two. I only have one.

Writing Transparency 100   © Macmillan/McGraw-Hill

Writing Transparency 100

SCORING RUBRIC

4 Excellent	**3** Good	**2** Fair	**1** Unsatisfactory
Ideas and Content Subject of poem is engaging and clearly developed	**Ideas and Content** Subject of poem is well developed	**Ideas and Content** Subject of poem is presented, but not always clearly	**Ideas and Content** Subject of poem is poorly developed
Organization Lines follow structure of a poem and break so rhythm is maintained	**Organization** Lines follow structure of a poem and break appropriately	**Organization** Some lines break in a way that interferes with comprehension	**Organization** Lines are structured more like a paragraph than a poem
Voice Expresses personality and enthusiasm of writer	**Voice** Expresses writer's personality	**Voice** Writer's voice is present but weak; lacks enthusiasm for subject	**Voice** Flat and does not convey interest in the subject
Word Choice Consistent use of precise words	**Word Choice** Adequate use of precise words	**Word Choice** Some exact words selected	**Word Choice** Few or no vivid words used
Sentence Fluency Sentences flow well; rhythm is evident when lines are read aloud	**Sentence Fluency** Good phrasing and rhythm to lines	**Sentence Fluency** Many lines lack proper phrasing and rhythm	**Sentence Fluency** Incomplete or confusing sentences
Conventions Mostly free of errors in spelling, mechanics, and usage	**Conventions** Minor errors in usage, spelling, and mechanics	**Conventions** Many errors in spelling, usage, and mechanics	**Conventions** Repeated errors in spelling, mechanics, and usage

Word Study

Objectives

- Apply knowledge of word meanings and context clues
- Analyze and complete analogies
- Use academic language: *analogies*

Materials

- Vocabulary Transparency 49
- Vocabulary Strategy Transparency 50
- Leveled Practice Books, p. 182

Vocabulary

hives (p. 267) boxes or houses that bees live in

architects (p. 271) people who design buildings

structures (p. 272) things that are built

contain (p. 272) to hold inside

retreats (p. 279) goes back

shallow (p. 268) not deep

shelter (p. 279) something that covers or protects

ELL — Access for All

Ask Questions Ask questions such as the following using the vocabulary: *What does a nest contain? What structures do animals build? If it's raining and you are outside, what could you use as a shelter?* Help students answer in full sentences.

Review

Vocabulary

 Words in Context

EXPLAIN/MODEL

Review the meanings of the vocabulary words. Display **Transparency 49.** Model how to use word meanings and context clues to fill in the first missing word.

Transparency 49

architects hives shelter structures
contain retreats shallow

Last week I helped my grandfather tend his honeybees. The bees live behind his house in boxes called (1) <u>hives</u>. That's where they store their honey. Grandpa checks often to see how much honey they (2) <u>contain</u>.

Later we went down to the pond. Beavers build strong houses there. They build these (3) <u>structures</u> out of sticks, stones, and mud. Beavers are wonderful (4) <u>architects</u>!

The beavers' dam has made a deep pond where once there was only a (5) <u>shallow</u> stream. The beavers have built a (6) <u>shelter</u>, called a lodge, in the pond. We walked quietly, hoping to see a beaver. When a beaver hears someone, it (7) <u>retreats</u> quickly to the safety of the lodge.

Vocabulary Transparency 49

Think Aloud The first paragraph tells about honeybees. The bees live in boxes. The missing word is the name for those boxes. I know that bees live in hives. The missing word, then, is *hives*.

PRACTICE

 Help students complete item 2. Then have students use context clues to write missing words for items 3–7 on a separate piece of paper. Students can exchange papers, check answers, and explain context clues they used to figure out the missing words.

Remind students that they can use the Glossary on pages 408–422 to confirm word meanings.

 **SKILL**
ANALOGIES

EXPLAIN/MODEL

An **analogy** is two pairs of words that have the same relationship. For example, *big is to little as deep is to shallow* is an analogy. The pairs of words (*big/little* and *deep/shallow*) are antonyms.

Display **Transparency 50.** Model how to complete item 1. Explain the relationship using a sentence, such as *Blue is the color of the sky.*

 Transparency 50

Analogies

wide school painting grass cold night

1. blue is to sky as green is to <u>grass</u>
2. sun is to day as moon is to <u>night</u>
3. shallow is to deep as narrow is to <u>wide</u>
4. architect is to building as artist is to <u>painting</u>
5. desert tortoise is to heat as polar bear is to <u>cold</u>
6. president is to country as principal is to <u>school</u>

Vocabulary Strategy Transparency 50

PRACTICE

 Help students complete item 2. Then have students write the correct words to complete items 3–6 on a separate sheet of paper. They can explain the relationship of the word pairs in each analogy.

Quick Check Can students use context clues to figure out word meanings and analyze and complete analogies?

During **Small Group Instruction**

If No → **Approaching Level** Vocabulary, p. 285O

If Yes → **On Level** Options, pp. 285Q–285R

Beyond Level Options, pp. 285S–285T

ELL Access for All

Understand Relationships Provide many simple examples of the kinds of analogy relationships students will need to know such as antonyms, synonyms, and examples. Then coconstruct other examples with students. It is through extensive practice that students will begin to understand analogies.

Vocabulary

Have students complete analogies using last week's vocabulary words, such as *on* is to *off* as *whispered* is to *screamed*; *chapter* is to *book* as *news story* is to *newspaper*. Students can create analogies for the remaining words.

On Level Practice Book O, page 182

An **analogy** shows how two pairs of words are alike. Analogies can help you understand the meanings of words based on their relationship to other words. The relationship may show similarities, opposites, parts of a whole, or some other connection.

wing is to **bird** as **paw** is to **cat**
desert is to **hot** as **arctic** is to **cold**

A. Circle the correct word to complete each analogy.
1. **bee** is to **hive** as **bear** is to _____
   (a. den) b. nest c. mound d. burrow
2. **fast** is to **rabbit** as **slow** is to _____
   a. prairie dog (b. snail) c. shallow d. long
3. **shallow** is to **deep** as **small** is to _____
   a. tiny b. hollow (c. big) d. bottom
4. **lodge** is to **pond** as **nest** is to _____
   a. tall (b. tree) c. water d. woods
5. **insect** is to **spider** as **worm** is to _____
   (a. bird) b. bear c. ant d. fish

B. Complete the analogy. Possible responses provided.
6. cup is to ___water___ as bowl is to ___soup___
7. sneaker is to foot as ___watch, bracelet___ is to wrist.
8. peanuts is to elephant as fish is to ___dolphin___

 Approaching Practice Book A, page 182
 **Beyond Practice Book B,** page 182

Word Study

Objectives

- Use syllabication rules to break multisyllable words into parts
- Decode multisyllable words with the V/CV and VC/V pattern
- Identify open and closed syllables in words with the V/CV or VC/V pattern
- Decode words with *qu* /kw/

Materials

- Leveled Practice Books, p. 183

Practice Identifying Syllables Write two-syllable words on the board with the V/CV and VC/V pattern. Model the pronunciation of each word, have students repeat, and then help them determine where the syllable division should be. Students will need extra modeling.

On Level Practice Book O, page 183

Two-syllable words may have the **V/CV pattern** or the **VC/V pattern.** When the first syllable ends with a vowel, it has the V/CV pattern and is pronounced with the long vowel sound.
fla / vor   si / lent

When the first syllable ends with a consonant, it has the VC/V pattern and is pronounced with the short vowel sound.
nap / kin   wat / er

Divide each underlined word into syllables. Then write whether the vowel sound of the first syllable is long or short.

1. The <u>pilot</u> spotted a buffalo herd from the plane. **pi/lot; long**

2. Would that monkey eat a <u>lemon</u>? **lem/on; short**

3. A turtle is one animal with a <u>mobile</u> home. **mo/bile; long**

4. Many animals seem <u>clever</u> because they build such good shelters. **clev/er; short**

5. The nature center has a <u>model</u> of a prairie dog's burrow. **mod/el; short**

6. The snake was <u>silent</u> as it slithered toward the rabbit. **si/lent; long**

7. Can you name an animal that lives in the <u>desert</u>? **des/ert; short**

8. The bear sleeps soundly in its <u>cozy</u> den. **co/zy; long**

★ **Approaching Practice Book A,** page 183

◆ **Beyond Practice Book B,** page 183

Phonics

Words with the V/CV and VC/V Pattern

 EXPLAIN/MODEL

- A syllable is a word part with one vowel sound.

- When a two-syllable word has a VCV (vowel-consonant-vowel) pattern, it usually divides into syllables between the first vowel and the consonant (V/CV), as in *pilot*. When a syllable ends in a vowel, it usually has a long vowel sound and is an open syllable. The syllable *pi* in *pilot* is an open syllable.

- In some two-syllable words with the VCV pattern, the first syllable has a short vowel sound, as in *cabin*. These words divide into syllables between the consonant and the second vowel (VC/V). The first syllable is a closed syllable.

Write: r o/b o t
      V/C V

Think Aloud This word has two syllables. I see the VCV pattern. I will try dividing the word between the vowel and the consonant so that the first syllable is *r-o*. I know that a syllable that ends in a vowel has a long vowel sound. I will say the first syllable with the long *o* sound, /rō/. When I say both syllables, I get /rō/ /bot/. *Robot* is a word I know. I divided the word into syllables correctly.

PRACTICE/APPLY

Display: *baby, cabin, river, motor, silent, robin, crater, clover.* Have students label the VCV pattern in each word, draw a line between the syllables, and try pronouncing the words. If a word sounds wrong, they should redivide the syllables and try again.

Decode Multisyllable Words Write these words on the board: *frequently, grocery, calendar, cucumber,* and *production.* Model how to decode *frequently,* focusing on the V/CV pattern and the /kw/ sound in the second syllable. Work with students to decode the other words.

Quick Check	Can students decode words with the V/CV and VC/V pattern?

During **Small Group Instruction**

If No → **Approaching Level** Phonics, p. 285P

If Yes → **On Level** Options pp. 285Q–285R

Beyond Level Options pp. 285S–285T

Vocabulary Building

Oral Language

Expand Vocabulary Work with students to brainstorm the names of animals that build their homes, and write the words on a web like the one below.

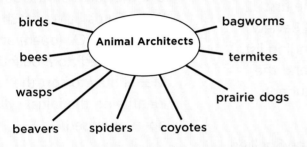

birds — Animal Architects — bagworms
bees — termites
wasps — prairie dogs
beavers — spiders — coyotes

Vocabulary Building

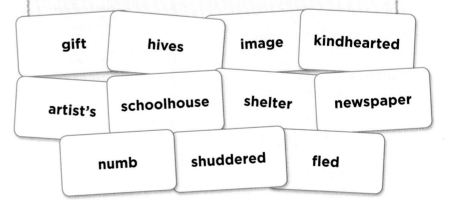

Onomatopoeia Many words for animal sounds resemble the sounds they name. For example, owls *hoot* and geese *honk*. Brainstorm words that describe the sounds that animals make. Write them on a chart.

animal	sound word
cat	meow, purr
crow	caw
bee	buzz
pig	oink, grunt
dog	growl, woof, arf

Then have students think of other words that sound like what they describe, such as *swish, whiz,* and *clink.* Challenge students to find an example of onomatopoeia from among this year's spelling and vocabulary words. (purr, squawk, crackle, click, clap)

Apply Vocabulary

Write a Paragraph Have students use the words *hives, architects, structures, contain, retreats, shallow,* and *shelter* in a paragraph about animal homes. Students can read their paragraphs aloud.

Spiral Review

Vocabulary Game Divide the class into small groups. Give each group a set of **Vocabulary Cards** for *gift, hives, image, kindhearted, numb, shuddered, fled, artist's, schoolhouse, shelter,* and *newspaper.*

- Each group places the cards facedown. A player in each group takes a card and, without revealing the word, provides clues for the group by drawing pictures on the board or on chart paper.

- The student in the group who guesses the word correctly then takes a turn at selecting a card and drawing a picture to define it.

- The group that guesses all of the words in the pile in the least amount of time wins.

gift	hives	image	kindhearted
artist's	schoolhouse	shelter	newspaper
	numb	shuddered	fled

5 Day Spelling

The V/CV and VC/V Pattern

Spelling Words

pilot	planet	label
diner	model	cozy
tiger	shady	silent
favor	robot	spider
lemon	tiny	frozen

Review follow, basket, Sunday

Challenge melon, stomach

Dictation Sentences

1. He is the pilot of the plane.
2. She had lunch at the diner.
3. The tiger has stripes.
4. He did a favor for his friend.
5. The lemon is sour.
6. We live on the planet Earth.
7. I built a model of a house.
8. It is shady under the tree.
9. The bug moves like a robot.
10. Snails have **tiny** shells.
11. He reads the label on the jar.
12. Animals like cozy homes.
13. The crowd was silent.
14. The **spider** weaves a web.
15. The lake is frozen.

Review Words

1. We will follow you in our car.
2. They brought a basket of fruit.
3. The concert is on Sunday.

Challenge Words

1. May I have a slice of melon?
2. He had a full stomach.

Note: Words in **bold** type are from *Animal Homes*.

Display the Spelling Words throughout the week.

Day 1 — Pretest

ASSESS PRIOR KNOWLEDGE

Use the Dictation Sentences. Say the underlined word, read the sentence, and repeat the word. Have students write the words on **Spelling Practice Book** page 153. For a modified list, use the first 12 Spelling Words and the 3 Review Words. For a more challenging list, use Spelling Words 3–15 and the Challenge Words. Have students correct their own tests.

Have students cut apart the Spelling Word Cards BLM on **Teacher's Resource Book** page 90 and figure out a way to sort them. Have them save the cards for use throughout the week.

Students can use Spelling Practice Book page 154 for independent practice.

Day 2 — Word Sorts

TEACHER AND STUDENT SORTS

- Review the Spelling Words, point out the open or closed syllable at the beginning of each word, and discuss meanings.

- Use the cards on the Spelling Word Cards BLM. Attach the headings V/CV (open) and VC/V (closed) to a bulletin board. Model how to sort the words by identifying the initial syllable as open or closed.

- Have students take turns choosing cards, sorting them, and explaining how they sorted them.

- Then have students use their own Spelling Word Cards. After placing the headings on their desks, they can sort the Spelling Words three times. Have students write their last sort on Spelling Practice Book page 155.

Spelling Practice Book, pages 153–154

Fold back the paper along the dotted line. Use the blanks to write each word as it is read aloud. When you finish the test, unfold the paper. Use the list at the right to correct any spelling mistakes.

1. _____	1. pilot
2. _____	2. diner
3. _____	3. tiger
4. _____	4. favor
5. _____	5. lemon
6. _____	6. planet
7. _____	7. model
8. _____	8. shady
9. _____	9. robot
10. _____	10. tiny
11. _____	11. label
12. _____	12. cozy
13. _____	13. silent
14. _____	14. spider
15. _____	15. frozen
Review Words 16. _____	16. follow
17. _____	17. basket
18. _____	18. Sunday
Challenge Words 19. _____	19. melon
20. _____	20. stomach

Spelling Practice Book, page 155

pilot	favor	model	tiny	silent
diner	lemon	shady	label	spider
tiger	planet	robot	cozy	frozen

Rhyme Time

Write the spelling word that rhymes with each word below.

1. chosen _frozen_
2. table _label_
3. flavor _favor_
4. lady _shady_
5. nosy _cozy_
6. rider _spider_

Syllable Patterns

How a word is divided into syllables may depend on whether the vowel in the first part of the word is long or short. If the first syllable has a short vowel sound, it is usually divided after the consonant. If the first syllable has a long vowel sound, it is usually divided after the vowel. Divide each spelling word into syllables.

7. pilot _pi-lot_
8. planet _plan-et_
9. robot _ro-bot_
10. model _mod-el_
11. diner _di-ner_
12. silent _si-lent_
13. tiger _ti-ger_
14. lemon _lem-on_
15. tiny _ti-ny_

Day 3 · Word Meanings

DEFINITIONS

Display the definitions below. Have students write the clues and the Spelling Words that go with them in a word study notebook.

1. someone who flies a plane (pilot)

2. a wild cat with stripes (tiger)

3. a yellow, sour fruit (lemon)

4. not sunny (shady)

5. a bug with eight legs (spider)

Challenge students to come up with clues for other Spelling Words, including Review Words and Challenge Words.

Have partners write a sentence for each Spelling Word, leaving a blank where the word should go. Then have them trade papers and write the missing word.

Day 4 · Review and Proofread

SPIRAL REVIEW

Review the VC/CV pattern. Write *follow, basket,* and *Sunday* on the board. Have students identify and underline the first syllable of each word.

PROOFREAD AND WRITE

Have students correct the errors.

1. The lemmon is tinny. (lemon, tiny)

2. The pillot flew a sillent plane. (pilot, silent)

BLIND SORT

Partners use their Spelling Word Cards. Each writes the headings V/CV (open) and VC/V (closed) on a sheet of paper and then take turns. One draws cards and says the words. The other writes. After both have finished, they can check each other's papers.

Day 5 · Assess and Reteach

POSTTEST

Use the Dictation Sentences on page 285G for the Posttest.

If students have difficulty with any words in the lesson, have them place them on a list called "Spelling Words I Want to Remember" in a word study notebook.

WORD STUDY NOTEBOOK

Challenge students to search for other words with the open-syllable V/CV and closed-syllable VC/V patterns in their reading for the week and write them in a word study notebook under the heading "Other Words with Open and Closed Syllables."

Spelling Practice Book, page 156

pilot	favor	model	tiny	silent
diner	lemon	shady	label	spider
tiger	planet	robot	cozy	frozen

What's the Word?
Complete each sentence with a spelling word.

1. The black **spider** was spinning a new web.
2. The large, **shady** oak tree is home to many animals.
3. The Bengal **tiger**, which is a kind of large cat, lives in India.
4. Birds build nests on every part of the **planet** Earth.
5. Many fish live beneath the surface of a **frozen** pond.
6. The black bear slept in his **cozy**, warm den all winter.
7. It takes many **tiny** ants to build an anthill.
8. Bugs were living in the **lemon** tree and eating the sour fruit.
9. The owl was as **silent** as a mouse as she landed in her nest.
10. I made a clay **model** of a beehive for my science project.

Define It!
Write the spelling word that has the same meaning as each word or phrase below.

11. A tag **label**
12. A machine that looks like a person **robot**
13. A small restaurant **diner**
14. Special help given to a friend **favor**
15. A person who steers a plane **pilot**

Spelling Practice Book, page 157

There are six spelling mistakes in this report. Circle the misspelled words. Write the words correctly on the lines below.

King of the Jungle

Some people think that the lion is the king of the jungle, but lions do not even live in forests. The real king of the jungle is the (tigger)!

I did a report on these large cats. Here are a few things I learned. These animals live in Asia, not in Africa, as many people think. They are (tiene) when they are born, only 2 or 3 pounds, but they grow fast. The biggest one on the (plannett) weighs more than 1,000 pounds! Because they live alone, they can be (siellent) as they walk through the (shadey) forest looking for food.

The next time someone calls a lion the king of the jungle, do me a (faiver) and tell them the truth!

1. **tiger**
2. **tiny**
3. **planet**
4. **silent**
5. **shady**
6. **favor**

Writing Activity
Imagine that you are an insect living in your backyard. Write a paragraph describing something about your life in this backyard home. Use at least four spelling words in your description.

_____

_____

_____

_____

Spelling Practice Book, page 158

Look at the words in each set below. One word in each set is spelled correctly. Look at Sample A. The letter next to the correctly spelled word in Sample A has been shaded in. Do Sample B yourself. Shade the letter of the word that is spelled correctly. When you are sure you know what to do, go on with the rest of the page.

Sample A:
- Ⓐ wagon
- Ⓑ wagen
- Ⓒ waggon
- Ⓓ waggen

Sample B:
- Ⓔ pallace
- Ⓕ pallase
- Ⓖ palase
- Ⓗ palace

1.
- Ⓐ pilote
- Ⓑ pilot
- Ⓒ pillot
- Ⓓ pielot

2.
- Ⓔ dinar
- Ⓕ dinnar
- Ⓖ dyner
- Ⓗ diner

3.
- Ⓐ tiger
- Ⓑ tigger
- Ⓒ tyger
- Ⓓ tiggur

4.
- Ⓔ favur
- Ⓕ favvor
- Ⓖ favor
- Ⓗ favore

5.
- Ⓐ lemone
- Ⓑ lemon
- Ⓒ lemmon
- Ⓓ lemmin

6.
- Ⓔ planet
- Ⓕ plannet
- Ⓖ planit
- Ⓗ plannit

7.
- Ⓐ modell
- Ⓑ model
- Ⓒ moddel
- Ⓓ modul

8.
- Ⓔ shadey
- Ⓕ shadie
- Ⓖ shady
- Ⓗ shadee

9.
- Ⓔ robbut
- Ⓕ robat
- Ⓖ robot
- Ⓗ robbat

10.
- Ⓐ tinee
- Ⓑ tinnie
- Ⓒ tiney
- Ⓓ tiny

11.
- Ⓔ labbel
- Ⓕ labil
- Ⓖ label
- Ⓗ labul

12.
- Ⓐ cozzy
- Ⓑ cozie
- Ⓒ cosie
- Ⓓ cozy

13.
- Ⓔ silente
- Ⓕ silent
- Ⓖ sillent
- Ⓗ silant

14.
- Ⓔ spidur
- Ⓕ spiddar
- Ⓖ spider
- Ⓗ spidder

15.
- Ⓔ frozen
- Ⓕ frowzen
- Ⓖ frausen
- Ⓗ frauzen

Pronoun-Verb Contractions

Daily Language Activities

Use these activities to introduce each day's lesson. Write the day's activities on the board or use **Transparency 25.**

DAY 1
1. eric said were best friends. **2.** Weve built a birdhouse. **3.** its amazing and youv'e got to see it. (1: Eric; we're; 2: We've built; 3: It's; you've)

DAY 2
1. My cat sleeps if shes tired. **2.** sometimes she'll sleep until I come home. **3.** Were best friends and Ill always love her. (1: she's; 2: Sometimes she'll; 3: We're; I'll)

DAY 3
1. My cat loves sleeping in it's basket. **2.** Your having fun playing with you're cat. **3.** The kittens are ready for they're dinner. (1: its; 2: You're; your; 3: their)

DAY 4
1. Wel'l visit the farm tommorow. **2.** The farmers animals stay in the cozzy barn at night. **3.** Ive playd in he's barn. (1: We'll; tomorrow; 2: farmer's; cozy; 3: I've played; his)

DAY 5
1. how many tinny chicks are they're. **2.** I'ave counted eigt of them. **3.** We'l take care of they (1: How; tiny; there?; 2: I've; eight; 3: We'll; them)

Tip: Language Variations
Some students may have difficulty using contractions or understanding what they stand for, since there may be no direct equivalent in their languages. Some languages may even drop the verb *to be* altogether. Model correct usage by correctly restating what students say.

Day 1 · Introduce the Concept

INTRODUCE PRONOUN-VERB CONTRACTIONS

Present the following:

- A **contraction** is a shortened form of two words.

- An **apostrophe** replaces letters that are left out in a pronoun-verb contraction.

he's = he + is	they're = they + are
she's = she + is	I've = I + have
it's = it + is	you've = you + have
I'm = I + am	we've = we + have
you're = you + are	they've = they + have
we're = we + are	

 See Grammar Transparency 121 for modeling and guided practice.

Grammar Practice Book, page 153

- A **contraction** is a shortened form of two words.
- An **apostrophe** ['] replaces letters that are left out.

I am = I'm	we are = we're	I have = I've
he is = he's	you are = you're	you have = you've
she is = she's	they are = they're	we have = we've
it is = it's		they have = they've

Rewrite each sentence and replace the underlined words with a contraction.

1. <u>We are</u> learning about animal homes.
   We're learning about animal homes.

2. <u>They are</u> different for each kind of animal.
   They're different for each kind of animal.

3. <u>It is</u> important for animals to have the right place.
   It's important for animals to have the right place.

4. <u>I am</u> fascinated by many of the animals' homes.
   I'm fascinated by many of the animals' homes.

5. My brother says that <u>we have</u> seen otters on the riverbank.
   My brother says that we've seen otters on the riverbank.

6. <u>He is</u> hoping to see the otters come out of their home.
   He's hoping to see the otters come out of their home.

7. <u>We are</u> bringing a camera to the river.
   We're bringing a camera to the river.

8. <u>You are</u> going to get copies of all the pictures!
   You're going to get copies of all the pictures!

Day 2 · Teach the Concept

REVIEW PRONOUN-VERB CONTRACTIONS

Review with students what a pronoun-verb contraction is.

INTRODUCE MORE PRONOUN-VERB CONTRACTIONS

- A **contraction** is a shortened form of two words.

- An **apostrophe** replaces letters that are left out in a pronoun-verb contraction.

I'll = I + will	you'll = you + will
he'll = he + will	it'll = it + will
she'll = she + will	they'll = they + will
we'll = we + will	

 See Grammar Transparency 122 for modeling and guided practice.

Grammar Practice Book, page 154

- Remember, a **contraction** is a shortened form of two words.
- An **apostrophe** ['] replaces letters that are left out. Here are more contractions.

I have = I've	I will = I'll	we will = we'll
you have = you've	he will = he'll	you will = you'll
we have = we've	she will = she'll	they will = they'll
they have = they've	it will = it'll	

Underline the two words in each sentence that you can make into a contraction. Then write each sentence with the contraction.

1. <u>We have</u> seen two beavers building a home in our pond.
   We've seen two beavers building a home in our pond.

2. <u>It will</u> be fun to watch them work.
   It'll be fun to watch them work.

3. <u>You will</u> see them when you come over.
   You'll see them when you come over.

4. <u>I have</u> read about beavers and their homes.
   I've read about beavers and their homes.

5. <u>She will</u> find branches for their home.
   She'll find branches for their home.

6. <u>He will</u> build with branches and mud.
   He'll build with branches and mud.

7. <u>They will</u> build an underwater door to their home.
   They'll build an underwater door to their home.

8. <u>They have</u> lots of building to do!
   They've lots of building to do!

Day 3 — Review and Practice

REVIEW PRONOUN-VERB CONTRACTIONS

Review forming contractions with pronouns and verbs.

MECHANICS AND USAGE: SPELLING CONTRACTIONS AND POSSESSIVE PRONOUNS

- Do not confuse possessive pronouns with contractions.

- The words *it's, you're,* and *they're* are **contractions.** They have an apostrophe that stands for letters that are left out.

- The words *its, your,* and *their* are **possessive pronouns.** They do not have an apostrophe.

- Pay attention when spelling contractions. Make sure the apostrophe is in the correct place.

 See Grammar Transparency 123 for modeling and guided practice.

Grammar Practice Book, page 155

- A **contraction** is a shortened form of two words. An **apostrophe** replaces letters that are left out. Examples: *I'm, he's, it's, we'll, they've*
- A **possessive pronoun** takes the place of a possessive noun. It shows who or what owns something. Examples: *my, his, its, our, their*

Circle the correct word to complete each sentence. Write C if the answer is a contraction and P if the answer is a possessive pronoun.

1. (Its, It's) possible that anmals live near your home. __C__
2. (Your, You're) lucky if you find animals to watch. __C__
3. (I've, Iv'e) spent a lot of time watching animals near my home. __C__
4. We've seen birds build nests in the tree in (our, our's) yard. __P__
5. My neighbor said he's seen rabbit holes near (he's, his) house. __P__
6. Now (we're, were) watching a squirrel build a nest in a tree. __C__
7. Mom said the squirrel wants to hide (it's, its) nuts in the nest. __P__
8. (Well, We'll) make sure to tell you when the nest is finished. __C__
9. (I'll, It'll) be fun to watch the squirrels work. __C__
10. The animals look in the fields for (their, they're) food. __P__

Day 4 — Review and Proofread

REVIEW PRONOUN-VERB CONTRACTIONS

Review how to spell pronoun-verb contractions, paying attention to apostrophe placement. Review how a possessive pronoun is different from a contraction.

PROOFREAD

Have students correct errors in the following sentences.

1. Wer'e going camping. (We're)
2. Its going to be fun. (It's)
3. I wonder if sh'ell bring her sleeping bag. (she'll)
4. Maybe wee'll have a fire. (we'll)
5. They'ave stayed at this campsite before. (They've)

 See Grammar Transparency 124 for modeling and guided practice.

Grammar Practice Book, page 156

- A **contraction** is a shortened form of two words.
- An **apostrophe** ['] replaces letters that are left out.

Proofread the paragraph. Circle any incorrectly written contractions.

(I'm) planning to become a zoologist someday. That's someone who studies animals. Until then I can learn a lot by watching and reading about animals. There are plenty of rabbits in our backyard. (They've) built their warren near our fence. (I've) seen rabbits hop across the yard. Then suddenly (theyre) gone down the hole into the warren. I (cant) go down there, so I read about what (its) like inside.

Writing Activity

Rewrite the paragraph. Write each contraction with the apostrophe in the right place. Make sure possessive pronouns and contractions are used correctly.

I'm planning to become a zoologist someday. That's someone who studies animals. Until then I can learn a lot by watching and reading about animals. There are plenty of rabbits in our backyard. They've built their warren near our fence. I've seen rabbits hop across the yard. Then suddenly they're gone down the hole into the warren. I can't go down there, so I read about what it's like inside.

Day 5 — Assess and Reteach

ASSESS

Use the Daily Language Activity and page 157 of the **Grammar Practice Book** for assessment.

RETEACH

Display the contractions *we're, she'll, they've,* and *I'm* on the board. Have students identify the two words that make up each contraction. Then have them create contractions from *he is, we have, they are,* and *you will.* Ask students to distinguish between meanings and spellings of *they're/their, you're/your,* and *it's/its.* Have students write sentences using the contractions.

Use page 158 of the Grammar Practice Book for additional reteaching.

 See Grammar Transparency 125 for modeling and guided practice.

Grammar Practice Book, pages 157–158

A. Is the underlined contraction correctly written? Write *yes* if it is. Write *no* if it is not and then write the word correctly.

1. Were buying a new cage for our hamster. __no; We're__
2. Its going to have tunnels for him to crawl through. __no; It's__
3. He's going to have a lot of fun playing in the tunnels. __yes__
4. It'll be like the tunnels he would dig in the desert. __no; It'll__
5. I'm looking forward to seeing him play. __yes__

B. Write the contraction for the underlined words.

6. You are not going to believe this. __You're__
7. We have got an owl living in a tree in our yard. __We've__
8. It is the biggest bird I have ever seen. __It's__
9. You will have to come over and see it sometime. __You'll__
10. My sister says she is going to videotape it flying. __she's__
11. I hope it will stay all summer. __it'll__
12. It is very fun to watch it fly. __It's__

Administer the Test

Weekly Reading Assessment,
Passage and questions, pages 309–316

ASSESSED SKILLS

- Description
- Vocabulary Words
- Analogies
- The V/CV and VC/V Pattern
- Pronoun-Verb Contractions

Macmillan/McGraw-Hill

Administer the **Weekly Assessment** from the CD-ROM or online.

Weekly Assessment, 309–316

Fluency

Assess fluency for one group of students per week. Use the Oral Fluency Record Sheet to track the number of words read correctly. Fluency goal for all students: **97–117 words correct per minute (WCPM).**

Approaching Level	Weeks 1, 3, 5
On Level	Weeks 2, 4
Beyond Level	Week 6

Fluency Assessment

Alternative Assessments

- **Leveled Weekly Assessment,** for Approaching Level, pages 317–324
- **ELL Assessment,** pages 152–153

ELL Assessment, 152–153

Diagnose	IF . . .	Prescribe — THEN . . .
VOCABULARY WORDS VOCABULARY STRATEGY Analogies Items 1, 2, 3	0–1 items correct . . .	Reteach skills using the **Additional Lessons**, page T10 **LOG ON** Reteach skills: Go to **www.macmillanmh.com** **CD ROM** Vocabulary PuzzleMaker Evaluate for Intervention.
COMPREHENSION Skill: Description Items 4, 5, 6,	0–1 items correct . . .	Reteach skills using the **Additional Lessons**, page T5 Evaluate for Intervention.
GRAMMAR Pronoun-Verb Contractions Items 7, 8, 9	0–1 items correct . . .	Reteach skills: **Grammar Practice Book,** page 158
SPELLING The V/CV and VC/V Pattern Items 10, 11, 12	0–1 items correct . . .	**LOG ON** Reteach skills: Go to **www.macmillanmh.com**
FLUENCY	89–96 WCPM 0–88 WCPM	**AUDIO CD** Fluency Solutions Evaluate for Intervention.

READING
Triumphs
AN INTERVENTION PROGRAM

Also Available

To place students in the Intervention Program, use the **Diagnostic Assessment** in the Intervention Teacher's Edition.

Leveled Reader Lesson 1

Objective	Read to apply strategies and skills
Materials	• **Leveled Reader** *Amazing Mammal Builders* • chart paper
	• **Approaching Practice Book A,** p. 180

PREVIEW AND PREDICT

Show the cover. Read the title and have students preview the photos and captions. Ask what this book might be about. What do mammals build?

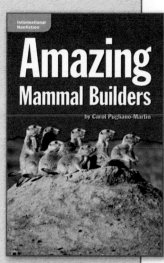

Leveled Reader

VOCABULARY WORDS

Review the vocabulary words. As you read, discuss each word as it comes up: *hive, shelter, architects, structures,* p. 3; *shallow, contain,* p. 4; *retreat,* p. 12. Help students identify context clues, such as *tools, job, design,* and *build* for *architects* and *structures* on page 3.

STRATEGY
SUMMARIZE

Remind the group that summarizing an article means restating the most important information in their own words. As you read, help students identify the most important facts in the descriptions of the structures mammals build. Read pages 2–3 aloud and model summarizing.

Think Aloud The Introduction tells me that mammals build structures where they can live and raise their young. That seems important, judging from the title of the book. As I keep reading, I will look for more information about those structures.

SKILL
DESCRIPTION

Remind students that nonfiction writers sometimes organize information by describing a topic using details and examples. During and after reading, discuss how harvest mice and pack rats build nests. Help students create Description Webs.

■ How can we briefly state the topic of this chapter? Give some details.

■ Do the descriptions seem well-organized? Give examples.

READ AND RESPOND

Have the group read to the end of Chapter 1 orally. Help students identify and analyze descriptions. Provide fluency support.

Fluency: REPEATED READING

Model reading the expository nonfiction passage on **Practice Book** page 180. Have the group echo-read the passage. Then have partners practice reading it to each other. Circulate and provide corrective feedback.

Approaching Practice Book A, page 180

As I read, I will pay attention to the genre of the passage.

	Birds aren't the only animals that build nests. Harvest
9	mice are nest builders as well. Their materials are long
19	strips of grass. Their tools are their teeth and tiny claws.
30	Harvest mice build their nests in fields. Their nests are
40	shallow and small. They often hang between two grass
49	stems.
50	Harvest mice use these grass stems to climb up into
60	their nests. These nests contain fur. This fur keeps their
70	babies warm in their home.
75	Pack rats build nests too. Their nests are made from
85	sticks and grass. But these little creatures have an eye for
96	shiny things. They collect anything that sparkles. For
104	example, glass, mirrors, coins, and spoons are some of
113	their favorite things. 116

Comprehension Check

1. Where can you find the nest of a harvest mouse? **Main Idea and Details**
   Harvest mice build their nests in fields.

2. What do you think a pack rat's nest might look like? **Draw Conclusions**
   messy; made of sticks and grass; contain shiny things, such as pennies or glass

	Words Read	–	Number of Errors	=	Words Correct Score
First Read		–		=	
Second Read		–		=	

Leveled Reader Lesson 2

Objective Read to apply strategies and skills

Materials • **Leveled Reader** *Amazing Mammal Builders* • chart paper

VOCABULARY WORDS

As students review the first half and preview the second, point out and discuss the vocabulary words. Ask volunteers to state briefly what each word means and to give an example of when they might use the word.

SUMMARIZE AND PREDICT

Have students summarize how harvest mice and pack rats build nests. Review the titles of Chapters 2 and 3 and ask students to predict what they will learn in the rest of the book.

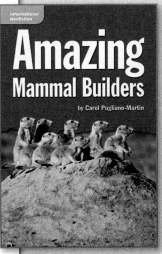

Leveled Reader

SKILL
DESCRIPTION

Ask students to keep these questions in mind as they read.

■ How do prairie dogs build their homes? How do beavers build theirs?

■ Which do you think is safer: a home underground or a home in the middle of a pond? Why?

You may wish to help students make a Description Web for each chapter.

READ AND RESPOND

Read to the end of the selection with the group. Remind students to review what they have read, summarizing the text regularly to help them focus on the topic. Discuss what kind of homes prairie dogs and beavers build. Have students share personal responses. Are mammal builders truly "amazing"? Why or why not?

Fluency

Objective Read with increasing fluency

Materials • stopwatch • **Approaching Practice Book A,** p. 180

TIMED READING

Have students do a final timed reading of the passage. They should

■ begin reading the passage aloud when you say "Go."

■ stop reading the passage after one minute when you say "Stop."

Keep track of miscues and coach students as needed. Discuss what they find hardest about reading a nonfiction book such as this aloud. Help students record and graph the number of words they read correctly.

Student Book

Web Spinners
by Steven Kistner

Analogies Review analogies. Have students complete the following: *retreat* is to *turn back* as *nap* is to (*sleep*); *shelter* is to *protect* as *encyclopedia* is to (*inform*); *shallow* is to *deep* as *hard* is to (*soft*); *buildings* are to *structures* as *apples* are to (*fruits*).

Comprehension

Objective	Identify description text structure in nonfiction
Materials	• **Comprehension Transparencies 25a** and **25b**

SKILL
DESCRIPTION

Remind students that description is a text structure using details and examples to tell about a topic. Nonfiction authors may use description that helps readers "see" details and understand the topic.

Display **Transparencies 25a** and **25b.** Read aloud the second paragraph of "Web Spinners."

Think Aloud This paragraph tells about the silk threads that spider webs are made from. It describes the thread as very thin but strong. The thread comes from glands in the spider's stomach.

Have students underline descriptive details in the article. Discuss how the descriptions help readers experience information with all five senses.

Vocabulary

Objective	Apply vocabulary word meanings and complete analogies
Materials	• **Vocabulary Cards** • **Student Book** *Animal Homes*

VOCABULARY WORDS

Review the vocabulary words using the **Vocabulary Cards.** Then help students locate and read the vocabulary words in *Animal Homes*. Have them read the words aloud and tell in their own words what each word means based on context. Then review the definitions in the Glossary.

ANALOGIES

Explain that an analogy compares the relationships of two pairs of words. Write the following analogy: *Bears are to dens as bees are to hives*. Discuss how this analogy compares two kinds of animals and their homes: *Bears and bees are animals; dens are where bears live, so hives must be where bees live*.

Discuss the first half of each analogy below. Then ask students to choose the best word to complete the analogy.

- *bird* is to *chirp* as *wolf* is to _____ (fur, howl) *(howl)*
- *fish* is to *swim* as *bird* is to _____ (sing, fly) *(fly)*
- *shallow* is to *stream* as *deep* is to _____ (desert, ocean) *(ocean)*
- *architects* are to *structures* as *spiders* are to _____ (webs, insects) *(webs)*

Phonics

Objective   Recognize VCV patterns in two-syllable words

WORDS WITH THE V/CV AND VC/V PATTERN

Write *pilot* and *shady*. Say each word and have students echo you. Clap the syllables with students. Draw a square around the VCV pattern in each word, explaining that the *y* in *shady* is considered a vowel. Point out the first vowel sound is long.

Write these spelling words: *diner, tiger, favor, robot, tiny, label,* and *spider*. Have students say the words and clap the syllables. Ask a volunteer to draw a square around the VCV pattern in each word. Then share examples of words with the VCV pattern in which the first vowel sound is short: *lemon, planet, model*. Have students repeat the words and identify the pattern.

Additional Lessons

Use your **Quick Check** observations to help you identify students who might benefit from additional instruction. See page T5 for comprehension support and page T10 for vocabulary support.

Vocabulary

Objective   Apply vocabulary word meanings
Materials   • **Vocabulary Cards**

VOCABULARY WORDS

Display the **Vocabulary Cards** from this week and last week. Read each word and discuss its definition. Then play a guessing game. Provide students with these clues:

- I am thinking of a word that is something that you might buy or get delivered in the morning. It contains articles, advertisements, and information. What is the word? (newspaper)

- I am thinking of a word that is a verb. It means to turn back because of danger. An antonym for this word is *advances*. What is the word? (retreats)

Challenge students to create and share clues for the remaining words.

Make Connections Across Texts

Objective   Compare descriptions across texts
Materials   • **Student Book** *Animal Homes*   • **Leveled Reader** *Amazing Mammal Builders*

SKILL
DESCRIPTION

Have the group summarize and discuss *Animal Homes* and *Amazing Mammal Builders*. Ask students to compare and contrast descriptions of animal homes. How similar were the authors' descriptions of prairie-dog burrows and beaver lodges?

Student Book

Leveled Reader

Leveled Reader Lesson

Objective   Read to apply strategies and skills

Materials   • **Leveled Reader** *Amazing Bird Builders*   • **On Level Practice Book O,** p. 180

PREVIEW AND PREDICT

Show the cover and read the title of the book. Ask students to predict why the author thinks some birds are amazing builders.

Leveled Reader

STRATEGY
SUMMARIZE

Remind students that summarizing, or briefly stating the most important ideas, can help them understand nonfiction text. As students read, have them look for important ideas about the structures that birds build. Read pages 2–3 aloud. Model how you summarize.

Think Aloud   The Introduction gives a lot of information. I might summarize it like this: Birds, like other animals, are amazing builders, and they use different materials to make their nests. I'll keep reading to learn more about how birds build their nests.

SKILL
DESCRIPTION

Review that authors sometimes use examples and details that describe a topic. As students read, have them focus on each topic looking for examples and details that describe the structures tailorbirds and weaverbirds make in Chapter 1. Students may make a Description Web to help them summarize the information.

READ AND RESPOND

Have students read to the end of Chapter 1, looking for descriptions of tailorbird and weaverbird structures. Encourage them to summarize as they read. Discuss how the vocabulary words are used in this book.

Then have students read to the end of the book. Discuss other bird structures and details that describe them. Have students share personal responses.

Fluency: REPEATED READING

Model reading the fluency passage for *Amazing Bird Builders* and have students echo-read each sentence on **Practice Book** page 180.

Have students work in pairs, taking turns reading the passage and listening for tempo. Remind them to pay attention to the genre of the passage and to read nonfiction with interest. Listen and offer feedback.

ELL Leveled Reader
Go to pages 285U–285V.

On Level Practice Book O, page 180

As I read, I will pay attention to the genre of the passage.

	Many different kinds of animals build their own
8	homes. Their homes are structures that shelter them
16	from the cold and the rain. They are also places where
27	they can retreat from danger. Beavers build lodges, bees
36	build **hives,** and birds build incredible nests where they
45	hatch their eggs and raise their babies.
52	Have you ever seen a bird's nest? Some are made of
63	twigs and are round and shallow. Others are made of
73	grass and are long and deep. Still others are made from
84	mud and look like small cups. There are even birds that
95	use their own saliva, or spit, when they build a nest.
106	Many birds' nests contain feathers and hair. This makes the
116	nest a soft place for their babies, or chicks, to sleep. Birds
128	are some of the most amazing **architects** in the animal
138	world! 139

Comprehension Check

1. Compare and contrast different birds' nests? **Compare and Contrast**
   Compare: Many nests contain feathers and hair.
   Contrast: Nests are different sizes and shapes, and are made with different materials.
2. What does the word saliva mean? **Context Clues**
   Saliva is spit.

	Words Read	–	Number of Errors	=	Words Correct Score
First Read		–		=	
Second Read		–		=	

Vocabulary

Objective Apply vocabulary word meanings and complete analogies
Materials • **Vocabulary Cards**

VOCABULARY WORDS

Discuss which words students find hardest. Distribute the **Vocabulary Cards** for *hives, architects, structures, contain, retreats, shallow,* and *shelter.* Tell students not to look at their card but to show it to the group. The group gives clues about the word, and the student must guess it correctly.

ANALOGIES

Discuss each analogy. Have students choose the best word to complete it.

- Tall is to height as shallow is to ___. (depth, width) (depth)
- People are to houses as bees are to ___. (hives, honey) (hives)
- Sticks are to nests as bricks are to ___. (eagles, houses) (houses)
- Artists are to paintings as ___ are to blueprints. (architects, builders) (architects)

Leveled Reader

Student Book

Literary Elements

Objective Identify simile and rhythmic pattern in limericks
Materials • **Student Book** "Home Sweet Home," "Limerick"

SIMILE AND RHYTHMIC PATTERN

Review the two limericks on **Student Book** pages 282–283. Discuss the authors' use of figurative language and rhythmic patterns.

Discuss what a limerick is and what its rhyme scheme is. Ask students to give one example of a simile in these poems and discuss the humorous elements in "Home Sweet Home" and "Limerick."

Student Book

Make Connections Across Text

Objectives Make connections across texts and analyze descriptions
Materials • **Student Book** *Animal Homes* • **Leveled Reader** *Amazing Bird Builders*

SKILL
DESCRIPTION

Have students compare and contrast *Animal Homes* and *Amazing Bird Builders.* Discuss how each author uses description as a text structure. Ask: *Did you find out everything you wanted to know about animal homes? What else might you like to find out?*

Leveled Reader Lesson

Objective	Read to apply strategies and skills
Materials	• **Leveled Reader** *Amazing Insect and Spider Builders*
	• **Beyond Practice Book B,** p. 180

PREVIEW AND PREDICT

Show the cover and read the title of the book and its chapter headings. Ask students what structures they think insects and spiders build. Remind students to watch for vocabulary words as they read.

STRATEGY
SUMMARIZE

Ask students to explain what summarizing is and tell why it is useful. As students read the Introduction, have them summarize how insects and spiders build and what tools and materials they use.

Think Aloud The Introduction presents many different facts. I could summarize the information this way: Insects and spiders build structures without tools, making some materials with their own bodies. As I keep reading, I will look for more information about how they do this.

SKILL
DESCRIPTION

During and after reading, discuss the structures that honeybees, wasps, and termites build. Suggest that students create Description Webs to organize information. How does summarizing help them?

READ AND RESPOND

First, have students read to the end of Chapter 3. Discuss how the three insect structures described are similar to the homes we live in.

Next, have students finish the book. Discuss how insect and spider architects are different from human architects. Finally, have students share personal responses.

Fluency: REPEATED READING

Read the fluency passage and have students follow along on **Practice Book** page 180. Have students listen for how you pay attention to the genre of the passage as you read by adjusting your tempo.

Have partners take turns reading and offer corrective feedback. At the end of the week, partners should do a timed reading for one minute and see how many words they read correctly.

Leveled Reader

◆ **Beyond Practice Book B**, page 180

As I read, I will pay attention to the genre of the passage.

	Hives contain many wax structures called honeycombs. The
8	honeycombs are made with wax from the bees' stomachs. Honeybees
18	churn the wax out of their stomachs. Then they chew the wax to soften
32	it. The bees then mold the wax into hundreds of hexagonal, or
44	six-sided, cells.
46	The cells in a honeycomb are like little rooms. They are small holes
59	or spaces. Some of these cells are used as storage bins for the honey and
74	and pollen that bees eat. The queen honeybee lays eggs in the other cells.
88	Wasps are similar to honeybees, but they are also very different.
99	Like bees, they live in large groups with a queen. Wasps also build
112	nests with hexagonal cells. But they don't use wax. They make their
124	nests out of paper they make themselves!
131	How do they do it? Wasps scrape bits of wood from fence posts, old
145	boards, or dead trees. Then they chew the wood into a soft pulp by
159	mixing it with their saliva, or spit. They spread the pulp in layers and
173	shape it into cells. 177

Comprehension Check

1. Compare and contrast a honeycomb and wasp nest. **Compare and Contrast** Bees and wasps build nests with hexagonal cells. Bees use wax and wasps use paper to build the nests.
2. What are the cells of a honeycomb used for? **Main Idea and Details** for storing pollen and honey, and for laying eggs

	Words Read	−	Number of Errors	=	Words Correct Score
First Read		−		=	
Second Read		−		=	

Vocabulary

Objective Apply vocabulary word meanings
Materials • **Vocabulary Cards** • **Leveled Reader** *Amazing Insect and Spider Builders*

EXTEND VOCABULARY

Use the **Vocabulary Cards** to review the vocabulary words: *hives, architects, structures, contain, retreats, shallow,* and *shelter.* Discuss how the words are used in *Amazing Insect and Spider Builders.* Have students summarize the Leveled Reader using some of the vocabulary words.

Student Book

Literary Elements

Objective Analyze similes and rhythmic patterns and create a limerick
Materials • **Student Book** "Home Sweet Home," "Limerick"

SIMILE AND RHYTHMIC PATTERN

After rereading the two limericks on **Student Book** pages 282–283, review the two literary elements: rhythmic pattern and similes. Discuss how the rhythmic pattern adds to the "punch line" of the limerick. Then show how both limericks use similes to compare unlike things.

Have partners try to create limericks that compare unlike things. Remind them about the number and length of lines, and encourage them to write a good "punch line."

Self-Selected Reading

Objective Read independently and analyze descriptions
Materials • Leveled Readers or trade books at students' reading level

READ TO ANALYZE DESCRIPTIONS

Invite students to choose a nonfiction book for independent reading. For a list of theme-related titles, see pages T19–T20. Remind students to summarize the content as they read and to pay attention to how the author describes animals, objects, or people.

Afterward, have students summarize and compare information from their books. Ask them to describe one topic they read about to the group to see if they can convey as much detail as the author. If they cannot, discuss how summarizing what they have read can help them to identify and remember the most important information.

Academic Language

Throughout the week the English language learners will need help in building their understanding of the academic language used in daily instruction and assessment instruments. The following strategies will help to increase their language proficiency and comprehension of content and instructional words.

Oral Language For additional language support and oral vocabulary development, go to **www. macmillanmh.com**

Strategies to Reinforce Academic Language

■ **Use Context** Academic Language (see chart below) should be explained in the context of the task during Whole Group. Use gestures, expressions, and visuals to support meaning.

■ **Use Visuals** Use charts, transparencies, and graphic organizers to explain key labels to help students understand classroom language.

■ **Model** Demonstrate the task using academic language in order for students to understand instruction.

Academic Language Used in Whole Group Instruction

Content/Theme Words	Skill/Strategy Words	Writing/Grammar Words
architects (p. 261)	analogy (p. 262)	descriptive poem (p. 284)
homes (p. 261)	summarize (p. 263)	colorful and precise words (p. 284)
camouflage (p. 264)	relationship (p. 263)	lines and stanzas (p. 284)
	informational nonfiction (p. 264)	word choice (p. 284)
	limerick (p. 282)	contractions (p. 285l)
	simile (p. 282)	apostrophe (p. 285l)
	rhyme (p. 282)	possessive pronouns (p. 285J)
	rhythmic pattern (p. 282)	

ELL Leveled Reader Lesson

Before Reading

DEVELOP ORAL LANGUAGE

 Build Background Write the words *Architect* and *Builder* on the board and discuss their meanings. *Do animals build anything?* Discuss examples.

Review Vocabulary Write the vocabulary and support words on the board and discuss their meanings. Use each word in a sentence and check comprehension by asking students for other examples. *A bridge is built by people, so it's* man-made. *What other things are* man-made?

PREVIEW AND PREDICT

Point to the cover photograph and read the title aloud. Ask: *What is the bird building? How do birds build nests?* Explain that students will read about how birds build their nests.

Set a Purpose for Reading Show the Description Web. Ask students to complete a similar web to identify text structure.

During Reading

Choose from among the differentiated strategies below to support students' reading at all stages of language acquisition.

Beginning	**Intermediate**	**Advanced**
Shared Reading As you read, model how to find an example for the topic and details that describe it. Model how to use text, pictures, and captions to find information.	**Read Together** Read Chapter 1. Have students help find an example of a bird builder. Model how to use text, pictures, and captions to find details. Have students take turns reading the rest of the book. Ask them to use the strategy and fill in the web as they read.	**Independent Reading** Have students read the story. Write *Animal Builders* on top of the Description Web. Each day, ask them to use the strategy to fill in the web. Guide them to page 7 to use the information to complete the web.

After Reading

Remind students to use the vocabulary and story words in their whole group activities.

Objective

- To apply vocabulary and comprehension skills

Materials

- ELL Leveled Reader

ELL 5 Day Planner

DAY 1	• Academic Language • Oral Language and Vocabulary Review
DAY 2	• Academic Language • ELL Leveled Reader
DAY 3	• Academic Language • ELL Leveled Reader
DAY 4	• Academic Language • ELL Leveled Reader
DAY 5	• Academic Language • ELL Leveled Reader Comprehension Check and Literacy Activities

ELL Teacher's Guide for students who need additional instruction

Answer Questions

Test Strategy: Think and Search

EXPLAIN

- Good test takers think about where in the selection they are most likely to find the best answer to a question.

- **Think** about what the question asks you to find.

- **Search** the selection for the part or parts that will give you the correct answer.

- **Look for information:** There may be boldface print, headings, or text features to help you locate information. Look for information in more than one place.

MODEL

Remind students to record their answers on a separate sheet of paper.

Question 1 Read the question and all of the answer choices.

Think Aloud I know this question is asking me to look for information. Why is a tornado also called a twister? I will search for information related to the key words *tornado* and *twister* and look for answers there.

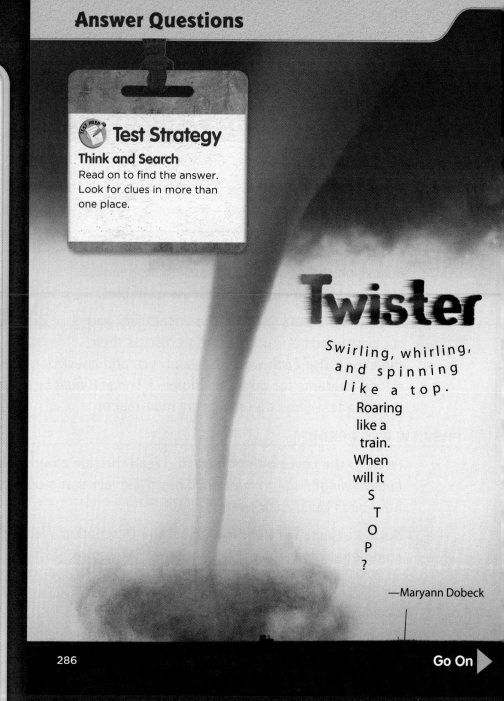

Test Strategy

Think and Search
Read on to find the answer. Look for clues in more than one place.

Twister

Swirling, whirling, and spinning like a top. Roaring like a train. When will it
S
T
O
P
?

—Maryann Dobeck

286

Go On ▶

Genre: Expository Writing

Expository writing gives information about a specific topic.

- **Main idea:** The writing introduces a main idea.
- **Details:** The main idea is supported by verifiable facts and details.
- **Summarizes:** The writing summarizes information from different sources.
- **Conclusion:** The writing draws a conclusion based on given facts.

TORNADOES: NATURE'S TOUGHEST STORMS

What Is a Tornado?

A tornado is a funnel of wind spinning very fast. Its wind can blow as fast as 300 miles per hour, which is almost six times the speed limit on a highway! Tornadoes can be caused by powerful thunderstorms called *supercells*. Cold, dry air mixing with warm, moist air makes a supercell. When the warm air in the supercell rises very quickly, it starts to spin into a tornado.

Tornadoes come in different shapes and sizes.

When a tornado reaches the ground, it begins to travel. The path of a tornado can be straight, zigzag, or circular. The damage along this path can be as wide as one or two miles and as long as 50 miles. Tornadoes typically touch down for only two or three minutes.

At first, a tornado's long cone shape is almost invisible. As it picks up dirt and other materials, the tornado becomes easier to see. A tornado can even pick up cars, trees, and parts of buildings.

Go On ▶ 287

The poem "Twister" uses the words *swirling, whirling,* and *spinning* to describe a tornado. All these words mean almost the same as *twisting.* The photograph on page 286 shows a tornado. Using this information, I think the answer to the question is B, the wind spins around. To make sure B is the best answer, I will look for more information. In the article, under the heading "What Is a Tornado?", I read that a tornado is a funnel of wind spinning very fast and that supercells spin into a tornado. The best answer is **B.**

GUIDED PRACTICE

Question 2 Read the question and all of the answer choices. Help students use Think and Search to answer the question.

Ask students to tell what words they have to look for in the text. (wind speed; power)

Point out the Fujita Pearson Tornado scale on page 288 that rates the power of tornadoes by wind speed. The two key words are in this part of the article. Give the following facts from the scale: A wind speed of 40–72 miles per hour can break tree branches. A wind speed of 261 miles per hour can lift up houses.

Ask students if a higher wind speed has more power. Could more power cause greater damage? (yes) So, the best answer is **C**. The greatest wind speed does the most damage.

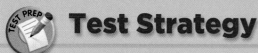
Answer Questions

APPLY

Question 3 Read the question and all of the answer choices.

- Have students use the **Think and Search** strategy to choose an answer.

- After students have chosen an answer ask: What did you think the question is asking you to do? (choose the best thing to do if a tornado is nearby)

- Where did you search for the answer? (in the passage and subheadings to find specific information about what people should do if a tornado is approaching)

- Where did you find information on what to do if a tornado approaches? (under the heading "Staying Safe in a Tornado" on page 288)

- The best answer is **C.**

Have students answer questions 4 and 5.

Question 4 Answer: Tornadoes can be formed from thunderstorms called supercells. Cold, dry air mixing with warm, moist air makes a supercell. When the warm air in a supercell rises quickly, it spins into a tornado.

Question 5 Possible answer: Loud winds and greenish skies are possible signs that a tornado is nearby. I should stay inside and find a place without windows, such as a cellar, bathroom, hallway, or closet. If I am in a car, I should stop and go inside a building as soon as possible.

The Dangers of Tornadoes

Tornadoes can be very dangerous. The Fujita Pearson Tornado Scale rates the power of tornadoes. Here's how it rates them:

F-0: Wind speed of 40–72 miles per hour. It can break tree branches and damage chimneys.

F-1: Wind speed of 73–112 miles per hour. It can damage roofs and overturn mobile homes.

F-2: Wind speed of 113–157 miles per hour. It can pick up trees and damage houses.

F-3: Wind speed of 158–205 miles per hour. It can destroy house roofs and walls, move cars, and overturn trains.

F-4: Wind speed of 207–260 miles per hour. It can knock down even strong walls in big buildings.

F-5: Wind speed of 261–318 miles per hour. It can lift up and carry houses. It can knock down anything in its path.

Staying Safe in a Tornado

Tornadoes are hard to predict. The sky might appear slightly greenish just before a tornado. Loud winds that sound like a train or an airplane might mean a tornado is very close.

The best place to take cover from a tornado is in a place without windows, such as a cellar, bathroom, hallway, or closet. People in cars should stop driving and get into a building as soon as possible.

Powerful tornadoes can turn sturdy homes to pieces.

288

Go On ▶

288

Directions: Answer the questions.

Tip

Look for information.

1. **According to the poem and the article, why is a tornado called a twister?**

   A   It twists things in its path.

   B   The wind spins around.

   C   It is like a puzzle.

   D   It is unpredictable.

2. **What is the relationship between wind speed and a tornado's power?**

   A   Wind speed doesn't matter.

   B   The slowest wind speed does the most damage.

   C   The greatest wind speed does the most damage.

   D   The greatest wind speed does the least damage.

3. **What do you think is the BEST thing to do if a tornado is nearby?**

   A   Get in a car and drive away from the tornado.

   B   Go to the top floor of the building.

   C   Go to a room that has no windows.

   D   Decide which path the tornado is taking.

4. **What causes a tornado to form?**

5. **The thunder is loud, and the sky looks green. What should you do? Use details from the selection in your answer.**

Writing Prompt

Some people get close enough to tornadoes to take photos and videos. Do you think this is a good idea? Write a two-paragraph speech explaining your point of view.

STOP 289

Writing Prompt

EXPLAIN

Before you begin, find the following information:

- What is the **mode** or **type** of writing?
- What is the **purpose?**
- Does the prompt tell me the **form** or **format?**
- Who is the **audience?**

MODEL/GUIDED PRACTICE

Discuss the writing mode. Read the prompt aloud. Reread the sentence "Do you think this is a good idea?" Ask: What is the sentence asking you to do? (to give your opinion)

Point out that students are going to write an explanation of why they think something.

Determine the purpose.
Ask: What clues in the prompt tell you what your writing should be about? (if you think it is a good idea for some people to get close enough to tornadoes to take photos and videos)

Determine the form and audience.
Ask students: What should be the format of your writing? (a two-paragraph speech) There is no specific audience stated, so write for your teacher.

ASSESS/CLOSE

Have students summarize the information they have found in the prompt and the clue words they used.

SCORING RUBRIC

4 Points	**3** Points	**2** Points	**1** Point
Writing is on topic. There is a beginning, middle, and end. Writing shows accuracy in punctuation and capitalization.	Writing is on topic. There is an attempt to sequence the events. Errors do not interfere with understanding.	Writing is generally on topic, but does not include sufficient order. Errors may make understanding difficult.	Writing may show little or no understanding of topic. There is an attempt to get words on paper. Writing shows no use of writing conventions.

Objectives

- Identify features of a compare-and-contrast article
- Plan and organize ideas for a compare-and-contrast article
- Draft and revise a compare-and-contrast article
- Proofread, publish, and present a compare-and-contrast article

Materials

- Unit Writing Transparencies 25–30

Features of a Compare-and-Contrast Article

- It tells how two things, ideas, or people are **both alike and different.**
- It **organizes details** in an **order that makes sense.**
- It uses **compare-and-contrast words** such as *both* and *unlike.*
- It **draws a conclusion** based on the comparison.

ELL | Access for All

Discuss and Write For the Prewriting step, have students in groups choose two jobs and compare and contrast them using the following questions: *What do people do? What clothes do they wear? Where do people work? What skills do people need? What makes a job interesting or fun to you?* This will help students build vocabulary and clarify ideas. Afterward, do the activity under Choose a Topic.

Descriptive Writing: Compare and Contrast

Read Like a Writer

Read the following excerpt from *Animal Homes* by Ann O. Squire. Explain to students that this excerpt is an example of writing that compares and contrasts. Have students follow along on **Student Book** page 266 as you read aloud. Ask students to listen for

- what two things are **both alike and different;**
- how the writer **organizes details;**
- examples of **compare-and-contrast words.**

Animal Homes

Animals need homes for many of the same reasons that people do. What are some of those reasons? Start by thinking about your own home, and the kinds of things you do there.

Eating is one very important thing you do every day. Your house has a kitchen where you store and prepare food. Some animals also keep food in their homes. Honeybees, for example, live in hives made up of waxy honeycombs. Each honeycomb has many six-sided cubbies, or cells, where the bees store their honey.

Discuss the Features

After reading, discuss the following questions with students.

- **How is a bee's home like a human home?** (Food is stored in both places.)
- **How is a bee's home different from a human home?** (A bee's home is a hive; a human home is usually a house.)
- **The writer organizes details by telling about what activity?** (eating and storing food)
- **What compare-and-contrast words does the writer use?** (same, also)

Access for All **Prewrite**

Set a Purpose Explain that one purpose or reason for writing a compare-and-contrast article is to describe how two things are both alike and different.

Know the Audience Have students think about who will read their articles, such as classmates or family members. Ask: *Who will your readers be? What do you want your readers to remember about the two things you are comparing and contrasting?*

Choose a Topic Ask students to brainstorm jobs they might like to do when they grow up. Ask the following questions to help students focus their ideas:

- What jobs seem fun or interesting to do?

- How are these jobs similar?

- How are they different?

- Why would you like to do one of these jobs?

Mini Lesson Organization

Display **Transparency 25** and explain that together you will follow David M.'s progress as he plans his compare-and-contrast article. Point out the following details in David's Venn diagram.

- He tells how the jobs of a baseball player and an actor are **alike.**

- He tells how the two jobs are **different.**

- He **organizes details** in an **order that makes sense.** He puts details about playing baseball on the left, details about acting on the right, and details about the way the two jobs are alike in the center.

Organize Ideas After discussing David M.'s Venn diagram, ask students to create a Venn diagram to plan their own compare-and-contrast articles. Use Transparency 25 to demonstrate how to organize ideas.

Peer Review

Think, Pair, Share Ask partners to discuss their Venn diagrams with one another. Encourage students to suggest additional details that might strengthen a partner's compare-and-contrast article. Students can share how their partners helped them.

Flexible Pairing Option Consider writing students' names on strips of paper. Pick two names at a time to match partners.

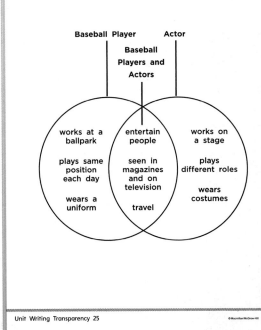

Writing Prompt

Write an article that compares and contrasts two things. You might want to compare and contrast two jobs. Choose jobs you would like to do when you grow up. Tell how the jobs are alike and different. Be sure to include compare-and-contrast words in your article.

Transparency 25

Baseball Player   Actor

Baseball Players and Actors

works at a ballpark | entertain people | works on a stage

plays same position each day | seen in magazines and on television | plays different roles

wears a uniform | travel | wears costumes

Unit Writing Transparency 25

Unit Writing Transparency 25

Practice Language and Models Show two objects. Write words such as *different, the same, both, but, too, unlike,* and *alike.* Help students use the words to compare the objects. You may also have students revisit the essay on **Student Book** page 182 and discuss the ways the author compares and contrasts information. Encourage students to use the sentences as a model for writing their sentences.

Transparency 26

Two Interesting Jobs
by David M.

The jobs of an actor and a baseball player are alike in many ways. They both gets paid to perform. They both gets paid to entertain people. Actors and ballplayers are often seen in magazines and on television. Their recognized everywhere they go. They gets to travel to many cities.

In other ways, actors and baseball players are different. A ballplayer works at a ballpark everyday. An actor works on a stage or on the set of a movie. A ballplayer learns how to play one position really well and wears one uniform. Actors learn how to become many different types of characters. They gets to wear many different costumes.

i think both jobs are interesting. Maybe I will try them both.

Unit Writing Transparency 26   © Macmillan/McGraw-Hill

Unit Writing Transparency 26

Draft

Mini Lesson | Similarities and Differences

Display **Transparency 26** and read it with students. As you discuss David M.'s draft, point out the following features:

- When I read David M.'s first sentence, I know right away that he is going to describe how the jobs of an actor and a baseball player are both **alike and different.**

- He organizes his **details in an order that makes sense.** In the first paragraph, he tells how the jobs are alike. In the second paragraph, he tells how the jobs are different.

- He includes **compare-and-contrast words** such as *both.*

- He ends by **drawing the conclusion** that both jobs would be interesting to try.

Point out that David will have the chance to revise and proofread his draft in later stages.

Review Your Venn Diagram Have students review their Venn diagrams before they begin writing. Suggest that they refer to their diagrams often as they write to keep the details of their comparisons in mind.

Write the Draft Remind students that their goal in writing a first draft is to get their thoughts on paper. They will have time to revise and proofread their work later. Share the following tips as students begin to write:

- Introduce the two jobs you are comparing and contrasting in your first sentence.

- Present your ideas and supporting details in a logical order.

- Include compare-and-contrast words.

Writer's Resources
Use the Library

As inspiration for their compare-and-contrast articles, suggest that students visit the school library to find nonfiction books about jobs that interest them. Remind them to use the library's card catalog or electronic catalog to search for material. Suggest that they consult the librarian if they need additional help locating what they want. Allow time for students to share the titles of any books of particular interest with their classmates. Encourage students to record new ideas they discovered during their visit to the school library.

Revise

Mini Lesson | Sentence Fluency

Display **Transparency 27** and discuss how David M. revises his compare-and-contrast article to make it excellent.

- In both the first and second paragraphs, he combines two sentences to make the writing less choppy. (Sentence Fluency)

- He deletes words from the phrase *on the set of a movie* to make the sentence read more smoothly. (Sentence Fluency)

- He revises his last sentence to make his conclusion a livelier and more personal statement. (Voice)

- He adds the compare-and-contrast words *also* and *in contrast* to show similarities and differences. (Word Choice)

Note that David M. will need to proofread his article to make final corrections.

Guide students to think about the following writing traits as they revise their compare-and-contrast articles.

Ideas and Content Can you add more details to help readers better understand how the two jobs are **alike and different**?

Organization Do you **organize details** in a way that readers will find easy to follow and understand? Do you need to rearrange any words or sentences?

Voice Does your writing show your interest in the topic and give a sense of your personality?

Word Choice Do you use **compare-and-contrast words** to clarify what is the same or different?

Sentence Fluency Do you use both short and long sentences? Do you vary the types of sentences you use?

Peer Review

Think, Pair, Share Have partners read one another's compare-and-contrast articles. Ask students to point out compare-and-contrast words and to suggest additional ones that might improve a partner's writing. Have students share how their partner's suggestions helped them.

Flexible Pairing Option Consider pairing students who wrote about similar jobs to enable them to discuss different points of view about these occupations.

Transparency 27

Two Interesting Jobs
by David M.

The jobs of an actor and a baseball player are alike in many ways. They both gets paid to perform. They both gets paid to entertain people. Actors and ballplayers are often seen in magazines and on television. Their recognized everywhere they go. They gets to travel to many cities.

In other ways, actors and baseball players are different. A ballplayer works at a ballpark everyday. An actor works on a stage or on the set of a movie. A ballplayer learns how to play one position really well and wears one uniform. Actors learn how to become many different types of characters. They gets to wear many different costumes.

Maybe I can be an actor in the winter and a baseball player in the summer! i think both jobs are interesting. Maybe I will try them both.

Have students read their articles aloud. Share these strategies.

SPEAKING STRATEGIES

- Speak with enthusiasm.

- Use props or drawings to illustrate the points you are comparing and contrasting.

- Pay attention to end punctuation. When you come to a question mark, remember to read with an asking voice.

LISTENING STRATEGIES

- Prepare to listen.

- Listen for similarities and differences.

Transparency 28

Two Interesting Jobs
by David M.

The jobs of an actor and a baseball player are alike in many ways. They both gets paid to perform. They both gets paid to entertain people. Actors and ballplayers are often seen in magazines and on television. Their recognized everywhere they go. They gets to travel to many cities.

In other ways, actors and baseball players are different. A ballplayer works at a ballpark every day. An actor works on a stage or on the set of a movie. A ballplayer learns how to play one position really well and wears one uniform. Actors learn how to become many different types of characters. They gets to wear many different costumes.

I think both jobs are interesting. Maybe I will try them both.

Unit Writing Transparency 28

Unit Writing Transparency 28

Proofread

Mini Lesson | Conventions

Display **Transparency 28** to point out examples of David M.'s proofreading corrections.

- He changes *gets* to the correct verb form *get*.

- He changes the possessive *their* to the contraction *they're*.

- He capitalizes the pronoun *i*.

Have students read and reread their compare-and-contrast article to find and correct usage errors. Review the use of proofreading marks on **Teacher's Resource Book** page 152. Have students apply them as they proofread. Remind students to indent paragraphs and use possessive pronouns correctly.

Peer Review

Think, Pair, Share Ask students to exchange papers and proofread their partner's edited article. Have partners carefully check the spelling of words with affixes.

TEACHER CONFERENCE

Before students finalize their articles, circulate among them and ask these questions to foster self-assessment:

- Did you tell how two things are alike and different?

- Did you present details in a logical order and use compare-and-contrast words?

- Did you draw a conclusion?

Publish

Have students write or type a final copy of their compare-and-contrast articles. Remind them to use appropriate spacing between words, sentences, and paragraphs and to use standard margins.

PRESENTATION

Have students bring or make props related to the two jobs they are comparing. Have students wear or display these props as they tell about each job.

Author's Chair Invite students who have developed strong comparisons to share their articles from the Author's Chair and to hold a question-and-answer session afterward.

 # Raising Scores

READ AND SCORE

Display **Transparency 29** and tell students to follow along as you read the compare-and-contrast article aloud. Then have students use their student rubric for Descriptive Writing: Compare-and-Contrast Article on page 157 of the **Teacher's Resource Book** to assess the writing sample.

Guide students to understand that this compare-and-contrast article is only a fair writing sample, which would score only a 2, and that they will work together in groups to improve it.

RAISE THE SCORE

Point out the following shortfalls in the writing sample:

Ideas and Content The writer has attempted to compare the jobs of a teacher and a doctor, but her first sentence does not clearly identify her purpose or main idea.

Organization Details do not follow in a logical order.

Word Choice The writer could use more compare-and-contrast words to clarify how the two jobs are alike and different.

Ask students to work in small groups and revise the compare-and-contrast article to raise the score. Remind them to refer to the student rubric.

SHARE AND COMPARE

Have groups share their revised versions with the class, explaining how they improved the writing. Then display **Transparency 30** to show the same compare-and-contrast article written at an excellent level. Have each group compare its revised version with the transparency. Remind students that although two versions vary, they may both be considered excellent papers. Then have students review the compare-and-contrast article they wrote to raise their scores.

Objective

- Revise a compare-and-contrast article to raise the writing score from a 2 to a 4.

CREATE A RUBRIC

Distribute copies of the blank rubric on page 159 or 160 in the Teacher's Resource Book. Remind students that the rubric should assess whether the compare-and-contrast article tells how two things are alike and different, presents details in an order that makes sense, and uses compare-and-contrast words. Students should include the following four levels to assess writing: Excellent, Good, Fair, and Unsatisfactory. They should discuss and apply rubrics independently and cooperatively.

 Transparency 30

Jobs That Help
by Kara P.

The jobs of a doctor and a teacher are alike in some ways. Doctors and teachers are both responsible for keeping their patients and students safe. Doctors and teachers have to go to college to learn how to do their jobs well.

In other ways, these two jobs are very different. Most doctors work in hospitals or in their offices. Teachers work in schools. Teachers are responsible for teaching many different subjects. Doctors try to focus on one area of medicine. Teachers work with the same group of students for a long period of time. Doctors see many different patients each day.

Doctors and teachers both have jobs that help other people. I think I want to be a doctor or a teacher when I grow up.

Unit Writing Transparency 30

Unit Writing Transparency 30

4-Point Rubric

Use this four-point rubric to assess student writing.

SCORING RUBRIC FOR DESCRIPTIVE WRITING: COMPARE AND CONTRAST ARTICLE

4 Excellent	3 Good	2 Fair	1 Unsatisfactory
Ideas and Content Presents a clear, original, and detailed comparison	**Ideas and Content** Presents a clear comparison; describes both similarities and differences	**Ideas and Content** Compares and contrasts two things, but lacks a sufficient number of details	**Ideas and Content** Does not compare two things
Organization Begins with a clear statement of the topic; logically organizes details; includes an effective closing	**Organization** Begins with a statement of the topic; logically organizes details	**Organization** Fails to state the topic clearly at the outset; may not order information in the most logical way	**Organization** Does not organize information in any logical way
Voice Reflects keen interest in the topic; relates the topic to the audience	**Voice** Reflects interest in the topic; relates the topic to the audience	**Voice** Reflects little personal involvement	**Voice** Reflects no interest in the topic
Word Choice Uses a variety of words to convey comparisons	**Word Choice** Uses a variety of compare and contrast words	**Word Choice** Uses few compare and contrast words; words are generally dull	**Word Choice** Uses no compare and contrast words; may misuse words
Sentence Fluency All sentences are clear and complete; the flow of the writing is uninterrupted; makes smooth connections between paragraphs	**Sentence Fluency** Sentences are clear and complete	**Sentence Fluency** Only some sentences are complete, clear, and easy to follow	**Sentence Fluency** Sentences are run on, incomplete, or confusing
Conventions Contains few or no mechanical, grammatical, and spelling errors; usage is standard throughout	**Conventions** Spelling, capitalization, punctuation, and usage are mostly correct	**Conventions** Makes frequent, noticeable mistakes that interfere with a reader's understanding of the text	**Conventions** Makes repeated and serious errors in grammar, spelling, mechanics, and usage
Presentation Text is easy to read; presentation is appropriate and appealing	**Presentation** Spacing and format support readability	**Presentation** Handwriting or word processing is inconsistent and may be difficult to read	**Presentation** Formatting is inconsistent or absent; spacing is random and confusing; handwriting is sometimes illegible

Refer to Anchor Papers for compare and contrast writing in the **Unit and Benchmark Assessment** pages 208–211 for a sample of each writing level.

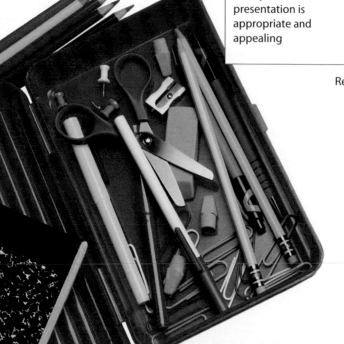

6-Point Rubric

Use this six-point rubric to assess student writing.

SCORING RUBRIC FOR DESCRIPTIVE WRITING: COMPARE AND CONTRAST ARTICLE

6 Exceptional	**5** Excellent	**4** Good	**3** Fair	**2** Poor	**1** Unsatisfactory
Ideas and Content Crafts a detailed comparison; shares fresh insights and observations	**Ideas and Content** Crafts a cohesive and carefully detailed comparison; makes some fresh observations and connections	**Ideas and Content** Presents a solid and clear comparison with details that help a reader understand the main idea	**Ideas and Content** Attempts to compare but includes ideas or details which do not fit the topic	**Ideas and Content** Has little control of task or seems unsure of the topic; ideas are vague	**Ideas and Content** Does not compare two occupations; writer is unfocused, or unsure of what she/he wants to say.
Organization Has a thoughtful sequence of facts and ideas; strong beginning and satisfying ending; details strengthen comparisons	**Organization** Presents a well-planned strategy that helps the reader follow and understand the comparisons	**Organization** Presents facts and observations in a logical sequence; has a clear beginning and ending	**Organization** Attempts to structure a comparison, but the logic is sometimes difficult to follow	**Organization** Has no clear structure; details don't fit where they are placed	**Organization** Shows extreme lack of organization; ideas are not connected; details, if presented, are incomplete, irrelevant, or vague
Voice Shows originality and involvement with the topic; brings a genuine personal style to the task	**Voice** Shows originality and strong involvement with the topic	**Voice** Tries to convey an authentic personality; shows involvement with the topic	**Voice** Does not sound authentic or natural	**Voice** Is not involved in sharing observations with a reader	**Voice** Does not address an audience at all; does not have a sense of sharing a personal message or style
Word Choice Careful choices make the comparison unusually precise and interesting	**Word Choice** Makes thoughtful use of accurate, colorful language; points of comparison are clear and interesting	**Word Choice** Communicates the main idea; uses a variety of words that fit the task	**Word Choice** May attempt to use a variety of words, but some are used inaccurately	**Word Choice** Words are dull, general, or inaccurate	**Word Choice** Uses words that do not compare, or are vague and confusing
Sentence Fluency Simple and complex sentences flow in a natural rhythm; writing is easy to follow when read aloud	**Sentence Fluency** Crafts well-paced, simple, and complex sentences that flow naturally	**Sentence Fluency** Uses simple and complex constructions, with stronger control of simple sentences	**Sentence Fluency** Most sentences are readable but show little variety in length and pattern	**Sentence Fluency** Sentences may be choppy or awkward; patterns are monotonous	**Sentence Fluency** Sentences are incomplete, rambling, or confusing
Conventions Is skilled in most writing conventions; proper use of the rules of English enhances clarity, meaning, and style; editing is largely unnecessary	**Conventions** Shows skill in most writing conventions; needs little editing	**Conventions** May make some errors in spelling, capitalization, punctuation, or usage which do not interfere with meaning; some editing is needed	**Conventions** Makes noticeable errors that interfere with meaning	**Conventions** Makes frequent errors in spelling, word choice, punctuation, and usage	**Conventions** Frequent and serious errors in spelling, punctuation, and usage make the text hard to read
Presentation Text is easy to read whether typed or handwritten; formatting is appropriate and consistent	**Presentation** Margins are mostly even; font style and size are appropriate; handwriting is legible	**Presentation** Text is readable, although formatting is at times inconsistent	**Presentation** Margins and handwriting are variable; formatting is at times inappropriate	**Presentation** Text is difficult to read; formatting and spacing are not uniform	**Presentation** Handwriting is illegible; type size and font are inappropriate; lacks any consistent formatting

Refer to Anchor Papers for writing that compares in the **Unit and Benchmark Assessment** pages 208–211 for a sample of each writing level.

Working with Graphics

Objectives

- Practice using tools in a paint program
- Learn to scan a picture and save to desktop

Materials

- www.macmillanmh.com/reading
- paint program at Computer Literacy at www.macmillanmh.com/reading
- scanner

Vocabulary

graphics pictures that are created, stored, or printed on a computer

paintbrush tool a tool in a paint program used to draw graphics

fill tool a tool in a paint program used to fill an area with a solid color

color palette a set of available colors

scanner an input tool that puts words and pictures into the computer

ACCESS PRIOR KNOWLEDGE

Discuss with students:

- What are some ways people use drawings and **graphics**?

- How can **graphics** help you with a school project or with your homework?

EXPLAIN

Introduce the lesson vocabulary by writing each word on the board and asking for its definition.

- Discuss with students the different types of **graphics** you can create with or import into a paint program. What are the various things you can do with the graphics?

- Explain that students will use a paint program on the computer to create their own graphics.

MODEL

- Open the paint program from the Computer Literacy section at **www.macmillanmh.com/reading**. Show students how to use the shape icons to draw shapes. Demonstrate how to use the **paintbrush tool** to free draw. Have students practice both.

- Using the **fill tool**, show students how to select a color from the **color palette** and fill in the shape that was already created.

- Using the select option, demonstrate how to select the free-drawn object and move it around the page. Then delete it.

Productivity Tools

- **Scanners** are used to input information, both graphics and words, into a computer.

- Show students how to place a picture on the scanner and press the start button to scan.

- Save the scan onto the desktop.

- Demonstrate how to import the scan into the paint program and edit. If possible, have students do the same.

GUIDED PRACTICE

Have students connect to **www.macmillanmh.com/reading** and go to the Computer Literacy Lesson for Grade 3 Unit 5.

Remind students to save their work regularly!

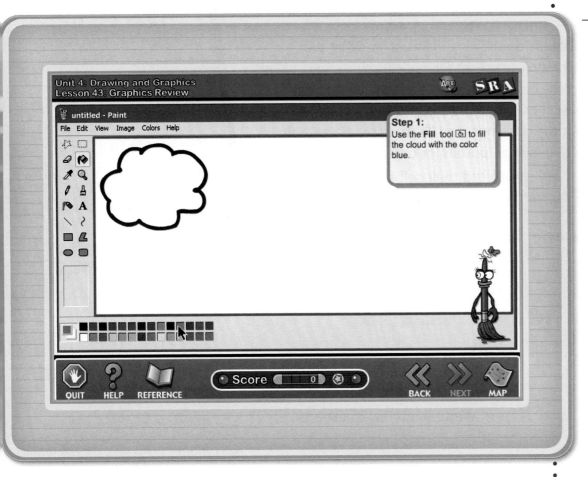

The online practice lesson is an excerpt from SRA TechKnowledge. For information about the full SRA TechKnowledge program, go to **www.sratechknowledge.com**.

Leveled Practice

Approaching Level

Have students draw a free-form drawing with the paintbrush tool. Have them write a short paragraph to describe their drawing.

On Level

Have students scan a picture of their choosing. Have them import the document into the paint program, edit it, and save it to the desktop.

Beyond Level

Have students scan a picture of an animal home and import it into the paint program. Have them import the document into the paint program and use the drawing tools to add in an appropriate animal.

Theme Project Wrap-Up

Research and Inquiry

After students complete Step 1, Step 2, Step 3, and Step 4 of their project, have them work on the following:

Step 5 **Create the Presentation** Have students share what they learned in their library research and interviews by making a class scrapbook about the challenges they investigated. Students should plan a design or layout, use their notes to write descriptive paragraphs about the challenge, and illustrate the paragraphs with photographs, drawings, posters, or other visuals.

When students have completed their self-selected or cross-curricular projects, plan a time when they can present.

Step 6 **Review and Evaluate** Use these questions to help you and students evaluate their research and presentation.

Teacher Checklist

Assess the Research Process

Planning the Project
- ✔ Participated in discussion.
- ✔ Narrowed the topic.
- ✔ Identified an interviewee.

Doing the Project
- ✔ Wrote interview questions.
- ✔ Conducted an interview.
- ✔ Synthesized information.

Assess the Presentation

Speaking
- ✔ Spoke clearly, using appropriate pacing.
- ✔ Made eye contact.
- ✔ Maintained a clear focus.

Representing
- ✔ Planned a design or layout.
- ✔ Wrote labels for pictures and photos.
- ✔ Let everyone see their pages.

Assess the Listener

Listening
- ✔ Listened without interrupting.
- ✔ Made eye contact with the speaker.
- ✔ Related prior experiences to those of the speaker.
- ✔ Asked at least one relevant and thoughtful question.

Student Checklist

Research Process
- ✔ Did you investigate a challenge?
- ✔ Did you identify a source whom you could interview?
- ✔ Did you prepare questions?

Presenting

Speaking
- ✔ Did you present clearly?
- ✔ Did you stay on the topic?
- ✔ Could you answer your audience's questions?

Representing
- ✔ Did you use illustrations to help explain the challenge?
- ✔ Did you arrange your pictures and words effectively?
- ✔ Did you make sure everyone got to see your pages?

SCORING RUBRIC

4 Excellent	**3** Good	**2** Fair	**1** Unsatisfactory
The student: • presents the information in a clear and imaginative way. • uses words and visuals that effectively present important information. • may offer sophisticated personal reflections.	The student: • presents the information in a fairly clear way. • uses words and visuals that present relevant information. • may offer thoughtful personal reflections.	The student: • struggles to present the information clearly. • may use adequate words and visuals. • may offer irrelevant personal reflections.	The student: • may not grasp the task. • may present sketchy information in a disorganized way. • may have extreme difficulty with research.

 Home-School Connection

Invite family members, other students, and members of the community to attend students' presentations of their projects. Make sure to include people who gave interviews.

- Introduce each guest by name and describe his or her relationship to students or the community. Remind students to respect the age, gender, social position, and cultural traditions of those who view their projects.

- Videotape the presentations for family members to borrow or to show at the parent/teacher conferences. Include a question-and-answer period for students to respond and pose follow-up questons. Remind students that, while they may use informal language when speaking to classmates, they should speak more formally to adults.

End-of-Unit Assessment

Administer the Test

Unit 5 Reading Assessment, pp. 81–96

TESTED SKILLS AND STRATEGIES

COMPREHENSION STRATEGIES AND SKILLS

- Strategies: Make Inferences and Analyze, Summarize
- Skills: Sequence, Cause and Effect, Fact and Opinion, Make and Confirm Predictions, Description

VOCABULARY STRATEGIES

- Word Parts
- Context Clues
- Analogies

TEXT FEATURES AND STUDY SKILLS

- Calendar
- Editorial
- Map
- Skim and scan a nonfiction article

GRAMMAR, MECHANICS, USAGE

- Pronouns (subject and object, possessive)
- Capitalizing I and proper nouns
- Apostrophes
- Pronoun-verb contractions
- Pronoun-verb agreement
- Contractions and possessive pronouns

WRITING

- Descriptive Writing

Use Multiple Assessments for Instructional Planning

To create instructional profiles for your students, look for patterns in the results from any of the following assessments.

Fluency Assessment

Plan appropriate fluency-building activities and practice to help all students achieve the following goal: **97–117 WCPM**

Running Records

Use the instructional reading level determined by the Running Record calculations for regrouping decisions.

Benchmark Assessments

Administer tests three times a year as an additional measure of both student progress and the effectiveness of the instructional program.

Technology

Progress Reporter
Macmillan/McGraw-Hill

- Administer the **Unit Assessment** electronically.
- Score all tests electronically.
- Available on CD-ROM or online.

Analyze the Data

Use information from a variety of informal and formal assessments, as well as your own judgment, to assist in your instructional planning. Students who consistently score at the lowest end of each range should be evaluated for Intervention. Use the **Diagnostic Assessment** in the Intervention Teacher's Edition.

Diagnose		Prescribe
ASSESSMENTS	**IF...**	**THEN...**
UNIT TEST	0–23 questions correct	Reteach tested skills using the **Additional Lessons** (pp. T1–T12).
FLUENCY ASSESSMENT		
Oral Reading Fluency	89–96 WCPM	Fluency Solutions
	0–88 WCPM	Evaluate for Intervention.
RUNNING RECORDS	Level 30 or below	Reteach comprehension skills using the **Additional Lessons** (pp. T1–T5). Provide additional Fluency activities.

For users of DIBELS

Use the results from the DIBELS Progress Monitoring tests to confirm instructional decisions.

DIBELS LINK

PROGRESS MONITORING
Use your DIBELS results to Inform Instruction.

IF...
DIBELS Oral Reading Fluency (**DORF**)   0–109

THEN...
Use the Fluency Solutions Audio CD.

For users of TPRI

Use the scores from the TPRI Inventory tests to confirm instructional decisions.

TPRI LINK

PROGRESS MONITORING
Use your TPRI scores to inform instruction.

IF...
Graphophonemic Awareness	Still Developing
Reading Fluency/Accuracy	Frustrational on Grade 3, Story 1
Reading Comprehension Questions	0–5 correct

THEN...
Use the Fluency Solutions Audio CD. Use the Comprehension Skills **Additional Lessons** suggestions in the above chart.

Glossary

INTRODUCTION

Introduce students to the Glossary by reading through the introduction and looking over the pages with them. Encourage the class to talk about what they see.

Words in a glossary, like words in a dictionary, are listed in **alphabetical order.** Point out the **guide words** at the top of each page that tell the first and last words appearing on that page.

ENTRIES

Point out examples of **main entries,** or entry words and entries. Read through a sample entry with the class, identifying each part. Have students note the order in which information is given: entry word(s) with syllable division, pronunciation respelling, part of speech, definition(s), example sentence(s).

Note that if more than one definition is given for a word, the definitions are numbered. Note also the format used for a word that is more than one part of speech.

Review the **parts of speech** by identifying each in a sentence:

Interjection	article	noun	conjunction	adjective	noun
Wow!	A	dictionary	and	handy	glossary

verb	adverb	pronoun	preposition	noun
tell	almost	everything	about	words!

HOMOGRAPHS/HOMOPHONES/HOMONYMS

Point out that some entries are for multiple-meaning words called **homographs.** Homographs have the same spellings but have different origins and meanings, and, in some cases, different pronunciations.

Explain that students should not confuse homographs with **homophones** or **homonyms.** Homophones are words that have the same pronunciation but have different spellings and meanings. Homonyms are words that have the same pronunciation and spelling but have different meanings. Provide students with examples.

PRONUNCIATION KEY

Explain the use of the pronunciation key (either the short key, at the bottom of every other page, or the long key, at the beginning of the Glossary). Demonstrate the difference between primary stress and secondary stress by pronouncing a word with both. Pronounce the words both correctly and incorrectly to give students a clearer understanding of the proper pronunciations.

WORD HISTORY

The Word History feature explains the **etymology** of select words. Explain to students that etymology is the history of a word from its origin to its present form. A word's etymology explains which language it comes from and what changes have occurred in its spelling and/or meaning. Many English words are derivatives of words from other languages, such as Latin or Greek. Derivatives are formed from base or root words. Many everyday words have interesting and surprising stories behind them. Note that word histories can help us remember the meanings of difficult words.

Allow time for students to further explore the Glossary and make their own discoveries.

Glossary

What Is a Glossary?

A Glossary can help you find the **meanings** of words in this book that you may not know. The words in the Glossary are listed in **alphabetical order**. **Guide words** at the top of each page tell you the first and last words on the page.

Each word is divided into syllables. The way to pronounce the word is given next. You can understand the pronunciation respelling by using the **pronunciation key** on page 409. A shorter key appears at the bottom of every other page. When a word has more than one syllable, a dark accent mark (´) shows which syllable is stressed. In some words, a light accent mark (´) shows which syllable has a less heavy stress. Sometimes an entry includes a second meaning for the word.

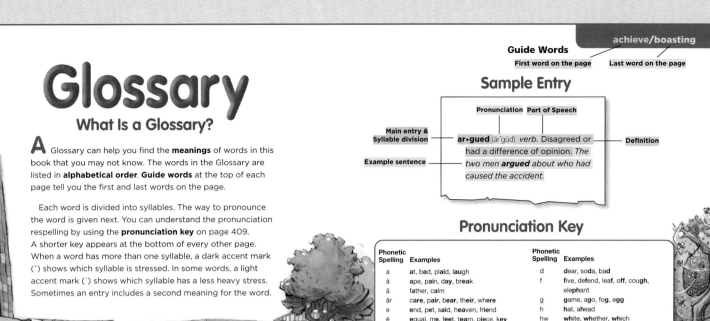

Guide Words
First word on the page   Last word on the page
achieve/boasting

Sample Entry

Pronunciation   Part of Speech
Main entry & Syllable division → **ar•gued** (är´gūd) *verb.* Disagreed or had a difference of opinion. *The two men **argued** about who had caused the accident.* ← Definition
Example sentence →

Pronunciation Key

Phonetic Spelling	Examples	Phonetic Spelling	Examples
a	at, bad, plaid, laugh	d	dear, soda, bad
ā	ape, pain, day, break	f	five, defend, leaf, off, cough, elephant
ä	father, calm	g	game, ago, fog, egg
âr	care, pair, bear, their, where	h	hat, ahead
e	end, pet, said, heaven, friend	hw	white, whether, which
ē	equal, me, feet, team, piece, key	j	joke, enjoy, gem, page, edge
i	it, big, give, hymn	k	kite, bakery, seek, tack, cat
ī	ice, fine, lie, my	l	lid, sailor, feel, ball, allow
îr	ear, deer, here, pierce	m	man, family, dream
o	odd, hot, watch	n	not, final, pan, knife, gnaw
ō	old, oat, toe, low	ng	long, singer
ô	coffee, all, taught, law, fought	p	pail, repair, soap, happy
ôr	order, fork, horse, story, pour	r	ride, parent, wear, more, marry
oi	oil, toy	s	sit, aside, pets, cent, pass
ou	out, now, bough	sh	shoe, washer, fish, mission, nation
u	up, mud, love, double	t	tag, pretend, fat, dressed
ū	use, mule, cue, feud, few	th	thin, panther, both
ü	rule, true, food, fruit	th	these, mother, smooth
ù	put, wood, should, look	v	very, favor, wave
ûr	burn, hurry, term, bird, word, courage	w	wet, weather, reward
ə	about, taken, pencil, lemon, circus	y	yes, onion
b	bat, above, job	z	zoo, lazy, jazz, rose, dogs, houses
ch	chin, such, match	zh	vision, treasure, seizure

Aa

a•chieve (ə chēv´) *verb.* To do or carry out successfully. *Did Thomas **achieve** his goal of cleaning his desk before the bell rang?*

ap•pli•an•ces (ə plī´əns əz) *plural noun.* Small machines or devices that have particular uses, such as toasters, refrigerators, and washing machines. *The store was crowded because of the sale on kitchen **appliances**.*

ar•chi•tects (är´ki tekts´) *plural noun.* People who design buildings and supervise their construction. *A group of **architects** showed up at the empty lot and began planning the building they wanted to make there.*

ar•gued (är´gūd) *verb.* Disagreed or had a difference of opinion. *The two men **argued** about who had caused the accident.*

ar•tist's (är´tists) *possessive noun.* Belonging to a person who is skilled in painting, music, literature, or any other form of art. *The chef uses an **artist's** touch when he puts the toppings on his famous desserts.*

au•to•mat•i•cal•ly (ô´tə mat´ik əl lē) *adverb.* Gets done without a person's control. *Digestion takes place in the body **automatically**.*

Bb

batches (bach´əz) *plural noun.* Groups of things prepared or gathered together. *Tracey and Darryl made several **batches** of cookies for the bake sale at the library.*

beamed (bēmd) *verb.* **1.** Shined brightly. *The sun **beamed** down on the field.* **2.** Smiled brightly. *Marleigh **beamed** when she thought about the joke Raffi told yesterday.*

blos•somed (blos´əmd) *verb.* Grew or developed. *The student kept practicing until she **blossomed** into a wonderful violinist.*

boast•ing (bōst´ing) *verb.* Talking with too much pride. *Everyone got annoyed when Lisa started **boasting** about her new bicycle.*

busi•ness (biz´nis) *noun.* **1.** The work a person does to earn a living. *Kenneth worked in the fashion **business** for eight years.* **2.** The buying and selling of things; trade. *The kite shop does good **business** in the summer.*

Cc

cap•ture (kap´chər) *verb.* To catch and hold a person, animal, or thing. *The park rangers were trying to **capture** the bear that was roaming the picnic area.*

clumps (klumps) *plural noun.* Groups or clusters. *After Jennifer went swimming, she had **clumps** of knots in her long hair.*

com•bine (kəm bīn´) *verb.* To join together; unite. *We will **combine** eggs, flour, and milk to make batter for pancakes.*

com•mu•ni•ty (kə mū´ni tē) *noun.* **1.** A group of people who live together in the same place. *Our **community** voted to build a new library.* **2.** A group of people who share a common interest. *The scientific **community** is involved in important research projects.*

con•flict (kon´flikt) *noun.* A strong disagreement. *The school board is in **conflict** with the mayor's office about where to build the playground.*

con•struc•tion (kən struk´shən) *noun.* The act or process of building something. *It was interesting to watch the **construction** of the new grocery store.*

con•tain (kən tān´) *verb.* To hold inside. *The storage boxes **contain** clothes.*

at; āpe; fär; câre; end; mē; it; īce; pîerce; hot; ōld; sông; fôrk; oil; out; up; ūse; rüle; pùll; tûrn; chin; sing; shop; thin; this; hw in white; zh in treasure.

The symbol ə stands for the unstressed vowel sound in about, taken, pencil, lemon, and circus.

con·ver·sa·tion (kon´vər sā´shən) *noun.* Talk between two or more people. *It was difficult to have a* **conversation** *with Jerry because of all the loud construction noises.*

crate (krāt) *noun.* A box made of pieces of wood. *The grocery store worker emptied the* **crate** *filled with grapes onto the fruit stand.*

crouch (krouch) *verb.* To stoop or bend low with the knees bent. *The firefighters had to* **crouch** *to pick up the hose.*

Dd

de·clared (di klârd´) *verb.* Stated strongly and firmly. *They* **declared** *that they were right and nothing would change their minds.*

de·mand (di mand´) *noun.* An urgent requirement or need. *Katie knew there was a* **demand** *for blankets at the dog shelter.*

de·serve (di zûrv´) *verb.* To have a right to something. *I believe I* **deserve** *to be on the soccer team because I practiced after school and on weekends.*

de·ter·min·a·tion (di tûr´mə nā´shən) *noun.* A firm purpose. *Miguel's* **determination** *made him study very hard to get the best test score in the class.*

di·rec·tions (di rek´shənz) *plural noun.* **1.** Lines leading to a place or point. *The class decided to walk in two different* **directions**: *the boys headed for the lake, and the girls went toward the woods.* **2.** Orders or instructions on how to do something or how to act. *Follow the* **directions** *on the package to cook the soup.*

dis·ap·pear (dis´ə pîr´) *verb.* To stop existing or become extinct. *Elephants began to* **disappear** *because so many people hunted them for their tusks.*

dis·pute (dis pūt´) *noun.* A disagreement. *I had a* **dispute** *with my sister about her messiness.*

down·town (doun´toun´) *adjective.* Located in the main part or business district of a town. *My mother works in the* **downtown** *office.*

Ee

en·clos·ure (en klō´zhər) *noun.* A place that is surrounded by a fence or wall on all sides. *The animals were kept in an* **enclosure** *until their owners came to pick them up.*

e·quip·ment (i kwip´mənt) *noun.* Anything that is provided for a special purpose or use. *The firefighters showed the class all the different* **equipment** *they have and how it is used.*

es·cape (es kāp´) *verb.* To become free. *The students wanted the bell to ring so they could* **escape** *the heat of the classroom.*

ex·act (eg zakt´) *adjective.* Very accurate. *I need to know the* **exact** *time because I can't be one minute late.*

ex·ist·ed (eg zis´təd) *verb.* Was real. *Tyler couldn't believe that a movie theater once* **existed** *where his house now stood.*

Ff

fab·ric (fab´rik) *noun.* A material made from fibers, such as cotton, silk, or nylon. *My mother bought the* **fabric** *to make our costumes.*

Word History

Fabric has a complicated history, from the Latin *faber,* meaning "workman," and *fabrica,* "craft" or "workshop," to the Old French *fabrique,* and finally the Middle English *fabryke,* which meant "something constructed."

fled (fled) *verb.* Ran away from something. *Many families* **fled** *the hurricane coming toward them.*

form (fôrm) *noun.* The outline of something; shape. *Steve saw the dim* **form** *of the Golden Gate Bridge through the fog.*

func·tion (fungk´shən) *noun.* A specific use or purpose. *An usher's* **function** *is to help people find their seats.*

at; āpe; fär; câre; end; mē; it; īce; pîerce; hot; ōld; sōng; fôrk; oil; out; up; ūse; rūle; pûll; tûrn; chin; sing; shop; thin; this; hw in white; zh in treasure. | The symbol ə stands for the unstressed vowel sound in about, taken, pencil, lemon, and circus.

Gg

ge·o·met·ric (jē´ə met´rik) *adjective.* **1.** Consisting of or decorated with lines, angles, circles, triangles, or similar shapes. *The rug in my bedroom has a* **geometric** *design of blue circles and yellow squares.* **2.** Having to do with geometry. *A cone is a* **geometric** *shape.*

gift (gift) *noun.* Something given to someone, such as a present. *Nigel received a special* **gift** *on his birthday.*

grace (grās) *noun.* Beautiful movement, or style. *The dancer moved with* **grace** *on the stage.*

grown·ups (grōn´ups) *plural noun.* Adults. *The children were playing games while the* **grownups** *prepared the dessert.*

grum·bled (grum´bəld) *verb.* Complained in a low voice. *The class* **grumbled** *when the teacher gave them a lot of homework to do over the holiday.*

Hh

harm·ing (härm´ing) *verb.* Doing damage to or hurting. *The construction company was told that it was* **harming** *the environment because it cut down so many trees.*

his·tor·i·cal (hi stôr´i kəl) *adjective.* Having to do with history. *This book contains* **historical** *information, such as how our town began and who its leaders have been.*

hives (hīvz) *plural noun.* Boxes or houses for bees to live in. *We were warned to stay away from the bee* **hives** *that were in the park.*

Ii

im·age (im´ij) *noun.* A picture of a person or thing. *I still have an* **image** *in my head of the beautiful sunset at the beach.*

Word History

Image comes from the Latin *imago,* or *imitari,* "to imitate."

in·di·vid·u·al (in´də vij´ū əl) *adjective.* Single; separate. *The coffee was served with* **individual** *packets of sugar.*

in·flu·enced (in´flū ənst) *verb.* Had an effect on, especially by giving suggestions or by serving as an example. *The older members of my family* **influenced** *me in many ways when I was growing up.*

in·gre·di·ent (in grē´dē ənt) *noun.* Any one of the parts used in a recipe or mixture. *The baker was missing one* **ingredient** *for making a cake.*

in·ter·rupt·ed (in´tə rup´təd) *verb.* Broke in upon or stopped something or someone. *A loud car alarm* **interrupted** *our teacher from speaking.*

in·ter·viewed (in´tər vūd´) *verb.* Obtained information from someone by asking questions. *Last night my favorite actress was* **interviewed** *on television.*

in·volved (in volvd´) *adjective.* Taken up with. *Many students said that they wanted to become* **involved** *in raising money for the park.*

Kk

kind·heart·ed (kind´här´tid) *adjective.* Having or showing a friendly or gentle nature. *The* **kindhearted** *woman put food outside her house for birds to eat during the winter.*

Ll

leak·y (lē´kē) *adjective.* Having a hole or small opening that water, light, or air can pass through. *The* **leaky** *hose caused a big puddle whenever I tried to water the plants.*

lone·some (lōn´səm) *adjective.* Not often visited by people; deserted. *The* **lonesome** *house in the swamp was a sad sight.*

at; āpe; fär; câre; end; mē; it; īce; pîerce; hot; ōld; sōng; fôrk; oil; out; up; ūse; rūle; pûll; tûrn; chin; sing; shop; thin; this; hw in white; zh in treasure. | The symbol ə stands for the unstressed vowel sound in about, taken, pencil, lemon, and circus.

bringing the most good luck. *Of all the contest winners, James was the **luckiest**; he won the grand prize.*

Mm

mag·nif·i·cent (mag nif´ə sənt) *adjective.* Very beautiful and grand. *We walked through the **magnificent** garden and admired all the beautiful flowers.*

mar·mo·sets (mär´mə zetz´) *plural noun.* Small, tropical monkeys with claws, soft thick fur, tufted ears, and long tails. *Michael enjoyed watching the **marmosets** at play.*

mas·ter·piece (mas´tər pēs´) *noun.* **1.** A great work of art. *The painting Mona Lisa by Da Vinci is thought to be a **masterpiece**.* **2.** Something done with great skill. *Her plan to surprise her brother on his birthday was a **masterpiece**.*

marmoset

Nn

na·tive (nā´tiv) *adjective.* Originally living or growing in a region or country. *The cheetah is **native** to sub-Saharan Africa.*

need·y (nē´dē) *adjective.* Very poor; not having enough to live on. *Food and clothing were donated to **needy** families in the area.*

news·pa·per (nüz´pā´pər) *noun.* A publication printed on sheets of paper that contain news and are published every day or every week. *Many people read the **newspaper** every morning on the way to work.*

numb (num) *adjective.* Lacking feelings. *The members of the basketball team were **numb** after they lost the championship game.*

Oo

of·fi·cial (ə fish´əl) *adjective.* Coming from or approved by authority. *The referee announced the **official** score of the basketball game.*

or·gan·i·za·tion (ôr´gə ni zā´shən) *noun.* A group of people joined together for a specific purpose. *Her father joined a business **organization**.*

done, thought of, or used for the first time; new. *There are not many **original** ideas coming out of Hollywood anymore.* **2.** Able to do, make, or think of something new or different. *One doesn't need to be an **original** thinker to watch television.* **3.** Relating to or belonging to the origin or beginning of something; first. *The **original** owners moved out of the house years ago.*

own·ers (ō´nərz) *plural noun.* People who possess something. *Sarah was very proud that the knitting shop was doing well because she was one of the **owners**.*

Pp

per·son·al·i·ty (pûr´sə nal´i tē) *noun.* All the qualities, traits, habits, and behavior of a person. *It was in her **personality** to always be cheerful.*

pit·i·ful (pit´i fəl) *adjective.* Making people feel sorrow for. *The boy standing outside in the cold without his coat looked **pitiful**.*

Things that are owned by someone. *Many of his **possessions** were stolen by thieves who broke into his house.*

pow·ered (pou´ərd) *verb.* Filled with the energy to function or operate. *The toy truck was **powered** by batteries.*

pre·served (pri zûrvd´) *verb.* Protected; kept from harm. *The refrigerator door was closed so that the food's freshness could be **preserved**.*

pride (prīd) *noun.* **1.** A person's feeling of self-respect, dignity, and self-worth. *Although Rhonda did not score an A in science class, she never lost her sense of **pride**.* **2.** A company of lions. *The antelope were startled by a small **pride** moving in their direction.*

at; āpe; fär; câre; end; mē; it; īce; pîerce; hot; ōld; sông; fôrk; oil; out; up; ūse; rūle; púll; tûrn; chin; sing; shop; thin; <u>th</u>is; hw in white; zh in treasure.

The symbol ə stands for the unstressed vowel sound in about, taken, pencil, lemon, and circus.

---

pro·duce (prə düs´ *for verb*; prō´düs *for noun*) *verb.* To make or create something. *The class was asked to **produce** a play about the signing of the Declaration of Independence. noun.* Farm products, such as fruits and vegetables. *Mom likes to buy fresh **produce** from the farmer's market.*

profits (prof´its) *plural noun.* Amounts of money earned on sales. *The difference in **profits** that winter between the two shops was small.*

pro·tect (prə tekt´) *verb.* To defend from harm. *Mr. Trang put on a heavy overcoat to **protect** himself from the cold.*

pur·chased (pûr´chəst) *verb.* Got something by paying money for it. *Lester's mother **purchased** a bicycle to give to him for his birthday.*

Qq

quar·rel·ing (kwôr´əl ing´) *verb.* Having a heated argument. *My uncles were always **quarreling** about which baseball team was better.*

Rr

rebuild (rē bild´) *verb.* To build again or repair. *The farmer wanted to **rebuild** his shed after the storm blew it down.*

rec·i·pes (res´ə pēz) *plural noun.* Lists of ingredients and instructions for making something to eat or drink. *My mother has many cookie **recipes**.*

rent (rent) *noun.* A payment for the use of something. *The **rent** for the house was more than he was willing to pay. verb.* **1.** To get the right to use something in return for payment. *Katie and Jill planned to **rent** an apartment together once they finished college.* **2.** To give the right to use something in return for payment. *The landlord wanted to **rent** out the apartment to a quiet tenant.*

re·quire·ments (ri kwīr´mənts) *plural noun.* Things that are necessary; demands or needs. *There were certain **requirements** the students had to meet before they could move on to the next grade.*

re·search (rē´sûrch, ri sûrch´) *noun.* A careful study or investigation in order to learn facts. *A lot of **research** had to be done before the paper could be written.*

> **Word History**
>
> The Old French *recerchier*, which means "to search closely," is where the word research comes from.

re·solve (ri zolv´) *verb.* To settle, explain, or solve. *Barry can **resolve** the situation by offering to pay for anything that has been broken.*

re·spect (ri spekt´) *verb.* To have or show honor or consideration. *It is important to **respect** the opinions of others, even if you don't agree with everything they say.*

re·treats (ri trēts´) *verb.* Goes back or withdraws, as from danger. *A tigress **retreats** when it realizes it is outnumbered. plural noun.* Places to go to for safety, peace, and comfort. *Staying in **retreats** was a helpful way for Bob to leave his problems behind him.*

ru·ined (rü´ind) *verb.* Damaged greatly or harmed. *The flood **ruined** all our carpets in the basement.*

Ss

sched·ule (skej´ül, əl) *noun.* A list of times, events, or things to do. *He checked his **schedule** to make sure he would be available.*

> **Word History**
>
> Schedule has a long history: starting with the Greek *skhida*, "to split"; the Latin *scida*, "papyrus strip"; the Old French *cedule*, and Middle English *sedule*, which both mean "slip of parchment" or "paper, note."

at; āpe; fär; câre; end; mē; it; īce; pîerce; hot; ōld; sông; fôrk; oil; out; up; ūse; rūle; púll; tûrn; chin; sing; shop; thin; <u>th</u>is; hw in white; zh in treasure.

The symbol ə stands for the unstressed vowel sound in about, taken, pencil, lemon, and circus.

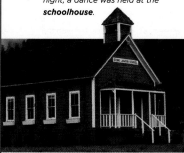

building used as a school. *On Friday night, a dance was held at the* **schoolhouse**.

scram·bled (skram´bəld) *verb.* Moved or climbed quickly. *We all* **scrambled** *to the finish line in the three-legged race.*

screamed (skrēmd) *verb.* Made a loud cry or sound. *The woman* **screamed** *when she saw her baby crawling close to the pool.*

seized (sēzd) *verb.* Took hold of or grabbed. *The guard* **seized** *the money out of the thief's hand.*

sep·a·rate (sep´ə rāt´) *verb.* To set apart or place apart. *After the big fight, we had to* **separate** *the cat and the dog and put them in different rooms.*

coming of one thing after another in a fixed order. *The* **sequence** *of even numbers from one to ten is 2, 4, 6, 8, 10.* **2.** A series of connected things. *A* **sequence** *of drawings showed the figure moving from left to right.*

ser·vi·ces (sûr´vis əz) *plural noun.* A variety of tasks or acts done for others, usually for pay. *The car wash provided other* **services**, *such as dusting and vacuuming inside the car.*

shal·low (shal´ō) *adjective.* Not deep. *All the young children were playing in the* **shallow** *part of the pool.*

shel·ter (shel´tər) *noun.* Something that covers or protects. *Once it began to rain, the group immediately looked for* **shelter**.

should·n't (shŭd´ənt) *verb.* Contraction of should not. *You* **shouldn't** *run with scissors in your hands.*

shud·dered (shud´ərd) *verb.* Trembled suddenly. *The house* **shuddered** *during the earthquake.*

side·walks (sīd´wôkz´) *plural noun.* Paths by the side of the street or road, usually made of cement. *Vladimir and Bill were paid to shovel snow off the* **sidewalks** *around their apartment building.*

and well cared for. *Everyone admired the* **sleek** *poodle at the dog show.*

slee·py (slē´pē) *adjective.* Ready for or needing sleep. *After a big dinner, Raymond felt very* **sleepy** *and sat down on the couch.*

slo·gan (slō´gən) *noun.* A phrase, statement, or motto. *Today our teacher asked us to think up a* **slogan** *for our science club.*

sprout (sprout) *verb.* To begin to grow. *Maria was pleased to see that the sunflower seeds she planted were finally beginning to* **sprout**. *noun.* A new growth on a plant; bud or shoot. *There was a* **sprout** *on the plant that would soon become a leaf.*

keeping things for future use. *Mr. Chen used his garage mainly for* **storage**.

strolled (strōld) *verb.* Walked in a slow, relaxed manner. *The tourists* **strolled** *through the streets looking at all the big buildings and store windows.*

struc·tures (struk´chərz) *plural noun.* Things that are built, such as buildings. *From so far away, the* **structures** *on the horizon were hard to make out.*

Word History

Structure comes from the Latin word *struere*, which means "to construct."

stur·dy (stûr´dē) *adjective.* Strong or solid. *The new table is very* **sturdy**, *and we are able to put many heavy boxes on it.*

sup·ply (sə plī´) *noun.* An amount of something needed or available for use. *We had a* **supply** *of candles and batteries in the closet in case of an emergency.*

at; āpe; fär; câre; end; mē; it; īce; pîerce; hot; ōld; sông; fôrk; oil; out; up; ūse; rûle; pûll; tûrn; chin; sing; shop; thin; **this**; hw in white; zh in treasure.

The symbol ə stands for the unstressed vowel sound in about, taken, pencil, lemon, and circus.

420

421

---

sway (swā) *verb.* To move or swing back and forth or side to side. *The trees began to gently* **sway** *in the tropical wind.*

Tt

tast·y (tās´tē) *adjective.* Having a pleasant flavor. *The freshly baked brownies were very* **tasty**.

tend (tend) *verb.* To look after or take care of something. *It was the farmer's job to* **tend** *to the cows and chickens and make sure they had enough food.*

thrilled (thrild) *verb.* Filled with pleasure or excitement. *The team members were* **thrilled** *when they heard their best player was not badly injured.*

tour (tûr) *noun.* A trip or journey in which many places are visited or many things are seen. *The guide led a* **tour** *through the museum and explained all the famous artwork.*

trad·ers (trā´dərz) *plural noun.* People who buy and sell things as a business. *The* **traders** *went to the settlers to sell them blankets and clothes.*

Vv

vol·un·teers (vol´ən tîrz´) *plural noun.* People who offer to do things by choice and often without pay. *Several* **volunteers** *showed up to help clean up the park and paint the fence.*

Ww

wailed (wāld) *verb.* Made a long and sad cry, especially to show grief or pain. *The baby* **wailed** *when she dropped her toy.*

Yy

ya·poks (yə poks´) *plural noun.* Tropical aquatic opossums with dense fur, webbed feet, and long tails. *The young* **yapoks** *huddled together beneath the shade of the palm tree.*

yearned (yûrnd) *verb.* Felt a strong and deep desire. *The school team* **yearned** *for the chance to play.*

422

Comprehension

Objective: Use text clues to review sequence

Sequence

Intervention/Remediation

Materials *Boom Town*, Student Book pp. 154–175

Review Ask: *Do you put the toothpaste on your brush before or after you brush your teeth?* Explain that the story events similarly move in a time order.

Explain Say: *In a story, sequence is the order in which events happen. Sometimes authors will use signal words such as* first, then, next, *and* last *to show the order of events.* Read page 158 aloud. Ask students to tell the sequence involving Pa.

Model Say: *The signal word helps me know that the first thing Pa does is take a bath. The signal word* then *tells me that the next thing he does is sing and tell stories.*

Guided Practice Read aloud the first paragraph on page 164. Ask: *When does this event happen? How can you tell?*

Corrective Feedback

If students are unable to identify sequence, ask: *On which day of the week does Pa come home? What did Amanda give her Pa? What did Pa do then?*

Practice Read aloud the rest of page 164. Have student pairs write the story events in order in a sequence chart and then use their charts to retell the events.

Corrective Feedback

If students have trouble identifying sequence, review the definition of sequence and have students restate it in their own words. Draw a time line on the board and have students read one paragraph at a time on page 164 and write the events in order.

Sequence

Materials Student Book or Leveled Reader

Explain Write the following on the board: *There was not one cloud in the sky when Mike and Henry first pushed the sailboat out into the water. Twenty minutes later they noticed the sky was getting dark. Then Mike turned the sailboat around and headed for home. The wind grew stronger as they neared land, but at last they arrived home safely.* Read the paragraph aloud. Tell students that they'll write the sequence of events in the story.

Guided Practice Draw a sequence chart on the board. Ask students to identify signal words such as *first, then,* and *at last* and use the signal words to complete the chart.

Practice Have students choose a previously read story in their books. Have them organize the main story events in a sequence chart and use the chart to summarize the story for a partner.

Group Story

Materials index cards

Explain Write sequence signal words on separate index cards. Tell students they will work together to make up a sequence of events for a story.

Guided Practice/Practice Mix up the cards and distribute them to students. Have students stand and organize themselves in a logical sequence according to the signal words. Tell students a story starter. Using their signal words, have them add a sentence or two to tell what happens next in the story.
Visual/Auditory/Kinesthetic

Comprehension

Objective: Review using signal words with cause and effect

Cause and Effect

Intervention/Remediation

Materials *Beatrice's Goat*, Student Book pp. 188–209

Review Say: *If you forget to eat lunch, how will you feel? That you forgot to eat lunch is a cause— it's why you feel hungry. That you feel hungry is an effect or result of forgetting to eat.*

Explain Say: *To find a cause, ask yourself, "Why did this happen?" To find an effect, ask, "What happened?" Cause and effect words include* so, because, due to, since, *and* as a result. Read aloud the second paragraph on page 193. Ask why the students bring the benches outside and identify the cause and the effect.

Model Say: *In the story, the students bring benches outside because they want to work in the shade. The cause is that it's cool in the shade. The effect is that the students bring benches outside.*

Guided Practice Read the first paragraph on page 198 aloud. Have students determine why Beatrice names her goat Mugisa.

Corrective Feedback

If students have difficulty identifying cause and effect, ask: *What does the name* Mugisa *mean? Why is* Mugisa *a good name for the goat?*

Practice Read aloud the remaining text on page 198. Have students complete a cause-effect chart to identify why Beatrice gives Mugisa lots of grass and water.

Corrective Feedback

Have students restate the definitions of cause and effect in their own words. Then have students identify causes and effects using everyday examples, such as banging a pot to get attention.

Cause and Effect

Explain Write on the board: *My shoes are soaked because I stepped in a puddle. Due to the heavy rain, I was late for school. A driver didn't notice the puddle in the street and as a result she splashed me. My backpack is ripped, so the water soaked my homework. Since my homework was ruined, I have to do it over again.* Tell students they will use signal words to identify causes and effects.

Guided Practice Read aloud the paragraph and have students identify the signal word in the first sentence. *(because)* Then have students identify the cause *(I stepped in a puddle)* and the effect *(My shoes are soaked)* in the sentence.

Practice Have students copy the paragraph, circle each signal word and draw one line under each cause and two lines under each effect.

If...Then Circle

Materials pencil, paper

Explain Tell students they will write causes and effects about sports or other fun activities.

Guided Practice/Practice Have students, stand in a circle, and fold a piece of paper in half the long way and write *Cause* at the top of one half and *Effect* at the top of the other. Say: *If you kick a ball, what happens to the ball? Kicking the ball is a cause. The ball moving away is an effect. Think of other effects that happen as you play a game or sport. Write one cause on your paper, and then pass your paper to the left. That person writes the effect of your cause. Then write a new cause on your paper and pass it to your left. Repeat until you get your own paper back again.*
Visual/Kinesthetic

Objective: Review fact and opinion

Fact and Opinion

Intervention/Remediation

Materials *A Carousel of Dreams*, Student Book pp. 222–225

Review Say: *A fact is something that can be proved to be true. An opinion is something you believe about something.*

Explain Say: *To prove a fact you might ask an expert or look in a book. An opinion is what someone thinks, believes, or feels about something.* Read aloud the first sentence on page 222 and ask students to identify one fact and one opinion.

Model Say: *I can prove that Riverbank State Park is in New York City by getting its address. The signal word* probably *lets me know it's the author's opinion that the carousel is fantastic.*

Guided Practice Read aloud the first sentence on page 223. Ask: *What word signals the opinion in this sentence?* (believed) *What information in the sentence can be proved?* (he held drawing classes in Riverbank State Park)

Corrective Feedback

Ask: *Who believed that kids should be a part of the project? Does everyone agree? Is this a fact or an opinion? Did Milo Mottola hold drawing classes at the park? Is that a fact or opinion? Why?*

Practice Have partners read the rest of page 223 together and find two more facts and opinions on the page.

Corrective Feedback

Have students restate the definitions of a fact and an opinion in their own words. Create a fact and opinion chart and list facts about the students and their opinions about various subjects.

Fact and Opinion

Explain Write the following on the board: *My mother is the best cook in our neighborhood. We have a garden, so lots of our food is fresh. When she cooks a chicken, she puts lemon and garlic inside. That makes it taste delicious!* Tell students they will identify facts and opinions.

Guided Practice Read the paragraph aloud and have students circle provable facts and underline the opinions or what the person believes in the paragraph. Write their responses in a fact and opinion chart.

Practice Read the following paragraph aloud and have students identify facts and opinions: *I went with my friends to see* The Return of the Snake *at the movies last night. It's the movie that has Pete Brown in it. Pete Brown is one of the best actors today. In this movie, he plays a writer. I think he wasted his talent on this film. This has to be the worst movie I ever saw.*

Movie Reviews

Materials paper, pencils

Explain Have students think of movies they have seen recently. Discuss what they liked or didn't like about them. Tell students they will write a review of a movie to share their opinions about it.

Guided Practice/Practice Remind students that their movie review should tell facts about the movie, the actors, and the plot. It should also include students' opinions about the movie, the actors, and the plot. Ask volunteers to read their reviews aloud. Have the other students raise their hands each time they hear an opinion.
Visual/Auditory

Comprehension

Objective: Make and confirm predictions using story clues

Make and Confirm Predictions

Intervention/Remediation

Materials *The Printer*, Student Book pp. 234–251

Review Remind students that a prediction is an educated guess about what might happen.

Explain Say: *When we make predictions as we read, we look for story and picture clues and use our own knowledge and experiences. As we read on, we might rethink and revise our predictions.* Read the text on pages 237–239 aloud, and ask students to make predictions about things or ideas that will be important in the story.

Model Say: *The boy says his dad feels sad because the other printers haven't ever spoken to him. Since the title of this story is* The Printer, *I think the story will be about the boy's dad and friendship.*

Guided Practice Read aloud page 240 and have students predict what will happen next. Have students complete a predictions chart and then confirm or revise their predictions.

Corrective Feedback

Ask: *What would you do if you saw a fire? Do you think the boy's dad will help the other printers? How might he do that?*

Practice Read aloud pages 243–247. Using a prediction chart to organize clues, have students predict what the printers will do. Partners can revise or confirm their predictions as they read.

Corrective Feedback

Guide students as they restate in their own words the process of making and confirming predictions. Give them two possible predictions and have them explain the clues that make one choice better.

Make and Confirm Predictions

Explain Write on the board: *Coach Davis signaled to Marvin to take the pitcher's mound. This was Marvin's first game. As Marvin walked out onto the field, his knees started shaking. He could barely stand. Jason, the catcher, gave Marvin an encouraging smile. Although Marvin was a good pitcher in practice, his first pitch sailed over Jason's head.*

Guided Practice Read the text aloud and have students predict what they think will happen next and back up their predictions with story clues. Then write on the board and read aloud: *Jason came out to the mound and told Marvin to imagine that this was a practice. Marvin closed his eyes and visualized his pitch. Then he focused on Jason's mitt and threw the next pitch.*

Practice Have students compare their predictions with what happened in the story. Then have them make a new prediction about how the story might end.

The Unfinished Skit

Materials paper, pencils

Explain Tell students they will make predictions about what will happen in a skit.

Guided Practice/Practice Have teams plan a skit, keeping notes about what will happen. Players should perform the first half of their skit and stop; the others should predict how the skit will end. Have players complete their skits as the others confirm or revise their predictions.
Visual/Kinesthetic/Auditory

Comprehension

Objective: Use description to understand nonfiction text

Description

Intervention/Remediation

Materials *Animal Homes,* **Student Book pp. 264–279**

Review Ask students to describe your classroom. Explain that description is one way that nonfiction authors organize their writing.

Explain Say: *When authors write descriptions they use examples and details to show the characteristics and qualities of something.* Read aloud page 267 and have students listen for the characteristics and qualities that describe a honeycomb.

Model Say: *The author gave many details about a honeycomb. She wrote that it is waxy. It's made up of little cells that bees use for storing honey. Each cell has six sides.*

Guided Practice Read aloud the second paragraph on page 271. Ask students to listen for examples and details that tell what a weaverbird's nest is like. Use a description web to record descriptive words.

Corrective Feedback

Ask: *What is the weaverbird's nest made of? What does the bird do with the grass? What does the bird make first? What does the nest look like? Is it hollow or solid?*

Practice Have students choose another animal home from the selection to describe and use a web to record that description.

Corrective Feedback

Review that a description gives details about something so the reader is able to picture it in his mind. Have students restate the definition in their own words, then describe a simple object, recording their observations in a web.

Description

Explain Write the following on the board: B*obwhites get their name from the sound of their whistle. It seems to chirp, "bob-white." This small bird is a member of the partridge family. It is rusty brown, with dots of white feathers on its chest.* Tell students they will describe a bobwhite.

Guided Practice Read the text with students. Draw a circle on the board and write *bobwhites* inside it. Then draw smaller circles around it with lines to the main circle. Have students identify descriptive characteristics of a bobwhite as volunteers record them on the description web.

Practice Write the following on the board and read it aloud. Have students draw a description web to identify the characteristics of a sea urchin. *What looks like a cactus but lives under water? It's a sea urchin. Unlike fish, sea urchins have no backbones but they do have plenty of sharply pointed spines. These spines, like the spines on a cactus, are very painful if stepped on.*

Mmm-Mmm Good!

Materials **paper, pencils, crayons, or markers**

Explain Tell students that when writers write descriptions, they use their senses: sight, hearing, touch, taste, and smell.

Guided Practice /Practice Have students name their favorite foods. Ask volunteers to tell what their foods look, smell, feel, and taste like. Tell students to use a description web to organize the characteristics of their favorite food and then write a short description.
Visual

Vocabulary

Objective: Review compound words

Compound Words

Intervention/Remediation

Materials *Boom Town*, Student Book pp. 154–175

Review Write *fireplace* on the board and point out that it is made of two smaller words.

Explain Write *bathtub* on the board. Say: *Sometimes you can figure out the meaning of a compound word by putting together the meanings of the two small words. A bathtub is a tub in which you take a bath.* Read aloud the first paragraph on page 160. Ask students to identify and define the compound word.

Model Say: *I hear two small words in the word gooseberries. It doesn't make sense that gooseberries are berries made from a goose, so I'll look up gooseberries in the dictionary.*

Guided Practice Read aloud the first paragraph on page 167. Have students identify the compound word and use a dictionary to look up its meaning. *(blacksmith: a person who makes tools and other things out of iron)*

Corrective Feedback

Have students examine page 167 for words made up of two smaller words. Have them copy the compound word they find on paper and circle the two words that make it up.

Practice Have students scan pages 171–172 for compound words. Have them list the words they find and their meanings.

Corrective Feedback

Have students state the definitions of a compound word in their own words. Then write a list of compound words on the board and have students circle words that form each one.

Compound Words

Materials *paper, pencil*

Explain Write on the board: *One afternoon as we were walking barefoot along the seashore, my grandfather and I spotted a seashell crawling in the sunshine.* Read the sentence aloud and tell students to listen for compound words.

Guided Practice Ask volunteers to underline the compound words in the sentence. Then have students tell the meaning of each, using a dictionary as needed.

Practice Write the following on the board *The butterfly fluttered around the rooftop of the doghouse before settling on my windowsill.* Have students write each compound word and its meaning.

Compound-Word Riddles

Materials paper, pencil

Explain Tell students they will draw pictures to make compound-word riddles.

Guided Practice/Practice Draw on the board a sketch of a person standing on top of a mountain. Beside it write a plus sign. Then draw a chair. Ask students to guess the compound word your riddle pictures. *(highchair)* Have students brainstorm compound words they know. Tell students to draw their own compound-word riddles. Then display the riddles and have students try to guess them.

Visual

 **Vocabulary**

Objective: Recognize and use word families

Word Families

Intervention/Remediation

Materials *Beatrice's Goat*, Student Book pp. 188–209

Review Ask: *What is the same about these two words:* schoolgirl, schoolbooks? Say: *The words are related. They both have the base word* school.

Explain Say: *Just as people are related in families, words are related in word families if they share a common base word.* Read aloud the first sentence on page 190. Tell students to think about the two words that make up *crossroads*.

Model Say: *I know that* crossroads *contains two small words—*cross *and* roads. *This word means a place where one road crosses another. I know a related word—*crosswalk.

Guided Practice Draw a word web for *cross* and one for *road*. Have students add related words and tell their meanings. Encourage them to use a dictionary to find related words.

Corrective Feedback

Write pairs of words on the board, such as *doorbell* and *windowsill*. Have students determine which word is related to *doorstep* and what it means.

Practice Ask a volunteer to read the first sentence on page 202. Tell children that *water* is a base word that has a large family. Have students draw a word web and write at least four words that have *water* as a base word.

Corrective Feedback

Have students define word families, in their own words. Then make a list of several words related to water, such as *waterfall* and *waterlog* have students tell how they are related.

Word Families

Explain Write the following on the board: *It was such a sunny day that Josh put on his sunglasses. As he walked, he noticed yellow sunflowers. It was hot in the sunshine, so Josh hurried to the store. He needed to buy some suntan lotion. He didn't want to get sunburn.* Read the paragraph aloud. Tell students they will identify related words and their meanings.

Guided Practice Ask volunteers to draw a line under each related word in the first sentence and identify the base word. Then have them tell the meaning of each word.

Practice Have partners draw a word web and write in it all the related words from the paragraph and their meanings. In the middle of the web, tell students to write the base word they identified earlier.

Let It Snow

Explain Tell students that they will pantomime words related to the base word *snow*.

Guided Practice/Practice Write *snow* in the middle of a word web. Have students brainstorm several words that belong to this word family. Have students choose a word and pantomime it as the class guesses the related word.
Visual/Kinesthetic

 **Vocabulary**

Objective: Use context clues to understand figurative language

Context Clues (Figurative Language)

Intervention/Remediation

Materials *The Printer*, Student Book pp. 234–251

Review Say: *Writers often use figurative language to paint a picture in the reader's mind. They may use words or phrases in unusual ways—ways that may be somewhat different from their dictionary meanings.*

Explain Say: *To figure out what the figurative language means, you have use the context.* Read aloud the last sentence on page 237. Help students compare how the word *spat* is usually used and how it is used in the sentence.

Model Say: *I am surprised to see that the author uses* spat *to talk about how the newspapers came out of the presses.* Spat *is the past tense of the verb* to spit. *Because the author uses the word* spat *in this way, I get a picture of the newspapers flying out of the presses as if spat from a mouth.*

Guided Practice Read aloud the third paragraph on page 240 and ask students to compare the ways in which *roar* is usually used and how it is used in this context.

Corrective Feedback

If students have trouble identifying the meanings of words and phrases used figuratively, have them draw silly pictures. For example, draw a lion roaring at a printing press.

Practice Have students explain the phrase "roared into life" on page 247.

Corrective Feedback

If students still have trouble, help them think of other uncommon items that might roar, such as a car engine or traffic.

Context Clues (Figurative Language)

Explain Write on the board: *The boy's shoes _____ as he crept down the darkened staircase. The _____ of the doorbell startled him. The door _____ as someone began pounding on it.* Tell students that they will complete each sentence using figurative language.

Guided Practice Read the first sentence aloud. Have students brainstorm figurative language that describes sound. (Examples: squeaked, tapped, whispered)

Practice Have students complete the other two sentences using figurative language. Ask volunteers to read their sentences and explain the figurative language they chose.
Auditory

Sounds like an Animal

Materials drawing paper, pencils, crayons or markers

Explain Tell students they will write sentences that show how things sound like animals.

Guided Practice/Practice Have students brainstorm sounds that people and animals make, such as *hiss, groan, purr,* and *chirp.* Have them fold a paper in half. On one side have them write a sentence that tells about an animal and the sound it makes. On the other side have them write a sentence to show how an object can make a similar kind of sound. Have students illustrate their sentences and share them with the class.
Visual/Auditory

Vocabulary Strategy

Objective: Use possessives correctly

Possessives

Intervention/Remediation

Materials "Smooth Riding," Student Book p. 221, *A Carousel of Dreams,* Student Book pp. 222–225

Review Say: *To show ownership, we use the possessive form of the word. Instead of saying "the red bed that belongs to the cat," we can say, "the cat's red bed." To write a possessive we usually add an apostrophe and* s *to the end of the noun.*

Explain Say: *Read aloud the entry for 1903 on page 221.*

Model Say: *I can tell that* brothers' *is a possessive because of the apostrophe at the end. Because* brothers' *ends in* s *and an apostrophe, it must be a plural. So the first flight belonged to more than one Wright brother.*

Guided Practice Read aloud the last two sentences on page 222. Say: *Identify two words that sound the same—one is a plural (kids) and one is a possessive (kids').* Discuss how students can tell what each word means.

Corrective Feedback

If students have trouble identifying possessives, have them list classmates' names and classroom objects. Then have students create a possessives list.

Practice Ask students to find and explain the possessive on page 224. (Tennessee's) Point out the difference between possessives and contractions.

Corrective Feedback

Help students create a possessives chart with examples found in their weekly reading. Separate singular and plural possessives.

Possessives

Explain Write on the board: *It was the day of the third graders field trip.* Tell students they will decide if an underlined word is a possessive and if so, where the apostrophe should go.

Guided Practice Read the sentence aloud. Ask: *Does something belong to the third graders?* (yes, the field trip) *Is* third graders *a plural that ends in* s? (yes) *How do we make a plural a possessive?* (Add an apostrophe after the *s.*)

Practice Write these sentences on the board: *Two boys forgot their permission slips. The boys parents had to drive to school. Tims mother and Jakes dad were not happy.* Have students copy the sentences and add apostrophes to form possessives for the underlined words if needed. *(boys, boys', Tim's, Jake's)*
Visual

Possessive Hold-Up

Materials index cards, pencils

Explain Give each student two index cards. Have the students write *'s* on one card and just an apostrophe on the other card. Tell students that they will hold up the card to show how to form each possessive.

Guided Practice/Practice Write these words on the board: *kid, Miss Brown, boys, teachers, bear.* As you point to each word, say the possessive form as part of a phrase such as *one kid's toys.* Have students hold up the correct index card to show how to change *kid* to *kid's.* Ask a volunteer to write the possessive on the board. Continue with the other nouns.
Auditory/Kinesthetic

Vocabulary Strategy

Objective: Recognize analogy relationships

Analogies

Intervention/Remediation

Materials "Web Spinners," Student Book pp. 262-263, Animal Homes, Student Book pp. 264-279

Review *An analogy shows the relationship between pairs of words.*

Explain Read aloud the text on page 263 under the headings "Cellar Spiders" and "Water Spiders." Write on the board: *Cellar spiders are to cellars as water spiders are to ponds. Both pairs of words tell where a certain kind of spider makes its home. Both pairs of words in an analogy must have the same relationship.*

Model Read aloud the first sentence on page 268. Say: *I know that the weather is cold in winter, so the relationship here is what the weather is like in a season. It is hot in the summer, so an analogy could be,* cold *is to* winter *as* hot *is to* _____.

Guided Practice Write on the board: *silver is to metal as burrow is to* _____. Read aloud the second paragraph on page 268. Ask, *what is the relationship between* silver *and* metal? (silver is a kind of metal) *A* burrow *is a kind of what?* (hole).

Corrective Feedback

If students have trouble completing analogies, discuss the word relationships.

Practice Write this analogy on the board and have students complete it:
bird is to nest as beaver is to _____ (lodge)

Corrective Feedback

If students have trouble, review that analogies show a relationship between two pairs of words.

Analogies

Explain Write on the board: *tall is to* _____ *as* _____ *is to* _____. Tell students that they'll write an analogy that uses the word *tall.*

Guided Practice Have students brainstorm synonyms for *tall.* Ask a volunteer to write one in the first blank. Discuss what the first pair of words tells about the relationship. Have students then suggest other pairs of synonyms to complete the analogy such as *shut* and *closed.* Repeat the activity using antonym pairs.

Practice Write on the board: **1,** *fish is to* _____ *as* _____ *is to* _____ **2,** *run is to* _____ *as* _____ *is to* _____. Have students work with partners to complete each analogy. Ask volunteers to share their analogies and have other students identify the relationships. Visual/Auditory

The Analogy Game

Materials index cards, long strip of paper, pencils

Explain Tell students that they will play a game by making analogies.

Guided Practice/Practice Write these synonym pairs on 14 separate index cards: *begin, start, yell, shout, go, leave, right, correct, kind, helpful, make, build, look, see.* On the strip of paper write: _____ *is to* _____ *as* _____ *is to* _____. Mix up the cards and distribute equally to players. Player 1 puts a card face up on the first blank on the analogy strip and reads it aloud. Play goes around the circle as players take turns putting down cards to complete the analogy with synonyms. If a player doesn't have the needed synonym card, play passes to the player on the left. The person who is out of cards first wins. Visual

 # Study Skill

Objective: Understand how to read a calendar and a newspaper editorial

Calendar and Newspaper (Persuasive Editorial)

Intervention/Remediation

Materials "How to Earn Money!" **Student Book** pp. 178-181, blank calendar

Review Ask volunteers to name the days of the week and the months of the year. Ask: *Thanksgiving is always on the fourth Thursday in November. Where could I look to find what date Thanksgiving is this year?* (a calendar)

Explain Display the calendar on page 180. Say: *This is a calendar page. Calendars show the months, weeks, and days of the year. They help us keep track of things such as birthdays, holidays, and tasks we must do. A calendar shows all twelve months of the year. The days of the week are along the top of the page. The number in each box is the date. This calendar shows the dates in May.*

Guided Practice/Practice Help students find May 20 and tell what day of the week it is. (Tuesday) Help them find the date for the fourth Saturday in May and name that day's task. (Buy dog shampoo) Give each student a blank calendar page for July. Tell them to plan three activities during vacation. Have them choose dates and record them on the calendar. Tell them to note on their calendars that the 4th of July is a holiday. Display calendars and have students answer classmates' questions.

Corrective Feedback

If students have trouble reading a calendar, have them put a finger on a given date and follow it up to the day of the week and the month. Have students use those three pieces of information to tell the complete date.

Intervention/Remediation

Materials "Ugandan Girl Reaches Goal" Student Book pp. 212-215

Review Say: *A fact is something that can be proven to be true. An opinion is what someone thinks, feels, or believes about a topic.*

Explain Say: *Much of what you read in the newspaper is supposed to be facts and not the writer's opinion. But newspapers do have special columns called editorials. Editorials give the editor or publisher's opinion on a subject. The purpose of an editorial is to persuade readers to think, believe, or act in a certain way. Editorials use facts to support the editor or publisher's opinion. Look at the editorial on page 214.* Read aloud the headline, byline, and first two sentences of the editorial.

Guided Practice/Practice Ask: *What does the headline tell you about the topic of this article?* (It's about education and what Beatrice thinks about it.) *What does the first sentence tell you about what the editor thinks?* (Education is very important.) *Which clue words let you know that this is the editor's opinion?* (should be) *What fact does the editor tell in the second sentence?* (Beatrice Biira grew up in Uganda.)

Corrective Feedback

If students have difficulty identifying the characteristics of an editorial, make a checklist for students to use. Include questions such as: *Does this appear in a newspaper? Does it express a clear opinion? Are there facts to support an opinion? Does the writer want the readers to think, believe, or act in a certain way?*

Study Skill

Objectives: Skim and scan a nonfiction article and read a map

Skimming and Scanning and Maps

Intervention/Remediation

Materials "Visions of the Future from the Past," Student Book p. 220, previously read nonfiction Leveled Readers, paper, pencils

Review Say: *When you research a topic, you can't read every page of every book to find the information you need. First, glance at the headings to see if they seem like they will have information you need. Then quickly read the first few sentences of paragraphs to get main ideas.*

Explain Say: *Skimming and scanning are strategies good readers use to locate information quickly in an article. When you scan a page, you move your eyes quickly over text to pick out key words. Then slow down and read the text to see if it has the information you need. When you skim, you read small bits of information, such as headings and the first few sentences in each paragraph to figure out the main ideas and important details.*

Guided Practice/Practice Help students scan page 220 for references to Leonardo da Vinci. Help them skim to find out when he lived. (1400s) Then give each student a previously read nonfiction Leveled Reader. Have students skim and scan for questions to ask about the book. Have them trade books and questions with a partner, then skim and scan to find the answers.

Corrective Feedback
If students have difficulty using skim and scan to quickly find information, write on a sticky note a key word to look for on a page. Put the note at the top of the page. Have the student quickly trace a finger across each line to scan for the key word.

Intervention/Remediation

Materials "Smokejumpers," Student Book pp. 254-257

Review Say: *I use a map when I drive to a new place. The map shows where things are. Driving maps also have special symbols that show highways and rivers and towns.*

Explain Display the map on page 255. Say: *A map is a flat drawing of a place such as a city, state, or country. The title of this map is "California Fire Danger." That's what this map is all about. Maps have special features that give readers information. The box on the left of this map is the map key. It shows what different colors mean. The star on the right of the map is called a compass and it tells where the four main, or cardinal, directions are. This compass uses initials to show the directions north (N), south (S), east (E), and west (W).*

Guided Practice/Practice Ask: *What does the color yellow stand for in this map?* (high fire danger) *How do you know?* (find the yellow bar in the map key) *Is the high fire danger in the north or the south of California?* (south) Distribute other maps to Student Partners and have them explain what their maps show and identity features like the map key and compass.

Corrective Feedback
If students have difficulty locating information on the map, have them first trace a finger from each color on the map to its color on the key and tell what the color stands for. Then discuss the cardinal directions and have students trace a finger from each direction to its respective part of the map.

The Babe & I

by David A. Adler

Before Reading

BUILD BACKGROUND

Explain that the Great Depression was a time in the late 1920s and 1930s when people in America had a hard time finding work and earning money. Brainstorm a list of "known" items for a KWL chart about the Great Depression. Ask students: What do you picture in your mind when you hear the words "Great Depression"?

PREVIEW AND SET PURPOSES

Have students look at the cover illustration and read the title. What clues from the cover illustration can students find to show what the story is about? Have students set a purpose for reading, such as to find out what it might be like to meet a famous baseball player.

During Reading

APPLY COMPREHENSION SKILLS AND STRATEGIES

Following are suggestions for dividing the reading into manageable sections. For each section, Think Alouds and discussion questions are provided. Use these to review comprehension strategies and skills taught in this unit.

Pages 1–8

STRATEGY
MAKE INFERENCES AND ANALYZE

Think Aloud I know the author doesn't always tell me everything. Sometimes I have to use what I read and what I know to figure things out. I learn that during the Great Depression almost everyone is poor and out of work. The boy realizes his father lost his job and is now selling apples. If I lost my job I'd probably be embarrassed to tell people. I think that the boy's father doesn't tell his family he lost his job because he is embarrassed. The author didn't tell me this, but I used clues in the story and what I know to figure this out.

Make and Confirm Predictions The boy finds out his father no longer has his regular job. What do you predict will happen? Do you think the boy will tell his father that he knows? Do you think the father will tell his family? Explain. (Predictions will vary. The boy might feel too bad to talk about it with his father. The father might eventually have to tell his family because they would notice that he isn't bringing home paychecks anymore and he might feel bad about hiding the truth.)

Objectives

- Make inferences and analyze
- Make and confirm predictions
- Summarize
- Identify sequence of events

Genre Historical Fiction

Approaching Level

Summary

As a boy sells newspapers during the Great Depression to help his family make ends meet, he meets Babe Ruth.

 **for your information**

Set in New York City in 1932, this story takes place during the Great Depression, when jobs and money were hard to come by. Many families depended on extra income from their children to get by, so children got jobs as newsies—newspaper sellers—to help out.

Classroom Library

Cross-Curricular Connection

Kids at Work

Have students find out more about the kinds of jobs children had to do during the Great Depression. Students can use their school or class library, or a reputable search engine. Discuss their findings and talk about whether children could or should do this kind of work today, and why or why not.

Cross-Curricular Connection

Newspaper Earnings

Babe Ruth gave the boy $5 for a newspaper. How many newspapers would the boy have had to sell to earn that much? (Remind students that the boy sold papers for 2 cents each, then had to give a cent back to the newspaper company.)

Pages 9–18

STRATEGY
MAKE INFERENCES AND ANALYZE

Think Aloud   Sometimes I'm not sure why something happens in the story because the author doesn't tell me. For example, at first I wasn't sure why the boy wanted a baby carriage. I know he sells newspapers and he wants to be able to bring more of them to Yankee Stadium, but he needs something to carry the papers in. When I put these clues together, I see that the boy wants to use the carriage to carry newspapers. Using information in the story helped me figure this out.

 Make and Confirm Predictions The boy gets a job as a newsie and brings money home. His mother tells him not to let his father know. What do you predict will happen? Will his father find out? (Predictions will vary. Students may say that the father might see his son working out on the streets. Or the father will find out because he will see the money in the jar.)

Pages 19–end

STRATEGY
SUMMARIZE

Think Aloud   I want to stop and summarize what has happened. The boy gets a job selling newspapers to help his family. He and his friend Jacob sell newspapers outside Yankee Stadium. Babe Ruth buys a newspaper from the boy and gives him five dollars. Summarizing helped me remember the most important information.

 Sequence What events lead up to the two boys seeing Babe Ruth play baseball? (First, Babe Ruth buys a paper from the boy; next, the boy uses the money to buy two tickets to the game; last, Babe Ruth comes up to bat.)

 After Reading

LITERATURE CIRCLES
Use page 174 in the **Teacher's Resource Book** to review Speaking and Listening guidelines for a discussion. Have students discuss the book in small groups. Ask:

- What do you think it was like growing up in the Great Depression?

- Why do you think the boy says he and Babe Ruth are a team? Why does he say he and his dad are a team?

Write About It
Point out that the boy in the story got a job to help his family make ends meet. Have students think of a time they helped their family, such as a time they helped a parent clean the house or fix a meal. Have them write a personal narrative about how they helped, telling what happened first, next, and last. Remind students to use possessive pronouns correctly.

The Year of Miss Agnes

by Kirkpatrick Hill

Before Reading

BUILD BACKGROUND

Explain that in the past, in some parts of the country, a school had just one teacher who taught all subjects to all of the children. Brainstorm a KWL chart about what students know about schoolhouses. Ask students:

- What do you see in your mind when you think of a one-room schoolhouse?

- What might be some of the advantages and disadvantages of going to school in one room with all the kids in town?

PREVIEW AND SET PURPOSES

Have students look at the cover illustration and read the title. Read a page or two aloud to give students a sense of what the book might be about. Then have students set a purpose for reading, such as to find out whether Miss Agnes is a good teacher.

During Reading

APPLY COMPREHENSION SKILLS AND STRATEGIES

Following are suggestions for dividing the reading into manageable sections. For each section, Think Alouds and discussion questions are provided. Use these to review comprehension strategies and skills taught in this unit.

Chapters 1–6

MAKE INFERENCES AND ANALYZE

Think Aloud I know that I have to use what I read and what I know to understand more than the author tells me. As I read descriptions of the village, the new teacher, and the schoolhouse, I can infer that this town is small and far away from other towns and that the people are poor. I will look for more information about the people and the way they live. I can use this information to make more inferences about what living in this village was like.

Make and Confirm Predictions The village gets a new schoolteacher because the last one did not stay. Make a prediction. Do you think Miss Agnes will stay for long? (Readers' predictions will vary. Miss Agnes has sinus problems so she won't be able to smell the fish. At least this won't be the reason she leaves.)

Objectives

- Summarize
- Make inferences and analyze
- Identify sequence of events
- Make and confirm predictions

Genre | Historical Fiction

"The genius...lies in the characters' absolute presence."
—*New York Times Book Review*

The Year of Miss Agnes

Kirkpatrick Hill

ALADDIN HISTORICAL FICTION

On Level

Summary

Ten-year-old Frederika tells about the year Miss Agnes came to her Athabascan village in Alaska to be the town's one and only schoolteacher.

 for your information

Set in Alaska in 1948, this book gives a child's view of life in a small Alaskan Native American village. The families depend on the rivers and the woods for food—whole families leave town during winter and summer to gather food. The book provides wonderful descriptions of the clothing and other items people make.

Cross-Curricular Connection

Maps

Miss Agnes shows her students a map of Alaska and helps them locate places they know. Have students find a map of their state and locate their town. Partners can locate lakes, rivers, mountains, and other physical features of their state. Then ask them to locate Alaska and England to see how far away from home Miss Agnes was.

Cross-Curricular Connection

Sketch a Setting

What does spring camp look like? Have students reread the description on page 104 and use their imaginations to draw what they think the camp looks like.

Chapters 7–11

STRATEGY
SUMMARIZE

Think Aloud I want to stop and summarize what has happened so far before I read on. Miss Agnes is the new teacher at the village school, and she is teaching the kids all kinds of new things. The kids really like her, and she thinks every child should go to school, even Bokko, who is deaf.

Sequence How does Bokko start going to school? What happened first, next, and last to cause this to happen? (First, Bokko comes to school to deliver Fred's forgotten lunch; next, Miss Agnes talks to Bokko and Fred's mother; last, Bokko comes to school and Miss Agnes and the class learn sign language.)

Chapters 12–17

STRATEGY
MAKE INFERENCES AND ANALYZE

Teacher Think Aloud I learn that the kids leave school at times to go and help their families catch and dry fish. I can infer because of their poverty that finding food is more important for these families than going to school.

Make and Confirm Predictions Miss Agnes plays a record of the King's Choir in England and talks about how pretty the flowers are there. Fred thinks Miss Agnes will stay only one year. What do you predict will happen? (Readers' predictions will vary. Miss Agnes does plan a trip to England, but she returns for the next school year, surprising her students.)

After Reading

LITERATURE CIRCLES

Use page 174 in the **Teacher's Resource Book** to review Speaking and Listening guidelines for a discussion. Have students discuss the book in small groups, using questions such as these:

- Based on the descriptions in this book, what do you think it was like to be a child growing up in this village in 1948?

- Why do you think Miss Agnes leaves the map and the pictures on the wall at the end of the school year?

Write About It

Reread pages 21 and 22 aloud, focusing on the descriptions of the mittens and boots Mamma sews. Point out phrases that help readers "see" the mittens, pom-poms, and boots in their minds. Then have students choose an object to describe. Tell them to use descriptive words to tell about the object so that someone who has never seen one can understand what it looks like. Remind students to check their writing to be sure that pronouns and verbs agree.

Amelia and Eleanor Go for a Ride

by Pam Muñoz Ryan

Before Reading

BUILD BACKGROUND

Explain that women and girls have more freedom today than in the past. We read about things that only a few women did in the past, such as driving a car or flying a plane, that many women do today. Create a two-column chart titled: Women in the Past and Women Today. Have students brainstorm items for each column. Ask:

- How are jobs for women different today? What kinds of jobs did women have long ago?

Summarize with students what their chart shows.

PREVIEW AND SET PURPOSES

Have students look at the cover illustration and read the title. Read a page or two aloud to give students a sense of what the book might be about and when and where the action might take place. Then have students set a purpose for reading, such as to find out what happens on the plane ride.

During Reading

APPLY COMPREHENSION SKILLS AND STRATEGIES

Following are suggestions for dividing the reading into manageable sections. For each section, Think Alouds and discussion questions are provided. Use these to review comprehension strategies and skills taught in this unit.

Pages 1–9

STRATEGY
MAKE INFERENCES AND ANALYZE

Think Aloud I use what I read and what I know to infer parts the author doesn't tell me. As I read about Eleanor and Amelia, I can infer from their actions that they are both very independent and courageous people. They did things that not many women were doing. I will look for more information that helps me make inferences about the characters in the book.

Make and Confirm Predictions What do you predict Eleanor and Amelia will talk about during dinner? (Students' predictions will vary. They might suggest the women will talk about flying, living in the White House, or Eleanor's new car.)

Objectives

- Summarize
- Make inferences and analyze
- Identify sequence of events
- Make and confirm predictions

Genre Historical Fiction

Beyond Level

Summary

During an elegant dinner at the White House, Amelia Earhart and Eleanor Roosevelt decide to go for a ride in an airplane.

 for your information

This book tells the story of an airplane ride taken by Amelia Earhart and Eleanor Roosevelt. Eleanor Roosevelt was the wife of Franklin Roosevelt, President of the United States. Amelia Earhart had become the first female pilot to fly solo across the Atlantic Ocean. On April 20, 1933, when Amelia was a guest at the White House, she and the First Lady, an airplane enthusiast and amateur pilot herself, took a flight over Washington, D.C. This book offers a fictionalized version of that event.

Pages
10–17

Social Studies
Cross-Curricular Connection

First Ladies

Have students do research to identify women who have accomplished "firsts" in their field, such as the first woman doctor, supreme court justice, or astronaut. Have them write a brief report on the woman they choose.

Political Women

Have students do research to identify female world leaders, past and present. Ask them to choose one woman leader and write a short biography of her, using books from the classroom or school library, or a reputable source on the Internet.

STRATEGY
MAKE INFERENCES AND ANALYZE

Think Aloud   The author doesn't always tell me everything. For example, she doesn't say why Amelia arranges a flight for her and Eleanor. I know that Eleanor is interested in aviation and received her student-pilot's license. She also gets excited when she hears what it is like to fly at night. When I put these clues together, I see why Amelia decides to arrange for the two of them to take a flight that night.

Make and Confirm Predictions During the dinner party, Amelia suggests she take Eleanor on a flight over the city. What do you predict will happen? (Students' predictions will vary. They may suggest that the women take a flight the next day. In fact, they take a flight that very night.)

Pages
18–end

STRATEGY
SUMMARIZE

Think Aloud   I want to stop and summarize what has happened. After their flight, Amelia and Eleanor answer questions from a group of reporters. Then, Eleanor drives both of them around in her new car. Summarizing is a good way to remember the most important parts of the book.

Sequence What happens after they get out of the plane? (First, they answer questions from a group of reporters; next, they go for a ride in Eleanor's new car; last, they return to the White House just in time for dessert.)

After Reading

LITERATURE CIRCLES

Use page 174 in the **Teacher's Resource Book** to review Speaking and Listening guidelines for a discussion. Have students discuss the book in small groups. Ask:

- Who was Amelia Earhart? Who was Eleanor Roosevelt? Why were they famous?

- Why was it unusual for a woman to fly a plane in the 1930s?

- Why do you think Amelia and Eleanor were friends? How are they similar? How are they different?

Write About It

Reread pages 14 and 15 aloud, where Amelia describes what it is like to fly at night. Emphasize phrases that help readers "see" the experience in their minds. Then have students describe an experience of their own. Tell them to use descriptive words so that readers can see what happened in their minds. Remind students to be sure that they capitalize the pronoun *I* as well as proper nouns.

	WEEK 1	**WEEK 2**
by the Authors and Illustrators	**Levitin, Sonia.** *Nine for California.* **Scholastic, 1996.** Mama and her five kids embark on a long journey to join Pa in a faraway place called California during the Gold Rush. `ON LEVEL`	**McBrier, Page.** *Oliver and the Lucky Duck.* **Troll, 1986.** Oliver helps a wild duck with a broken wing and hopes to keep it as a pet after it heals. `BEYOND`

Related to the Theme

WEEK 1	**WEEK 2**
Leedy, Loreen. *Follow the Money.* **Holiday House, 2002.** A quarter describes all the ways it is used from the time it is minted until it is taken back to the bank. `APPROACHING`	**Chinn, Karen.** *Sam and the Lucky Money.* **Lee & Low Books, 1995.** Sam receives some money for Chinese New Year and decides to give it to someone less fortunate. `APPROACHING`
Murphy, Stuart. *Sluggers' Car Wash.* **HarperCollins, 2002.** The 21st Street Sluggers hold a car wash to raise money, and learn how to keep careful financial records. `APPROACHING`	**Battle-Lavert, Gwendolyn.** *The Shaking Bag.* **Whitman, 2000.** An elderly African American woman shares all she has and is repaid with a bag that provides for all her needs. `APPROACHING`
Halperin, Wendy Anderson. *Once Upon a Company.* **Orchard Books, 1998.** Three siblings decide to start a wreath-making business to begin earning money for college. `ON LEVEL`	**Bunting, Eve.** *So Far From the Sea.* **Clarion, 1998.** Laura pays one last visit to her grandfather's grave at the Manzanar Relocation Camp to leave a memento of her love for him. `ON LEVEL`
Mollel, Tolowa. *My Rows and Piles of Coins.* **Clarion, 1999.** A Tanzanian boy saves the money he has earned to buy a bicycle so that he can help his parents carry their goods to market. `ON LEVEL`	**Hill, Kirkpatrick.** *The Year of Miss Agnes.* **Aladdin, 2002.** Miss Agnes takes over a one-room schoolhouse on the Alaskan frontier and makes a difference in the lives of the kids. `ON LEVEL **`
Cribb, Joe. *Money.* **Knopf, 1990.** Discusses how coins and banknotes are made, the value of money, and how to collect coins in order to increase the value of your collection. `BEYOND`	**Borden, Louise.** *The Greatest Skating Race: A World War II Story From the Netherlands.* **Simon & Schuster, 2004.** A brave Dutch boy, inspired by a famous skater, leads other children to safety. `BEYOND`
Kiefer, Jeanne. *Jobs for Kids: A Smart Kid's Q & A Guide.* **Millbrook Press, 2003.** Questions and answers are posed for the five most popular jobs for kids as well as other ways they can make money. `BEYOND`	**Gerstein, Mordicai.** *The Man Who Walked Between the Towers.* **Roaring Brook, 2003.** The inspirational story of Philippe Petit's tightrope walk between the World Trade Center Towers. `BEYOND`

* **Main Selection from Student Book**
** **Classroom Library Title**

WEEK 3	WEEK 4	WEEK 5
Editors of TIME for Kids. *TIME for Kids: Butterflies!* **HarperTrophy, 2005.** There are 20,000 different kinds of butterflies in the world. Every butterfly begins as a tiny egg that hatches into a caterpillar. BEYOND	**Uhlberg, Myron.** *Flying Over Brooklyn.* **Peachtree, 1999.** It is 1947, and over 25 inches of snow have blanketed Brooklyn. A magical retelling of the event. ON LEVEL	**Squire, Ann O.** *Growing Crystals.* **Children's Press, 2002.** Beautiful color photographs and a clear, concise writing style explain how to identify and appreciate crystals. ON LEVEL
Bradley, Kimberly. *Energy Makes Things Happen.* **HarperCollins, 2003.** A good introduction to basic scientific concepts, such as the transfer of energy from one thing to another. APPROACHING	**Adler, David.** *The Babe and I.* **Harcourt, 1999.** A young boy's adventure selling newspapers at Yankee Stadium, and the hero he met there one day. APPROACHING **	**Rockwell, Anne F.** *Two Blue Jays.* **Walker, 2003.** A class watches outside their window as two blue jays build and guard their nest, lay their eggs, and raise their young. APPROACHING
Walker, Sally, and Feldmann, Roseann. *Wheels and Axles.* **Lerner Publications, 2001.** This book uses color photos of children to reinforce straightforward explanations of how wheels and axles work. APPROACHING	**Gayle, Sharon.** *Teddy Roosevelt: The People's President.* **Aladdin, 2004.** Roosevelt was a war hero, a champion of the environment, and the youngest United States president at that time. APPROACHING **	**Swinburne, Stephen R.** *Safe, Warm and Snug.* **Harcourt, 1999.** Tells how a variety of animals, including kangaroos and pythons, protect their unborn and young offspring from predators. APPROACHING
Stringer, John. *The Science of a Spring.* **Raintree Steck-Vaughn, 2000.** Simple text explains why springs act the way they do, based on elementary concepts. ON LEVEL	**Border, Louise.** *Fly High! The Story of Bessie Coleman.* **McElderry, 2001.** Bessie was the first African American to earn a pilot's license. ON LEVEL **	**Dowson, Nick.** *Tigress.* **Candlewick, 2004.** A mother tigress searches for a new den for her cubs and teaches them all they need to know until they are ready to be on their own. ON LEVEL
Toci, Salvatore. *Experiments with Motion.* **Children's Press, 2003.** Projects and experiments explore motion and the forces that cause motion. ON LEVEL	**Winter, Jonah.** *Roberto Clemente: Pride of the Pittsburgh Pirates.* **Atheneum, 2005.** Roberto Clemente's greatness extended beyond the baseball field. ON LEVEL **	**Squire, Ann O.** *Animal Homes.* **Children's Press, 2001.** Explains why animals need homes, how they build them, and what they do inside them. ON LEVEL*
Lafferty, Peter. *Force and Motion.* **Dorling Kindersley, 2000.** Explores the principles of force and motion and how they have been applied from ancient to modern times. BEYOND	**Bolden, Tonya.** *Portraits of African-American Heroes.* **Dutton, 2003.** Presents 20 profiles of remarkable men and women who changed their communities and their country. BEYOND	**Madgwick, Wendy.** *Animaze: A Collection of Amazing Nature Mazes.* **Knopf, 1992.** Text and illustrations of mazes that depict the habitats and living conditions of animals worldwide. BEYOND
Sauvain, Philip Arthur. *Motion.* **New Discovery, 1992.** Defines motion, describes different types of motion, and discusses how motion is used in bicycles, escalators, and other machines. BEYOND	**DeLaCroix, Alice.** *The Hero of Third Grade.* **Holiday House, 2002.** Randall pretends to be an anonymous hero until his class plans a fund raiser and he decides being himself is good enough. BEYOND	**Settel, Joanne.** *Exploding Ants: Amazing Facts About How Animals Adapt.* **Atheneum, 1999.** Examples of animal behavior and some of the ways animals find food, shelter, and safety in the natural world. BEYOND

Selection Honors, Prizes, and Awards

Boom Town
Unit 5, p. 154
by **Sonia Levitin**

Author: Sonia Levitin, ALA Notable Children's Book (1970) for *Journey to America* and (1973) for *Who Owns the Moon?*; Golden Spur Award and the Lewis Carroll Shelf Award (1978) for *The No-Return Trail*; ALA Best Book for Young Adults Award, PEN Los Angeles Award for Young Adult Fiction, National Jewish Book Award from the Jewish Book Council, and the Sydney Taylor Book Award (1987) for *The Return*

Beatrice's Goat
Unit 5, p. 188
by **Page McBrier**

IRA Teachers' Choice (2002), African Studies Association Africana Children's Book Award Honor Book (2002), Bank Street College of Education "Best Children's Books of the Year" (2002), and the Christopher Award (2002)

Unit 1

Week	Vocabulary	Spelling			
1 **First Day Jitters** *Leveled Readers:* *The New House* *The New Kid* *The New Hometown* *The First Day*	downstairs nervous fumbled chuckled nonsense trudged	clap step **sick** rock	luck crop snack **mess**	head shut miss stamp	jump click pond
		Review Words: cat man can			
		Challenge Words: bathtub anthill			
2 **Dear Juno** *Leveled Readers:* *The E-Mail Pals* *Dear Ghana* *Faraway Home* *Letters to Africa*	crackle announced soared starry envelope photograph	date **fine** rose lake	life home safe rice	globe **plane** wise smoke	grade **smile** come
		Review Words: clap sick crop			
		Challenge Words: sneeze escape			
3 **Whose Habitat Is It?** *Leveled Readers:* *A Year at the Pond* *Saving the Rainforest* *The Deep Green Forest* *The Rainforest*	neighborhood content addressing resort	fail bay pail ray	plain tray trail May	braid sway gray plays	**paint** snail great
		Review Words: safe rice globe			
		Challenge Words: lady afraid			
4 **Penguin Chick** *Leveled Readers:* *The Blue Whales of* *Antarctica* *The Weddell Seals of* *Antarctica* *The Wandering* *Albatross* *The Weddell Seals*	fierce whips echoes shuffles huddle junior down	gold bowl soak sold	**snow** loaf roast coast	scold coal slow **grows**	show float blow
		Review Words: snail plain gray			
		Challenge Words: window program			
5 **The Perfect Pet** *Leveled Readers:* *The Rescue* *Charlie's Pet Problem* *Dan's Idea* *Charlie Has a Problem*	perfect challenge healthy satisfy manage scratch appetite	mild sky pie might	**find** fight ties **right**	fry tight child flight	bright buy dye
		Review Words: soak bowl gold			
		Challenge Words: wind children			

Key Spelling words in bold appear in the selection.

Unit 2

Week		Vocabulary	Spelling			
1	**The Strongest One**	decorated	heel	bean	free	**street**
		symbol	seal	creek	green	**freeze**
		darkened	**weak**	speaks	clean	field
	Leveled Readers:	gnaws	week	team	cream	
	How Fly Saved the River	securing				
	Clever John	weakest	**Review Words:**	right	pie	child
	Dorje and the Lost Treasure					
	John's Plan		**Challenge Words:**	sixteen	peanut	
2	**Wolf!**	passion	**chick**	chum	hatch	stretch
		admire	**much**	lunch	cheese	watching
	Leveled Readers:	concentrate	pitch	ditch	bench	crunching
	Running with Wolves	splendid	teacher	cheek	chunk	
	Katie and the Wolf	bothering				
	A Dog's Life	dangerous	**Review Words:**	weak	green	seal
	The Wolf	ached				
			Challenge Words:	catcher	sandwich	
3	**What's in Store for the Future?**	objects	thick	shock	**them**	month
		entertainment	**this**	**fish**	washing	dishpan
		predictions	truth	**what**	wheel	weather
	Leveled Readers:	computers	whales	sixth	pathway	
	Incredible Inventions:					
	Everyday Wonders		**Review Words:**	lunch	chick	pitch
	Computers					
	On the Move		**Challenge Words:**	shadow	thicken	
	The Incredible Invention					
4	**The Planets in Our Solar System**	solar system	thread	stream	three	strong
		easily	scrubs	scratch	screens	scraped
		farther	spree	spread	spray	strength
	Leveled Readers:	main	screams	throne	throw	
	What's in the Sky?	dim				
	The International Space	temperatures	**Review Words:**	thick	washing	whales
	Station	telescope				
	Exploring Space	probably	**Challenge Words:**	streamer	scribble	
	Living on a Space					
	Station					
5	**Author: A True Story**	talented	wrap	knots	knock	gnaws
		single	knit	**wrote**	wreck	write
		proper	gnat	knight	know	**wrong**
	Leveled Readers:	excitement	wrists	sign	wring	
	Laura Ingalls Wilder	acceptance				
	E.B. White, Writer	useful	**Review Words:**	throw	spray	scratch
	Sequoyah: The Gift of					
	Writing		**Challenge Words:**	wristwatch	knapsack	
	A Great Writer					

Unit 3

Week	Vocabulary	Spelling			
1 **Stone Soup** *Leveled Readers:* The Popcorn Dancers The Fox's Banquet The Duke's Banquet The Fox's Dinner	guests banquet agreeable curiosity gaze untrusting	bark shorts sharp sore	hard storms **yard** sport	sharks porch pour **story**	chore wore carve
		Review Words: knots		sign	wrong
		Challenge Words: orchard		artist	
2 **One Riddle, One Answer** *Leveled Readers:* The Monster's Riddle Magpie's Mystery Adding with Kevin The Mystery of the Magpie	wearily depart suitable increase observed advised discouraged	stairs mare bear bare	share wear dares chairs	glare pairs hare **their**	pears square haircut
		Review Words: sport		sore	hard
		Challenge Words: airport		beware	
3 **Saving the Sand Dunes** *Leveled Readers:* Endangered Animals of the Everglades Water in the Desert Estuaries: Where Oceans and Rivers Meet Life in the Desert	preserve restore suffered rainfall	turns first herds learn	purr third earn nurse	perch girls firm word	**world** serve worth
		Review Words: bare		bear	stairs
		Challenge Words: perfect		Thursday	
4 **The Jones Family Express** *Leveled Readers:* A Different World Storm Surprise A Long Way to Go The Hurricane	annual potential expensive politely package wrapping innocent aisles	loop rude **look** clue	spoon tube **shook** blue	cubes goose mules gloom	true shoe stew
		Review Words: firm		turns	learn
		Challenge Words: classroom		childhood	
5 **What Do Illustrators Do?** *Leveled Readers:* Drawing Animals Drawing Faces Drawing Landscapes How to Draw Faces	instance illustrate style textures sketches suggestions	coy soil foil toil	coins **point** noise loyal	boiled spoiled enjoys voice	choice soybean joyful
		Review Words: spoon		rude	shook
		Challenge Words: noisy		checkpoint	

Key Spelling words in bold appear in the selection.

Unit 4

Week		Vocabulary	Spelling			
1	**Cook-A-Doodle-Doo!** *Leveled Readers: From Farm to Dinner Table: Food's Great Journey Oops! Food Surprises Follow the Pizza Trail Fun Food Surprises*	magnificent masterpiece ingredient recipes tasty	yawn **taught** **salt** lawn	halls hauls hawks **squawk**	bought bawls drawing caused	paused crawled coughing
			Review Words: joyful		coins	spoiled
			Challenge Words: walrus		autumn	
2	**Seven Spools of Thread** *Leveled Readers: Androcles and the Lion A True Hero The Lost Brocade The Diamond*	beamed argued possessions fabric purchased quarreling	found town **shout** owl	couch bow scout round	plow crowd **proud** clouds	**ground** louder bounce
			Review Words: drawing		lawn	hauls
			Challenge Words: snowplow		outline	
3	**Washington Weed Whackers** *Leveled Readers: Resources All Around Us Enjoying Our Natural Resources Energy and Our Natural Resources Sky, Sea, and Earth*	native shouldn't research sprout clumps	cell gems age place	gyms city cents price	space nice giant **changes**	pages gentle message
			Review Words: crowd		clouds	found
			Challenge Words: giraffe		celebrate	
4	**Here's My Dollar** *Leveled Readers: Our City Gardens Patching a Playground Service Dogs in the Neighborhood Kids Make a Difference*	tour volunteers community thrilled slogan grownups deserve interviewed	sale sail beet beat	rode road rowed its	it's **your** you're there	they're peace piece
			Review Words: city		gems	space
			Challenge Words: seen		scene	
5	**My Very Own Room** *Leveled Readers: The Slightly Tipping Tree House A Winter Adventure The Science Fair Safe in the Storm*	separate determination storage crate exact ruined luckiest	**years** twins trays states	ashes foxes inches flies	cities ponies bunches alleys	lunches cherries daisies
			Review Words: sale		rode	you're
			Challenge Words: heroes		libraries	

Unit 5

Word List

Week		Vocabulary	Spelling			
1	**Boom Town** *Leveled Readers:* Children at Work: Colonial America; Children at Work: On the Frontier; The Work They Did: The Immigrant Experience; Frontier Children	sidewalks grumbled traders blossomed wailed lonesome	airplane daytime birthday daylight	hairdo notebook birdhouse barefoot	headlight sometime someone newspaper	**sidewalks** basketball **stagecoach**
			Review Words: states		inches	cities
			Challenge Words: somebody		handwriting	
2	**Beatrice's Goat** *Leveled Readers:* Henry Bergh and the ASPCA; John Muir: Friend of Nature; Alexander Fleming and His Great Discovery; John Muir	gift yearned tend produce sturdy schoolhouse kindhearted	names **named** naming hopes	hoped hoping dances danced	dancing drops dropped dropping	wraps wrapped wrapping
			Review Words: airplane		birthday	newspaper
			Challenge Words: driving		traded	
3	**A Carousel of Dreams** *Leveled Readers:* Making Waves; Thrills and Chills; Up, Down, or Open- Moving Machines; What a Ride!	powered declared existed artist's pride	tries tried trying dries	dried drying hurries hurried	hurrying studies studied studying	plays played playing
			Review Words: dances		hoping	wrapping
			Challenge Words: obeyed		worrying	
4	**The Printer** *Leveled Readers:* Blizzard Heroes; Hurricane Heroes; Earthquake Heroes; Keeping Us Safe	screamed numb escape fled shuddered image newspaper	basket rabbit napkin letter	invite bedtime mammal number	**fellow** chapter follow problem	chicken butter Sunday
			Review Words: tried		studies	drying
			Challenge Words: splendid		complete	
5	**Animal Homes** *Leveled Readers:* Amazing Mammal Builders; Amazing Bird Builders; Amazing Insect and Spider Builders; Bird Builders	hives architects structures contain retreats shallow shelter	pilot diner tiger favor	lemon planet model shady	robot **tiny** label cozy	silent **spider** frozen
			Review Words: follow		basket	Sunday
			Challenge Words: melon		stomach	

T26

Key Spelling words in bold appear in the selection.

Unit 6

Week		Vocabulary	Spelling			
1	**A Castle on Viola Street** *Leveled Readers:* *Heat Wave* *Emergency!* *New Neighbors* *The Flood*	downtown appliances owners construction equipment leaky	able purple riddle handle	towel eagle puzzle **castle**	**little** nickel camel pickle	travel tunnel squirrel
			Review Words: spider		tiny	planet
			Challenge Words: motel		couple	
2	**Wilbur's Boast** *Leveled Readers:* *The Elephant's Boast* *Mike's Surprise* *The Grizzly and the* *Frigate Bird* *Animal Friends*	conversation interrupted boasting sway scrambled seized rebuild	**untied** repay disagree preheat	unafraid **return** preschool dislike	disappear resell precook prepay	unbeaten reprint unwrap
			Review Words: nickel		handle	pickle
			Challenge Words: unlucky		recover	
3	**An American Hero Flies Again** *Leveled Readers:* *Symbols of America* *Getting Out the Vote* *Three Great Americans* *Vote!*	historical dispute automatically requirements	sister sailor dollar toaster	winter doctor **later** dancer	mayor writer silver cellar	trailer December **author**
			Review Words: resell		prepay	unwrap
			Challenge Words: circular		editor	
4	**Mother to Tigers** *Leveled Readers:* *Painting Birds: The Life of* *John James Audubon* *Jane Goodall* *Gerald Durrell* *Jane Goodall and the* *Chimpanzees*	strolled pitiful sleepy crouch official sleek grace	careful cheerful helpful colorful	harmful peaceful **pitiful** painless	priceless helpless sleepless rainless	helplessly carefully peacefully
			Review Words: doctor		dollar	December
			Challenge Words: wonderful		cloudless	
5	**Home-Grown Butterflies** *Leveled Readers:* *The Curious World of* *Beetles* *Purple Loosestrife: The* *Beautiful Invader* *Aliens in the Water* *The Marsh Monster*	disappear protect harming involved supply capture enclosure	because rubber about puddle	alive behind before around	better **attract** kettle hammer	attend tickle **people**
			Review Words: peaceful		helpless	carefully
			Challenge Words: believe		beaver	

Bb

Key 3.1 = Grade 3, Book 1

Dd

Ee

Ff

Key 3.1 = Grade 3, Book 1

Hh

Ii

Jj

Ll

Mm

Key 3.1 = Grade 3, Book 1

Key 3.1 = Grade 3, Book 1

Key 3.1 = Grade 3, Book 1

Uu

Vv

Key 3.1 = Grade 3, Book 1

Ww

Key 3.1 = Grade 3, Book 1

Acknowledgments

The publisher gratefully acknowledges permission to reprint the following copyrighted material:

"Animal Homes" by Ann O. Squire. Copyright © 2001 by Children's Press®, a Division of Scholastic Inc. All rights reserved. Reprinted by permission.

"Beatrice's Goat" by Page McBrier, illustrations by Lori Lohstoeter. Text copyright © 2001 by Page McBrier. Illustrations copyright © 2001 by Lori Lohstoeter. Reprinted by permission of Atheneum Books for Young Readers, an imprint of Simon & Schuster Children's Publishing Division.

"Boom Town" by Sonia Levitin, illustrations by Cat Bowman Smith. Text copyright © 1998 by Sonia Levitin. Illustrations copyright © 1998 by Cat Bowman Smith. Reprinted with permission by Orchard Books a Grolier Company.

"A Castle on Viola Street" by DyAnne DiSalvo. Copyright © 2001 by DyAnne DiSalvo. Reprinted with permission of HarperCollins Children's Books, a division of HarperCollins Publishers.

"The Caterpillar" by Christina Rossetti from BOOK OF POEMS by Tomie dePaola. Text copyright © 1988 by Tomie dePaola. Reprinted with permission.

"A Child's Call to Aid the Zoo" by Jim Davis. Copyright © 2003 by Jim Davis. Reprinted with permission by The Fresno Bee, a division of the The McClatchy Company.

"Cook-a-Doodle Doo!" by Janet Stevens and Susan Stevens Crummel, illustrations by Janet Stevens. Text copyright © 1999 by Janet Stevens and Susan Stevens Crummel. Illustrations copyright © 1999 by Janet Stevens. Reprinted with permission of Harcourt Brace & Company.

"Home Sweet Home" by John Ciardi from THE HOPEFUL TROUT AND OTHER LIMERICKS by John Ciardi. Text copyright © 1989 by Myra J. Ciardi. Reprinted with permission by Houghton Mifflin Company.

"Home-Grown Butterflies" by Deborah Churchman from RANGER RICK®. Copyright © 1998 by National Wildlife Federation. Reprinted with permission of the National Wildlife Federation, May 1998.

"Monarch Butterfly" by Marilyn Singer from FIREFLIES AT MIDNIGHT by Marilyn Singer. Text copyright © 2003 by Marilyn Singer. Reprinted with permission by Atheneum Books for Young Readers, an imprint of Simon & Schuster's Publishing Division.

"Mother to Tigers" by George Ella Lyon, illustrations by Peter Catalanotto. Text copyright © 2003 by George Ella Lyon. Illustrations copyright © 2003 by Peter Catalanotto. Reprinted by permission of Atheneum Books for Young Readers, an imprint of Simon & Schuster's Publishing Division.

"My Very Own Room" by Amada Irma Pérez, illustrations by Maya Christina Gonzalez. Text copyright © 2000 by Amada Irma Pérez. Illustrations copyright © 2000 by Maya Christina Gonzalez. Reprinted with permission by Children's Book Press.

"The Printer" by Myron Uhlberg, illustrations by Henri Sørensen. Text copyright © 2003 Myron Uhlberg. Illustrations copyright © 2003 by Henri Sørensen. Reprinted with permission by Peachtree Publishers.

"Seven Spools of Thread: A Kwanzaa Story" by Angela Shelf Medearis, illustrations by Daniel Minter. Text copyright © 2000 by Angela Shelf Medearis. Illustrations copyright © 2000 by Daniel Minter. Reprinted with permission by Albert Whitman & Company.

"Think of darkness" by David McCord from MORE RHYMES OF THE NEVER WAS AND ALWAYS IS by David McCord. Copyright © 1979,

1980 by David McCord. Reprinted with permission of Little, Brown and Company (Canada) Limited.

"Wilbur's Boast" (from "CHARLOTTE'S WEB") by E. B. White, illustrations by Garth Williams. Text copyright © 1952 by E. B. White. Text copyright © renewed 1980 by E. B. White. Illustrations copyright © renewed 1980 by Estate of Garth Williams. Reprinted with permission by HarperCollins Publishers, a division of HarperCollins Publishers.

ILLUSTRATIONS
Cover Illustration: Scott Gustafson

12-13: Shane McGowan. 14-39: Janet Stevens. 44: Tim Johnson. 50-73: Daniel Minter. 76: Tim Johnson. 83: Rick Nease for TFK. 84: Jack Thomas. 108-109: Traci Van Wagoner. 110: Tim Johnson. 116-139: Maya Christina Gonzalez. 142: Wetzel & Company. 144: Tim Johnson. 146-149: Wetzel & Company. 154-177: Cat Bowman Smith. 180: Wetzel & Company. 182: Tim Johnson. 188-211: Lori Lohstoeter. 216: Tim Johnson. 221: (tl) Topham/The Image Works. 222: (cr) Mario Ruiz/Time Life Pictures/Getty Images. 234-253: Henri Sørensen. 255: Robert Schuster. 258: Tim Johnson. 282-283: Amy Ning. 284: Tim Johnson. 294-315: DyAnne DiSalvo. 320: Tim Johnson. 326-338: Garth Williams. 344: Tim Johnson. 354: Library of Congress, Prints & Photographs Division. 362-379: Peter Catalanotto. 380-381: Nicole Rutten. 382: (tc) Tim Johnson. 402: Tim Johnson. 405: Joe Taylor. 408-409: Lindy Burnett.

PHOTOGRAPHY
All Photographs are by Macmillan/McGraw Hill (MMH) except as noted below:

10-11: (bkgd) © Gabe Palmer/CORBIS. 11: (inset) C Squared Studios/Getty Images. 38: Courtesy Susan Stevens Crummel. 40: Comstock/Alamy. 41: Premium Stock/CORBIS. 42: (tl) Foodpix/Getty Images; (br) Royalty Free/CORBIS. 43: Steve Niedorf Photography/The Image Bank/Getty Images. 44: (bkgd) Wetzel&Company; (b) Michael Newman/Photo Edit Inc. 45: Judd Pilossof/FoodPix/Getty Images. 46-47: (bkgd) © James Marshall/CORBIS. 47: (inset) Royalty-Free/CORBIS. 48: (t) Myrleen Ferguson Cate/Photo Edit Inc; (bl) Richard Hutchings/Photo Edit Inc. 49: Myrleen Ferguson Cate/Photo Edit Inc. 72: (tcl) Courtesy Angela Meaderis; (cr) Courtesy Daniel Minter. 74: Tom & Dee Ann McCarthy/CORBIS. 75: Ellen Senisi/The Image Works. 76: Royalty-Free/CORBIS. 77: (tl) Tom McCarthy/ Photo Edit Inc; (tc) Emma Lee/LifeFile Photos Ltd./Alamy; (tr) Photodisc/Getty Images. 78: (bl) Peter Lillie/OSF/Animals Animals; (br) Wolfgang Kaehler/CORBIS. 78-79: (t) Michael Gadomski/Animals Animals. 79: (bl) David Hall/Photo Researchers; (br) Doug Wechsler/Animals Animals. 80: Barry Iverson for TFK. 81: (tl) Don Enger/Animals Animals; (tr) W. Perry Conway/CORBIS; (tcl) Nature's Images/Photo Researchers; (tcr) S. Michael Bisceglie/Animals Animals; (cl) Gregory Ochocki/Photo Researchers; (cr) Nigel Dennis/APBL/Animals Animals; (bcr) Photolink/Photodisc/Getty Images; (bl) Stephanie Harvin. 82: Jack Thomas. 83: Joel W. Rogers/CORBIS. 86: (cl) Tom Myers/Photo Researchers; (bl) Courtesy Jean Mahoney. 88: SuperStock/AGE Fotostock. 89: (bkgd) Dian Lofton for TFK. 89: (c) Burke/Triolo Productions/Brand X/Alamy. (cr) Tracy Montana/PhotoLink/Getty Images; 90-91: (bkgd) Ben Osborne/Getty Images. 91: (inset) Photodisc/Getty Images. 92: (bl) ©Peter Kaplan/Photo Researchers. 92-93: (t) ©Nancy Rotenberg/Animals Animals/Earth Scenes. 93: Heifer International. 94: (bc) ©Robert Cranston/RJ's Images of Nature. 94-95: (bkgd) Wetzel & Company. 95: (c) Darrell Wong/The Fresno Bee. 96: (bc) Courtesy Stacey L. Caha. 96-97: (bkgd) Wetzel & Company. 97: (bc) Courtesy of The Fresno Bee. 98: (bl) Courtesy Stacey L. Caha. 98-99: (bkgd) Wetzel & Company. 99: (tc) ©Robert Cranston/RJ's Images of Nature. 100: (tc) David Hunter/The Fresno Bee. 100-101: (bkgd) Wetzel & Company. 101: (bc) Courtesy Stacey L. Caha. 102: (bc) Courtesy Stacey L. Caha. 102-103: (bkgd) Wetzel & Company. 103: (tc) Courtesy Stacey L. Caha. 104: (tc) Courtesy Stacey L. Caha. 104-105: (bkgd) Wetzel & Company. 105: (bc) ©Robert

The publisher gratefully acknowledges permission to reprint the following copyrighted material.

"A Bear in the Family" by Ben Mikaelsen from *Boys' Life*, February 1997, Vol. 87 Issue 2. Copyright © 1997 by Boy Scouts of America. Used by permission of Boy Scouts of America.

Illustration Credits

150B: Renato Alarcao. 177B: Ken Bowser. 183F: Francesco Santalucia. 183U: Gideon Kendall. 217F: Francesco Santalucia. 217U: Gideon Kendall. 229F: Francesco Santalucia. 229U: Gideon Kendall. 253B: Ken Bowser. 259F: Francesco Santalucia. 259U: Gideon Kendall. 285F: Matt Straub. 285U: Gideon Kendall. 289K: Jenny Vainisi. T19: Renato Alarcao.

Photography Credits

All photographs are by Macmillan/McGraw-Hill (MMH) and Ken Karp for MMH except as noted below:

150I: Michael Newman/PhotoEdit, Inc. 211B: Image Source/Getty Images, Inc. 281B: Rob & Ann Simpson/Visuals Unlimited. 289C: Ryan McVay/Getty Images, Inc. 289F: Gabe Palmer/CORBIS. 289G: Royalty-Free/CORBIS.

Cranston/RJ's Images of Nature. 106: (tcl) Courtesy Gary Soto. 106-107: (bkgd) Wetzel & Company. 107: (br) ©Robert Cranston/RJ's Images of Nature. 110: Superstock/Alamy. 111: (tcl) Steve Gorton/DK Images; (2) Thinkstock/Alamy. 112-113: (bkgd) ©Michael Mancuso/Omni-Photo Communications Inc. 113: (inset) Comstock. 114: (t) Tom Stewart/CORBIS; (b) Michael Pole/CORBIS. 115: C Squared Studios/Getty Images. 138: Courtesy Children's Book Press. 140: (bkgd) Esselte/Phototone/Earthlink Textures; (b) Marvin Koner/CORBIS. 141: (t) Farrel Grehan/CORBIS; (b) Western Pennsylvania Conservancy/Art Resource, NY. 142: (bkgd) Esselte/Phototone/Earthlink Textures; (r) Angelo Hornak/CORBIS. 143: Catherine Karnow/CORBIS. 144: Scholastic Studio 10/Index Stock Imagery. 145: Royalty-Free/CORBIS. 146: (l) Bettmann/CORBIS. 146-149: Wetzel & Company. 147: (tr) Image Farm; (inset) The Granger Collection, New York. 148: Bettmann/CORBIS. 150-151: (bkgd) The Image Bank/Getty Images. 151: (inset) Photodisc/Getty Images. 152: (t) Charles O'Rear/CORBIS; (cl) Michael Newman/ Photo Edit Inc; (bl) David Young-Wolff/Photo Edit Inc. 153: Michael Newman/ Photo Edit Inc. 176: (tcl) Courtesy Scholastic; (cl) Courtesy Cat Bowman Smith. 178: Bronwyn Kidd/Getty Images. 179: Lynda Richardson/CORBIS. 181: Ariel Skelley/CORBIS. 182: Amy Etra/Photo Edit Inc. 183: PhotoLink/Getty Images. 184-185: (bkgd) ©Ben Osburn/Getty Images. 185: (inset) David Buffington/Getty Images. 186: (t) Courtesy of the Heifer Organization; (bl) Gunter Marx Photography/CORBIS. 187: Tom Stewart/CORBIS. 210: (tr) Courtesy Simon & Schuster; (cl) Image Farm; (inset) Courtesy Simon & Schuster. 212: (tc) Courtesy of Heifer International; (tr) Freeman Patterson/Masterfile. 212-213: (bl) Freeman Patterson/Masterfile. 213: (br) Courtesy of Heifer International. 214: (cr) Courtesy of Heifer International. 214-215: (t) Freeman Patterson/Masterfile. 215: (c) Courtesy of Heifer International. 216: David Young-Wolff/Photo Edit Inc. 217: (tl) Image Source/Alamy; (cr) Royalty-Free/CORBIS. 218-219: (bkgd) Orion Press/Stone/Getty Images. 220: (tl) Library of Congress, Prints and Photographs Division; (tr) NASA; (bl) Bettmann/CORBIS; (br) Gianni Dagli Orti/CORBIS. 221: (tr) AP-Wide World Photos; (c) C Squared Studios/Photodisc/Punchstock; (bcl) SSPL/The Image Works; (bl) James Keyser/Time Life Pictures/Getty Images. 222: Christopher Hornsby. 223: Mario Ruiz/Time Life Pictures/Getty Images. 224: Courtesy of Libertyland Amusement Park, TN. 226: (tcl) Ross W. Hamilton/The Oregonian; (bcl) AP-Wide World Photos. 228: Ryan McVay/Photodisc/Punchstock. 229: (c) Photodisc/Getty Images; (cr) C Squared Studios/Getty Images; (br) Ryan McVay/Photodisc/Getty Images; (b) Dian Lofton for TFK. 230-231: (bkgd) © Philip Rostron/Masterfile. 231: (inset) Siede Preis/Getty Images. 232: Jim Vecchi/CORBIS. 233: L. Rue III/Bruce Coleman. 252: (tcl) Courtesy Peachtree Publishers, Ltd; (cl) Courtesy Peachtree Publishers, Ltd. 254: (t) Michael S. Yamashita/CORBIS; (tr) Tim Matsui/Liaison/Getty Images. 255: Richard Swanson//Time Life Pictures/Getty Images. 256: (t) Michael S. Yamashita/CORBIS; (b) Stephen Ferry/Liaison/Getty Images. 257: Tim Matsui/Liaison/Getty Images. 258: Bob Daemmrich/The Image Works. 259: Steve Cole/Getty Images. 260-261: (bkgd) MITSUHIKO IMAMORI /MINDEN PICTURES. 261: (inset) C Squared Studios/Getty Images. 262: (t) Gerry Ellis/Minden Pictures; (bl) Adam Wolfitt/CORBIS. 263: (tl) Pat O'Hara/CORBIS; (cr) Joe McDonald/CORBIS. 264-265: (bkgd) Diana L. Stratton/Tom Stack and Associates. 265: (l) Esselte/Phototone/Earthlink Textures. 266: Fritz Polking/Peter Arnold. 267: (bc) Ken Kavenaugh/Photo Researchers; (inset) Scott Camazine/Photo Researchers. 268: Jerry L. Ferrara/Photo Researchers. 269: (cl) John D. Cunningham/Visuals Unlimited; (b) Leonard Lee Roe III/Photo Researchers. 270: © SuperStock / SuperStock. 271: David Hosking/Stone/Getty Images. 272: (t) Mark Boulton/Photo Researchers; (tr) Kjell B. Sandved/Visuals Unlimited. 273: (tcl) © SuperStock / SuperStock; (tr) Bruce M. Herman/Photo Researchers; (bcr) Michael Giannechini/Photo Researchers. 274: Glen Oliver/Visuals Unlimited. 275: E. R. Degginger. 276: (tl) Jeff Lepone/Photo Researchers; (tcr) E. R.

Degginger/Photo Researchers. 277: Craig K. Lorenz/Photo Researchers. 278: (tl) Randy Wells/CORBIS; (tc) David M. Schleser/Natures Images Inc/Photo Researchers; (b) Kim Heacox/Stone/Getty Images. 279: (tc) M. H. Sharp/Photo Researchers; (cl) M. H. Sharp/Photo Researchers; (br) Joe McDonald/Visuals Unlimited. 280: (l) SuperStock; (tl) Courtesy Scholastic; (bc) Gary Meszaros/Dembinsky Photo Associates; (bcr) SuperStock. 280-281: (bkgd) Raymond Gehman/CORBIS. 281: (tc) M. H. Sharp/Photo Researchers; (b) Kim Heacox/Stone/Getty Images. 284: Photodisc Blue/Getty Images. 285: (bkgd) Wetzel and company; (tr) Anup Shah/The Image Bank/Getty Images. 286-287: (bkgd) Eric Nguyen/Jim Reed Photography. 287: (cr) Jim Reed Photography. 288: (t) Dean Schoeneck/Jim Reed Photography; (bcr) Jim Reed/CORBIS. 290-291: (bkgd) Rudi Von Briel/Photo Edit Inc. 291: (inset) C. Borland/PhotoLink/Getty Images. 292: (t) Siede Preis/Getty Images; (b) Henry Diltz/CORBIS. 293: (cl) Dennis MacDonald/Photo Edit Inc; (cr) David Hiller/Photodisc blue/Getty Images. 314: Courtesy DyAnne Disalvo-Ryan. 316: (t) Tim Matsui/Getty Images; (bl) Billy Hustace/Stone/Getty Images. 317: Erik S. Lesser/Getty Images. 318: (t) Erik S. Lesser/Getty Images. 318-319: (b) Mark Peterson/CORBIS. 320: Michael Newman/Photo Edit Inc. 321: CheapShots/Alamy Images. 322-323: (bkgd) Chuck Place/Place Stock. 323: (inset) Photodisc/Getty Images. 324: (t) G.K. & Vikki Hart/Getty Images; (bl) Premium Stock/CORBIS. 325: Juniors Bildarchiv/Alamy. 338: (l) Photo by Donald E. Johnson; (2) Courtesy Estate of Garth Williams c/o Frost National Bank. 340: Lawrence Manning/CORBIS. 341: Philippe McClelland/Stone/Getty Images. 342: (t) Agnes Overbaugh; (b) Siede Preis/Getty Images. 343: Rick Friedman/CORBIS. 344: Ryam McVay/Getty Images. 346-347: Photodisc/Getty Images. 348: Stephen Jaffe/AFP Photo/NewsCom. 349: (tr) Kim Kulish/CORBIS. 350: (bkgd) AP-Wide World Photos; (bl) Courtesy NASA. 351: (bc) NASA; (br) Time Life Pictures/Getty Images. 352: (b) NASA/Getty Images/NewsCom. 353: (tc) Courtesy NASA; (tr) NASA/Reuters/NewsCom. 354: Library of Congress, Prints & Photographs Division. 356: Digital Vision/Punchstock. 357: (tc) Burke/Triolo Productions/Brand X/Alamy; (cr) Nancy R. Cohen/Getty Images; (b) C Squared Studios/Getty Images; (bkgd) Dian Lofton for TFK. 358-359: (bkgd) © Najlah Feanny/CORBIS. 359: (inset) G.K. & Vikki Hart/Getty Images. 360: Frank Siteman/Photo Edit Inc. 361: (tcr) Courtesy of Texas Hearing and Service Dogs; (cr) Lawrence Migdale/Photo Researchers. 378: Courtesy Simon & Schuster. 382: Frank Siteman/Photo Edit Inc. 384-385: (bkgd) © Adam Jones/Visuals Unlimited. 385: (inset) Pat Powers and Cherryl Schafer/Getty Images. 386: Millard H. Sharp/Photo Researchers. 387: (tr) Ken Thomas/Photo Researchers; (c) Valerie Giles/Photo Researchers. 388-389: William Dow/CORBIS. 390: (c) Ralph A. Clever/CORBIS; (bl) J.H. Pete Carmichael; (br) J.H. Pete Carmichael. 391: J.H. Pete Carmichael. 392-393: (t) J.H. Pete Carmichael. 393: (bl) Whit Bronaugh. 394-395: Whit Bronaugh. 395: (tl) J.H. Pete Carmichael. 396-397: Craig W. Racicot/Game Day Pictures. 398: (l) J.H. Pete Carmichael; (2) Ralph A. Clever/CORBIS; (3) J.H. Pete Carmichael. 398-399: (bkgd) Getty Images. 399: (l) Craig W. Racicot/Game Day Pictures; (2) Whit Bronaugh. 400: (b) Bill Beatty/Animals Animals/Earth Scenes. 400-401: (bkgd) Craig Tuttle/CORBIS. 401: (t) Sharon Cummings/Dembinsky Photo Associates; (c) MENDEZ, RAYMOND/Animals Animals/Earth Scenes. 402: Bryan Peterson/Getty Images. 403: Siede Preis/Getty Images. 404: Steve Ruark/Syracuse Newspapers/The Image Works. 405: Royalty Free/CORBIS. 406: Jerry/Express news/CORBIS Sygma. 410: Robert Glusic/Getty Images. 411: Skip Nall/Getty Images. 412: Steve Mason/Getty Images. 413: (l) Siede Preis/Getty Images. 413: (2) Siede Preis/Getty Images. 414: (l) Steve Cole/Getty Images; (r) David Seed Photography/Taxi/Getty Images. 416: ©Tom J. Ulrich/Visuals Unlimited. 417: Doug Cheeseman/Peter Arnold. 418: Photolink/Getty Images. 420: ©Michael T. Sedam/CORBIS. 421: Siede Preis/Getty Images. 422: (t) MedioImages/Picture Quest; (b) ©Margot Granitsas/The Image Works.

424